MARKETS OF CIVILIZATION

THEORY IN FORMS

A series edited by Nancy Rose Hunt
and Achille Mbembe

MARKETS OF CIVILIZATION

Islam and Racial Capitalism in Algeria

MURIAM HALEH DAVIS

DUKE UNIVERSITY PRESS
Durham and London 2022

Designed by A. Mattson Gallagher
Typeset in Garamond Premier Pro, Univers, and Clarendon
by Westchester Publishing Services

Library of Congress Cataloging-in-Publication Data
Names: Davis, Muriam Haleh, author.
Title: Markets of civilization : Islam and racial capitalism in
Algeria / Muriam Haleh Davis.
Description: Durham : Duke University Press, 2022. | Includes
bibliographical references and index.
Identifiers: LCCN 2021052363 (print) | LCCN 2021052364
(ebook) | ISBN 9781478015871 (hardcover) |
ISBN 9781478018506 (paperback) | ISBN 9781478023104
(ebook)
Subjects: LCSH: Race—Religious aspects. | Islam and politics—
Algeria. | Muslims—Algeria—Economic conditions. | Algeria—
History—1830-1962. | Algeria—History—1962-1990. | France—
Colonies—Economic policy. | Algeria—Colonial influence. |
BISAC: HISTORY / Africa / North | POLITICAL SCIENCE /
Colonialism & Post-Colonialism
Classification: LCC DT285 .D37 2022 (print) | LCC DT285
(ebook) | DDC 305.6/97065—dc23/eng/20220420
LC record available at https://lccn.loc.gov/2021052363
LC ebook record available at https://lccn.loc.gov/2021052364

Cover art: Bachir Yellès, "Plan Quadriennal" postage stamp,
Algeria, 1970s. Courtesy of the artist.

Duke University Press gratefully acknowledges the Humanities Institute at the University of California Santa Cruz, which
provided funds toward the publication of this book.

For my parents

CONTENTS

AFCAL	Association pour la formation et le perfectionnement des cadres agricoles d'Algérie
ALN	Armée de libération nationale
AUMA	Association des 'ulémas musulmans algériens
BNASS	Bureau national d'animation du secteur socialiste
CACAM	Caisse algérienne de crédit agricole mutuel
CAPER	Caisse d'accession à la propriété et l'exploitation rurale
CDC	Caisse des dépôts et consignations
CEDA	Caisse d'équipement du développement de l'Algérie
CGP	Commissariat général au plan
CHEAM	Centre des hautes études sur l'Afrique et l'Asie modernes
CIRL	Centre international d'études pour la rénovation du libéralisme
CREA	Centre de recherches économiques appliquées
DRS	Défense et restauration des sols
ENA	Étoile nord-africaine
FA	Fédération anarchiste
FAO	Food and Agriculture Organization of the United Nations
FFS	Front des forces socialistes
FIDES	Fonds d'investissement pour le développement économique et social
FIO	Fédération internationale d'oléiculture

FIS	Front islamique du salut
FLN	Front de libération nationale
GPRA	Gouvernement provisoire de la République Algérienne
ICO	Information et correspondance ouvrière
IEDES	Institut d'études du développement économique et sociale
INA	Institut national agronomique
INSEE	Institut national de la statistique et des études économiques
IRFED	Institut international de recherche de formation éducation et développement
MNA	Mouvement national algérien
MPS	Mont Pèlerin Society
MTLD	Mouvement pour le triomphe des libertés démocratiques
OAS	Organisation de l'armée secrète
OCDE	Organisation de coopération et de développement économiques
OCRS	Organisation commune des régions sahariennes
OECE	Organisation européenne de coopération économique
OFALAC	Office algérien d'action économique et touristique
ONACO	Office national de commercialisation
ONRA	Office national de la réforme agraire
PCA	Parti communiste algérien
PCF	Parti communiste français
SAP	Sections agricoles de prévoyance
SAS	Sections administratives spécialisées
SCET	Société centrale d'équipement du territoire
SEAA	Secrétariat d'État chargé des affaires algériennes
SEDES	Société d'études pour le développement économique et social
SGCI	Secrétariat général du comité interministériel pour les questions de coopération économique européenne
SIP	Sociétés indigènes de prévoyance
UGTA	Union générale des travailleurs algériens

In transliterating words from Arabic, I have used a modified version of the guidelines of the *International Journal of Middle East Studies* (*IJMES*), omitting all diacritics except for the ayn (') and hamza ('). I have adopted the most common spellings for proper names (i.e., Ben Bella rather than Ibn or Bin Balla, Oran rather than Wahran), at times leaving out the ayn or hamza (as with Ferhat Abbas). In general, I have used the more common spelling in the body of the text (fellah, Abdel Nasser), but opted for a more accurate transliteration when citing these terms in the endnotes (fallah, 'Abd al-Nasir).

Working between common French and English transliteration produced a few inconsistencies. For example, the definite article in Arabic is often written *al-* in English, but I have kept the original spelling when quoting from French sources (as in El Khayen or el baraka). I have followed a similar strategy in my endnotes; when French sources use a spelling different from my transliteration, I remain true to the former. For example, while I have transliterated the term for ex-combatants from the War of Independence as *anciens mujahidin* in the text, the term sometimes appears as *anciens moudjahidine* when I cite French archives. The notes also alternate between French and English titles for organizations. I have opted to use English names when the French translation is clear (Direction of the Plan and Economic Studies, General Planning Commission), but otherwise used the original French (Caisse d'accession à la propriété et l'exploitation rurale). My goal has been to make these terms legible for my readers so they can navigate archival catalogs or follow up on my references. In documenting the many organizations that played a role in economic development, as well as their acronyms, readers will find English translations in parentheses following the original French.

This book analyzes how the market acts as a moral system that permeates the most unexpected domains. As a result, I am reluctant to say that I have accumulated intellectual debts or created obligations of reciprocity. Instead, this work reflects forms of collectivity and the contributions of friends and colleagues who have shared insights, resources, and care. Despite the idealist fantasies that underpin intellectual production, I have benefited from institutional support to complete this research, including grants from the Social Science Research Council (SSRC) and the American Institute for Maghreb Studies (AIMS). The Institut d'histoire du temps présent (IHTP) and NYU's global research initiative generously offered me an intellectual community in Paris as I finished the dissertation. A Fulbright fellowship allowed me to spend a year at the European University Institute (EUI) as a Max Weber postdoctoral fellow. A Hellman fellowship supported subsequent archival research, and the IMéRA in Marseille provided a space of discussion and camaraderie. The UCHRI and the Humanities Institute (THI) at the University of California at Santa Cruz (UCSC) allowed me to workshop the manuscript and provided assistance with the final publication.

Many people have shaped my thinking about race, religion, and colonialism. At Georgetown University, Paul Betz and Frederick Ruf gave me the confidence to test out new ideas as an undergraduate. Osama Abi-Mershed, Ahmad Dallal, and Judith Tucker anchored my theoretical interests in a study of the Middle East and North Africa. Discussions with David Theo Goldberg have been fundamental to my own conception of racial difference. At NYU, Frederick Cooper provided guidance at every stage of this project, generously engaging with my work while helping me find my voice as a historian. Zachary Lockman's insights encouraged me to situate my research on the Maghreb in the broader framework of Middle Eastern studies, and

I am especially grateful for his encouragement and warmth. My reflections on the environment were shaped by exchanges with Karl Appuhn, who emboldened me to tackle more material questions. Working with Neil Brenner gave me the opportunity to deepen my reflections on political economy, often over a very early morning coffee. Language training from Belkacem Baccouche, Rakan Abdo, and, more recently, Atika Mekki gave me "access" to Arabic sources but, more importantly, allowed me to learn from the lives and literatures I encountered in the Middle East and North Africa.

In Algeria, a number of people showed me the ropes (and bus routes, as the need arose). Bobby Parks has provided advice, beverages, and humor since we first met in Oran in 2006. No one goes to Algeria without receiving lessons in political engagement, and Daho Djerbal generously offered them from his office, classroom, and home. Guillaume Michel and the residents of the Glycines taught me a great deal about Algeria and provided hospitality as well as lodging. I would like to thank Selma Kasmi, Moustafa, Ahderrahmane Krimat, and the Achrati family for making me feel welcome. I continue to learn from Hakim Addad on both sides of the Mediterranean.

In France, Giulia Fabbiano has provided much laughter as well as shelter from all storms. I am also grateful for the friendship of Augustin Jomier and M'hamed Oualdi. Sara Adjel, Noureddine Amara, Raphaëlle Branche, Charlotte Courreye, Jocelyne Dakhlia, Thierry Fabre, Claire Fredj, Houda Ben Hamouda, Jim House, Arun Kapil, Dorothée Kellou, Nadia Marzouki, Gilbert Meynier, David de Paco, and Malika Rahal were excellent company and shared scholarly insights. I would also like to thank all those who agreed to be interviewed and helped me navigate the archives, particularly Odile Fleury and Mahmoud Ourabah. Antoine Bernard de Raymond offered feedback on what is now the second chapter, and Awel Houati shared photos from Algiers that I analyze in the epilogue. Farida Souaih and Neïl Belakhdar patiently answered lingering questions about translation and transliteration. The Yellès family generously allowed me to use artwork by Bachir Yellès for the cover.

My colleagues at UCSC have sustained me personally and intellectually over the past five years. Jennifer Derr, a careful reader of this book, helped me navigate assistant professorship and went to bat for me when I was content to remain on the bench. Nidhi Mahajan, who is equally magnanimous with her humor and intellect, is one of the main reasons I am glad to have landed in Santa Cruz. Alma Heckman has been a constant pillar of support and occasional source of feline paraphernalia. I am grateful to Marc Matera for taking on the roles of colleague, reader, and confidant. The Center for

Cultural Studies at UCSC offered a forum to workshop the project and also provided an intellectual community. Mark Anderson, Hillary Angelo, Dorian Bell, Terry Burke, Julia Clancy-Smith, Yasmeen Daifallah, Mayanthi Fernando, and Juned Shaikh generously offered much-valued feedback during the writing process. A number of friends, including Benjamin Breen, Hunter Bivens, Vilashini Cooppan, Amy Ginther, Camilo Gómez-Rivas, Jo Isaacson, Kate Jones, Greg O'Malley, Roya Pakzad, Emmanuelle Salgues, Elaine Sullivan, and Jerry Zee have kept me afloat in an unfamiliar habitat. The insights of a number of graduate students—particularly Jack Davies and Ingy Higazy—were helpful in the last phases of writing.

Many friends read chapters of the manuscript, offered advice, or provided moral support at crucial moments. Darcie Fontaine has done all three, patiently responding to queries on everything from minute details to metaphysical conundrums. I thank her and Sandrine Sanos for always being in my corner, especially during the last few rounds of revisions. I sometimes wonder if first exploring Marseille on long walks with Pascal Menoret kept me coming back. Arthur Asseraf offered debate and advice at critical moments in the writing process, instinctively sensing when I needed snark, sincerity, or a reminder to stop working. Hesham Sallam has kept me laughing since 2006 and sets the bar for generosity so high that it is hard for the rest of us to clear it. Ziad Abu-Rish somehow manages to, however. Sherene Seikaly has been a political and intellectual role model as well as interlocutor. Bassam Haddad has created spaces for engagement, debate, and activism. Susan Slyomovics's mentorship has been indispensable.

Tony Alessandrini has been a generous reader and editor while also providing many of us with a model of what solidarity looks like in practice. Frederik Meiton has patiently allowed me to talk through ideas since our first year at NYU. Megan Brown and Dónal Hassett read chapters and were partners in commiseration, reflection, and frivolity. Todd Shepard offered guidance on the archives and beyond. Venus Bivar, Jeffrey Byrne, J. P. Daughton, Samuel Dolbee, Omnia El Shakry, Idriss Jebari, Laleh Khalili, Lilith Mahmud, James McDougall, Roxanne Panchasi, Paul Silverstein, Judith Surkis, Diren Valayden, Elizabeth Williams, and Madeline Woker offered critical feedback during the long journey from dissertation to monograph. Max Ajl, Samuel Everett, Philip Grant, Aaron Jakes, Jennifer Johnson, Abhishek Kaicker, Emily Marker, Fatima Mojaddedi, Hussein Omar, Terry Peterson, Elilzabeth Perego, Sara Rahnama, and Alex Winder continue to be wonderful fellow travelers. Thanks also to Chris Silver, who helped me access documents during COVID-19.

I was fortunate to work with Elizabeth Ault at Duke University Press, who expressed early enthusiasm for this project. Benjamin Kossak assisted with the nuts and bolts of getting the manuscript into production. I am grateful to the two anonymous reviewers who provided detailed feedback and engaged with my arguments. Joshua Cole also offered a particularly close and generous reading of the manuscript. Anitra Grisales, Ross Lipton, and S. C. Kaplan helped me with the editing process, making my writing stronger and arguments clearer in the process.

This book could not have been written without friends and family outside the academy who provide the necessary conditions to survive within it. Kimi Kobayashi, Jocelyn Sze, Lauren Farley, Heather Foster, Andy Masloski, and Sophia Qureshi have been with me through the thick and the thin. Laura Hartwick and the ladies of Bonny Doon have kept me sane during the weekly grind of writing and teaching. Frédéric and Marie-Christine Serres offered me a second home in Tours filled with warmth, cats, and a steady supply of Poire Williams. None of this would have been possible without the support of my parents, who followed me down the long and winding path that led to this book. Thomas Serres read chapters, debated concepts, scoured archives, and fixed sentences. Crucially, the support he provides resolutely defies all logics of exchange or obligation.

It must be emphasized that the destiny of modern civilization as developed by the white peoples in the last
two hundred years is inseparably linked with the fate
of economic science.

Ludwig von Mises, *Human Action: A Treatise on Economics*

INTRODUCTION

On April 1, 1947, the Swiss diplomat William Rappard gave the opening lecture at the first meeting of the Mont Pèlerin Society. Organized by Friedrich Hayek, the gathering brought together dozens of economists, intellectuals, and politicians who were committed to promoting free enterprise and a competitive market economy. According to Rappard, they sought to reinvent a postwar liberal order during a "tragic age" when economic man "everywhere [had] been obliged to put on a national uniform and seek national security more than general welfare."[1] Rappard had dedicated his career to the principles of economic liberalism, in both Europe and its empire. He had spent eighteen years as the director of the mandates section at the League of Nations, which was responsible for administering the colonies carved out of the Ottoman and German empires after World War I, and headed the Swiss delegation to the International Labor Organization from 1945 to 1956.[2] Though committed to the cause of world peace, he maintained that colonialism was necessary since vital resources were often located in countries whose native populations lacked the capacity to properly exploit these potential sites of development.[3]

It was perhaps these professional experiences that led him to reflect on the alleged universality of Adam Smith's writings, which "assumed that the average man always and everywhere, sought to obtain the maximum of material satisfaction at a minimum cost of effort."[4] In his speech Rappard also recounted his time in Algeria during the landing of the Allied forces in November 1942. He had been "impressed by the sight of the Arabs seated on the curb of the sidewalks," he said, who "seemed quite indifferent to what was going on" and were "absolutely idle." A French friend explained that "the Arabs in Algiers never did any more work than was absolutely necessary," noting that attempts by the French governor general to double their rations had actually reduced their productivity.[5] This led Rappard to conclude that the figure of economic man—homo economicus—was based on a Scottish template. He was, at heart, an industrious "Nordic mountaineer" who loved freedom and viewed wealth in a positive light. Rappard then asked: Would Smith have defended the universality of homo economicus if he had been "reared among the sun-baked race of Arabs who prefer leisure to work, security on the lowest scale to the insecurity of initiative and therefore equality to liberty?"[6] Rappard's comments echoed the concerns of colonial officials, who had long tried to increase the productivity of native subjects. His comments also revealed a concern that racial differences, and their attendant cultural codes, would be insurmountable sources of resistance to human and economic development. As European countries embarked on colonial development programs after World War II, economists and politicians revisited older debates on the relationship between race and the economy in which cultural superiority was assumed to be the key factor in Europe's material development. In the process, they promoted market exchange as an essential weapon in defending Western civilization and combating the twin threats of totalitarianism and decolonization.[7]

Rappard's musings on cultural difference and the drive to secure material wealth highlight that postwar economic reforms were articulated in the long shadow of empire. In the eighteenth and nineteenth centuries the figure of homo economicus had emerged as a model of human behavior against the foil of Ottoman piracy. Philosophers pointed to the economic and political backwardness of so-called Oriental despotism, which was organized around an "economy of enjoyment" rather than production.[8] Orientalist fantasies about Islam crystallized in the figure of homo islamicus during the nineteenth century. This trope expressed the widespread understanding that Muslims were fundamentally distinct from so-called Western man, the economically self-interested individual who epitomized the liberal subject of European modernity.[9] As I demonstrate in this book, the twin figures of homo economicus and homo islamicus were also invoked by the colonial administrators, economists, and politicians who implemented economic reforms in late colonial and postcolonial Algeria.

This book contends that Algeria provides a useful case study for scholars working outside the Atlantic world interested in how "rights in property are contingent on, intertwined with, and conflated with race."[10] The following chapters trace how colonial officials and metropolitan planners identified the economic capacities of Muslims as a key variable in the success of developmental policies.[11] In drafting economic blueprints, they drew on ethnographic knowledge that reified the existing boundaries between ethnic and religious groups. They also sought to confront the "obstacles" that traditional strategies for organizing families, property, and wealth posed to economic growth.[12] In the process, economism, a belief that economic factors are the motor of social and political action, emerged as a technology of racial difference; the tension between homo economicus, the exemplar of European economic modernity, and homo islamicus, the model of native social practices, provided a basic grammar that structured debates on colonial policy. The tension between these two figures was especially evident in the decades leading up to decolonization, when French officials intensified their attempts to bring Algerian natives into the fold of a productive market economy and redefined French empire as a "modernizing mission."[13] It also influenced Algerian attempts to define national identity after 1962, when Islam was considered fundamental to the creation of revolutionary subjects.

Racial Regimes of Religion

The French state progressively occupied Algerian territory over the course of the nineteenth century, establishing a system of rule in which religion represented a set of origins and imagined bloodlines that structured access to property, citizenship, and livelihood.[14] Islam did not merely justify unequal access to economic value but rather constituted the very terms in which economic policies were envisaged and implemented. This book argues that Islam formed the basis of a racial regime of religion, revealing the porous boundary between race and religion. It considers different moments in which colonial officials, social scientists, French politicians, and Algerian nationalists debated economic policies in light of their understandings of the economic aptitudes and capacities of Muslims. Drawing on archival material and interviews, it analyzes how the French and Algerian states introduced economic and social reforms from the interwar period (1918–39) to the first years of Algerian independence under President Ahmed Ben Bella (1962–65).

The heart of this narrative arc takes place in the late 1950s, when the Algerian War of Independence (1954–62) and European integration led French officials to introduce the Constantine Plan, which outlined major economic and social reforms. Against the backdrop of the Cold War, liberal politicians articulated the need to include Algeria in the nascent European Economic Community and insisted on an intimate link between economic development and military pacification. After World War II, politicians across Europe adopted liberal economic policies and tried to disavow the importance of racial categories in organizing economic and political inequalities. Rather than demonizing Islam or espousing arguments based on biological racism, observers described Muslims as particularly susceptible to pan-Islamism, a political threat that mirrored the dangers of communism.[15] The French scholar René Jammes, for example, wrote that both Muslims and communists were inherently against free thought and concluded that a Muslim was, in many ways, "very close to a material communist." The difference between them, he argued, was "purely formal"—Muslims proclaimed fidelity to Allah, while communists worshiped the "laws of nature."[16]

Jammes's comments underscore how the geopolitical realities of postwar Europe shaped dominant attitudes to economic orthodoxies and religious attachments. Liberal economists repurposed Smith's writings to address the threat of totalitarianism, which they saw emanating from diverse sources, including communism and fascism.[17] The body of thought they developed from the late 1930s to the 1960s has come to be understood as an early articulation of neoliberalism in France.[18] Yet there are good reasons to study how decolonization shaped these economic debates. Broadening the geographic scope challenges the notion that the history of economic thought is the purview of a narrow circle of intellectuals in Europe and helps foreground the role of race in fashioning the modern subject as one who embodied the values of individualism, progress, and private property. Economists and philosophers long debated whether these principles could apply to so-called Oriental subjects, understanding their alleged fatalism and communalism to be rooted in Islam.[19]

As feminist critics have noted, the figure of the rational European individual (man) was also the subject of property and self-interest.[20] Anxieties about gender also played out in discussions on economic prosperity in Algeria as colonial officials sought to protect the virility of empire against racial degeneration. Issues of sexual practice and the question of polygamy became a pretext for excluding Algerian Muslims from French citizenship after 1865.[21] Liberal notions of the self were defined against subjects—colonized populations and women—who were supposedly governed by dangerous passions rather than self-interest. This provided a ready vocabulary for making sense of pan-Islamism and communism after World War II.[22] From the 1950s to the present, economic reforms promoted by local governments and international financial institutions have ushered in new forms of dispossession, as Julia Elyachar has brilliantly elucidated in the case of Egypt. Even if organizations such as the World Bank and IMF now shy away from the patently Eurocentric vocabulary of civilization, they nevertheless promote specific social values in the name of an allegedly universal form of economic rationality.[23]

Following the work of Edward Said, postcolonial theory and representations of Islam have often been analyzed separately from the material ways in which capitalism organized the distribution of resources.[24] Yet by insisting that the realm of economic interest was constructed against the passionate attachments of religion and race, this book indicates one possible rapprochement between political economy and postcolonial theory. The notion that universal human interest constitutes a self-evident domain underpins many Marxist approaches, which argue that "no matter what the subjective clothing, objectively constituted needs, aspirations, and capacity will express themselves in resistance to exploitation and oppression everywhere and in all times."[25] These debates intensified after the 2013 publication of Vivek Chibber's *Postcolonial Theory and the Specter of Capital*, which defends the use of universal categories in studying global capitalist development. In particular, Chibber takes issue with postcolonial approaches that highlight the specificity of capitalism in colonial contexts and critique the Eurocentrism of orthodox Marxism.[26]

This argument overlooks the fact that philosophers and political theorists upheld the ability to recognize supposedly objective interests as a mark of European (masculine) individuality.[27] An awareness of material self-interest was understood to be a civilizational capacity that certain people did not possess. Put differently, the ability of Europeans to recognize allegedly universal interests was defined against the inability of colonized subjects to embody the values of economic modernity. In Algeria, appeals to "universal human interests" were part of colonialism's lexicon for maintaining the division between subjects and citizens. Moreover, the conceptual distinction between homo economicus and homo islamicus had concrete effects on how capitalism was introduced and organized.

Muslims were not the only religious group whose racialization dovetailed with economic anxieties regarding the global capitalist order. In the nineteenth century, politicians often conflated Jewishness and communism, resulting in the widespread fear that Judeo-Bolshevism was a major threat to Europe.[28] The figure of the Jew, like that of the Muslim, had been associated with deviant economic behaviors and served as a foil for a French identity grounded in Christianity.[29] Moreover, the consolidation of France's colonization of North Africa in the late nineteenth century coincided with the rise of the myth of Jewish financial power. This should encourage us to think relationally about anti-Semitism and the racialization of Muslims.[30] If the entanglements between anti-Semitism and French attitudes toward Islam are increasingly well-trodden territory, we might ask why there has been such reluctance among scholars of French history to treat Islam as a racial category.[31] Part of the reason surely resides in a modern attachment to the division between race and religion. For many observers, race is understood to be based on "permanent" features such as skin color, biology, or physiognomy, while religion is presumed to describe the more flexible realm of belief, ritual, and faith.

This analytic division between race and religion underpins current debates in France over Islamophobia and "Islamo-leftism." Those who deny that Islamophobia is a form of racial discrimination often argue that it is fundamentally misguided to draw on the vocabulary of race when discussing religion, which they claim is a personal choice.[32] Yet such a reading reveals a basic misunderstanding of race as an analytical category. As Stuart Hall reminds us, "the discursive conception of race—as the central term organizing the great classificatory systems of difference in modern human history—recognizes that all attempts to ground the concept scientifically... have been shown to be untenable."[33] In this book, I treat religion as a particular expression of racial thought that was used to categorize humanity and that emerged in specific historical contests over symbolic and material resources. Ethnologists and anthropologists often invoked biology, bloodlines, and origin when determining racial categories. But they also referenced religion as a factor that shaped biological reproduction and was responsible for specific cultural or physiological traits.

In recent decades, scholars of the French empire have shown that race was a factor in constructing and policing colonial legal structures, categories of citizenship, and boundaries of national belonging.[34] The field has also seen heated debates over the role of republicanism in promoting inequalities.[35] Focusing on the legal frameworks of the empire, however, risks reproducing the color-blind fantasies of the French state, whose republican values discourage explicit references to the racial categories that structure economic and political precarity. Rather than studying the mechanisms of formal belonging, this work focuses on economic policies to elucidate the functioning of a racial regime of religion. On the basis of religion, Muslims in Algeria were disproportionately subjected to racism as Ruth Wilson Gilmore defines it: "state-sanctioned or extralegal production and exploitation of group-differentiated vulnerability to premature death."[36] This is not to claim that Islam inevitably operated as a racial category wherever European colonialists encountered indigenous Muslims, although a number of scholars have fruitfully investigated the racialization of Islam on a global scale and have questioned the analytic distinction between race and religion. Cemil Aydin argues that the concept of the "Muslim world" has offered a racialized language for understanding Islam from the late nineteenth century to the present, while other scholars have focused on how the American War on Terror has created a global geography of Islamophobia that overlaps with racial categories.[37] My research, however, highlights Algeria's status as a settler colony and the need to remain attentive to specific racial formations.

The history of colonial Algeria elucidates how Islam emerged as a racial sediment or remainder even as the allegedly secularizing force of modernity perpetuated the myth that religion had been expunged from the scientific interpretation of nature.[38] Centuries before the "new imperialism" in Africa, religious prejudice had taken the shape of biological racism in Europe. During the early modern period, Spain and Portugal defined religious categories in terms of *limpieza de sangre* (purity of blood) and policed what they feared were "false" conversions, revealing how declarations of religious belonging surpassed the frame of theological commitments.[39] Race and religion were also intimately linked in Latin America, where understandings of human differentiation into castes had been imported from the Iberian Peninsula. In colonial India, the notion of caste introduced a social hierarchy centered on religious notions of purity and pollution that were also expressed in biological terms.[40] Other examples of colonization within Europe, such as the British conquest of Ireland, also blurred the line between religious and racial conflicts.[41]

This book places the history of economic development in colonial and postcolonial Algeria within larger discussions about racial capitalism that expose how understandings of human difference determined which kinds of bodies would be subjected to extraction, violence, and legal exception. In the 1970s, South African Marxists used the notion of racial capitalism to theorize the capitalist system's coexistence with, and indeed reliance on, native reserves created for black Africans. Inhabitants of these Bantustans provided occasional wage labor but were mostly dependent on a subsistence economy and extended kin relations. Discussions of capitalist economic organization structured by noncapitalist societies were subsequently revisited by scholars working on the Atlantic slave trade and settler colonialism in sub-Saharan Africa. Cedric Robinson, for example, insists that the racialism of the feudal order in Europe was foundational for the emergence of capitalist society.[42] A number of scholars, including W. E. B. Du Bois, Oliver

Cromwell Cox, C. L. R. James, and Stuart Hall, have exposed the intimate relationship between capitalism and race, showing that racial thought cannot be invoked as a mere justification for the inequalities produced by the capitalist system.

A number of questions arise when engaging with these debates in light of the specific racial formation introduced by French colonialism: What does it mean to use the tools of racial capitalism in a context where religion—not skin color—served as the basis for legal exclusion and economic precarity? If debates on race tend to be informed by American history, how can historians working on other racial formations develop a vocabulary for thinking about racial capitalism? We should also be wary of invoking race to describe every instance of human difference, which voids the historical and analytic power of the term.

In bringing the theoretical apparatus of race to bear on religion, my approach differs from ontological approaches to blackness as well as from sociological and phenomenological approaches to Islam. Those looking for a history from below will almost certainly be disappointed. Scholars have documented the fluidity of religious and economic power, notably in the context of *zawiyas*, the religious institutions rooted in popular forms of Islam that were loci of anticolonial resistance in the nineteenth century.[43] Islamic traditions affected patterns of economic power, land use, and even the accumulation of merchant capital. For example, religious notables were exempt from taxation, but they also controlled *hubus* properties, which had been granted as religious endowments.[44] Qur'anic laws relating to inheritance structured land tenure across the region and played an important role in the organization of merchant capital in the Middle East and North Africa from the sixteenth to the nineteenth century.[45] Major religious institutions, such as al-Azhar in Egypt, had a hand in managing the flow of wealth and collecting taxes.[46]

Islam established a set of imaginaries that governed aspects of the daily lives of Algeria's inhabitants and contributed to their understanding of geopolitics.[47] Yet religion was not only a lived reality; it was also an object of government. Understandings of racial-religious difference played a central role in how planners, experts, and politicians on both sides of the Mediterranean conceived and implemented economic policies. There is certainly much to say about how individuals navigated categories fabricated by the colonial state and understood their own identities in Algerian society. This book, however, takes a different tack, charting how the French racial state drew on economic policies to "fashion, modify, and reify the terms of racial expression, as well as racist exclusions and subjection" in Algeria.[48]

The legal status of Algeria, which was not technically a colony but rather incorporated into the French nation as three departments, is fundamental to this story.[49] The establishment of a settler colony relied on a central contradiction: while Algerian territory was assimilated to mainland France after 1848, political rights were nevertheless foreclosed to the majority of the population until the mid-twentieth century. The French state classified native Algerians (i.e., those living in the territory prior to the French invasion) as either Muslim (*indigènes musulmans* or *musulmans d'Algérie*) or Jewish (*israélites indigènes*). When Jews achieved French citizenship *en bloc* in 1870, the adjective *Muslim* became legally synonymous with native status. Stated differently, the epistemic violence of the colonial system made Islam synonymous with the status of an *indigène*—a word with deeply pejorative connotations in French. Meanwhile, the adjective *algérien*—the most obvious descriptor for the original Muslim and Jewish inhabitants—was appropriated by European settlers at the end of the nineteenth century and again during the interwar period. Because this book is interested primarily in the state's production and management of racial categories, it at times employs the term *native* to refer to Muslims who were subjected to the exceptional legal practices reserved for indigenous subjects. The following chapters argue that this slippage must be understood in terms of the material structures of race and work to expose the deep entanglements among religious, racial, and national categories that were fashioned over 132 years of colonial rule.

The Political Economy of the French Empire

Prior to the French invasion in 1830, Algeria was a province of the Ottoman Empire whose rural economy depended on the production of agricultural surplus.[50] Land could belong to the state (*beylik*), be held collectively by groups belonging to a particular lineage (*'arsh*), or be possessed by individuals (*milk*). A sharecropping system, in which workers received a share of the harvest in exchange for their labor, also developed in parts of the territory.[51] In addition, access to the Mediterranean provided a major source of revenue for the Barbary corsairs who ransomed slaves captured as far afield as Iceland or Ireland. Trans-Saharan caravans linked Algeria to its African hinterland, helping Jewish and Ibadi merchants acquire wealth.[52] The increased presence of Europeans in the nineteenth century introduced new commodities and shifted existing trade routes, though it was not until the twentieth century that "maritime traffic replaced the ship of the dessert."[53]

The French invasion of Algeria in 1830 was driven by domestic political concerns and justified by economic motivations. King Charles X claimed that the conquest would end the activities of Barbary corsairs and settle French debts resulting from the purchase of wheat during the revolutionary wars. It was not until 1848 that Algerian territory was legally annexed to the mainland in a decision that subsequently led to the expropriation of native lands. The settlement of Europeans on Algerian territory required significant economic investment. Direct and indirect taxes disproportionately targeted Muslim Algerians, who financed economic development that largely benefited the settler population, such as the construction of basic infrastructure. Algerians provided cheap labor for Europeans, working as sharecroppers and wage laborers. This trend accelerated after the introduction of vineyards to Algeria in the 1860s.[54] Agricultural capitalism found fertile ground in the expropriation of native labor and benefited from colonial credit structures. While some economists, such as Jean-Baptiste Say, advocated for the introduction of a liberal market economy as part of a call for "virtuous empire" in the early years of colonization, the laissez-faire model of settlement gave way to official colonization in the 1840s.[55] The late nineteenth century saw the consolidation of a system of colonial capitalism in which the large-scale confiscation of land, alongside fiscal measures that disproportionately extracted wealth from indigenous Algerians, led to widespread rural impoverishment.[56]

By the beginning of World War I, the Algerian economy was a classic example of the colonial pact, in which territories in Africa or Asia provided primary materials for Europe and markets for manufactured goods. As Rosa Luxembourg wrote in 1913, "next to tormented British India, Algeria under French rule claims pride of place in the annals of capitalist colonization."[57] This situation led many observers to conclude that Algeria suffered from a so-called dual economy, where a capitalist European sector existed alongside a native economy defined by precapitalist modes of production.[58] It was not until the interwar period that the colonial pact was questioned by colonial officials, who for the first time started to promote a strategy of modernization and state investment.

Scholars remain divided over how to understand the turn to economic development during the interwar period. French historian Jacques Marseille argued that the main sectors of imperial capitalist accumulation ceased to be profitable after World War I, leading to a "divorce" between empire and metropolitan capital.[59] Empire, he claimed, had become a financial burden rather than a motor of economic growth for the metropole. Algeria was especially to blame for this crisis since the territory was responsible for more than half of all spending in the French empire from 1945 to 1958.[60] Marseille's analysis opened the door to arguments that increased state investment should be viewed as an act of political generosity, not as an indication of economic pragmatism. A student of Marseille, Daniel Lefeuvre, subsequently illustrated France's supposed magnanimity by observing that metropolitan France continued to buy goods from Algeria at inflated prices in the early 1930s despite the global financial crisis.[61]

Specialists of French empire have taken issue with the empirical grounding of Marseille's work.[62] But this revisionist analysis cannot be understood outside of the seemingly inexhaustible polemics in France regarding colonial memory.[63] A parliamentary law passed in 2005 included an article requiring high school teachers to inform students about the "positive role" of colonization, particularly in North Africa. Although the article was repealed by presidential decree, the political debates set the stage for Lefeuvre's second book, published in 2006, which lamented the display of "repentance" for French colonialism.[64] This reading of economic policy is symptomatic of the tendency to prioritize quantitative approaches that view economic history in terms of profitability in order to provide a cost-benefit analysis. These debates generally overlook how economic discourses have "enabled signs of power to function" and offered the promise of sociological transformations.[65] Undoubtedly, colonial officials viewed rising poverty levels after World War I as a threat to imperial rule and felt compelled to introduce economic reforms to bolster native welfare.[66] But colonial officials were not inspired by generosity; they adopted the doctrine of economic development (or *mise en valeur*) because they believed it was necessary to preserve French colonial influence. In tethering political economy to a seemingly rational description of material interests, Marseille and Lefeuvre provide a sanitized account of the economics of empire. A more complete analysis of how their studies were informed by discourses that espoused a "triumphant neoliberal globalization" remains to be written.[67]

Other scholars, less infatuated with quantitative approaches, have taken up William Sewell Jr.'s injunction to study the "economic life" of French empire.[68] This research considers the embedded nature of economic activities to be a rich site for understanding "social ties, cultural assumptions, and political processes."[69] While acknowledging that political economy generated myths about race—positing certain groups as more productive than others, for example—this approach often treats race as an ideological justification for capitalism's uneven exploitation of the workforce. By contrast, my research insists that the very articulation of economic orthodoxies and the concomitant appeal to capacities, social structures, and moral codes was itself a technology of racial difference. Colonial officials certainly invoked a lack of productivity to stigmatize certain populations, but articulations of liberal economic orthodoxies were themselves inseparable from the genealogy of racial thought.

After World War II, economic development on both sides of the Mediterranean sought to abolish the forces of "conservativism and restriction" associated with state protection.[70] The resulting commitment to a market economy reshaped the understandings of racial difference that had been established in the nineteenth century. Economic planners were increasingly confident about the transformational capabilities of market incentives, thanks to the new social scientific tools at their disposal. They drew on the postwar disciplines of economic planning, rural sociology, and behavioral psychology to improve the material conditions of Algerians. Rather than casting native subjects as fanatical or biologically inferior, however, they focused on the economic capacities of Muslim inhabitants. This reflected a broader shift following World War II, when the Holocaust prompted many scholars and politicians to replace scientific understandings of race with discourses that centered on cultural difference.[71] The transition from biological to cultural racism, which occurred in the crucible of decolonization and the Cold War, also influenced economic orthodoxies. Colonial officials and economic planners subsequently "recast racial difference in terms of economic futures" and articulated a new language for understanding poverty and underdevelopment.[72]

State support for colonial development increased after World War II. Efforts to restructure the French Empire led to the creation of the French Community in 1958, which eliminated references to France's imperial project overseas. This gradual, if largely symbolic, retreat from empire increasingly prioritized liberal colonial development and European integration. The Fonds d'investissement pour le développement économique des territoires d'outre-mer (FIDES; Investment Fund for the Economic and Social Development of Overseas France) was created in 1946 to encourage the modernization of French colonial territories in Africa. Though Algeria was not included in this organization, it became an integral part of the European Economic Community after the signing of the Treaty of Rome in 1957.

The close links between mainland France and its three Algerian departments came into stark relief during the Algerian War of Independence

(1954–62). The ensuing political crisis brought down the Fourth Republic in 1958, as right-wing partisans of French Algeria staged a coup against the government. This prompted Charles de Gaulle to come out of retirement in order to lead the country and create the Fifth Republic. The day before the constitution was adopted, he announced an ambitious program of social and economic reform in Algeria, known as the Constantine Plan. He gave the following orders to Paul Delouvrier, who was in charge of its execution: "You must pacify and administer [Algeria], but at the same time, you must transform it."[73] De Gaulle hoped that by bringing Algeria into the orbit of material progress, he would undercut the economic misery that animated the anticolonial uprising. This vision clearly did not come to pass, as Algeria won independence just four years later.

My analysis of the political economy of late colonial Algeria is consistent with the findings of Samir Saul, who rejects the claim that decolonization was driven by the imperatives of French capitalism.[74] Rather than being seduced by the economic profits of empire or clinging to a last-ditch attempt to save colonial rule, French officials hoped that the Constantine Plan would give rise to a symbiotic economic relationship after independence. A sovereign Algeria seemed increasingly probable after de Gaulle's speech on September 16, 1959, which proposed self-determination as a potential solution to the crisis. The extreme violence of the war, which included the exercise of torture, the introduction of regroupment camps, and the use of psychological warfare, has led historians to consider economic development as a palliative measure to maintain French sovereignty. This view, in which the plan was too little, too late, was undoubtedly shared by some colonial officials at the time. Yet the following chapters do not focus on the alleged failures or successes of the Constantine Plan. Instead, they chart how it attempted to transform Muslims into subjects who owned property, used credit, calculated future profitability, and employed heavy machinery to harvest crops.[75] Rather than political arguments about French sovereignty, this book is interested in how late colonial capitalism operated "through racial projects that assign[ed] differential value to human life and labor."[76]

Figures of Economic Modernity

The Constantine Plan is but one example of how debates on political economy relied on assumptions about religious and racial difference.[77] Max Weber famously explained the flourishing of capitalism in Europe in terms of the Protestant belief that material success was a sign of divine election. The problem with Islam, he argued, was that it emphasized pre-determination rather than predestination.[78] While Calvinists were driven to hard work, believing that material success signaled that they were among the elect, Muslims, in contrast, suffered from fatalism. These differences in behavior were not rooted exclusively in religious dogma, however. Weber viewed religion as a force that shaped biological reproduction and explained the geographical isolation and marriage patterns that gave rise to cultural traits. Moreover, in the introduction to *The Protestant Ethic*, he admitted the importance of hereditary and biological factors in creating attitudes toward capitalism, hoping that advances in neurology and psychology would confirm his analysis.[79]

The figures of homo islamicus and homo economicus are figments of a collective imagination; the individual who perfectly embodies the self-interested principles of the market, or who exemplifies the alleged fatalism of religion, cannot be found in the archives. The fact that these subjects are ideal forms rather than identifiable actors does not diminish their ability to shape the course of history. But this does not mean that we should banish them to the world of theory—a realm supposedly separate from "real" empirical events. As Georg Simmel has written, conceptual forms not only provide patterns for social relationships, but they also allow events to be legible over time and space, synthesizing "fundamental categories of life."[80] Homo economicus and homo islamicus emerged through the historical experience of colonization and structured the possible futures envisioned by colonial administrators, social scientists, and Algerian nationalists. Admittedly, colonial officials and economic planners never expressed a singular view of economic development or the capacities of Muslims to contribute to material progress. Despite this lack of consensus, homo economicus and homo islamicus provided a vocabulary for debates on economic policy in Algeria.

Just as focusing on the peasant or proletariat enabled historians to recount disparate events in a singular narrative and join the particular to the generalizable, an account of these two figures reveals assumptions about human nature that shaped colonial governance and economic thought. When Ranajit Guha, one of the founders of the subaltern studies group, argued that the Indian peasant was "denied recognition as a subject of history," he did not mean that Indians refused to engage in agriculture.[81] Instead, he highlighted how colonial mindsets imposed a "cultural value form" that made certain subjectivities illegible.[82] If homo islamicus and homo economicus present a conceptual dichotomy, this is not to deny the rare historical examples of Algerian natives who were able to accumulate capital or to argue that Islamic thought has remained silent on questions of economic organization.[83] Rather, the coherence attributed to each of these signifiers is the result of a colonial governmentality that depended on an analytic distinction between Western rationality and Eastern spirituality. The partitioning of Islam from economism helps explain why, to quote Max Weber, "certain types of rationalization have appeared in the Occident, and only there."[84] My intent is not to reproduce a reified understanding of the economy and Islam as two separate domains but rather to trace how this worldview undergirded the construction of colonial governance.

Chapter 1 begins by studying the implantation of a settler colony in Algeria over the nineteenth and early twentieth centuries. It demonstrates how French colonial rule established a racial regime of religion that was constructed around Islam and argues that a racial fix reconciled the tension between the two imperatives of encouraging European settlement and introducing a rational capitalist economy. The seizure of native lands was underpinned by a racial genealogy that defined Arab Muslims, in contrast to Berbers, as inherently ill-adapted to agriculture. As Islam became the pillar of legal and economic exclusion over the course of the nineteenth century, European settlers and Algerian Jews experienced a form of whitening. Colonial administrators and metropolitan observers posited an essential opposition between homo islamicus and homo economicus, and their policies also foreclosed Algerian Muslims from the quintessential figure of European economic modernity: the proletariat.[85]

In the aftermath of World War I, colonial officials and metropolitan economists advocated for greater investment in infrastructure as they began to view Algerians as potential sources of human capital instead of mere recipients of French aid. Chapter 2 therefore focuses on the interwar period, in which planners sought to include Algeria in an economically integrated Europe and asked whether a rapprochement between homo islamicus and homo economicus was indeed possible. It traces how the emerging geographic unit of Eurafrica blended a new technocratic vocation with an older racial discourse on the Mediterranean. Writers and colonial officials resurrected the figure of the "Mediterranean man" to describe Algeria as a cultural and racial melting pot, which in reality foregrounded the European settler inhabitants and relegated Arab Muslims to a marginal role. These tropes also had a concrete influence on economic policy: the standardization of crops such as olive oil and wine, symbols of Mediterranean identity par excellence, discouraged the agricultural techniques and preferences associated with

Muslim producers. At the same time, these measures promoted financial support and a system of classification that bolstered European production.

Chapter 3 focuses on the role of social Catholics and colonial administrators such as Paul Delouvrier in French economic planning. After World War II, economists and technocrats—a class of state experts who took the reins of the Fourth Republic—expressed a newfound confidence in the ability of economic planning to transform homo islamicus into homo economicus. This was particularly evident in the Constantine Plan. Consistent with neoliberalism's tendency to forget or "wipe away the terms of reference" that structure racial domination, the Constantine Plan effectively elided the racial regime of religion constructed by the colonial state.[86] In adopting new social scientific tools, often imported from the United States, planners analyzed economic disparities in a color-blind framework that denied the historical link between Muslim natives and poverty.

The modernizing planners of the Fifth Republic nevertheless expressed anxiety that the peasant, an important symbol of French national identity, was vanishing due to postwar reconstruction. In Algeria, colonial officials understood the *fellah* (plural, *fellahin*; Arabic for peasant or farmer) as a particularly stubborn version of homo islamicus. According to this view, their deep connection to religion prevented them from embracing the values that defined the French peasant. In the eyes of French officials, Muslims were resistant to adopting the norms of private property, growing crops for export rather than subsistence, or grasping the notion of credit. This essentialized notion of the fellah, which became a symbol for Algerian nationalism, was also shaped by the work of sociologists and revolutionaries such as Pierre Bourdieu and Frantz Fanon.

Chapters 4 and 5 investigate how a range of actors sought to refashion the relationship between homo islamicus and homo economicus after independence. The fifth chapter focuses on the presidency of Ahmed Ben Bella (1962–65) and the policies of agricultural self-management and land reform. These initiatives were the cornerstone of Ben Bella's attempt to introduce an authentically Algerian socialism based on Islam. For the postcolonial regime, questions of planning aimed not only to redistribute economic resources, but more fundamentally to instigate the sociological transformation of Algerian citizens. In 1962, Layashi Yaker, Algeria's representative to the United Nations, argued before the UN General Assembly that "the transformation of colonized man into productive man" would be the basis of Algerian policy.[87] By positing a specifically Algerian socialism rooted in Islam, Ben Bella drew on the local vernacular of religion to forge an indigenous articulation of economic policy in the context of decolonization.

French experts had cast Islam as inherently resistant to a market economy, but Ben Bella upheld Islamic history as proof that Algerians had an innate propensity for socialism. The politics of the Non-Aligned Movement also forced him to navigate Algeria's sometimes fraught relationship with pan-Africanism and pan-Arabism. The racial legacies of French empire had defined a "white" North Africa in contrast to a "black" sub-Saharan Africa, while also isolating Algeria from the eastern Mediterranean. This colonial history helps explain why Islam, rather than Arabness, provided the cornerstone for the revolutionary identity of the model citizen in the new nation-state. Ben Bella's vision deviated from the political aims and economic orthodoxies of colonial development, but it nevertheless perpetuated the assumption that economic planning should express a set of essential civilizational attributes rooted in Islam. This echoed the experience of state-building across the Middle East and North Africa, as intellectuals and politicians debated how the racial formations constructed by imperial policies would be expressed in a national frame after decolonization.

While the ideology of the Algerian nation-state promoted an anti-capitalist orientation through appeals to Islam, French leftists understood the implications of Algerian independence differently. The final chapter shows how decolonization fashioned economic orthodoxies in France by analyzing how radical Third Worldists and officials engaged in cooperation policies viewed the place of religion in postcolonial economic development. While secular leftists often viewed official references to Islam as an indication of a feudal mentality, liberal *coopérants* believed that Islam would play an important role in development by providing a cultural framework. Put differently, while French liberals engaged with cultural difference in the service of development programs, the far left understood religious difference as an obstacle to international socialism. While the former adopted a culturalist reading of Islam that overlooked how religion had structured underdevelopment, the latter maintained that religion had no place in a properly revolutionary society. Told from this vantage point, the story of postcolonial Algeria demonstrates how decolonization shaped the analytic models available for thinking about race and capitalism in France.

Algerian intellectuals sought new tools to make sense of national identity and economic underdevelopment after 1962. The epilogue returns to Algeria, focusing on Salah Bouakouir, a technocrat who worked on the Constantine Plan, and Malek Bennabi, a philosopher best known for his notion of colonizability. Despite holding divergent political views on French colonialism, their trajectories demonstrate how debates on economic orthodoxy and technical expertise shaped national identity after independence. While controversies surrounding Bouakouir's place in official narratives reflect contests for nationalist legitimacy, the continued relevance of Bennabi's writings illustrates the tensions resulting from postcolonial developmental policies. His invocation by Algerian protestors and analysts of the Hirak, the popular struggle against the regime that began in 2019, demonstrates how Algerians continue the work of decolonization as they challenge dominant discourses on national identity and economic development.

1.

SETTLING THE COLONY

Karl Marx arrived in Algiers on February 20, 1882, hoping to cure a lung condition that had worsened after the death of his wife, Jenny. His doctors suggested that the Mediterranean climate might bring relief, though Marx would have preferred to seek treatment on the French Riviera.[1] His skepticism was well-founded; it rained almost every day in March, and he spent much of his time undergoing medical treatments that produced no discernible benefits. Yet these adverse circumstances did not stop Marx from noticing the city's charms. He stayed at the Victoria Hotel, which offered spectacular views of the Bay of Algiers. Despite his ailing health, he appreciated the scenery, making a short visit to the botanical gardens and even frequenting a Moorish café. Writing in relatively good spirits to Friedrich Engels, he announced that he had shaved off his "prophetic" beard because of the sun.[2]

Algiers, too, was undergoing dramatic changes in the early 1880s. Between 1876 and 1882 the country had seen three major revolts against the colonial order. Despite signs that these uprisings were motivated by the continued violence of the occupation, French observers often interpreted these incidents as proof of Islamic fanaticism.[3] Transformations were also visible in the landscape of the city. In one of the main squares in Algiers stood a statue of General Thomas Robert Bugeaud. Just around the corner was the Bank of Algeria, a monument to colonial capital. Place Bugeaud was a physical representation of the merger between economic interest and military might.[4] Despite Bugeaud's use of physical violence to "pacify" the colony, he believed that French colonialism would introduce common material interests and thereby bring the European and native populations closer together. "France wants to govern you so that you prosper," he wrote, promising Algerians that colonialism would ensure that each person could "peacefully enjoy the fruit of his labor."[5] Despite his claim that fostering mutual interests would extinguish native resistance, the prosperity of the settler colony in fact relied on the plunder of Algerian society.

Marx and Engels had penned a few articles on Algeria for the *New American Encyclopedia* in 1857. A few years before traveling to Algiers, Marx carefully read the work of Maxime Kowaleski, whom he had met in London, taking extensive notes on the Russian's observations regarding Algeria's precolonial system of collective land tenure. By the 1880s Marx is reputed to have shed some of his teleological fervor and begun questioning the modernizing narratives that featured prominently in his 1853 writings on colonial rule in India.[6] He nevertheless repeated a number of preconceived notions about Algerian society during his stay. His attitude toward Islam was consistent with his view on religion in general, which he believed was a consequence of the alienation that was rooted in material conditions.

Marx understood Algerian traditions of land use in terms of a Germano-Slavic tradition, overlooking how family structures and social hierarchies influenced by Islam prevented lands from being truly collective.[7] His attempt to understand material practices independently from religious forms obscured how Islam shaped the organization of material resources as well as how it could serve as the basis for radical anticolonial claims.[8] For example, in recounting a visit to the Moorish café, Marx wrote that while the Muslim's hatred of Christianity stemmed from a deep desire for equality, the natives were "damned" without a truly revolutionary movement.[9] He thus cast Islam as a potential source of equality, but believed that religious commitments had to be channeled into an understanding of economic exploitation. In this regard, the story of Marx in Algeria remains one of "secular messianism" that viewed religious sentiments as irrelevant to understanding the predominant economic model. Cedric Robinson has argued that this perspective was based on Europe's own historical experience despite Marxism's universal claims.[10] Furthermore, he maintains that racial distinctions were central to the historical development of capitalism and class consciousness.[11]

This chapter demonstrates that Islam was the basis of a racial regime of religion, which underpinned the economic structures of the settler colony. The French state's legal definition of Algerian Muslims as "natives" shaped discriminatory patterns of access to life, livelihood, and property. Islam not only indicated a set of transcendental beliefs but erected a legal edifice that dictated personal status laws, land tenure, and citizenship status. Over the long nineteenth century, deepening economic inequalities consolidated the belief that Muslims were fundamentally inferior to Europeans. Long-standing assumptions about Islam also influenced the ways in which land confiscation, taxation laws, and systems of labor were introduced in practice.

Capital accumulation was an uneven process in Algeria. It did not begin in earnest until the 1880s, and even in the late nineteenth and early twentieth centuries a series of obstacles endemic to the settler colony—limited access to credit, markets, and wage labor—put certain limits on the development of agrarian capitalism.[12] The tension between the political need to settle the land and the economic imperative to introduce a system of rationalized capitalism was resolved by a racial fix as beliefs about Islam justified economic policies that promised social transformation rather than profit. The concept of a racial fix is rooted in David Harvey's argument that capitalism relies on a "spatial fix," or temporary solution to solve the crises of overaccumulation.[13] For Harvey, the surpluses of capital and labor endemic to capitalism are absorbed through geographic and temporal expansion. In this chapter, however, I use the concept to explore how race served as a "fix" for a series of contradictions that emerged from attempts to introduce capitalist development in a settler colony.

Historians of French Algeria have long debated the relationship between capitalism and colonialism, seeking to determine the "relative weight of economic and political factors" in the colonization of Algerian territory.[14] In many ways, this tension stems from the political imperatives of settler colonialism. While liberal economists believed that settlement could introduce capitalist values, including a commitment to individual liberties, legal formalism, private property, and abstract labor power, the act of settling Europeans on Algerian land often violated these very principles.[15] This chapter traces how the contradiction between capitalism and settlement was worked out through a racial fix that staved off impending crisis, at least until the early years of decolonization.

In the long nineteenth century, vocabularies of racial difference upheld the inability of certain populations to participate in the common bonds of proprietorship, individualism, and economic exchange that had become touchstones of political and economic modernity after the French Revolution. Understandings of the religious-racial difference of Muslims not only justified unequal access to material resources, however. They also served to conceptualize and organize the political economy of the settler colony by shaping strategies of primitive accumulation and expropriation.

Prior to the invasion of Algeria, French intellectuals and politicians often identified North Africa as the locus of Islamic despotism, portraying the region as a foil for Europe's liberal ideals. These Orientalist visions subsequently informed the decisions of colonial administrators who drafted policies relating to the organization of labor and property. Rather than confront the ways that settler colonialism foreclosed Algerian Muslims from entering the universalizing process of capital accumulation and economic development, colonial officials invoked the alleged racial-religious difference of the native population to establish a dichotomy between homo islamicus and homo economicus. Racial understandings of Muslims evolved from early debates on the racial degeneration of the native population to the Arabophile tendencies of the Second Empire and finally the turn to association under the Third Republic. Many of the shifts in colonial governance were rooted in political expediency rather than ideological coherence. By the end of the nineteenth century, however, the cumulative effect of these policies was to establish a racial regime of religion that marginalized native inhabitants while naturalizing the presence of European settlers on Algerian land.

"Piracy and Pederasty"

The expansion of the Ottoman Empire provoked a mixture of religious, cultural and economic anxieties among European writers, philosophers, and politicians. Algiers became a base for Ottoman corsairs in the early sixteenth century and came to occupy a mythical place in the European imagination as the front line in the struggle between Christianity and Islam.[16] In the seventeenth century, many European observers understood hostilities between the Barbary corsairs and the French navy as a crusade, while Algerian corsairs often framed the competition for trade and influence as a jihad.[17] From the end of the seventeenth through the eighteenth century, environmental factors, moral capacities, and religious beliefs provided important criteria for human classification. During the Enlightenment, Europe's self-understanding developed in opposition to the figure of the Turk, who represented the tyranny, excess, and cruelty of Islam.[18] Both geography and religion explained the licentious nature of the East and its inhabitants; Montesquieu, for example, described hot climates as fertile ground for the development of despotic rule and slavery.[19] The nineteenth century saw the formation of a self-consciously liberal tradition of political thought that was defined by a focus on individual rights and hostility to monarchical power. Debates on the so-called eastern question were fundamental for defining Europe as a "transcendental idea, composed of a set of Enlightened ideals differentiated from a prior historical moment," while intellectuals portrayed the lands of Islam as replete with moral, sexual, and political depravity.[20]

The literary and philosophical expressions of these Orientalist tropes are well known, but many European observers also located the corrosive moral influence of Islam in Ottoman economic practices: notably, so-called white slavery that subjugated Europeans for economic and military gain. Some politicians believed that piracy was a geopolitical threat to Europe and a moral vice that prohibited North Africans from adopting the more virtuous economic activities of agriculture and trade.[21] The enslavement of Europeans also carried the threat of religious conversion—a particularly repulsive notion as Islam was believed to impart the vices of "piracy and pederasty" among converts, in the words of one sixteenth-century French court cosmographer.[22] In this light, many French observers viewed North Africa as a source of contagion that risked bringing illness and sodomy to Europe.

French officials expressed moral outrage over "white slavery" more vehemently, and earlier, than they did in their campaigns to eliminate African slavery in the Maghreb. In reality, the French state continued to tolerate the enslavement of Africans after the practice was legally abolished throughout the empire for a second time in 1848.[23] Scholars remain divided over whether blackness served as an indelible mark of inferiority given that sub-Saharan Africans were but one category of enslaved peoples. There is a general consensus, however, that forms of Mediterranean captivity were more flexible than the better-known example of chattel slavery in the Atlantic world. Some have attributed this to Islamic law, which outlined a number of ways that slaves might attain freedom, even though the legal stipulations forbidding the enslavement of fellow Muslims were clearly ignored in practice. While enslaved people were undoubtedly subjected to violence and exploitation, Gillian Weiss argues they nevertheless "maintained kinship ties and legal statuses" and thereby avoided the "social death" characteristic of Atlantic slavery.[24]

As a result, there was no rigid racial order based solely on either religion or skin color in Ottoman Algeria. The Ottoman ruling class incorporated ethnic elements from throughout the empire, most notably from the Balkans. Descendants of mixed North African and Turkish origins, known as Kouloughlis, formed a local elite. Algerians who claimed Andalusian heritage, often referred to as *Moors*, were yet another component of the urban elite. Before hardened racial categories that separated settler from native emerged at the end of the nineteenth century, important divisions existed within religious communities that were based on socioeconomic status, language, regional origins, and skin color. French writers also used terms such as *Moors, Bedouins, Turks*, and *Kouloughlis* inconsistently.[25] Despite this ethnic diversity, however, some French observers saw Islam as a blanket threat to European civilization and Christendom.

Like many countries in North Africa, Algeria was gradually drawn into the economic orbit of Europe at the end of the eighteenth century. The revenue from privateering decreased, and agricultural activities henceforth formed the basis of the Algerian economy. Ottoman Algeria had supplied France with wheat during the Revolutionary and Napoleonic periods. These unpaid debts supposedly led Hussein Dey to strike French counsel Pierre Duval with a fly whisk in 1827 and impose a French blockade of Algiers. After a long standoff, Charles X announced plans to invade Algeria on March 2, 1830, which he hoped would bolster the waning influence of the Bourbon restoration. This attempt to use military aggression to secure domestic support failed miserably, however. On June 12, the French fleet anchored to the west of Algiers. Charles's regime fell the next month. The liberal July Monarchy that came to power after the conquest was now saddled with the task of crafting policy in Algeria.

Capacities of Belief

In the decade that followed, French politicians, economists, merchants, and military figures failed to reach a consensus on how to govern Algeria. Debates in the Chamber of Deputies revealed divisions among those who advocated for settling the territory, withdrawing from it altogether, or following a policy of limited occupation. This last strategy proposed that the French state would concentrate on governing the coastal regions and rely on Turkish or native intermediaries in the rest of the territory. Some liberals who supported colonial settlement admired the nobility of the Arab population and hoped for a "fusion" of the races. Others rejected this vision, believing that Muslims were inherently backward and fanatical. Eventually, in light of continued armed resistance, even a committed liberal like Alexis de Tocqueville revised his earlier convictions. After visiting Algeria in 1841, he considered the prospect of racial fusion to be a flight of fancy and adopted the more classic view of Arabs as savage and ignorant.[26] The questions of settlement and racial mixing were discussed alongside prospects for financial gain as politicians, merchants, and administrators asserted that Algeria would provide a market for manufactured goods from the metropole, a foothold for trading with the African interior, and a new source of grain.

The French state wasted little time in introducing economic measures that dispossessed Algerian natives. Ottoman policy had placed any unoccupied land (*beylik*, or public domain lands) under the authority of the *dey* or one of his representatives, but the French state was committed to introducing a system of private property.[27] Land ordinances passed in 1844 and 1846 invalidated all unconfirmed land titles that had been granted before the conquest, stipulating that uncultivated land would become part of the state's domain.[28] The French state also increased its landholdings by confiscating *hubus* properties, which had been held in a religious trust, heightening the belief of many Algerians that colonization represented a fundamental threat to Islam.

French officials often invoked the economic aptitudes of Muslim Algerians when designing measures to seize native property. Nineteenth-century land laws stemmed from the physiocratic understanding that private property, rather than trade, created value. This posited a link between the creation of economic wealth and the civilizing capacities of those who worked the land. Those deemed capable of creating value through commercial transactions were viewed as more civilized than individuals who practiced subsistence agriculture or pastoralists who used land sporadically for grazing livestock. Land that was uncultivated, or did not have a title, was deemed to be legally vacant.[29] These seizures undoubtedly contravened the right to personal property, but the racial inferiority of Muslims as evidenced by their relationship to the land justified the confiscation of Algerian territories for European settlement.

Debates on the economic capacities of Muslims dovetailed with arguments regarding colonial policy. An 1848 report by the Algerian Society of Paris, a group dedicated to studying and defending French interests in Algeria, wrote that the native could only be an obstacle to settlement because Muslim fanaticism would not allow Algerians to be governed by Christians.[30] It discussed three possibilities for surmounting this obstacle: extermination, transplantation, and education.[31] While favoring the last strategy, the report nevertheless wondered if France could overcome native fanaticism. Ultimately, the committee proclaimed that because Algerian Muslims were "not an element that [could] help in colonization," it was necessary to limit their lands and hand them over (*livrer*) to European settlers.[32]

It was not uncommon for colonial officials and settlers to describe Arabs as ignorant, lazy, or fanatical in justifying France's expropriation of land. Gaston de Raousset-Boulbon, who expounded his theories of colonialism while living in Algeria after 1845, wrote, "France did not sow its blood and gold in Algeria to be satisfied with the insignificant tribute of two million natives and to abandon the vast Tell region to a backward and powerless population. The land belongs to he who … knows how to develop it [*la mettre en valeur*], and European colonization unites the right of conquest with that of superior exploitation."[33] Echoing Locke's claim that labor was constitutive of property, Raousset-Boulbon maintained that European settlers had the right to seize Algerian property because they could cultivate the soil. When his hopes for fortune in Africa were ruined by the 1848 revolution, he set his sights on a new colonial frontier and left Algeria for San Francisco in search of gold.

As colonial officials articulated a hierarchy of races based on their perception of the capacities of indigenous Algerians for productive labor at the end of the nineteenth century, they wed older notions of Islamic fanaticism to biological racism. Writing in 1847, the director of the Ministry of Arab Affairs, Eugène Daumas, and his colleague Paul Fabar claimed it was possible to distinguish between Arab and Kabyle physiognomy through facial shapes as well as through eye and skin color. They concluded that physical traits corresponded to certain moral tendencies and argued that Arabs were essentially lazy and repulsed by labor.[34] The racial distinction between Kabyles and Arabs resonated with the belief, widespread during the colonial period, that the Berberophone population—especially in Kabylia—was only superficially Muslim. This meant that they would be more useful to agriculture, especially in the harvesting of olives.[35] Anthropologists and ethnologists understood Berbers to be distinct from Arabs, sometimes viewing them as a separate race. It was their allegedly tepid attachment to Islam, however, that brought them closer to French civilization. Despite the relatively positive representations of Berber Algerians, they were still denied citizenship along with Arabs in 1865.[36]

The colonial tax system also highlights how beliefs about religious and ethnic categories underpinned material calculations.[37] David Todd notes that, until 1919, there was a "differential system of land taxation, based on ethno-religious distinctions between Christian Europeans, Kabyles, Arabs, and indigenous Jews."[38] The French state extracted economic value from indigenous Muslims through the introduction of the so-called Arab tax: proportional taxes on agricultural products from which settlers were exempt. Moreover, in 1855, authorities introduced the *centimes additionnels* (additional centimes) to finance public works. This payment was required in cash rather than foodstuffs, thereby obligating Algerian farmers to enter into a market society. The result of these policies was devastating. As members of an Algerian commission in Constantine explained in 1869, "Never has anyone in the world been subjected to the fiscal obligations imposed by two religions, except for us Muslims, who are required to pay taxes according to both Muslim and French law."[39] In 1875, over fifteen million francs was collected through the Arab tax, at a time when the yearly budget was thirty-two million francs. The European community, meanwhile, which was just one-sixth of the population, possessed over 40 percent of the territory's total wealth.[40]

Some French politicians paradoxically believed that levying taxes would convince the natives of France's civilizational superiority. A parliamentary commission that visited Algeria in 1833 reported that, even if the costs of extracting tax revenue were higher than the yield, it was imperative to introduce a form of tribute so that "the Arabs will believe that this civilization, which we praise to them, may be worth something, and that the harm we do not do to them is evidence of our sense of justice rather than of our weakness."[41] French officials believed that exposing natives to credit would impart an awareness of the intimate relationship between civilization and commerce. In this sense, contact with economic rationality became an important tool for the civilizing mission, even as armed resistance added to the costs of colonization.[42] When tensions arose between the desire for economic profit and the goal of European settlement, the language of race and the promise of racial transformation trumped economic concerns.

Many who supported colonization also believed that settlement would encourage racial regeneration among the settlers. This was especially important given the pervasive worry that urbanization and industrialization were causing national decline and moral corruption in the metropole. In the first decades of the occupation the French state pursued a policy of official colonization that encouraged poor laborers to settle in Algeria, where they would find honest work in farming.[43] It paid the costs of relocating to North Africa and required workers applying for passports to provide certificates attesting to their moral and physical aptitudes. Those considered "morally or professionally deficient" were denied authorization.[44]

Gender anxieties also motivated attempts to ensure the moral fabric of settler society. Even before the French conquest, economic prosperity was expressed in an overtly sexual vocabulary. In 1796, French writer and diplomat Jacques Grasset de Saint-Sauveur wrote, "The Turks and Algerians, not anxious for large families, behave as true pirates on the marital bed. They ravage the fields of sensual delight without making any effort to have them bear fruit."[45] This observation reflected the belief that Qur'anic precepts perverted sexual and economic intercourse, causing both intimate and material unions to be unproductive. After the conquest, colonial discourses celebrated the supposed virility of the colonial endeavor and romanticized the patriotic image of *la mère patrie* (the mother-fatherland) in order to dispel any threats of sexual promiscuity or deviance.[46] Sexual acts threatened to undermine the racial boundaries of the settler colony, leading the French state to regulate brothels and introduce a distinct status for prostitutes as early as 1831.[47]

In 1848, Théodore Fortin d'Ivry, a supporter of colonial settlement, argued that Algerian natives were incapable of organizing around a common interest because Islam promoted fatalism, sexual depravity, and polygamy.[48] The sexual imagery of settlement and the feminization of Algerian land were clearly spelled out by the journalist Alexandre Gresse, known for his Bonapartist sentiments. In 1860, he wrote that the agricultural vocation of the Algerian colony would address the uncontrolled proliferation of industrial workers—a threat he referred to as a "proletariat leprosy."[49] Gresse claimed: "The inert and fecund soil still waits for the hands that will open its bosom; yet this call, this ardent supplication, is not heard. We turn disdainfully away from agriculture; the always benevolent old mother.... [I]t is she whom one will perhaps have to court so that she consents to facilitate colonization."[50] This text was published the year that Napoleon III visited Algeria and began conceptualizing a new model of colonization based on Saint-Simonian principles. Yet despite this ideological reorientation, the sexual nature of conquest remained a common trope. The Saint-Simonians posited that France and Algeria would be joined through the nuptial bed of common labor.[51] In the realms of economic policy and colonial law, fantasies of sexual difference and racial fusion continued to underpin the discriminatory and violent measures introduced by the colonial state.[52]

Citizen and Subject

In 1848, as the July Monarchy succumbed to the wave of revolution sweeping Europe, a colony of more than a hundred thousand Europeans had sprung up on the southern shore of the Mediterranean. The same year, Algeria was assimilated to France as three new departments. These events were related: as workers rebelled in mainland France in June 1848, Louis-Eugène Cavaignac, a senior military general in Algeria, returned to Paris in order to quell the uprising.[53] Numerous French officials and politicians embraced the idea of sending the "dangerous classes" to colonize Algeria, prompting the government to pay for the relocation of eighteen thousand settlers in the following months. The policy of official colonization was largely a failure, however,

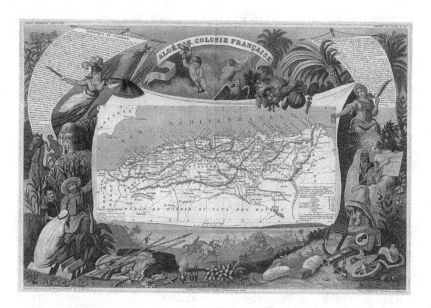

Figure 1.1 Map of Algeria, 1856. Courtesy of David Rumsey Map Collection, Stanford University Libraries.

as many settlers died of diseases and others protested against the difficult conditions. The end of the Second Republic and the introduction of the Second Empire in 1852 brought major changes to French policy in Algeria. The reign of Napoleon III, which lasted until 1870, introduced a liberal economic vision that sought to colonize the territory through large-scale investments and private capital.

Inspired by the Saint-Simonians in general, and Michel Chevalier's *Système de la Méditerranée* in particular, Napoleon III believed that economic integration would bring peace to Europe.[54] Henri de Saint Simon died in 1825, but disciples of his utopian socialism brought his vision to Egypt and then Algeria, where they supported public works projects and sought to create a union between the Orient and Occident. One of the founding fathers of the movement, Prosper Enfantin, left the metropole with twenty supporters in the early 1830s for Egypt, where he dreamt of building a canal linking the Mediterranean and the Red Sea. Although Enfantin returned to France in 1837, his supporters subsequently found the political will to translate their socialist utopian ideas into governmental policy in Algeria.[55] The Emir 'Abd al-Qadir's resistance to the French in the first decade of the occupation proved costly and made the assimilationist hopes of the civilizing mission seem increasingly untenable. The Saint-Simonians subsequently argued that engaging in commercial transactions could bring together disparate racial groups without causing them to lose their essential characteristics, a view of racial difference that came to be known as association.

The Saint-Simonian dictum, "Each according to his capacity, and each capacity according to its works," was fundamental to the goal of creating an "Arab Kingdom" in Algeria. Followers also saw Algerians as a foil for the French proletariat and believed that Europeans should engage in industry while Arabs were better suited to agriculture.[56] By viewing the proper economic roles of the Arab and European communities in Algeria in terms of natural aptitudes, they imposed a racial logic on the division of labor.[57] Napoleon III envisioned an economic system in which the pastoral instincts of the native population would complement the industrial interests of the European settlers. Convinced that Algerian Muslims were not capable of comprehending the distinction between spiritual and temporal commitments, Ismayl Urbain, Napoleon's advisor, declared that it was necessary to codify Islamic law, particularly in matters of family and property. This reified a domain of religious obligations and contributed to defining Algerians as Muslims above all else. Rather than apply the universal legal principles of common law, French officials often invoked Islam as the basis for economic policy. For example, officials in the Ministry of War defended attempts to "fix" Arab tribes on the land (*cantonnement*) by appealing to an understanding of Qur'anic law. They argued that according to Islamic tradition, usufruct was determined solely by the prince or ruling figure, who ruled in the image of God on earth.[58] Thus, while the seizure of lands by the state might seem like outright confiscation to Europeans, the Saint-Simonians postulated that natives would see these measures as repossession by a higher administrative power.

The Sénatus-Consulte of 1863 was the centerpiece of French property law in Algeria. Ostensibly introduced to protect native rights by delimiting tribal lands, it divided up individual territories among members of *douars* (the main unit of governance) and stabilized landholdings by granting titles.[59] The law formalized the distinction between 'arsh (tribal) and *milk* (private) lands and required land titles for individual holdings. It also allowed the state to sell land that had been recognized as milk, which opened up native lands for European investment.[60] Colonial officials sometimes assumed that property inhabited by a Berber-speaking population was milk rather than 'arsh, extrapolating from the belief that Berbers were more capable of adapting to sedentary lifestyles.[61] Rural Algerian Muslims lost an average of 14 percent of their most productive lands between 1863 and 1870, belying claims that the Sénatus-Consulte was designed to protect native property rights.[62]

Algerian territory became an integral part of France in 1848, but the inclusion of the native inhabitants was much less straightforward. After the revolution of 1848, there was increasing consensus among French thinkers and politicians that it was no longer possible to divide humanity into the categories of free men and slaves. France's first colonial empire, which had lasted until 1814, included holdings in North America and the Caribbean. This early experience of imperial rule, especially the Atlantic revolutions of the eighteenth century, imparted clear lessons regarding the dangers of slave colonies. French politicians and lawmakers thus sought to refashion imperial rule in light of universal rights, giving rise to an alternative classification that distinguished between subjects and citizens.[63] While citizens enjoyed full political rights, subjects were denied political expression and a range of legal and economic protections.

The Sénatus-Consulte of July 1865 affirmed that Algerian Muslims were French nationals while withholding the full rights of citizenship, according them a legal status that was inferior to that of the European settlers. According to this law, both *indigènes israélites* (indigenous Jews) and *indigènes musulmans* (indigenous Muslims) were governed by their respective personal status and therefore could not be subject to the French civil code. Even as it was envisioned as a "liberalizing step away from wars of conquest and towards the incorporation of the Algerians," the Sénatus-Consulte was an important moment in the transformation of Islam into a marker of racial difference.[64] This was not inevitable, nor did it apply in all French imperial holdings. In Senegal, the *originaires* (African inhabitants of the Four Communes) were allowed to maintain both Muslim personal status and French citizenship. Similarly, in French India, a person could become a naturalized French citizen while maintaining their personal religious status.

Questions of sexual practice and family law were central to establishing the difference between Algerian Muslims and Europeans. In crafting the 1865 Sénatus-Consulte, French jurists identified polygamy and child marriage as evidence of Muslim deviance while asserting that these practices were essential to Islam.[65] Respect for these religious imperatives meant that Algerians remained outside the fold of French citizenship. This was consistent with the policy of association, which upheld the need for native populations to evolve "along their own lines."[66] Rather than trying to transform Algerian Muslims into Frenchmen, colonial administrators adapted their methods of rule to suit the essential characteristics of the natives. This doctrine further entrenched the idea of religious-racial difference while maintaining the tantalizing possibility that Algerians could eventually make civilizational progress. In this way, association placed the universal principles of republicanism just out of reach on historical (rather than biological) grounds.[67] Under the liberal regime of the Second Empire, the claim that Algerians were not ready for individual property rights resolved the apparent tension between the universal precepts of political economy and their uneven application among native inhabitants. Extremely few Algerians applied for citizenship—1,309 men out of a population of 4 million between 1865 and 1899.[68] This likely reflects not only the reluctance of Muslims to give up their faith, but also the complicated bureaucratic procedures designed to reject applications for French citizenship that were introduced by the colonial state.[69]

"The End of a World"

Settlers viewed the economic liberalism and racial associationism of the Second Empire as a failed experiment, blaming the economic crisis of the late 1860s on the overly indulgent Arabophile tendencies of Napoleon III. As a result, politicians of the Third Republic changed course, making universal education and colonial expansion the twin pillars of national identity. The triumph of settler interests during this period also contributed to the rise of agrarian capitalism, which was bolstered by protectionist policies.[70] Despite this shift in economic policy, however, colonial administrators continued to invoke a racial genealogy of Algerian Muslims to identify ostensibly unproductive lands. The botanist-turned-senator of Oran, Auguste Pomel, wrote *Des races indigènes de l'Algérie et du rôle que leur réservent leurs aptitudes* (Of the indigenous races and the role reserved for them by their aptitudes) in 1871, wherein he repeated the myth that Arab Muslims were the direct descendants of Bedouin nomads, which allegedly explained why they were incapable of being successful farmers. He also argued that while Turkish oppression may have conditioned their dismal performance in farming, this was not the primary cause. Rather, he blamed "the inaptitude of the race to appropriate the resources of an agricultural regime and to live in a way not exclusively defined by pastoralism" and concluded that this vice was inherent in the social organization, beliefs, and "insufficient intellect of the Arabs."[71] Giving voice to settler opinion, he blamed the Second Empire for encouraging the Arab race to "turn in on itself" and deplete the soil.

Most settlers had opposed the Sénatus-Consulte of 1863 and now demanded that Algerian land be brought fully under French law. This resulted in the 1873 Warnier Law, which furthered native dispossession by establishing individual titles and dismembering collectively held 'arsh lands, making them available for purchase by Europeans. The introduction of individually held property, which was designed to encourage the sale of land to Europeans, was devastating. Much like the Dawes Act in the United States or the Torrens Act in Australia, this new system of property ownership was foundational to the construction of a settler colony. In the Algerian case, it invoked the long-standing trope of the Arab nomad, incapable of productively cultivating land, to justify the widespread dispossession of the indigenous population.[72] At the same time, however, the law allowed families to hold property collectively, reflecting the widely held belief that the family was an essential cultural unit among Algerian Muslims. It also included a provision that allowed individual family members to sell their shares in these collective holdings. According to Judith Surkis, this loophole reflected Auguste Warnier's optimism that Muslim family members would eventually appreciate the material benefits of selling their individual shares.[73] The Warnier Law provoked intense debates among jurists that centered on whether the social ties that defined homo islamicus (embedded in the Muslim family) would eventually be subsumed by economic reasoning.

The economic and physical violence inflicted on Algerian Muslims intensified under the Third Republic, which came to power in 1870. The establishment of large farms (contra the model of a small-scale family farm) was facilitated by the transition to a free market in land as well as the labor provided by native inhabitants.[74] The production of wheat and wine further increased the concentration of capital, particularly during the phylloxera crisis that decimated French vineyards in the 1870s.[75] When metropolitan winegrowers started to view Algerian wine as unwanted competition, they invoked the "unsavory and immoral habits" of their compatriots on the southern shore of the Mediterranean.[76] If settlers were subjected to disdain and even marginalization from mainland France, native Algerians undoubtedly suffered the most acute forms of precarity. The legal distinction between citizen and subject structured access to the security of one's self and property. It also facilitated the French state's extraction of value from Algerian natives.

One of the most extreme examples of how citizenship laws and economic exploitation worked together is the 1881 Native Code, which formalized the long-standing existence of extralegal punishments for Algerian

Muslims. These arbitrary and discretionary measures, which remained in place until 1944, included over forty infractions that were punishable only when committed by Muslims. Possible violations included threatening the security of settlers, failing to combat natural disasters, and participating in deforestation. Punishments led to the extraction of 1,658,958 francs in 1890, which could be paid in cash or forced labor.[77] As Sylvie Thénault argues, the difference in legal treatment was not merely punitive but resulted from a belief in the inherent lack of civilization among Arab Muslims, who were seen as incapable of respecting enlightened principles of justice and responding only to brute force.[78] In addition to imposing fines and seizing private property, the Native Code allowed the state to convert certain punishments into forced labor, so that from 1898 to 1910 the state extracted 600,000 days of work from Algerians.[79]

At the same time, the increased commercialization of agriculture, particularly of wheat and wine, led to the implementation of a system of agrarian capitalism supported by the state. The phylloxera crisis not only destroyed many of France's vineyards; it also boosted the large-scale agriculture that had been made possible by the availability of credit, construction of infrastructure, and favorable customs duties.[80] In 1884, a new law stipulated that all foreign products imported into Algeria would pay the same duties as those imported into France. But this did not apply to wine. Instead, the local government (rather than Paris) set the customs duties on foreign wine (known as an *octroi de mer*).[81] This economic autonomy irked metropolitan winegrowers, especially those from the Midi region, who criticized the allegedly poor quality of Algerian wines.[82] Winegrowers in Algeria also benefited from the availability of a cheap workforce. By the end of the century, European laborers were beginning to be replaced by Algerians who participated in the traditional sharecropping system (*khammès*) and worked for a fraction of the wages of their settler counterparts.

The introduction of a nascent agricultural capitalism did not encourage the full proletarianization of the native masses, nor did it obliterate precolonial social formations.[83] A complete transition to a system of rationalized capitalism was foreclosed by the alleged differences between settler and native, which were the foundation of the colonial system. In this instance, race was deployed to explain the discrepancy between the normal functioning of wage labor and the economic practices that benefited European settlement. According to some scholars, the Algerians who worked for a salary in the 1880s, mostly on farms owned by Europeans, formed a subproletariat rather than a classical Marxist or even agricultural proletariat.[84] A number of reasons explain this difference: First, Algerians working on French estates lacked the stability of traditional agriculture, as they were subject to the vagaries of seasonal employment as well as to high unemployment rates. In 1914, for example, the colonial state considered a mere 31 percent of the total population to be *actifs* or to have stable employment.[85] Second, agricultural workers were less well-off than even small farmers who owned their land and grew basic crops such as barley.[86] In this sense, their wages were less than the costs of biological reproduction. In fact, their wages were one-quarter to one-half less than those of their European counterparts.[87] Algerians did not experience the workplace as a site of exploitation, but rather had their labor expropriated as they labored under the threat of physical coercion.[88]

Theorists of colonial difference have highlighted how the European proletariat came to constitute a privileged figure in Western Marxism, as these individuals encapsulated the promise of revolution. They also seemed to possess a self-understanding that was "simultaneously the objective understanding of the nature of society."[89] Yet the ability of the proletariat to exchange his labor for wages was predicated on his liberation from the bonds of feudalism, physical coercion, and the violence of conquest that Marx associated with primitive accumulation.[90] Moreover, the romanticization of this ideal type contributed to the impression that laborers outside of Europe were somehow lacking or distorted in comparison. While works in subaltern studies have been particularly attuned to the question of difference in the lexicon of classical Marxism, a similar argument could be made in North Africa.[91] An industrial proletariat did not emerge until World War I, when a class of Algerian salaried workers constituted itself in France. In Algeria, however, the introduction of agrarian capitalism, lack of industrialization, and expropriation of native lands created a rural subproletariat. Algerians were denied the basic securities of employment and subjected to a discriminatory legal system that facilitated the extraction of value from Muslim inhabitants.

The reluctance of French politicians to apply a system of wage labor in Algeria was informed by the Paris Commune, a working-class revolutionary movement that ruled Paris from March to May of 1871. These events further ingrained the belief that the proletariat was a seditious political force as the French army violently suppressed the *communards*. In Algeria, the emergence of a proletariat seemed equally threatening; that same year, an anticolonial insurrection, led by Muhammad al-Muqrani, swept through eastern Algeria. French observers blamed the uprising on religious fanaticism, and the French state punished the native population with physical and economic violence.[92]

Introducing wage labor in this already volatile context seemed imprudent. The future subprefect of Orléansville (now Chlef) remarked, "The fall of the indigenous population into the status of a proletariat constitutes a serious danger for the future; it would take away from us our most powerful manner of acting on the conquered race, the threat of seizure and it would raise a social question in the colony that is especially ferocious as it would transpose onto antipathies of race or religion."[93] For many French administrators, the threat of mixing racial-religious divisions with class antipathies seemed fatal. Other politicians, however, including Arthur Girault and Auguste Warnier, believed that wage labor would ensure social peace.[94]

In Algeria, the constant threat of physical violence foreclosed the emergence of a proletariat. One settler wrote that he was comforted by the fact that "with the native (*indigène*), one [didn't] have to worry about the strikes or the pacts among workers to raise or maintain their salary, as [was] the case in the Midi region of France."[95] It was difficult for Algerians to negotiate the terms of their employment in an organized fashion, and they were also deprived of the social protections enjoyed by Europeans. For example, the minimum age for workers that was fixed for Europeans in Algeria in 1902 did not apply to Muslims.[96] Subjected to the confiscation of their most fertile lands and a broad array of exceptional punitive and financial measures, many Algerians suffered economic and physical violence, as captured in this Kabyle poem from 1899:

> Taxes struck us repeatedly
> Sixty *écus* per head each time;
> Bring them to us, or you'll see!
> People had to sell their fruit trees,
> And even their clothes;
> For them it was a dreadful time.[97]

Economic hardship only increased after the turn of the century, consolidating an economic and social dichotomy between the native and European inhabitants. The creation of *délégations financières* (Financial Delegations) in 1898 gave settlers the power to determine the state budget; two years later, the territory was granted financial autonomy from France.[98] Both of these measures allowed the colonial bourgeoisie to establish financial policies that benefitted the settlers at the expense of Algeria's Muslim inhabitants.[99] André Nouschi, a historian born in Algeria in 1922, confirms the devastation that resulted from these changes. In his study of the region of Constantine he recounts that, for many native Algerians, the turn of the century ushered in "the end of a world."[100]

An "Islamophobie Savante"

At the end of the nineteenth century, Europeans and native Algerian Jews were granted French citizenship, a right that the French state denied to Algerian Muslims. The introduction of naturalization laws coincided with the rise of social-scientific theories that viewed Islam as an essential marker of difference. George Trumbull IV notes that for Louis Rinn, the chief of native affairs in Algeria, "religion replaced the ethnologist's category of race."[101] This analysis reflects the sharper edges attributed to Islam at the end of the nineteenth century. At a moment when Europe was experiencing a resurgence of nationalist sentiment, the hardening of attitudes toward Islam was expressed in the social sciences as well as in the construction of an *Islamophobie savante*, or "scholarly Islamophobia." The Orientalist Ernest Renan is best known for his 1882 lecture "What Is a Nation."[102] Yet more than two decades before this speech, he outlined his emerging understanding of European identity against the foil of Islam. Maintaining that each race expressed its particular genius in the form of "religious legends," he nevertheless claimed that, with the exception of Persians, Islam represented a mixture of "inferior" human elements.[103] We will return to Renan's debate with Jamal al-Din al-Afghani in chapter 5, but it is striking that Renan's canonical definition of nationalism as a spiritual principle was presaged by his reflections on the intellectual poverty of Islam.[104]

Economists relied on civilizational hierarchies as they theorized the possibility of material advancement in the late nineteenth century. Pierre Paul Leroy-Beaulieu's *De la colonisation chez les peuples modernes*, published in 1874, repeated Saint-Simonian arguments that colonial development could be mutually beneficial rather than exploitative.[105] It also foreshadowed the popularity of *mise en valeur* during the interwar period. In 1887, Leroy-Beaulieu outlined the relationship between economic development and race in a publication dedicated to Algeria and Tunisia. Countering claims that Arabs were inherently inferior, he called for a policy of fusion. He clarified that this did not mean a "complete absorption" of one element into another so that differences between the two were "obliterated." Instead, he advocated for "a state of affairs where the two populations from different origins would be placed under the same economic and social regime."[106]

For Leroy-Beaulieu, a shared set of interests would allow two otherwise unassimilable elements to live in relative harmony.

In advocating for the expansion of French empire, the secular minister Jules Ferry echoed Leroy-Beaulieu's call for colonial development. He saw empire as a space for cultural expansion and a source of overseas markets, disagreeing with liberal economists who were weary of large-scale government investment.[107] Partisans of mise en valeur hoped that economic development would allow colonized people to participate in the process of material evolution even if their complete assimilation was unlikely. The economic sociologist Arthur Bochard, for example, believed that colonial officials had been wrong to think that France could conquer a foreign race by eliminating linguistic and cultural differences. He rejected cultural assimilation and stated that economic assimilation was the only policy suitable for the native population, writing, "It is first by the commonality of material interests that we will attach the Arab to us."[108] In the first decades of colonization, appeals to economic interests were less concerned with metropolitan capital accumulation than with safeguarding the existence of the settler colony.

Making the Settlers White

Over the course of the nineteenth century, European settlers gradually came to occupy a position of structural whiteness. In constructing racial hierarchies, French politicians and European settlers took lessons from other settler colonies such as America and Australia.[109] In 1888, the Algerian newspaper *Le petit colon algérien* ran an illustrated supplement on American cowboys that documented the transformation of racially mixed pioneers into ranchmen and the corresponding demise of the once noble Indians. The emerging class of cowboys, who had shed their initial heroism in order to become useful to society, turned the American desert into a productive land of cattle ranches.[110] This story would have been familiar to European settlers in Algeria, who saw their presence as a source of economic prosperity and held Muslim natives responsible for deforestation and desertification.[111] Although more than 68 percent of Europeans lived in cities in 1886, the vocation of agriculture was central to settler identity.[112] In fact, the French word for settler, *colon*, was synonymous with farming, which posed linguistic challenges in describing Europeans who did not engage in agriculture.[113]

In the context of French Algeria, whiteness does not refer to the racial identity of European settlers but indicates a set of social, legal, and economic privileges enjoyed by those in a position of dominance.[114] As Sara Ahmed reminds us, whiteness is not an "ontological given" but rather "that which has been received, or become given, over time."[115] In Algeria, this dominance was enshrined in personal status law, which was based on religious difference, and dictated whose lives would be subject to the punitive measures of the settler colony.[116] The structures of whiteness, which were available to native Jews as well as to Europeans, come into focus when contrasted with the violence exercised by the French state against Muslims. As Benjamin Stora claims, the unity of the settlers was due to a "shared fear of the Muslim majority."[117]

Christianity played a key role in constructing the position of whiteness enjoyed by European settlers. The dangers of racial mixing among Europeans, and the possibility that French civilization might be overrun by Spanish, Italian, or Maltese elements, were sources of considerable anxiety in mid-nineteenth-century Algeria. The French state even deployed missionaries to guard against the "decivilizing" effect that settlement might have on European inhabitants.[118] After early attempts to convert Algerian Muslims, particularly Berbers, failed, missionaries turned their attention to ingraining French values in the European population.[119] As Oissila Saaidia argues, unlike in France's old colonies, Catholicism in Algeria encouraged the segregation of the native and settler communities rather than their fusion.[120]

Muslims were not the only indigenous group whose religious attachments undermined their inclusion in French civilization. The capacity of Jews to exercise French citizenship had been questioned since the French Revolution.[121] In Algeria, indigenous Jews, like Muslims, were subject to personal status law, making them ineligible for the full rights of citizenship. This changed with the Crémieux Decree of 1870, which was the first legal measure that isolated the Muslim population as the undesirable element in settler society. The law granted Algerian Jews, except for those in the military regions of the south, access to citizenship *en bloc* and brought them under the French civil code.[122] Many Algerian Jews regarded metropolitan measures to "emancipate" them as an unwelcome intrusion, but Adolphe Crémieux, the president of the Alliance israélite universelle (Universal Israelite Alliance), viewed the law as tool to civilize the Jews of North Africa and to further their assimilation with the metropole.[123] Algerian Jews occupied an ambiguous place in the colonial hierarchy. While most were exempt from the discriminatory legal regime that applied to Algerian Muslims, they nevertheless suffered from the anti-Semitism that marked French political life, and many had had their citizenship revoked by the Vichy regime.[124]

The second development that consolidated the binary between settler and native society was the naturalization of European settlers. Immigrants from Italy, Malta, Spain, and Portugal had been fundamental for the colonization of Algeria, even if French officials viewed them as less desirable than northern Europeans in light of the mounting ethno-nationalism in Europe. However, the law of June 26, 1889 stated that a child born to European parents in France (and by extension, in Algeria) would automatically be considered French, spurring the creation of a so-called Franco-Algerian people (or a neo-Latin race). The demographic increase of Europeans, aided by a high rate of mixed marriages, enabled one colonial official to claim in 1900 that there were not two groups of people who lived in Algeria, foreigners (i.e., non-French Europeans) and French; instead, "there [were] only Algerians."[125] The new race of French people born in Algeria was understood to have a different temperament and language from metropolitan French people. They gradually constituted a coherent settler identity and came to be known as *pieds-noirs*.[126] During the nineteenth century, these individuals were identified as neo-French or simply as Algerian. The naturalization of Europeans consolidated the French presence on Algerian territory in the face of the native "Muslim element."[127]

The Third Republic attempted to weaken the bond between Catholicism and nationalism, notably with the 1905 law that separated church and state. Yet religion continued to dictate racial structures in Algeria. A 1907 decree stipulated that the 1905 law would be partially implemented in Algeria, but lawmakers refused to apply this law to Islam on security grounds, and the French government kept the clergy of all three monotheisms on its payroll.[128] The Catholic Church often served the interests of the colonial state, making Catholicism synonymous with being European. Just as it was clear that Algerians described as Muslim were indigenous, the word *rumi* referred to Christians who were assumed to be European.[129] In another telling turn of phrase, the term *petit blanc* indicated someone from the lower-middle-class settler population (i.e., not the *grands colons* [prominent settlers]) at the end of the nineteenth century. At the same time, the Arab quarters of Oran and Algiers came to be known as *villages nègres* (black villages), reminding us of the Manichean nature of the built environment under settler colonialism.[130] The color line that was gradually constructed over the course of the nineteenth century relied on the whitening power of Christianity as well as the marginalization of Algerian Muslims.

In addition to being France's closest settler colony, Algeria was key to fashioning the metropole's *politique musulmane* (Muslim policy) in the nineteenth century. As Henri Laurens observes, this phrase does not indicate a policy applied to Muslim-majority territories, but rather the "accounting for Muslim realities" in crafting the strategies for colonial governance.[131] The need to explicate the specificity of Islam was evident in attempts to understand indigenous culture or in devising political strategies as well as in debates on economic reforms. Homo islamicus emerged as a key figure in the imaginary of colonial officials who crafted land policies, labor laws, and systems of taxation. Material structures introduced new levels of precarity among Algerians, while colonial understandings of the inherent aptitudes of Muslims shaped the political economy of the settler colony. Even as the colonial administrators of the July Monarchy, Second Empire, and Third Republic held diverging views of Islam, they all invoked the racial-religious properties of native Algerians in justifying economic policies. The concept of a racial fix helps elucidate how long-standing beliefs about Muslims led officials to adopt policies that secured the existence of a settler colony, even if these measures at times compromised the basic principles of liberal capitalism.

World War I brought Algerians to French battlefields and factories, which prompted the question of whether colonial reforms would be offered as a reward for military service. As native subjects across the empire grew restless, the Communist International (Comintern) went so far as to call for the liberation of Algeria and Tunisia in 1922. The Parti communiste français (PCF; French Communist Party) nevertheless struggled to reconcile its opposition to colonialism with the conviction that class revolution should be the primary goal. Maurice Thorez, the leader of the PCF, considered Algeria a "nation in formation," implying that it was not yet ready to be granted autonomy. Even if Algeria had the right to a divorce, that did not make the act necessary, he argued. Speaking to a crowd of ten thousand people in Algiers on February 11, 1939, he iterated these points with a poster of a hammer and sickle in the background.[132] The iconography is hardly surprising, but it is notable that a Frenchman held the hammer while an Algerian farmer wielded the sickle. This image reinscribed the notion that Frenchmen inhabited the world of industry while the vocation of Arabs was essentially agricultural.

Thorez's speech made it clear that even if Algerian Muslims could be allies to the communists, they did not constitute a people in their own right. A perceived link between nationalism and race was fundamental to Thorez's denial of Algerian separatism as he saw "an Algerian nation" being "forged through the mixing of twenty races."[133] Albert Camus and writers associated with the Algiers school also depicted the territory as the epitome of Mediterranean hybridity. This view of racial integration mirrored broader economic and political shifts: after World War I, Algeria was increasingly seen as a lynchpin that assured commercial exchange and military security. In debating the possibilities for Algerian economic development, French planners and politicians often invoked a Eurafrican space that would join the northern and southern shores of the Mediterranean. As the next chapter demonstrates, colonial officials who sought to standardize and commercialize Algerian products for export to Europe marginalized native producers while mirroring the racial myths associated with a Mediterranean melting pot.

2.
A NEW ALGERIA RISING

In 1948, the French government released a promotional film that showed cargo ships transporting fruits and vegetables from Algeria to Europe. Thanks to French colonization, Algeria was no longer merely a source of basic foodstuffs but now offered high-quality produce that could be exported across the Mediterranean. Produced by the Office algérien d'action économique et touristique (OFALAC; Algerian Office of Economic and Touristic Action), which was responsible for expanding trade and publicizing Algeria's potential as a tourist destination, the film featured a map of the shipping routes that connected Algerian ports at Oran, Mostaganem, Bougie, Philippeville, and Bône to the French cities of Sète and Marseille as well as to the European capitals of London, Brussels, and even Stockholm. It assured viewers that each product was treated with the "same care and, one could say, the same love and with the ardent desire that they arrive at their destination in perfect condition to satisfy the pleasure of the far-away consumer."[1]

Grapes, olive oil, and citrus—three products that had been historically associated with French civilization in Algeria—featured prominently in the film. At one point, a blond mother offers her two young girls an orange, a fruit that produces "joy in the eyes of a child." A few minutes later, another woman picks Chasselas grapes, the most "delicate" variety, off the vine, further emphasizing the link between colonial agriculture and French domesticity. Alongside these images of economic modernity, other scenes displayed the production habits of indigenous Algerians. Berber women were shown collecting olives and then placing them on the back of a donkey for transport, illustrating the fact that most Algerian olive oil was produced by Muslims using traditional methods. The images shown in the film mirrored the touristic propaganda for Kabylia from other promotional videos; the traditional crop of olive oil served as a foil for the modernizing potential of wine and citrus.[2] The productive capacities of specific groups thus came into sharp relief through colonial propaganda that highlighted the commodification of agriculture.[3]

After World War I, colonial officials challenged the older representation of Algeria as an exotic, anachronistic landscape. Experts who worked for the Ministère de l'agriculture, OFALAC, and the Ministère d'État chargé des affaires algériennes (Ministry for Algerian Affairs) increasingly viewed the country as a space of mise en valeur, or economic development. Along with representatives of settler agriculture, planners debated which crops would be most suitable for market-oriented reforms and wondered if it would be possible to transform homo islamicus into homo economicus. As officials introduced concrete policies to develop agriculture, they drew on older notions of the economic aptitudes of natives and Europeans. Because olive oil was predominantly cultivated by Algerian Muslims, for example, some observers argued that any investment in modernizing its production would fail to secure a suitable return. In contrast, colonial officials saw wine and citrus as testaments to the ingenuity of the European settlers. This chapter analyzes OFALAC's modernization of agricultural commodities from the interwar period to the 1950s, charting how economic reforms built upon interwar ideas of mise en valeur while redefining understandings of racial difference in terms of capacities for market production.

Created in the wake of the global economic crisis of 1929, when Algerian producers faced increased competition from European countries, OFALAC introduced changes to the conditioning, standardization, and distribution of agriculture. While the organization improved the quality of Algerian produce and increased exports to Europe, it failed to integrate native producers into circuits of commercialization. Moreover, its touristic and literary activities marginalized Algerian Muslims by depicting the territory as a Mediterranean melting pot. After World War II, OFALAC's reforms reflected the growing importance attributed to economic development, which served as a new rationale for empire.

In response to the Cold War and rising anticolonial sentiment, politicians across Europe justified colonial rule by calling for the material advancement of indigenous populations. Many planners also promoted the inclusion of African territories in plans for European integration, a vision that animated attempts to create a Eurafrican economic space. Yet OFALAC's role in the standardization of olive oil and wine production highlights how the construction of a Eurafrican space articulated a new relationship between racial difference and capitalist development. Rather than invoking the nineteenth-century vocabulary of religious fanaticism and backwardness, colonial officials in the Fourth Republic defined the inferiority of Muslims primarily in terms of economic behaviors.

Colonial Reforms and Mise en Valeur

During the interwar period, French officials introduced a number of political and economic reforms in Algeria. World War I fundamentally changed the politics of empire by bringing many Algerians into direct contact with mainland France for the first time. Just under 173,000 Algerians served in the French army, 125,000 of whom fought on European battlefields. An additional 119,000 contributed to the so-called total war by working in French factories.[4] The Hexagon relied on its empire for sustenance and manpower: 90 percent of French wine came from the colonies, and France saved 707 million francs by purchasing foodstuffs from Algeria.[5] Some French politicians argued that the lives of the 25,000 Algerians who died in battle could be considered a repayment for French colonial investments, otherwise known as a blood tax.[6] After the war, French administrators were not alone in trying to balance native Algerians' demands for greater rights with the need to maintain racial difference in the empire. From British India to German East Africa, colonized subjects found their desires for economic development and political integration blocked by the same racial ideologies that had shaped recruitment patterns and military strategies during the war.[7] To the disappointment of those living under colonial rule, wartime sacrifices did little to ensure the full inclusion of colonized subjects in European nations.

For Algerians who demanded colonial reforms by asserting the financial, social, and cultural capital they had accrued through military service, the contradiction between the promises of universal republicanism and the reality of political discrimination was especially bitter.[8] Before World War I, the Young Algerians, a French-educated nationalist group, had issued a manifesto calling for equal taxation and the abolition of the Native Code. They were ultimately successful in achieving minor reforms, largely thanks to the loyalty demonstrated by Algerians on the battlefield; in 1917, Governor General Charles Jonnart proposed a law to expand citizenship rights and lessen economic inequalities. It was passed in 1919, albeit in watered-down form; the law offered limited political rights to 421,000 "deserving" Algerian Muslim men, especially veterans, and eliminated the much-hated Arab taxes. These measures were not radical enough for many Algerians, but European settlers rejected any meaningful inclusion of Muslims in politics.

Moreover, Algerians had to contend with the disastrous harvests and spread of disease that followed the end of the war, which caused many to leave the countryside and seek work in urban centers.

The contrast between the hopes generated by World War I and the continued political and economic subjugation of colonized peoples led to a surge in political agitation between the two world wars. An increase in union activity and public meetings, as well as the appearance of new forms of media including Arabic newspapers and radio, ushered in an age of mass politics.[9] Algerian nationalists expressed competing visions for reform and autonomy: Messali Hadj's party, the Étoile nord-africaine (North African Star), blended communism with Algerian traditions, appealing to workers in France and embracing separatism in the 1920s. Religious scholar Abd al-Hamid Ben Badis, on the other hand, made religion and the Arabic language the cornerstones of his demands for cultural recognition and political rights, forming the Association des ulémas musulmans algériens (AUMA; Jam'iyat al-'Ulama al-Muslimin al-Jaza'iriyyin; Organization of the Algerian Ulama), in 1931.[10] These political debates raised thorny questions of whether Algerians should renounce their personal status, which had been the condition for French citizenship under the 1865 Sénatus-Consulte. Influenced by the calls for Islamic revival prompted by the fall of the Ottoman Empire, Emir Khaled, grandson of the great emir 'Abd al-Qadir, insisted that the French state grant Algerian Muslims citizenship while allowing them to retain their language, culture, and religion.[11]

The rise in nationalist sentiments, coupled with the 1917 Bolshevik revolution, convinced some colonial administrators that political and economic reforms were necessary. In light of communist agitation, they worried that the poverty of Algerian natives and the creation of an urban subproletariat could become a threat to French control. Albert Sarraut, the governor general of Indochina who later became minister of the colonies, viewed the policy of mise en valeur as a bulwark against communist sentiments that would also convince native inhabitants of the superiority of Western values.[12] Influenced by the ethnological turn in colonial governance, Sarraut maintained that while a complete racial transformation of natives was impossible, economic prosperity was the key to racial harmony.[13] His later publications, particularly *Grandeur et servitude coloniales* (1931), built on the widespread sentiment that empire was an integral part of French national identity. In addition to the patriotic frenzy that accompanied the 1930 centennial celebration of France's conquest of Algeria, there were economic reasons for this bombastic confidence in *la plus grande France* (greater

France). During the 1920s the metropole had become more dependent on Algeria, which provided mainland France with most of its imported agricultural products and served as an outlet for French exports.[14] Sarraut's argument that the French state should finance infrastructure and public works in the colonies was ultimately rejected by the Ministry of Finance, but it foreshadowed the policy of large-scale colonial development adopted by France after World War II.

After the Great Depression, the profits from wine and grain—two pillars of the colonial economy—stagnated. Thanks to Algeria's southern Mediterranean climate, crops known as *primeurs*, such as artichokes, tomatoes, green beans, and grapes, had historically appeared in French markets weeks or even months before the same products were available in Europe. Yet cheaper goods coming from countries like Spain, which did not incur the costs of trans-Mediterranean shipping, became a worrying source of competition, leading Algerian producers to seek new strategies for exporting their goods to Europe. The Financial Delegations, the body that determined the Algerian budget, called for the establishment of an organization to oversee the commercialization of agriculture. The goal of the October 29, 1931, decree that created OFALAC was to "make Algeria known in all aspects and particularly to contribute to foreign trade and Algerian tourism."[15]

Most of OFALAC's activities concerned the standardization and commercialization of food products and the promotion of tourism.[16] One of the organization's first initiatives was to create a brand known as *Algéria* that would guarantee the origin and quality of agricultural products. Once a cooperative or producer was registered with OFALAC and paid the required fee, their products would be subjected to inspection (usually conducted at the port) and receive the *Algéria* label.[17] Hoping that a consistent product would justify higher prices, OFALAC officials passed a law in October 1935 mandating the standardization of certain crops. These measures boosted the export of agricultural products, notably citrus fruit.[18] OFALAC's experiments with standardization in Algeria were an important precedent for the development of a modern system of distribution in mainland France in the late 1930s.[19]

OFALAC also educated producers about agricultural markets by publishing guides that encouraged the cultivation of certain crops and warning of potential sources of competition. These economic questions were inseparable from colonial propaganda that bolstered the image of French Algeria. OFALAC organized traveling fairs to promote Algerian development and agriculture internationally, publishing a bimonthly magazine titled *Algeria*.[20]

Figure 2.1 Algerian produce being exported to France from the port of Oran, ca. mid-1950s. Source: Service historique de la défense, 1H/1185.

Though OFALAC was initially concerned with European settlers' agricultural production, by the 1940s, the organization's officials also wondered whether Algerian natives could participate in the commercialization and standardization of agriculture.[21]

OFALAC adopted a strategy of bulk shipping rather than relying on small-scale vendors. This decision reflected the transition from a system of colonial protection to a liberal economy based on competitive markets.[22] French sociologist Antoine Bernard de Raymond argues that standardization broke with the logic of "commerce" and prioritized distribution.[23] Instead of small-scale intermediaries organizing the sale of fruits and vegetables and waiting for consumers to purchase them in local markets, commercial networks were organized around a limited number of points of sale. Rather than being directed by many vendors and therefore vulnerable to

Figure 2.2 An OFALAC official inspects oranges before export. Screenshot from the film *L'Algérie, pays de la qualité*, le Gouvernement général de l'Algérie, 1948. Source: Institut national de l'audiovisuel, https://www.ina.fr/video/AFE00003973.

their speculative schemes, the flow of goods was centralized and rational- ized to ensure the availability of a diverse array of products at designated locations. In addition, uniform packaging assured that the presentation of fruits and vegetables was aesthetically pleasing. According to René Mayer, the general secretary of territorial planning who worked on development initiatives in the late 1950s, planners used the amount of packaging bought by producers (along with the consumption of electricity and the purchase of cement) as a general indicator of economic growth.[24] The introduction of refrigerated containers and new shipping practices were also central to ensuring the uniform quality of produce.

Many Algerians continued to be disappointed by France's meager reform efforts in the 1930s. In 1936, the Popular Front came to power, boosting hopes for economic and political reform. The same year, the Blum-Viollette Plan proposed naturalizing twenty thousand to twenty-five thousand Mus- lims without requiring them to renounce their personal status. Moreover, Minister of the Colonies Marius Moutet recommended increasing French investment in Algeria and reducing taxes on natives.[25] Both of these initiatives failed due to settler opposition, as did the request to finance a Colonial Fund for Economic Development.

The year that the Blum-Viollette proposal was defeated in the Senate, members of the Financial Delegations considered whether OFALAC should continue to grant bonuses to producers of high-quality olive oil, as it had since the introduction of a policy in 1934. A revealing quandry emerged: Should consumer demand determine financial support, in which case the limited commercial success of olive oil would discourage additional aid? Or would these bonuses increase the desirability of olive oil on the market given the elasticity of consumer demand? Maurice Raoux, a delegate from Oran, objected to the bonus. Citing the example of wine in the metropole, he claimed that a planned economy required limiting the production of certain crops. He asked, exasperated, "Is it really necessary to encourage a crop that doesn't pay?"[26] Charles Munck, a delegate from Bône who had created one of the first tobacco cooperatives, argued that the bonus could help to reeducate olive oil producers and consumers, many of whom were Algerian Muslims. Otherwise, he claimed, "if the native has no interest in using fresh olives, he will continue his ancient mistakes, especially in Kabylia."[27] This exchange reveals the tensions between an emerging class of liberal technocrats and more conservative defenders of economic protectionism.[28] Attempts to encourage the standardization and commercialization of Algerian agriculture raised pressing questions about whether Algerian Muslims could adopt the behaviors and mentalities necessary to navigate a market economy. In establishing networks of distribution based on standardization and in moving away from a subsistence economy, planners devised new systems of classification for both agricultural products and colonial labor.

The Mediterranean "Melting Pot"

As representatives of colonial agriculture sought new markets for Algerian exports, they looked to European countries besides France. Gabriel Audisio, best known as a writer and founding father of the École d'Alger (Algiers school), was also the director of OFALAC's Press and Information Services. Audisio's writings analyzed the civilizational composition of the region and highlighted the racial mixing of Mediterranean societies. The region had become central to imperial rivalries during the interwar period, as the British, French, and Italian empires all tried to establish hegemony overseas. Interwar articulations of *la plus grande France*, or *mare nostrum* (our sea) in the Italian context, expressed both a nostalgia for the Mediterranean's

Roman past and aspirations for future imperial expansion.[29] Both discourses positioned Europeans as the rightful inhabitants of the region and described Muslims as culturally inferior.[30]

As the Mediterranean became the site of ideological struggles between fascism and socialism, the region played an increasingly important role in liberal visions of European cooperation. The Paneuropa movement, founded in 1923, posited that an integrated Europe would allow countries that no longer had colonies, such as Germany, to contribute to African development. The first president of the Paneuropa league, Richard von Coudenhove-Kalergi, coined the term *Eurafrica*. The concept envisioned Africa as a source of raw materials that would benefit from the social, technical, and demographic capacities of Europe.[31] French leaders used international groups, including the League of Nations and the International Labor Organization, to advocate for the development of France's African colonies within a European framework. This geographical orientation was so essential to OFALAC's activities after World War II that a promotional brochure proclaimed, "Eurafrica is the order of the day."[32]

While Audisio and other liberal imperialists invoked Eurafrica to encourage a closer union between France and Algeria, some politicians viewed the concept as a tool of fascist appeasement.[33] Nazis used it to call for a redistribution of Britain's African territories among the Axis powers, and Italian fascists adopted the notion to advance corporatism and racial purity.[34] Yet despite the appeal of Eurafrica to those on the right, the concept was generally associated with liberal advocates of economic cooperation with Germany who hoped that European reconstruction and colonial development would promote national security and economic prosperity.[35] Beginning in 1956, the discovery of oil in the Sahara bolstered the appeal of making Algeria the cornerstone of Eurafrica.[36]

In 1950 Eirik Labonne proposed creating five *zones d'organisation industrielle et stratégique africaines* (ZOIA; African zones of industrial and strategic organization), which were to be analogous to the large-scale development undertaken by the Tennessee Valley Authority in the United States. Labonne insisted that "for the French Union, for the European Union, the Atlas mountains should be our Ural and Africa our Siberia."[37] This maximalist vision of Eurafrica stretched to the Congo and imagined that Africa would supply Europe with raw materials such as phosphates. Partisans of Eurafrica also advocated for the industrialization of Algeria, a measure that had first been proposed by the Vichy government. Labonne reiterated the security threat posed by underdevelopment, claiming that since "nature detests a vacuum,"

North Africa would soon turn to anarchy if it remained a "blank" economic space.[38] In the context of the Cold War, this possibility seemed particularly menacing. OFALAC thus reassured the public that Eurafrica carried "the promise of common peace" because it would draw on Europe's human and economic potential in developing Africa, which was "still mostly fallow, intellectually and materially."[39]

The emphasis on material progress and technical advancement, rather than on political sovereignty, allowed a wide variety of actors to invoke the concept of Eurafrica. The Eurafrican framework encouraged OFALAC officials to reflect on European integration when designing colonial policies. When the European Economic Community (EEC) was established in 1957, French officials, supported by Belgian and Italian colleagues, insisted that the colonial possessions of member states be incorporated.[40] When the European Organization of Economic Cooperation (OECE) discussed establishing standards for shipping and distribution, they included experts from OFALAC due to their considerable experience in this domain.[41] France's African colonies were so fundamental to European integration in the 1950s that Robert Schuman, the French minister and one of the founding fathers of European integration, referred to the EEC as a "Eurafrican plan."[42] A host of French politicians, including Jacques Soustelle and Robert Delavignette, argued that France's colonies on the continent should be administered along Eurafrican lines. African nationalists such as Félix Houphouet-Boigny of the Ivory Coast and Léopold Sédar Senghor of Senegal also adopted the language of Eurafrica to advocate for increased political representation in France.[43]

French Eurafricanists often stressed the commercial and military advantages of economic integration. Yet this geographic vision remained tied to the racialized myths that had underpinned understandings of Mediterranean space and European nationalism since the nineteenth century. Partisans of Eurafrica generally celebrated Latin roots and downplayed Germanic influences, a theme that had played a major role in the French (and later Italian) colonization of North Africa. This vision of a Latin North Africa was most famously espoused by Louis Bertrand, who invoked the scientific racism of Arthur Gobineau while highlighting the Greek and Roman origins of the settler population and celebrating the "homecoming" of Europeans to North Africa.[44]

Racial anthropologists studying Italy asserted a tension between its northern regions and the Mediterranean in light of Italian reunification.[45] In 1901, the Italian Giuseppe Sergi described a "Eurafrican species" comprising

Nordic, African, and Mediterranean groups.[46] A few years earlier, William Ripley had drawn on cranial morphology to establish the French Pyrenees mountains as a boundary between the Nordic and Mediterranean races. In Italy, however, he argued that a "corresponding transition, anthropologically, from Europe to Africa takes place more gradually, perhaps, but no less surely," dividing the Italian nation into two parts of "entirely different racial descent."[47] Rather than defining the Mediterranean race as a product of degeneration due to the racial mixing of the Nordic races with African elements, this framework asserted the existence of a unique Mediterranean race in Europe and North Africa. Interestingly, Ripley argued that the Berber population (a generic term he used for nonnomadic people in North Africa) enjoyed "isolation from all admixture with the other ethnic types of Europe."[48] While these authors included North Africans in their analysis of the Mediterranean race, they nevertheless saw Arabs and Berbers as being resistant to full racial integration. Drawing on the tools of anthropology and ethnology, they arrived at a similar conclusion to Bertrand, who had also described North Africans as external to Mediterranean civilization.

Audisio's writings explicitly rejected the narrowly racial definition of the Mediterranean found in Bertrand's notion of Latinity. Defining the region as a place of cultural exchange rather than biological purity, he claimed that "to identify the Latin phenomenon with the Mediterranean phenomenon is a serious confusion."[49] In his eyes, the Mediterranean was not an interior lake in Europe, but rather its own country (*patrie*).[50] This culturalist rendering of the Mediterranean nevertheless foreclosed the possibility that Algerian identity could be based on Arab or Muslim elements. Nor did it question the positive role of French colonialism. For Audisio, Muslims represented one of many layers of the region's history, but they could not play a determining role in the cultural or linguistic identity of Algeria. In an essay on Algerian literature, he asserted that the base element of Algerian identity was Berber and that other populations, such as the Phoenicians, Romans, Vandals, Arabs, Turks, and French, merely represented subsequent waves of conquerors. In trying to define Algerian literature, however, the foundational Berber element was of little use since it had not produced a written language. While positing that the Arabic language was in a state of decline, he claimed that the French invasion had helped revive this sleepy civilization. The literary stupor of the Arabs, he claimed, showed that the Maghreb was "not so profoundly an oriental country as one would like to think."[51] He went on to ask, "Isn't it mostly through French expression that native Algerians will find their best literary voice?" In arguing for the necessity of the French language, the civilizing mission of French empire was kept resolutely intact.

Audisio's writings should be analyzed in light of the broader tendency to emphasize racial hybridity during the interwar period. Writers who positioned Middle Eastern countries as Mediterranean effectively countered Arab nationalist claims rooted in Islam. Alluding to a Spanish-Arab brotherhood, some Spaniards framed their policies in Morocco as an act of fraternity rather than colonization.[52] In the Levant, the Maronite writer Charles Corm emphasized the Phoenician and Christian roots of the Lebanese people in a nationalist vision that simultaneously expressed his loyalty to the mandate government.[53] In the 1930s, Egyptian writer Taha Husain similarly argued that Egypt was a Mediterranean nation with ties to the north and west rather than a Muslim nation with ties to the east.[54] Much like understandings of the Mediterranean melting pot, Pharaonism and Phoenicianism were first articulated in the late nineteenth century by Europeans to legitimize colonial incursions. In the interwar period, however, local opponents of pan-Arabism repurposed these ideologies to provide a counternarrative of national belonging.[55]

Studies of racial hybridity from South America also influenced how scholars understood Algeria's racial formation. Fernand Braudel, France's most famous historian of the Mediterranean, taught secondary school in Algiers between 1923 and 1932 and considered Algeria a "failed Brazil" due to the emergence of rigid racial categories.[56] In Brazil, the celebration of a distinctively Portuguese style of colonization "occurred within a conceptual framework that elevated people who were of European origin over those of African origin or of mixed ancestry."[57] The emphasis on racial mixing espoused by the Algiers school was a clear rejection of the vision of a Latin Mediterranean. Yet French settlers who described Algeria as a Mediterranean melting pot nevertheless articulated a new cultural basis for excluding Muslim natives.

Postwar Modernization and the Redefinition of Race

Interwar discourses on racial hybridity were overshadowed by the onslaught of fascism and World War II. The Nazi occupation of France in 1940 had profound implications for the political and economic life of Algeria. Jews lost their French citizenship and had their businesses expropriated. Rather than seeing this racism as wholly imported from Europe, Daniel Schroeter argues that "colonialism's racialized logic facilitated the ready reception and implementation of racial legislation during the Vichy period."[58] The Vichy regime also made the first tentative efforts to industrialize Algeria, though most initiatives were not implemented by the Fourth Republic until after the war.[59] North Africa also played a central role in Vichy's defeat: in November 1942, Anglo-American forces landed in Morocco and Algeria, and Algiers served as the capital of the Free French Forces from 1942 until 1944.

During these years, OFALAC officials envisioned a "new Algeria" that broke with the economic, aesthetic, and racial structures of settler society. In 1943, directors of OFALAC wrote: "The general public has a vision of Algeria that is outdated, perpetuated by a historical imaginary that no longer corresponds to reality. Certainly, traditional Algeria, which was forged by Islam, maintains its power and still presents a vision of Orientalism that is one of the most attractive features of tourism in Algeria and the Sahara. But in the face of this traditional Algeria, a new Algeria is rising, which is thoroughly modern, which is too often ignored and imperfectly known."[60] The nineteenth-century desert landscapes of Orientalists were replaced with images of a new Algeria that had entered the world of development and consumerism.[61] The modernizing impulses of Vichy France continued under Charles de Gaulle's provisional government, which announced a commission for political, social, and economic reform. In 1944, the discriminatory and widely hated Native Code was abolished, and citizenship was offered to sixty-five thousand Algerian Muslims without requiring them to renounce their personal status. While questions of material prosperity took center stage after World War II, meaningful colonial reform remained out of reach. The 1947 Organic Statute established an Algerian Assembly and offered full citizenship to Algerian Muslims in mainland France, but not in Algeria.[62] Even if Algerian Muslims were afforded increased parliamentary representation, the double college system ensured their continued political subordination to European settlers.

The years following World War II highlighted the violent state of exception that governed French Algeria. As Europe celebrated liberation from Nazi Germany on May 8, 1945, protestors raised a version of the Algerian flag and expressed support for the imprisoned nationalist leader, Messali Hadj. In the weeks that followed, France's repression was brutal; after 102 Europeans were killed in Sétif the floodgates of colonial violence opened, killing several thousand Algerians in return.[63] The communist press offered an economic interpretation of this unrest, pointing to the widespread famine that had struck Algerian society during World War II.[64] Algerian intellectuals such as Mohammed Harbi and Kateb Yacine have argued that these massacres ushered in the War of Independence, which officially began on November 1, 1954.[65]

After World War II, France's civilizing mission was transformed into a modernizing mission, as the rise of communist and anticolonial movements prompted colonial officials to undertake ambitious reforms in agriculture, education, housing, and healthcare.[66] The French state created the Fonds d'investissement pour le développement économique des territoires d'outremer (FIDES; Investment Fund for the Economic and Social Development of Overseas France) in 1946, six years after the introduction of Britain's first Colonial Welfare Act. That same year, de Gaulle adopted the Monnet Plan to spur postwar reconstruction in France, and colonial officials introduced the Balensi Plan in Algeria, hoping that industrialization would alleviate the "Muslim problem" by increasing native employment.[67] Yet these initiatives did not take concrete form in Algeria until the first modernization plan that was partly funded by the Marshall Plan in 1949.[68] An article in the Egyptian newspaper *al-Ahram* in 1950 praised the changes brought to the Algerian landscape by these initiatives. It described Algiers as "a modern city competing with the grandest European cities in the Mediterranean basin," noting that industrial production had doubled since 1938 and that this provided hope for all of Algeria's "Arab siblings."[69] Seven years later, the outbreak of the War of Independence had significantly dampened this optimism. The Lebanese leftist journal *al-Adab* subsequently criticized those who used economic language to discuss the conflict, claiming that Algerians sought dignity and nationalism before bread.[70]

Encouraging economic development was one way that metropolitan officials sought to distance themselves from the racial discrimination of the colonial system, particularly in the aftermath of the Holocaust. The constitution of the Fourth Republic formally abolished empire, created the French Union, and repudiated racism, stating that "the people of France proclaim anew that each human being, without distinction of race, religion, or creed, possesses sacred and inalienable rights."[71] In this spirit, the French state, in conjunction with UNESCO, brought scholars together to discuss the question of race in the 1950s. The resulting consensus, sometimes known as the UNESCO tradition of antiracism, disavowed biological racism while upholding culture as an essential arena of human difference.[72] This reconceptualization of race was fundamental to postwar economic reforms. Rather than describing Algerian Muslims as inherently violent or backward, planners increasingly viewed the differences between natives and Europeans in terms of their cultural capacity to participate in a modern economy.

Symbolic Economies: Citrus, Wine, and Olive Oil

When crafting policies to standardize Mediterranean crops for export, French experts sometimes prioritized the economic aptitudes of producers over calculations of profit. It was impossible to separate the symbolic importance of products like wine and citrus, which represented the genius of French settlers, from concrete discussions on economic policy. Both products were primarily geared for export, and their cultivation had benefited from credit structures that disproportionately favored large settler holdings.[73] Rather than acknowledging the state's role in encouraging these products, or ascribing their success to colonial economic policies, French agriculturalists saw the proliferation of wine and citrus as resulting from the natural climatic features of the Mediterranean. Speaking at a professional meeting in Oran in 1960, the president of the Mediterranean Citrus Network, Vincent Juan, stated,

> Christians and Muslims have profoundly transformed this part of west Algeria through the inspiration of French genius. Here, like everywhere [in Algeria], one feels that no one would dream of detaching [Algeria] from the motherland (*la mère patrie*). The proof of this lies in the immense work accomplished in a milieu marked by unsuspected difficulties, by the uninterrupted efforts to create new plantations, by the continual development of industrial and commercial equipment, and by the development of ports that enrich the patrimony (*patrimoine*) of the French nation to which our land belongs.[74]

In promoting the economic interests of citrus growers, Juan celebrated France's success in transforming Algerian soil into French *terroir*.

For Algerian planners, the two most informative models for the modernization of the citrus industry were Israel and California.[75] In Israel, citrus fruits such as the Jaffa orange had a long history of Palestinian labor and Zionist commercialization.[76] During the mandate period, the citrus industry was "unique" among other areas of private enterprise in that its energies were concentrated "in the major ideological and symbolic arena that the Zionist Movement claimed as its own: agricultural settlement, return to the soil, acquisition of land, 'conquest of labor,' and relations with the local Arab population."[77] These deep resonances with the ideological role played by citrus in French Algeria were hardly accidental; Moshe Smilansky, a pioneer of the First Aliyah and president of the Farmer's Federation in Israel, had been inspired by Paul-Leroy Beaulieu.[78] French officials encouraged agricultural exchanges with Israel and sent students from the National School of Agriculture in Algiers to Israel in April 1958. An official publication explained France's attraction to Israel by proclaiming that "this is a people that knows what it wants and has faith in its future" despite its "isolation in the midst of a hostile world that unites its forces for future attacks."[79] One can imagine that for French administrators writing during the Algerian War of Independence, Israel's survival was a comforting thought.

The French state also sent agricultural experts to California to study its citrus industry and learn irrigation techniques. In January 1938, Audisio organized an exhibition on "Algeria, a French California" at OFALAC's Paris office.[80] The event was so successful that it ran for two weeks longer than planned, welcoming visitors until the end of March. California was considered by Israeli and Algerian citrus growers to be the epitome of a modern system of Mediterranean agriculture. In California, Israel, and Algeria, the history of citrus production both provided a romantic vision of territorial expansion and relied on the availability of cheap labor in a colonial context. The extensive branding that accompanied the growth of the citrus industry obscured the history of colonization and recounted a celebratory tale in which horticulture "civilize[d] and whiten[ed]" colonial territories.[81]

Yet it was wine, not citrus, that served as the bedrock of the colonial economy.[82] Historian Hildebert Isnard argues that "wine growing put in place the structures that conditioned the existence of modern Algeria."[83] The production of wine influenced Algerian migration, created an agricultural subproletariat, and organized regional spaces. Algerian Muslims tended to grow dry pulses and cereals, which procured thirteen thousand francs per hectare. Wine vineyards, which mostly belonged to European settlers, could yield one hundred forty thousand francs per hectare, while other varieties of fruit provided up to ninety-five thousand francs.[84]

Algerian wine was inseparable from colonial understandings of French terroir.[85] In 1937, the OFALAC *Bulletin*, which was edited by Audisio, published the following "Sonnet to Algerian Wine" by the music hall singer Lucien Boyer.

> Because it comforts and relieves us,
> We pour it, today, in all cabarets,
> And because it is mature before its age,
> It warms our hearts without exhausting our legs!

Yes, it is proud to be from its village!
It is tired of being used for strengthening clarets!
Thus, some tribunes in their Great Areopagus
Have often introduced unfair measures against it

And it, proud to be pure, to be frank, to be suitable,
Has seduced the good people and the army and…customs!
Its red or blond *chéchia* (traditional hat) provokes jealousy….

But one should not discriminate:
Because our Algeria is the New France,
And the wine it produces is our own (*de chez nous*)![86]

Boyer's mention of "strengthening" claret (a Bordeaux-style red wine) refers to the practice of using Algerian wine, commonly referred to as medicinal, as an additive to metropolitan wines due to its high alcohol content.[87] The French wine industry depended on Algerian wine for this purpose, but settlers resented their marginalization and demanded French subsidies.[88] The settler lobby had good reasons to be defensive: the appellation system created in the 1930s was in large part designed to protect French wine growers from Algerian competition on the French market.[89]

The specter of the European Common Market raised questions about the quantity of wine that could reasonably be exported to Europe. Even before the signing of the Treaty of Rome in 1957, the wine market in France suffered from overproduction. In January 1955, the minister of agriculture offered compensation to wine growers in Algeria for voluntarily uprooting their vineyards. Given the need for Algeria's agricultural production to conform to the dictates of the European market, the wine lobby argued for professional solidarity based on geographical and climatic features. A brochure for the Ninth International Congress of Wine and Vine of 1959, held in Algiers, quoted the French geographer Jean Despois, author of *L'Afrique blanche* (White Africa), saying that North Africa had "many more affinities with Europe than with Africa" due to its geographic position.[90] He concluded that "its populations have nothing in common with those of Black Africa, who live outside of the Sahara: by their white race, their lifestyle, their modes of alimentation and their spiritual attachments, they belong to the Mediterranean."[91] At the same meeting, Delegate General Paul Delouvrier insisted that the industriousness of European settlers had made Algeria into a French province. By helping to integrate North African territory into European civilization, both citrus and wine contributed to producing a

Eurafrican space in which the Mediterranean fostered commercial and civilizational links.

Despite much evidence to the contrary, French officials repeatedly claimed that the Islamic prohibition against wine—not colonial capitalism—was the main obstacle to the cultivation of indigenous vineyards. In 1960, the Institut des vins de consommation courante (Institute of Commercialized Wines), allowed an additional 450 hectares of vineyards to be grown in Algeria for the production of table wine. This prompted 776 individuals to submit requests to the organization, 420 of whom were Muslim.[92] Despite this show of native enthusiasm for the economic rewards of wine, planners continued to reinforce the idea that it was a European product. It is true that most large vineyards were run by the settler population. But labeling wine as European also suggested that settlers enjoyed a particular ability to cultivate vineyards, thereby strengthening the link between economic aptitude and European civilization.

The commercialization of agriculture had a very different impact on small-scale indigenous producers, who were increasingly reliant on European intermediaries with the necessary capital and infrastructure (such as olive oil refineries or centers for the conditioning of dates).[93] While native Algerians tended to consume unrefined (*brute*) olive oil, which was generally produced for their own communities, the more expensive, refined olive oil was intended for export. Colonial experts estimated that the Kabylia region produced half of Algeria's olives, while other oil-producing areas included Bougie (present-day Béjaïa), Bône (present-day Annaba), Oran, Tlemcen, and Mostaganem.[94] Tlemcen and Bône possessed a number of hydraulic presses, while Oran's producers employed modern presses that used a continuous method of extraction in which the entire process occurred in a closed system. Kabylia, on the other hand, had a higher concentration of small-scale, old-fashioned artisanal mills. Writing in 1948, the Constantine-born lawyer Mathéa Gaudry noted that twenty years prior, machines dating to Roman times were used to crush olives in the Aurès mountains.[95] Mills of wood and stone employed the traditional method (also known as the discontinuous method) for producing olive oil, in which each step of the extraction process—from crushing the olives to spreading and pressing the olive paste—was done separately. The resulting oil, which was highly acidic due to the fermentation of olives during the much longer production process, was often used for family consumption and had sentimental value.[96] Ancestral methods of production imparted a taste that carried traces of the trees and herbs that surrounded the olive groves in the mountains.[97] The modern continuous method, which separated the juice of the olive from

Figure 2.3 Display of Algerian wine at OFALAC's Paris location in 1947.
Source: Getty Images.

the oil using an automated centrifugal system, produced an oil that was much lower in acidity.

Algerian olive oil was increasingly commodified during the interwar period. After the Depression, countries such as Italy, which had historically purchased large quantities of olive oil from Algeria, were increasingly concerned with selling their own stock. This convinced some observers that France should encourage higher-quality production in Algeria by offering subventions and discouraging the practice of mixing olive oil with substances such as peanut oil.[98] Even as OFALAC officials realized that improving the quality of olive oil was important for commercialization, it was far from evident what benchmarks they should use. For example, while acidity could offer a rough index of quality (olives with five degrees of acidity could provide a more pleasing taste than those with less than one degree of acidity), the varieties of the olives and the soil in which they were grown also affected the resulting oil.[99] In the 1930s, OFALAC organized tasting committees to determine the culinary qualities of olive oil. As one memo noted, it was necessary to find people who possessed refined palates and would not show bias in favor of certain producers.[100]

Olive oil producers in the town of Seddouk acknowledged that their oil was higher in acidity and claimed that this taste was a local specialty and appreciated by certain consumers, particularly those who lived in the Midi. Writing to OFALAC, they noted that although their product was lauded by public opinion, it was punished by new regulations that prevented it from receiving a bonus.[101] Officials in the arrondissement of Dra El Mizan were forced to recognize that local tastes varied greatly: "The producer of olives will always prefer to give his olives to the local oil mill and to consume the oil of his olives that he considers to be more perfumed, fruitier, purer, and with all the other qualities that the peasants attach to the products of their soil."[102] But even if local preferences complicated the commodification of olive oil, the creation of a modern industry depended on implementing standards.

As with wine, the question of standardizing olive oil became more pressing in light of European economic integration in the 1950s.[103] Agricultural experts working for the French government sought to implement a system of classification that would regulate olive production and encourage its domestic consumption. To this end, the Conseil oléicole international (International Olive Oil Council) was set up under the auspices of the United Nations in 1959, the same year in which the International Accords for Olive Oil came into effect. The first International Conference of Olive Oil Technicians was held in Tangiers in May 1958. During the opening session, the president of the Fédération internationale d'oléiculture (FIO; International Olive Oil Federation) declared that "the olive grower has always been the precise expression of the immortal generosity and human solidarity of all people of Mediterranean origin."[104] He thus felt that defending this figure was a "secular testimony to the marvelous vicissitudes of our people."[105] The question of who constituted "our people" was open to interpretation; local producers of olive oil in Algeria viewed the standardization of this product as an attempt to undermine local traditions rather than an act of Mediterranean solidarity.

A law proposed by the French administration in 1960 highlights this point. It sought to exclude pomace oil (oil extracted from the olive pulp after the first press) from the products defined as olive oil. This would have made the French regulations stricter than the international accords signed in 1956. Widespread condemnation from olive producers ensued. Jacques Pélissier, the director of the Ministry of Agriculture and Forests, argued that discouraging the use of pomace oil would constitute a handicap for Algerian producers.[106] Similarly, the Bougie chamber of commerce declared that numerous Muslim producers would be "involuntarily in violation" of these laws.[107] Mustafa Tamzali, the vice president of the Algiers chamber of commerce and a well-known member of the olive oil profession, wrote the following to his colleagues:

> I beg you, Mister President, please try and intervene among the relevant ministers to bring their attention to the absolute necessity of maintaining the possibility of consuming lampante olive oils, oils made from olive pomace, and olive oils that are a mixture of refined and virgin oils in the upcoming legislation. In effect, the general agreement [on olive oil] already cited only considers oils that were obtained by a treatment of the pomace of the olive in a solvent, in their non-refined state, as "industrial oils." It would thus be illogical and economically incomprehensible for France to impose a set of laws that are so different from those of its partners and competitors in the Common Market.[108]

Tamzali argued that the exclusion of pomace and lampante oils (which came from lower-quality olives) from the definition of olive oil would be catastrophic for local producers. Three-quarters of Algerian olive oil contained lampante oil, and the local practice of using it to cut higher-quality oil would be all but impossible to eliminate. In this regard, attempts to standardize olive oil further marginalized local Muslim producers.

The specific economic and social role of olive oil in Algeria suggested that the territory would benefit from having its own representation in international governing bodies. Yet French officials struggled to determine the territory's role in the FIO. Algeria had initially been admitted to the private organization as an autonomous entity and was granted five seats on the General Committee in 1958.[109] The Office of Agriculture nevertheless decided that the French administration, rather than the Algerian Union of the General Confederation of Agriculture, would respond to queries. This was "to avoid that Algeria, a territory of French sovereignty, have on the national level an official representation distinct from that of the metropole."[110] While clearly an issue of political optics, the administration nevertheless claimed that native Algerian farmers (fellahs), who represented the least-developed sector of Algerian agriculture and produced the majority of olive oil, lacked the ability to assume this responsibility.[111]

French experts working for the Office of Agriculture (Direction de l'agriculture, du paysannat, des forêts et de la restauration des sols) often understood native producers' proclivity for subsistence agriculture as a defining element of Algerian culture. There are good reasons to believe that the lack of available capital was responsible for native Algerians' supposed inability to adopt modern production techniques. Crucially, very few of the long-term credits offered to wine producers were available for olive growers. Overlooking this fact, one report published by the Office of Agriculture claimed, "limited for numerous centuries to occupying the most inaccessible regions of Algeria, the Berber populations had to make a living off the soil, more or less isolated from the rest of the world, in order to maintain their existence."[112] The report continued, "Oriented toward a production that is purely familial, of which the surplus allowed for few exchanges, the olive tree, like the figs of Barbary, respond quite badly to the requirements of an open economy."[113] When planners did concede that subsidies would encourage Muslims to plant more olives, they made this aid contingent on the producer meeting certain technical standards.[114] Bonuses for growing olives were offered on the condition that producers follow the technical advice of the Sections agricoles de prévoyance (SAPs; Agricultural Welfare Societies), the organization responsible for modernizing traditional agriculture.[115] As a result, the large majority of producers who still used traditional methods could not benefit from these funds.[116]

While some planners supported the idea of aiding Muslims without stipulations, their colleagues retorted that the Kabyle mentality would prevent natives from using these funds effectively. For them, the poor condition of many olive plantations and rare use of fertilizer were explained by the economic capacities of the Kabyle peasant, who had "short-term vision" and was "marked by fatalism."[117] The modernization of olive oil thus failed to garner the same support as that of other crops such as wine and citrus. As colonial officials and French politicians sought to rationalize an emerging Eurafrican economy, their commitment to market exchange marginalized native producers. Economic development undertaken in the Mediterranean space mirrored the literary and anthropological definitions of the region discussed earlier. While the former excluded small-scale producers from Mediterranean economic markets, the latter minimized the cultural influence of Algerian Muslims in defining a Mediterranean aesthetic or racial type.

A commission to draft a policy for olive oil production met in the late 1950s. It noted that olive oil consumption was on the rise and had increased from 4.5 kilograms per inhabitant in 1953 to 6.5 kilograms in 1958. Members of the commission reported that native Algerians consumed almost seven times as much olive oil as Europeans.[118] They also expressed concern that the majority of olive oil was produced in Kabylia, where production focused on self-consumption, and identified a number of reasons for the stagnation of this sector: family production was antithetical to the temporal and economic sensibilities needed for industrialization, native Algerians did not see their mills as capital to be maximized, and Muslims appreciated acidity because of their "deformed" tastes. The commission therefore proposed educating individuals so that they would learn to prefer a superior quality of olive oil, seeking to transform the "taste of the [native] population who was content with the quality of the oil" that had been produced by traditional methods.[119] The standardization of olive oil, a seemingly neutral endeavor to promote higher-quality products, was informed by a racialized vocabulary for understanding the relationship of Algerian producers to capitalist notions of profit, time, and family.

Independence and National Purity

The symbolic and economic importance of colonial crops was not lost on members of the Algerian Front de libération nationale (FLN; National Liberation Front) who sabotaged settler-owned wine vineyards and called for a boycott of tobacco and alcohol during the War of Independence.[120] The Evian Accords, which had set the terms for Algerian independence in March 1962, envisioned the free marketing and exportation of Algerian wine to France.[121] But tense negotiations between the Algerian and French states continued through the 1960s as winemakers in both countries lamented official policies.[122] These discussions reflected the different national priorities of the two states and the obstinacy of colonial structures: Algeria remained economically dependent on French markets, while French officials came under increasing political pressure to curtail wine imports due to overproduction. After independence, the Algerian state nationalized French farms and adopted a socialist orientation, as evidenced by the introduction of self-management (see chapter 5 for a closer analysis). Despite the massive departure of French expertise and the definition of Algerian nationalism in terms of Islam, wine played a central role in the socialist sector, employing over half of all agricultural laborers from 1966 to 1967.[123] Although the Algerian state attempted to convert vineyards into other crops in the late 1960s, wine remained the most profitable agricultural export.

After independence, all producers—Algerian and French, from the socialist and private sectors—complained about the conditions for commercializing and exporting their wine.[124] A dual structure made it necessary to obtain certificates of origin that indicated whether the vineyard was run by Algerians (in the socialist sector) or French producers (in the private sector).

This created general confusion, as wine produced in Algerian territory could be labeled as French or Algerian. Adding to this chaos, French consular reports stated that one hundred thirty thousand individuals claiming to be part of the Algerian Armée de libération nationale (ALN; National Liberation Army; Jaysh al-Tahrir al-Watani al-Jaza'iri) were roaming the country and pillaging French stocks of wine. Given the young state's attempt to control the market, this was seen as an affront to national sovereignty, leading French and Algerian authorities to agree on the need to fight this "bandit" wine.[125] Nationalist sentiments undoubtedly influenced the wine market: French consumers, bitter after the passing of French Algeria, were reluctant to buy Algerian wine.[126] Much to the chagrin of many ex-settlers, President Ben Bella claimed he was unable to repatriate the large quantity of French wine that remained in Algeria.

Olive oil continued to be associated with Algerian peasants (fellahin) after 1962. The Algerian state confiscated many large estates, including the olive groves of Mustafa Tamzali. Nationalized on October 10, 1963, his company was renamed the Huileries modernes d'Algérie (Modern Oil Mill of Algeria). One worker who took over production after nationalization reported that while Tamzali had mixed olive oil with different substances, including horse fat, the socialist management committee now sold only pure olive oil.[127] Once a symbol of native backwardness, the quality and purity of olive oil became a sign of national identity and revolutionary ethos after independence.

After 1962, the organization of markets in olive oil and wine continued to reflect the symbolic importance of these products and their associations with Algerian or European identity. Algerian nationalists had rejected Eurafrica as a neocolonial imposition during the war, but decolonizing the Algerian economy proved challenging.[128] In the case of olive oil, the Algerian government forbade exports from the private sector and assumed a monopoly on the export of olive oil from the public sector.[129] This led to the bureaucratization of the industry, leading Algerian expert Rachid Oulebsir to argue that "Algerian producers were cut off from the world, strangers to the international agricultural fairs, where they had been replaced by 'officials'—bureaucrats who were only familiar with olive oil in a salad!"[130] Despite these attempts to bring production under state control, olive oil in Algeria is still often sold outside of official circuits, and its acidic taste and deep green color remain sources of pride. Today, less than twenty percent of olive oil in Algeria is produced through the modern continuous system. Most Algerian consumers continue to buy olive oil directly from their local mill, appreciating the specific properties of a product that is not adapted to the global market.[131]

OFALAC's activities continued after independence, even though most of its staff was repatriated to France, often to work for services dedicated to the repression of fraud. The organization was renamed the Algerian Office of Commercial Action in August 1962 (officials kept the same acronym and logo, however).[132] Its responsibilities overlapped with those of the Office nationale de commercialisation (ONACO; National Office of Commercialization) created in December 1962, as well as the Office nationale de la réforme agraire (ONRA; National Office of Agrarian Reform), which was given the exclusive right to commercialize products from the self-managed socialist sector.[133] Algerians regularly complained about the administrative and even moral shortcomings of ONACO, which was involved in a number of scandals, including the arrests of several of its employees, during the first years of independence.[134]

Agricultural fairs, which had been organized by OFALAC to promote tourism and trade, also continued despite Ben Bella's rhetoric of economic self-sufficiency. At the first fair after independence, held in Oran in 1964, Minister of the Economy Bachir Boumaza gave a speech proclaiming that "the number of visitors and the quality of the countries that participate in this fair attest to the emergence of Algeria on the international economic scene."[135] Speaking of the newly formed organization, he continued, "the Algerian Office of Commercial Action is the guardian and the guarantor of the quality of our products, and this is a great honor for the Algerian government, who would at no price export merchandise that gives an unfavorable image of the country." While seeking to diversify trade partners and break free of its dependence on France, socialist Algeria was nevertheless eager to present itself as a "country of quality."

In the 1950s, 90 percent of Algeria's exports were still destined for France. Moreover, the modernizing dictates of the Common Market made OFALAC's organizational structure, which was divided between agriculture and tourism, seem increasingly anachronistic. Salah Bouakouir, the secretary general of economic affairs, instructed the director of OFALAC "to completely re-orient their commercial practices" and work exclusively toward the export of Algerian agriculture to Europe.[136] Similarly, given the need to work with European organizations promoting economic cooperation such as the OECE, the head of the chamber of commerce argued that the tasks of agricultural standardization and tourist promotion should not be handled by a single organization and that rules coming from Geneva required "a real technician" to head OFALAC.[137]

The Fifth Republic, which came to power in 1958, represented the definitive victory of a modern Algeria over the settlers' nostalgic vision of the territory. Planners sought to "achieve a genuine symbiosis between the two shores of the Mediterranean" by investing in human capital.[138] The dream of economic integration continued to draw on Mediterranean tropes. In 1960, Jean Vibert, a top French official responsible for Algerian economic planning, discussed the conditions necessary for successful development in Algeria. He contrasted Mediterranean and industrial lifestyles, claiming that "sunshine plays an important role" in the Mediterranean lifestyle, "and the habits of eating are not the same either."[139] Further explaining the difference between these two sensibilities, he noted that Mediterranean culture was "folkloric" and "less inclined toward technology." Another major obstacle to development was that individuals were "more oriented toward the past than toward the future."[140] The Algiers school's depiction of Mediterranean culture—defined by the sun, eating habits, superstition, and a slow temporality—was an obstacle for planners who sought to create entrepreneurial subjects out of native Muslims and Europeans.

After 1958, economic development become a key weapon in attempts to pacify the violence of the Algerian War. Despite the crucial roles played by forward-looking technocrats, however, late colonial development did not represent a clean break from the racial myths of the 1930s and 1940s. De Gaulle gave the reins of economic planning to a new generation of technocrats, who reconceptualized the role of economic markets and drew on the postwar social sciences. These experts displayed an unprecedented confidence in France's ability to convert homo islamicus into homo economicus. Rather than a means of distributing goods more efficiently, these planners viewed the market economy as a technology of sociological transformation.

3.
DECOLONIZATION AND THE CONSTANTINE PLAN

In 1960, the renowned French Orientalist Jacques Berque published *Les Arabes d'hier à demain* (The Arabs, from yesterday to tomorrow). Although Islam had historically dominated the collective life of the Arabs, he argued, the Muslim world was gradually adapting to economic development and technical progress. The Occident was home to the working man (*l'homme ouvrier*), as exemplified by the figure of homo faber. Berque defined the Oriental as his very opposite, a *non-febvre*.[1] In describing a tension between theological attachments and the need for material development, Berque intervened in a heated discussion among scholars, colonial administrators, and economic planners. These disputes were especially relevant in the context of the Algerian War of Independence (1954–62), which had led French economists and politicians to reflect on the possibility of reconciling Islamic traditions with technological progress as part of the broader strategy of pacification.

In a debate with the Catholic thinker Louis Massignon the same year, Berque expressed his hope that Muslims would "become actors in industrial civilization."[2] If this transformation did not take place, he warned, they would "remain eternally opposed to the Other, and, refusing the Other, they would refuse themselves."[3] Massignon was skeptical of industrial civilization, however, which he viewed as a symptom of the rise of technocracy. After World War II, many French intellectuals became increasingly suspicious of the forces of technocracy, which they considered to be a sign that the government had adopted the ideals of administrative rationality and specific technical competency while abandoning the principles of political representation.[4] If industrial civilization could be described as a marriage between moral values and material needs, technocracy was associated with the rise of an administrative class linked to the state. Both of these terms were products of the economic and cultural changes that occurred during the Trente Glorieuses (thirty glorious years), a period of economic growth that followed France's liberation from Nazi occupation. During these decades, planners adopted neo-Keynesian economic policies, encouraging strong state intervention and promoting market-oriented reforms that would lead to the emergence of a consumer society. The term *Trente Glorieuses* was coined by the French economist Jean Fourastié, who worked at the Commissariat général au Plan (CGP; General Planning Commission), the institutional mecca of economic planning that had been created by de Gaulle in 1946.

The transition to a market economy brought about noticeable changes in the daily lives of Algerians. Historian Mohammed Harbi recounts his father's observation that Algeria no longer enjoyed a "redistributive economy" but rather was subject to an "economy of profit" after 1940.[5] Pierre Bourdieu, who did fieldwork during the Algerian War of Independence, put it slightly differently: he wrote that Algerian peasants were acutely aware that the traditional subsistence economy had been transformed and the "time of the shopping basket" had arrived.[6] The outbreak of the War of Independence in 1954 radically altered the political stakes of economic development, even as the French government refused to officially acknowledge that the conflict with Algerian rebels in fact constituted a war.[7] Nevertheless, de Gaulle tackled the question of underdevelopment in Algeria immediately upon his return to power. On October 3, 1958, the Resistance leader announced his vision for the Constantine Plan, a five-year initiative that sought to raise the standard of living in Algeria through social and economic development. The very next day, Muslim subjects were granted the status of full citizens, ending the legal separation between Europeans and natives that was rooted in the 1865 Sénatus-Consulte.[8] De Gaulle sought to encourage peaceful relations through economic and political integration, a strategy that politicians had also used in Europe after World War II.

Planners in Algeria were confronted with the fact that Muslims greatly outnumbered Europeans. This made Berque's speculations regarding the abilities of Muslims to participate in technological modernity especially pertinent.[9] Consistent with older strategies for colonization, postwar economic reforms were shaped by long-standing ideas about native Algerians. After World War II, however, the consolidation of economic planning as a discipline and the rising influence of the social sciences offered new tools for understanding this racial-religious difference. Civil servants trained at institutions such as Sciences Po, the École Polytechnique and the École nationale d'administration (ENA; National School of Administration) increasingly staffed the CGP, bringing with them a "more flexible, American-influenced practice of management."[10] They also tended to distance themselves from older views of colonization that overtly embraced military domination or beliefs in racial inferiority. Rather than adhering to the vision of *Algérie de papa*, these experts believed that contact with markets would foster social evolution among the native inhabitants.

This chapter reflects on how the postwar history of economic planning in France influenced colonial modernization and the racial regime of religion in Algeria. The roots of colonial development can be traced back to the interwar visions of social Catholics and modernizing liberals who tried to address the chronic instability of the Third Republic. Building on this tradition, architects of the Constantine Plan sought to avoid the extremes of laissez-faire capitalism and authoritarian communism. The economic historian Richard Kuisel has defined the "new synthesis" of a "Gallic style of economic management that blended state direction, corporatist bodies, and market forces" as an early form of neoliberalism.[11] Paul Delouvrier, responsible for implementing the Constantine Plan, possessed excellent credentials, having studied at Sciences Po before working with Jean Monnet on the first French plan for economic recovery (known as the Monnet Plan) in the Hexagon from 1946 to 1947.[12] State experts like Delouvrier used the language of the social sciences and advances in the disciplines of statistics, psychology, and management to elide the historical structures of economic and racial violence. They also accentuated the need to transform mentalities, instill economic aptitudes, and incentivize behaviors. Consistent with the postwar embrace of color-blindness, they avoided explicit references to race or religion, even though assumptions about the inherent aptitudes of Muslims were built into the plan. Put differently, the racial hierarchies constructed through colonization were embedded—though disavowed—in the Constantine Plan, which defined humanity in terms of market capacities and entrepreneurial activities. This economic language was rejected by Algerian nationalists in the FLN, who viewed this discourse as an attempt to sidestep the basic dynamics of colonization. Rather than refusing the economic modernization outlined by the Constantine Plan however, the FLN sought to use similar tools for different ends. Many Algerian nationalists engaged in the struggle for independence hoped to create revolutionary subjects who embodied the country's Arab Muslim personality.

France Reborn

Recent scholarship has traced the roots of France's postwar rebirth as a welfare state to the 1930s. During the interwar period, intellectuals and economists of different ideological stripes—including French socialists, liberals, and social Catholics—embraced planning as a tool that would prevent another economic depression, which many blamed on laissez-faire liberalism, and foster a "third way" between socialism and capitalism.[13] In response to the focus on rationalization and technical progress, some economists articulated a "person-centric" rhetoric of development.[14] Members of Economy and Humanism, a group founded by Père Louis-Joseph Lebret in 1941, argued that chaos was the "rotten fruit of liberalism," and rejected both liberalism and socialism in their 1942 manifesto.[15] The social Catholic group called for an economy based on human values rather than market logics; the principles of blood and work, they argued, could be better expressed through a communal economy (économie communautaire) that would diminish social and class conflict.[16] They adopted the notion of community to signal their hope that men would be brought together by the "fundamental human relations" of "blood, work, and place."[17] While skeptical of free market approaches, they saw communism and Marxism as denying basic human needs. The true goal of any economic system, they argued, was to "remake men" and ensure the spiritual values necessary for true fulfillment. A draft of Economy and Humanism's 1955 manifesto described Christianity as playing a "unifying role" that would encourage the "universal solidarity of all peoples" through economic planning.[18] Yet not all religions were discussed in such a positive light. The document associated Islam with an "extraordinary passivism" and described it as afflicted by a "conception of time that is diametrically opposed to the hectic and jostled life that is dear to the West."[19] Arabs, it claimed, remained "frozen in immobility," stirring from this unproductive slumber only if there was an opportunity to kill in the name of God.[20]

Economy and Humanism exemplified a Catholic rejection of the abstract egalitarianism featured in the republican motto "liberté, égalité, fraternité." Père Lebret and his followers believed it necessary to acknowledge the natural differences among individuals while simultaneously guarding society against the most pernicious effects of capitalism. In a draft of the 1955 manifesto, Lebret wrote, "It is natural for inequalities to exist based on human qualities, labor, or inheritance ... but we must abolish the institutional theft that is the permanent exploitation of others' labor."[21] The group's skepticism of republicanism and egalitarianism had clear resonances with the conservative ideology of Vichy. As John Hellman has shown, these intellectual entanglements were evident at the school established by Vichy in 1940 at Uriage, which brought together social Catholics and future modernizers, and where Delouvrier himself completed a six-week training program in the summer of 1942.[22] This institution also played an important role in articulating the need for a "national managerial elite" after 1945, providing a model for the creation of the ENA.[23] Unsurprisingly, the continuities with Vichy ideology were downplayed after the war.

State officials who advocated for economic planning often made their case by foregrounding the humanist values that would be imparted alongside material progress and efficiency. Pierre Massé, the general commissioner of planning from 1959 to 1966, frankly characterized the "spirit" of the plan as "the bringing together of the nation's economic and social forces."[24] He defined the French tradition of planning as "the search for a middle road reconciling an attachment to liberty and individual initiative with a common orientation of development."[25] As Kristen Ross has argued, postwar debates on humanism were inextricably entangled with modernization; as a result, economic planning became an episteme through which "man" was made recognizable.[26] Crucially, however, the remaking of economic modernity after World War II was underpinned by understandings of religion that had crystallized during colonization.

The struggle against communism, and the desire to navigate the extremes of laissez-faire liberalism and socialist planning, encouraged social Catholics to find common ideological ground with secular economists.[27] According to Philip Mirowski and Dieter Plehwe, liberals first expressed this need for a middle ground in the 1930s, engaging in debates that would form the basis of a "neoliberal thought collective" that took shape after World War II.[28] Many of these figures attended the Walter Lippmann Colloquium, which was organized in Paris in 1938 by Louis Rougier.[29] Mirowski and Plehwe's use of *neoliberalism* may be jarring for those who associate the term with the era of Margaret Thatcher, Ronald Reagan, and a hollowing out of welfare services. Yet scholars who study interwar economic debates have argued that neoliberal tendencies can be seen in earlier attempts to refashion liberal principles after the Great Depression.[30] While careful not to conflate the two iterations of neoliberalism, historians have pointed to similarities between the adoption of market-based policies in the 1970s and 1980s and the revival of a market economy in the 1950s, even as the latter was "tempered by public economic management and heightened self-organization among private economic interests."[31]

The 1938 Walter Lippmann Colloquium sought to "revive the capitalist process and . . . define the doctrine, the conditions for success, and the duties of a true liberalism."[32] The discussions also assumed academic forms, including the creation of a journal (*Cahiers du libéralisme*) and think tank, known as the Centre international d'études pour la rénovation du libéralisme (CIRL; International Center of Studies for the Renovation of Liberalism). Convinced of the need to articulate a new form of liberalism, members of this collective supported the values of competition and entrepreneurship. According to François Denord, a number of fundamental principles were introduced at the conference:

> For the first time, neoliberalism was defined by a set of postulates that constituted an agenda: the use of the price mechanism as the best way to obtain the maximal satisfaction of human expectations; the responsibility of the state for instituting a juridical framework adjusted to the order defined by the market; the possibility for the state to follow goals other than short-term expedients and to further them by levying taxes; the acceptance of state intervention if it does not favor any particular group and seeks to act upon the causes of economic difficulties.[33]

Presaging later neoliberal thinkers such as Gary Becker, these intellectuals viewed the market as the most efficient way to reconcile the interests of disparate groups in society.

World War II halted these reflections, but they resumed in 1947, when Albert Hunold and Friedrich Hayek brought together a group of intellectuals to discuss the future of liberalism, inaugurating the Mont Pèlerin Society (MPS). As Jessica Whyte has argued, these thinkers viewed the competitive market as "the product of an appropriate institutional framework and rule of law" and believed it symbolized a moral order built around the allegedly Western values of liberty, freedom, and individualism.[34] Collectivism and socialism emerged as the principal enemies. Scholars, journalists, politicians, and even a few corporate leaders came together to create a space for like-minded intellectuals to reflect on how to combat the encroachment of collectivism and totalitarianism. The statement of the group's aims spoke not only of the "moral and economic origins" of the postwar crisis, but also mentioned the importance of developing an international order that would be capable of "permitting the establishment of harmonious international economic relations."[35] Reflections on economic development in Algeria were central in crafting the economic orthodoxies and political frameworks designed to save France—and Europe—from the socialist threats emanating from the Third World.

In the 1950s, state planners and colonial officials in Algeria addressed the dual imperatives of metropolitan reconstruction and colonial development. In 1954, just one month before the outbreak of the War of Independence, Roland Maspétiol, a member of the Council of the State known for his defense of rural interests in France, spearheaded a report on the Algerian economy. Known as the Maspétiol Report, it characterized markets as a threat to traditional agriculture and reflected its author's nostalgic view of the peasantry, which he believed was the country's best defense against communism and fascism.[36] This would not be the last word on colonial development. Robert Lacoste, the governor general of Algeria from 1956 to 1958, endorsed the Special Powers Act that was passed by the French National Assembly in March 1956.[37] He also introduced a series of resolutions for economic development that reflected his involvement with CIRL in the late 1930s.[38] Unhappy with the Maspétiol Report, particularly its emphasis on the need for protection, he commissioned the Decennial Perspectives in March 1956. This blueprint for economic development was organized by the Kabyle *polytechnicien* and secretary general for economic affairs in Algeria, Salah Bouakouir. Its findings were then revisited by the Byé Commission in early 1958.[39] These economic reforms, conceived in the last hour of the Fourth Republic, brought together many individuals who would go on to contribute to the Constantine Plan, which embraced the principle of market incentives to incite social transformations.[40]

"An Economist Will Fix This"

Studying the history of economic planning on the southern shore of the Mediterranean allows us to see how colonial reforms shaped the early emergence of neoliberalism. It reveals the ways in which racial-religious differences were written into the modernizing worldview of the postwar period and emerging conceptions of market rationality. The officials who drafted the Constantine Plan were trained by the institutions responsible for postwar modernization in mainland France. Massé served as the general commissioner of the CGP from 1959 to 1966 and symbolized the apogee of planning in France after 1945.[41] He also played an important role in designing the Constantine Plan as the honorary president of the High Council of the Plan, the organization responsible for outlining its main objectives.[42] Similarly, Jean Vibert had worked on colonial questions at the CGP before Delouvrier hand-selected him to be director of the Constantine Plan. He has been credited with drafting the document, writing rapidly on blank sheets of paper and ringing the bell for his secretary upon the completion of each page.[43]

The preponderance of these state experts on the High Council of the Plan is best explained by the reforms to the recruitment procedure for high-ranking civil servants laid out by the 1946 Statut général des fonctionnaires (general statute for public employees). This law followed the 1945 ordinance that had created the ENA, which was responsible for training elite functionaries to occupy posts at the General Inspection of Finances, a prestigious institution in charge of modernizing the financial system after the war, as well as the Ministry of the Economy and Finances.[44] The ENA was based on the École Polytechnique, a school that had been created to train engineers, many of whom subsequently occupied high-ranking positions in the civil service and the army. The formation of this specialized corps of experts was rooted in de Gaulle's vision of a strong state in which power would be concentrated in an executive branch and supported by a loyal and specialized administrative class.[45] The École libre des sciences politiques (renamed Sciences Po in 1945) was henceforth viewed as a launching pad for the ENA; between 1952 and 1969, over three-quarters of the students who passed the entrance exam for the ENA had been trained at Sciences Po.[46]

De Gaulle's faith in expertise was fundamental to his handling of the Algerian War. In September 1958, when discussing the increasing violence of the conflict, he is reported to have exclaimed, "An economist will fix this for me."[47] True to this belief, many of the individuals who worked on the Constantine Plan had graduated from one of the elite schools and previously served as high-ranking public servants.[48] Members of this state elite—most notably Delouvrier—had also been shaped by their participation in the Resistance during World War II and bore the imprint of Catholic values.[49]

As a student at Sciences Po, Delouvrier rubbed shoulders with the modernizing elect of the Fourth Republic. He took classes with Jacques Rueff, who had been a member of the MPS before the war and was known for his opposition to Keynesianism.[50] Explaining how his studies helped him assimilate to the world of Parisian intelligentsia despite his upbringing in the Vosges mountains, he recounted, "Sciences Po introduced me to both modernity and current events: those two years were a breath of fresh air. With people who had responsibilities in the administration and the business world who talked to us about the concrete problems they were facing, I felt like a Parisian in the true sense, because the Parisian looks around, is free, and opens his eyes and ears."[51] Institutions including Sciences Po and the ENA fostered professional networks, ensured social assimilation, and propagated the economic orthodoxies espoused by those close to state power.[52]

After his studies, Delouvrier returned to Sciences Po as a professor. The class on political economy that he co-taught in 1949 illustrates the tendency of liberals to occupy a middle ground between socialism's heavy-handed engineering of markets and the laissez-faire approach that discouraged state intervention in the economy. He believed that markets were the most reliable aggregator of social dynamics and that competition was fundamental to the functioning of the economy. In the textbook that he wrote for the class, he expressed a preference for growth over stability, a reliance on the state to encourage competition, and support for the priority of the price mechanism.[53] Delouvrier was adamant, for example, that agricultural subsidies be tied to productivity. He therefore denounced the Office du blé (National Wheat Office), which had been created by the Popular Front in order to stabilize prices, complaining that they were set based on political concerns instead of market demand. While at the Inspection of Finances, Delouvrier worked with Monnet on the first French Plan in 1946 and was head of finance for the CGP.[54] He subsequently held a position at the Secrétariat général du comité interministériel pour les questions de coopération économique européenne (SGCI; General Secretary of the Interministerial Committee Responsible for Questions of European Economic Cooperation) before Monnet offered him the position of financial director at the High Authority of the European Coal and Steel Committee. Delouvrier also participated in drafting the Treaty of Rome, which established the European Economic Community.

In certain ways, Delouvrier was skeptical of democracy. He regretted that popular representation required politicians to abide by the wishes of their constituents, who often sought to protect themselves from the short-term discomfort required to ensure long-term prosperity. Subjecting farmers to the law of supply and demand was a politically risky project, he reasoned, and would inevitably face resistance from unions. Only a strong, stable government would be able to implement the necessary economic reforms. It was not only the syndicalists who needed to change their way of thinking, he argued. Most entrepreneurs, he lamented, particularly in France, lacked the sense of risk necessary to be enterprising actors (*entreprenants*).[55]

Interwar debates on how to resist Soviet-style planning, while encouraging state intervention in the economy, set the tone for the Fifth Republic. This revised version of classic liberal thought was harnessed to the twin projects of colonial development and European integration after 1958. In Algeria, planners refused economic protection, supported the free trade of goods with France, and placed great faith in the social sciences. The Constantine Plan relied heavily on private-public partnerships, using state subsidies to incentivize the private sector.[56] These policies reconfigured state management of the economy and provided a new language for describing the religious-racial difference of Algerians. They reproduced the classic colonial tropes of Oriental passivity and fatalism, but inscribed them in the languages of statistics, public opinion, and social sciences. In adopting this new vocabulary, state officials working with the CGP disavowed racial categories while simultaneously reiterating the idea that the difference between Europeans and Algerians resided in the social fact of Islam.

Archimedes's Lever

On November 1, 1954, the Algerian FLN perpetrated a series of coordinated attacks across the country. The group was initially composed of a few hundred militants who had splintered off from the Comité révolutionnaire d'unité et d'action (Revolutionary Committee of Unity and Action), which comprised former followers of Messali Hadj. Over the next six years, the FLN strove to win support and achieve legitimacy, at times using violence against Messalists to force Algerians to take sides. The divisions within the nationalist movement, which were geographical and linguistic as well as ideological, continued to mark Algerian politics after independence. The war also led to the fall of the Fourth Republic in France.

FLN militants were inspired by the revolutionary fervor that spurred the 1952 coup in Egypt and the fall of France in Indochina after Dien Bien Phu. Adopting a redemptive view of history, they envisioned the November 1 attacks as a way to assuage the humiliations of the Algerian people. The FLN's proclamation of October 31, 1954, which was broadcast on Algerian radio from Cairo, stated that the war's ultimate goal was the "restoration of the sovereign, democratic, and social Algerian state in the framework of Islamic principles."[57] Yet the precise political orientations of the FLN were not outlined until the Soummam Congress on August 20, 1956, where Algerian nationalists argued that the diplomatic isolation of France would be crucial in winning the war.[58] In trying to gain international recognition and the support of the local population, members of the FLN also sought to counter French claims that the colonizing power was the only force capable of providing material prosperity for the Algerian population.[59]

The months leading up to the Soummam Congress were marked by increased violence. On August 20, 1955, the armed wing of the FLN deployed thousands of fellahs in Philippeville (now Skikda) in order to intimidate Europeans and win over undecided Algerians. Seventy-one European civilians, twenty-one Algerian civilians, and thirty-one members of the police and army were killed in the violence; French reprisals in turn killed at least two thousand Algerians.[60] The event polarized the two sides of the conflict and set the stage for the Battle of Algiers in late 1956, when parts of the city were transformed into an urban combat zone. During the campaign, military generals were given free rein to quash the insurgency by whatever means necessary, which resulted in the systematic use of torture and the application of counterinsurgency techniques that had been developed by officers working for the infamous Fifth Bureau of the French army.[61] This approach to military strategy, first articulated in Indochina, focused on "intelligence gathering, population control, psychological warfare, and the moral conquest and transformation of the population."[62] The Constantine Plan borrowed heavily from these techniques, exemplifying how military strategies and development initiatives were complementary tools in French attempts to pacify Algeria.[63]

On May 13, 1958, a group of disgruntled colonial officials and army officers, including General Raoul Salan, attempted a coup against the French government. They called on former military hero Charles de Gaulle to return to public life. Just two days later, de Gaulle announced that he was ready to assume power. From there, things moved quickly: a referendum on September 28 ratified the new constitution, leading to the creation of the Fifth Republic.[64] On October 3, 1958, in the predominantly Muslim city of Constantine, de Gaulle announced the Constantine Plan. He outlined that fifteen billion francs would be dedicated to public works and urban development, housing would be constructed for one million individuals, four hundred thousand new jobs would be created, and two hundred fifty thousand hectares of land would be redistributed to Muslim farmers. Alongside these material commitments came the promise of "social promotion" to introduce quotas for public sector jobs in both Algeria and the metropole.[65]

A few months later, on December 19, de Gaulle sought to reinstate civilian control in Algeria. He replaced General Salan with two figures: Delouvrier became delegate general, and General Maurice Challe was named commander in chief of the French Armed Forces. Each man was also put in charge of a plan: Delouvrier took over the Constantine Plan, and Challe sought to weaken the FLN's military arm, the ALN.

Figure 3.1 Paul Delouvrier (*front, center*) with General Maurice Challe (*front, left*) in Algiers, 1958. Source: Getty Images.

Challe was committed to Algeria's political integration with France. When he felt that de Gaulle was wavering on his commitment to French Algeria in 1961, the General organized a failed putsch. Delouvrier, however, had been skeptical that Algeria would remain under French sovereignty and that economic development could halt the insurgency.[66] British consular sources reported that Delouvrier was "appalled at the fascist atmosphere of Algiers and at the wall of hostility he foresees in his task here."[67] Just one month after Delouvier's arrival in Algiers, the journalist Jacques Sallebert interviewed him on French national television. Delouvrier began the interview by detailing his illustrious career in economic planning, frankly admitting that he had no direct involvement in politics or Algerian affairs, and asserting that a new strategy was needed in Algeria. Sallebert presented

Delouvrier as a "new man" who had come to rectify a situation that was, "unfortunately, not new."[68]

In overseeing the Constantine Plan, Delouvrier employed the same principles that he had learned while working with Monnet, with whom he often conversed about the challenges he faced in Algeria.[69] He worried that previous plans had led to the "economic isolation of North Africa" and therefore advocated for a more liberal system in which the market could enact the necessary psychological changes.[70] To the chagrin of some of his colleagues, Delouvrier refused to instate protectionist policies, believing that the state should promote competition and help the private sector should it prove unable to generate investments itself.[71] He tried to adopt Monnet's approach of finding an "Archimedes's lever"—a strategic intervention that could have ripple effects on the entire economy.[72] As Monnet recounted in his memoirs, "psychological changes, which some seek through violent revolution, can be achieved very peacefully if men's minds can be directed towards the point where their interests converge. That point always exists, but it takes trouble to find it."[73] Monnet believed that an economic plan should satisfy collective interests so that people would be less tempted to instigate violent revolution. This message had obvious lessons for Delouvrier in Algeria, where he blended the technocratic tools for political and economic integration first developed in Europe with colonial techniques of counterinsurgency.

As emphasized by Massé, there was little doubt that the Constantine Plan inaugurated a fundamental chapter in the history of French economic planning.[74] Delouvrier claimed that it would enable France to "reconstruct part of its human capital."[75] Nevertheless, the experience of economic planning in Algeria differed from that in mainland France. René Mayer, a polytechnicien who served as the director of habitat for the Government General from 1957 to 1960 and was secretary general of territorial planning under the Constantine Plan from 1961 to 1962, recounted the following:

> The colonial administration in Algeria was months—or years—ahead of [the administration in] France. I had more liberty, I felt much more free. I started a number of initiatives in Algeria, I just had to go down two floors to see the General Director of Finances. If there was a financial problem, we would come [to] an agreement and it was done. Here [i.e., in France], to do the same thing you had to make the rounds of all the ministries…and before you could sign a decree, two years would have gone by, it wasn't the same government [that was in power], the

signatures that you have obtained were no longer valid. It was maybe for this reason that we were ahead [in Algeria].[76]

Mayer's statement captures the widespread feeling that metropolitan bureaucracy was an obstacle to innovation and that Algeria offered a more dynamic environment. Planners tended to view the colonies as blank slates where one could escape the entrenched struggles for power that marked mainland France.[77] Institutions such as the Caisse d'équipement du développement de l'Algérie (CEDA; Fund for the Development of Algeria), the funding body for the Constantine Plan, were at the forefront of marketing techniques. Moreover, the political imperatives of maintaining French sovereignty, at least in the earlier stages of the war, meant that considerable resources were available for development initiatives.

At the same time, planners were forced to confront the specificity of Algerian society and the fact that the majority of its inhabitants were Muslim. In February 1959, the director of the plan sent a memo to local officials that highlighted the necessity of framing the plan as a "development plan" and not a "plan of modernization and equipment," as the first postwar metropolitan plan had been called.[78] When asked about this discrepancy at a press conference, Delouvrier explicitly linked economic structures to psychological capacities. He claimed that, in Algeria, traditional agriculture was outside the monetary circuit and that "economic calculation, in the modern sense [was] not possible" for Algerian farmers.[79] In other words, modernization was possible only where there was already a "network of businesses" and farmers who were "relatively evolved."[80] In his eyes *développement* was the more appropriate term in Algeria, where one had to introduce entirely new initiatives among less-evolved economic actors.

While Delouvrier expressed certain reservations about the economic capacities of Muslims, his colleague Vibert was more optimistic that the Constantine Plan would prompt large-scale social transformations. In 1961, he asserted that,

> thanks to the Constantine Plan, homo economicus has been born. He has replaced homo Islamicus, who accepted an extremely low level of material needs and who, as a result, did not feel the need to work more than was necessary. He is slowly becoming homo economicus, who is driven by his needs just like his European counterpart and who, consequently, starts working and is concerned with the betterment of his output and bonuses, or with improving his skills and who … has the underlying yet profound desire to uplift his children and the next generation.[81]

In Vibert's formulation, Algerian natives would be transformed by their embrace of a capitalist economic sensibility. This was quite a shift from the civilizing missions' emphasis on cultural traits and language skills. Much like in the metropole, where welfare provisions targeting Muslims were based on essentialized accounts of an "Algerian mentality," economic planning in Algeria could not escape questions of religious-racial difference.[82]

The colonial administration often interpreted the so-called problem of Islam through the prism of gender. The Constantine Plan noted that "female evolution should play a determining role" in modernization and financed measures to give Algerian women access to education and the work force, including the civil service.[83] Propaganda for the plan lauded the formation of female itinerant social-medical teams and monitors who would teach Muslim women the fundamental skills of domesticity and hygiene. This was also the goal of the Mouvement de solidarité féminine (Movement of Feminine Solidarity), a charitable organization that included the wives of generals and colonels and was headed by Nafissa Sid Cara, the first Muslim woman to serve as a minister in a French government.[84] While it followed a long-standing pattern of European women striving to enlighten their native counterparts, it was also a "tool of military operations" largely funded by the army.[85]

In metropolitan France, postwar modernization sought to inculcate the correct forms of domesticity while simultaneously encouraging women to participate in market consumption.[86] Planning in Algeria also had to address women's attachment to Islam. A particularly dramatic example of this was the unveiling of Algerian women that followed the attempted coup on May 13, 1958. During these ceremonies, women literally burned their headscarves as proof that the policy of Franco-Muslim fraternization had been successful. While the French administration claimed that these were spontaneous acts, they had in reality been staged by the Fifth Bureau of the army. The ordinance of February 4, 1959, also targeted women in the hopes of weaking the grip of Islam in Algeria. It undermined Islamic marriage laws by imposing a minimum age for marriage and banning *djabr* (the right of the father or guardian to choose a husband).[87]

The Constantine Plan should be seen in light of these broader attempts to transform the Algerian population into modern subjects. While the French state had previously constructed a racial regime of religion on the basis of their understanding of Muslim sexuality and family traditions, they now sought to reform a discriminatory system by emancipating women. While modernizing initiatives in Algeria were in many ways similar to those in

Figure 3.2 Women at a fair in Algiers, ca. mid-1950s. Source: Service historique de la défense, 1H/1186.

mainland France, officials were forced to account for the role of Islam in Algeria as they articulated the postwar doctrine of economic planning.

Motors and Multipliers

Colonial officials working to implement the Constantine Plan often disagreed on which strategies to adopt. Should they introduce concrete benchmarks for economic development that would raise the Algerian standard of living? Or should they initiate psychological transformations through contact with economic markets? Debates often pitted officials who had a functionalist understanding of the plan against those who advocated for a more aspirational approach. The former argued that the plan was obligated to provide measurable economic results and achieve specific goals.[88] The latter were seduced by promises that economic planning could introduce social—and even racial—transformations. Planners such as Michel Picquard, in charge of economic affairs for the Constantine Plan, wrote to Delouvrier that the ultimate goal of development "consisted less of [achieving] statistical objectives than in [introducing] general orientations, with the actions and investments that they will engender."[89] According to partisans of this aspirational view, the plan had "no scientific value," and attempts to reevaluate the Decennial Perspectives had been "irrational."[90] In this regard, Delouvrier's vision for Algeria bore only the most superficial resemblances to nineteenth-century attempts to introduce progress among Algerian subjects. Instead, the Constantine Plan is better understood as an attempt to teach Algerians how to play an "economic game" that would permeate society and transform Muslim subjectivities.[91]

The aspirational approach dominated at the Direction du plan (Directorate of the Plan) based in Algiers, where officials tended to be more liberal than their counterparts in Paris. One memo from Algiers explained that the primary goal of the plan was to "allow the population to live and to employ its capacity for work more efficiently." It also specified that "no investment should be agreed to if it will not contribute *very directly* to this central objective."[92] Investments should have concrete results, it argued. For example, it was not enough simply to increase the number of children that went to school; schooling should provide children with training that would enable them to fulfill their economic and civil responsibilities. Similarly, the state should seek not merely to increase agricultural production but to encourage farmers to develop their own initiatives in order to improve their standard of living. This vision of progress reflected the technocratic belief that so-called multiplier effects would be an important factor in the success of any economic or social plan. The motor of development was not to be found in specific industries or geographical advantages but in the ability of Muslims to internalize the economic values of competition, profit, and responsibility.

Two of the proposed slogans (likely designed by the Fifth Bureau) to win over Algerians to the Constantine Plan reflected this desire to instill economic thinking in the native population: "I know how to work: The Constantine Plan" and "I buy for less [money]."[93] Other sayings targeting the Muslim milieu were "Lazy people refuse the Constantine Plan" and "I see far ahead: The Constantine Plan."[94] Yet planners worried that these slogans might give the impression that the state would provide aid directly to a structurally disenfranchised population, when the goal was instead to incentivize individual subjects to maximize their own efforts. Vibert stressed that "the final objective is to put the rural populations to work *for their own profit, and not as state employees*"; he added that the plan's ultimate goal was to incite individuals to "action" rather than "passive appreciation."[95]

Metropolitan planners who supported a functionalist approach suggested that development should raise the standard of living for the six million Algerians who practiced traditional agriculture, rather than modernize

Figure 3.3 An image from an article covering the 1961 traveling fair dedicated to the Constantine Plan, which opened in Oran. Source: Archives nationales d'outre-mer, BIB AOM 20327/1962.

agriculture in general. Their more liberal colleagues in Algiers flatly refused, insisting that "the objective of the plan should look to the advanced sector of the economy since it is the only section that can be rapidly modernized and that will provide the resources necessary for the continuation of the plan."[96] Defending the large difference between the credits allocated to agriculture (700 million francs) versus other investments (1.7 billion francs), Delouvrier exclaimed, "My feeling is that there are too many credits for agriculture because these are credits of charity destined to create sites that mostly serve to feed workers."[97] True to his belief that charity was to be avoided at all costs, he found the idea of financing traditional agriculture to be fundamentally misguided. As he saw it, the goal of the Constantine Plan was to stimulate economic growth, not to offer aid to individuals who did not serve the needs of a market economy.

European settlers worried about the deterioration of agriculture, which was a pillar of settler identity. During a meeting of the chamber of commerce, Colonel Raymond Peyronnet implied that agriculture was far nobler than industry. He lamented, "While the role of industry grows each day, it is still without doubt the land that has nourished, and will nourish, the people."[98] While debates over planning and agriculture centered on economic concerns in the Hexagon, this discussion revealed a central tension in Algeria: Would France pursue a dynamic, outward looking, industrial future linked to the Common Market? Or would it remain bound to the agricultural traditions that had been fundamental to the making of the settler colony? It was precisely this second possibility that modernizing technocrats such as Delouvrier fought against, believing that it represented a backward-looking image of empire that was increasingly anachronistic in the postwar period.

The Elision of Race

As French planners debated whether to invest in industry or agriculture, they were seduced by the postwar social sciences, particularly behavioral psychology and statistics. Statistical expertise had first impressed planners during the modernization movement associated with Vichy. Under the Marshall Plan approximately one thousand French officials traveled to the United States to learn about the new science of management that warned against centralization and encouraged entrepreneurial spirit.[99] They returned to France with an arsenal of social-scientific knowledge that allowed them to quantify public opinion and reflect on the factors responsible for human actions during war.[100] Many experts returned from these training programs convinced that planning was far more than a cold science of computation; instead, they viewed it as a technique that could account for a wide range of human emotions and aspirations.

Francis-Louis Closon was particularly enthralled by the possibilities that economic planning had to offer. He had spent time at the Rockefeller Center in the late 1930s and went on to become the director of the Institut national de la statistique et des études économiques (INSEE; National Institute for Statistics and Economic Studies), an organization that collects statistical information on the French economy and society. He wrote, "Forecasting the future, which used to be the activity of a few visionaries or poet-philosophers, has become an activity of research, supported by the scientific disciplines, by observations, by rational hypotheses, and calculation."[101] INSEE's activities in Algeria increased considerably after World War II, and its methods of conducting the census changed fundamentally during these years. The Organic Statute of September 20, 1947, forbade any distinction based on race, language, or religion.[102] In Algeria this meant that the census could not target specific ethnic groups, so Algerian Muslims were included in the umbrella category of the French population. In December 1947, Closon wrote to the Ministry of the Interior and posed the following dilemma: "All Algerians being French citizens, it seemed preferable to eliminate any differentiation between those of French origin and Muslims, including that between Muslims of civil status and those of Qur'anic status; it is glaringly obvious, however, that the statistical difference among these elements is of primordial interest."[103] He suggested two ways to rectify the situation: to organize the population on the basis of last names or to draw on the information regarding Algerians who had been naturalized after 1830, including tracking down information on their children. The paper trail, unfortunately, does not tell us how this particular dilemma was resolved. The anecdote nevertheless demonstrates how statistical information was rendered color-blind for political expediency even as planners acknowledged that racial-religious difference remained at the heart of colonial governance.

In some cases, economic categories allowed planners to sidestep the racial structures on which French Algeria had been built. Planners vehemently denied claims that Algeria was a barter economy (économie de traite), wherein a foreign minority controls trade to import manufactured goods while exporting raw materials. Instead, they maintained that Algeria was an example of a dual economy in which the European population represented the modern or evolved sector and native Algerians represented traditional forms of social and economic organization. In other words, Algeria was the model of "an economy where two economic systems at different technical stages live side by side."[104] This conveniently shifted the focus from racial exclusion to economic behaviors. For example, the Decennial Perspectives claimed that the "evolved" economy "include[d] around 3.2 million Muslims who increasingly participate in the Western lifestyle alongside 1 million Europeans."[105] By asserting that Muslims participated in Western (i.e. modern) ways of living, planning documents refuted any structural analysis that highlighted the correlation between race and poverty. The notion of a dual economy also allowed planners to argue that Muslims would be the principal beneficiary of general economic growth and that assisting the indigenous inhabitants did not require specific measures.[106] As they effectively rebutted allegations of racial and economic segregation, planners obscured the history of French Algeria, which had been built on the foundation of racial-religious discrimination.

After World War II, a number of international organizations used the Mediterranean as a geographical frame for development efforts.[107] Rather than acknowledging that colonialism had created significant disparities between the northern and southern shores, however, the lens of regional underdevelopment erased the history of empire, serving as a kind of antipolitics machine.[108] In contrast, a brochure published by Algerian nationalists in Cairo in the early 1950s noted that the success of settler farms had largely been due to the availability of credit and the construction of infrastructure that benefited the European population. Significantly, members of the Mouvement pour le triomphe des libertés démocratiques (MTLD; Movement for the Triumph of Democratic Liberties) framed the economic history of Algeria in terms of the racial discrimination (*al-tamyiz al-'unsuri*) that characterized colonial society rather than using the language of underdevelopment.[109] This drew attention to the fact that the modern settler economy did not merely exist parallel to Muslim society but in fact relied on native underdevelopment in a parasitic fashion.[110]

Once again, the General Planning Commission was adamant that "the modern economy in Algeria is not parasitic to the traditional sector but exists in parallel."[111] French propaganda compared Algeria under the Constantine Plan to the Mezzogiorno region in Italy rather than to Martinique, a classic case of colonial underdevelopment. A memo composed by the cabinet of the of delegate general claimed that a previous draft of the Constantine Plan had mapped the ethnic differences between Europeans and Muslims onto a class analysis, noting that settlers tended to be better off than the native population. It denounced this tendency that it claimed "contradict[ed] the analyses that are presented more or less everywhere, in which the ethnic distinction in Algeria does not have major economic relevance."[112] To avoid highlighting a correspondence between class and religion, officials working for the delegate general described patterns of inequalities in terms of economic growth.

Psychology, as well as statistics and economics, influenced how economists and colonial officials recast understandings of racial-religious difference. Under the Constantine Plan, planning itself was seen as a means of colonial propaganda; experts viewed these development initiatives as part of a broader "public relations campaign," which they deemed more palatable than the term *psychological warfare*.[113] Technocrats such as Delouvrier also called for the Constantine Plan to have an easily recognizable brand.

Official documents counseled that the plan should be shrouded in a certain "mystique," which required increased attention to marketing and packaging.[114] One memo cited the blue eagle of the Tennessee Valley Authority as an example of this strategy.[115]

Planners working on propaganda employed aesthetics reminiscent of the colonial policy of association in which "'religious' events were folklorized, rendered public, and emptied of their original significance."[116] This even extended to the colors used on posters. Planners decided that green should be used only for "benevolent allusions to Islamic beliefs" or the "diffusion of texts emanating from religious personalities."[117] They also stipulated that any potential slogan "should be short and if possible without a verb, expressing the idea of the future rather than the [reality of the] present."[118] Those working on publicity wondered how they could harness the power of that typically "Oriental" way of spreading information in Arab societies: the rumor. The Fifth Bureau of the army wrote that potential rumors should be well chosen, efficient, and—most of all—controllable. Propagandists for the Constantine Plan who worked for the Office of Psychological Action (Bureau psychologique) adopted the genre of the Arabic fable, modeling propaganda after well-known *Juha* stories when addressing Algerian Muslims.[119] Yet teaching Algerians about an economic plan presented a particular challenge in that, according to these experts, Muslims "were not economists."[120] The General Delegation of the Government in Algeria concluded that numbers should "give way to images that respond to the most immediate preoccupations" of this group.[121]

Not all officials agreed with Delouvrier's conviction that Muslims could participate in industrial civilization.[122] At a conference to foster cooperation between industrialists and the army in September 1958, Jean-Louis Fyot, who worked with the Société d'études pour le développement économique et social (SEDES; Society for the Study of Social and Economic Development), a consulting firm under the umbrella of the French state, asked, "Is it possible to phase out (*supprimer*) Islamic civilization while keeping its values, and the traditional structure of the Muslim world? Does it not risk being an obstacle to economic progress and the essential components of saving, investment, initiative, and the functioning of financial mechanisms, as well as a certain conception of action and spirit?"[123] In 1952 Fyot, a devoted Jesuit, had written *Dimensions de l'homme et science économique* (Dimensions of man and economic science), in which he argued that economists as well as philosophers should concern themselves with the love of God.[124] While Fyot's religious convictions may have influenced his reading of Islam, the military sympathizer Pierre Charrasse echoed his position. He argued that Muslims in Algeria were subjected to a "sterilizing tradition that renders all of our efforts at renovation vain if we cannot liberate them from it."[125] In stark contrast, those working for the Ministry for Algerian Affairs wrote, "nothing in the dogma or fundamental spiritual values of Islam clashes with our own values and conceptions."[126]

While there was no consensus on whether homo islamicus could, in fact, be made into homo economicus, planners agreed that they had to account for the specific racial-religious identity of Algerian natives. Some experts worried that the Constantine Plan failed to consider the different sensibilities of Algerians. One memo asked, "Will they feel comfortable in a conference room of the Town Hall designed by a Parisian architect? Will they not prefer to debate the problems of their commune in their own way, that of their ancestors: [seated in] a room of the *djemâ*, or on old rocks under a sacred olive tree?"[127] At other times it seemed that ignoring cultural differences would be more prudent. One of the proposed slogans, which planners borrowed from Louis Pasteur, was "I ask you neither your race nor your religion; I ask you what causes your suffering."[128] While the first approach transposed the colonial doctrine of association onto development, the second adopted the supposedly color-blind position associated with assimilation. Both versions assumed that Islam had to be accounted for in any economic program, whether directly (through the incorporation of motifs and cultural sensibilities) or indirectly (by recoding racial difference in the language of economic aptitudes). At the same time, the obvious correlation between the race and underdevelopment was effaced through a new language of economic development that naturalized the link between culture and economic capacities, thereby eliding how the colonial state had structured inequalities.

Builders and Destroyers

According to Jean Morin, who replaced Delouvrier as delegate general in November 1960, the Constantine Plan failed because Algerian terrorists could destroy faster than French planners could build.[129] The official newspaper of the FLN, *El Moudjahid*, put it differently, claiming that "the destroyers of a country can never be builders" and identifying French colonialism as the true source of destruction.[130] On September 19, 1958, the FLN created the Gouvernement provisoire de la République algérienne (GPRA; Provisional Government of the Algerian Republic), a government-in-waiting modeled on the French Provisional Government established by de Gaulle in London during World War II.[131] Members of this body were aware of the power of economic models to obfuscate the racial basis of French colonial policies. In the doctrine of regional planning, such as the model of poles of development espoused by François Perroux, for example, Algerian underdevelopment was the result of the excessive centralization of industrial development within the economic space of France.[132] The GPRA rejected this scalar framing and insisted that Algeria could not be understood as a poor region of France. It was only by studying the territory as a national unit and "a distinct economic entity" that it was possible to elucidate the link between racial and economic disparities.[133]

An article in the nationalist newspaper *Révolution Africaine* refused any attempt to locate Algeria in the Eurafrican or Mediterranean spaces discussed in the last chapter. Mourad Bourboune, an FLN militant who went on to direct Algeria's national theater, wrote that Louis Betrand was a "direct ancestor" of the far-right French paramilitary group, the Organisation de l'armée secrète (OAS; Secret Armed Organization). As for Albert Camus, Bourboune wondered if he "was not more pernicious than Bertrand, who at least had the honesty to show his true colors."[134] An earlier article in the same publication argued that the strategies of "free exchange, free movement of capital, and the freedom to set up companies" were fundamentally colonial in nature.[135] In public, Algerian nationalists tended to dismiss the Constantine Plan as a political slogan built on the colonial myth of economic integration. French officials might have imagined that they were "accumulating numbers and statistics," but they were in reality attempting to hide the economic facts of settler colonialism.[136] While colonial planners separated the construction of markets from the domain of formal politics, the FLN did the reverse. To the FLN, only those with political legitimacy had the right to intervene in economic policy.[137]

Internally, the FLN had a more nuanced position. Unlike French technocrats, who sought to use the market as a tool to transform homo islamicus into homo economicus, the FLN believed that economic policy could create a revolutionary national subject. A memo by the GPRA explained:

> The Constantine plan was specifically conceived to attempt to satisfy the economic needs of the worker in order to detach him from the revolution while assuring his material well-being. It is necessary to present the worker with an economic and social program and respond to his aspirations so that he connects with an ideal of the revolution. Capital

and foreign technology will have a place in Algeria in the sense that their investments and their activities will not constitute any political or economic assumptions for the Algerian people. The Algerian Revolution opens the way to a cultural regeneration for the Algerian people where their Arab-Muslim personality will adapt to the evolution of the modern world and offer its contribution to the universal patrimony.[138]

This passage highlights how the FLN's vision of the "new man," theorized in its most dramatic form by Frantz Fanon, relied on economic development as a blueprint for cultural authenticity. Unlike French administrators, Algerian nationalists did not associate an Arab-Muslim identity with particularistic orientations or economic backwardness. Instead, they affirmed that Islamic principles could serve as the basis for material prosperity. Algerian national-ists appropriated the economic grammar of the postwar period that under-stood economic organization as an expression of national identity, viewing the distribution of material goods as a way of fashioning revolutionary subjects. Moreover, they were not alone in rejecting the economism of the French state. Many Arab leftists across the region understood the question of economic organization to be secondary to that of sovereignty. Writing in the Lebanese journal *al-Adab* in 1957, the Syrian Ba'athist 'Abdallah 'Abd al-Da'im charged France with trying to hide the Algerian reality under the "language of numbers (*lughat al-arqam*)."[139] He alleged that Europeans "only [understood] the Algerian conflict from the perspective of econom-ics," which was a form of delusion given that the Algerian people were, in his eyes, struggling for pride and dignity.[140]

When the FLN inherited the achievements of the Constantine Plan after 1962, the concrete results of the reforms were modest. The plan's most notable accomplishments were in construction: eleven thousand urban housing units had been created in the first seven months of 1959, in con-trast to eighteen thousand in all of 1958.[141] Overall, thirty-three thousand (out of a forecasted forty-two thousand) apartments in urban areas were built under the plan. Yet the rate of economic growth for 1959 was hardly greater than 1 percent, whereas 1957 and 1958 had seen growth rates of 9 and 10 percent, respectively.[142] The progress in agriculture was also disappoint-ing, and Delouvrier was forced to concede that Algerian nationalists had successfully sabotaged the program for land reform through violence against property and individuals.[143] The progress made in industrializing Algeria was also paltry despite the generous encouragements offered by the French state; initiatives to modernize agriculture and introduce land reform faced similar frustrations.[144] By January 1959 the organization responsible for land reform, the Caisse d'accession à la propriété rurale (CAPER; Fund for the Purchase and Exploitation of Rural Property) held a meager twenty-nine thousand hectares, which represented 1 percent of European landholdings in Algeria.[145] Only 30 percent of the grain silos and cereal warehouses envisioned in 1960 were constructed. The social aspects of the program, however, were more successful, and the number of students who received an education actually exceeded initial goals.[146] Furthermore, the French state was able to secure the construction of certain large-scale public works projects, such as a steel plant in Bône and a dam at Bou Noumassa, soon to be centerpieces of the FLN's postcolonial industrialization strategy.[147]

It seems fair to conclude that the Constantine Plan failed to meet its stated goal of improving the lives of most Algerians. It did, however, develop a set of tools to translate older colonial notions of racial-religious difference into a corpus of technical knowledge. Rather than accounting for the structural inequalities bequeathed by the history of colonization, the Constantine Plan offered a language of cultural aptitudes that stressed the importance of entrepreneurship. It therefore represented an important chapter in the colonial history of neoliberalism, an economic and social worldview that has also been defined by its need to erase how the historical structures of race fashioned economic inequalities.[148]

On September 16, 1959, less than one year after Delouvrier had arrived in Algeria, de Gaulle pronounced a word that far-right defenders of French Algeria considered treasonous: self-determination. His speech was followed by a referendum, held in January 1960, that proposed three political options for Algeria: integration with France, association, or independence. Delouvrier later remarked that he had been a "prisoner of the economy" and had no say over the army, which he considered to be the decisive force in Algeria.[149] In November 1960, Delouvrier left Algeria and handed the reins of the Constantine Plan to Jean Morin.[150] The Constantine Plan officially ended with the demise of French Algeria less than two years later, but its initiatives nevertheless had important effects on the Algerian state after independence.[151] When asked about the cutoff date of the plan, Mahmoud Ourabah, who was general secretary of the Algerian Ministry of Planning from 1963 to 1970, responded:

> The Constantine Plan ended as do some streams (*oueds*) in the Sahara, because of the way things are. But what does it mean exactly, [to say] that the plan ended? Some projects took shape and continued [after inde-

pendence]. Algerians took over and these projects continued. Of course, things changed dramatically. The entire administrative structure left the country in [the span of] a few weeks.... But many Algerians jumped on the wagon and there was no clear break.[152]

Consistent with Ourabah's comments, scholars have noted the similarity between Delouvrier's attempt to build one thousand housing units under the Constantine Plan and the desire of Houari Boumediene, the second Algerian president, to build one thousand "socialist villages."[153]

In France, Delouvrier is best known for his role in the construction of the *villes nouvelles* in Paris, a major renovation plan in the 1960s that sought to decentralize urban space and construct housing. The initiative brought together multiple planners who had experience in Algeria.[154] Delouvrier was not the only high-ranking functionary to contribute to the spatial reorganization of France after decolonization. Olivier Guichard, who had directed the Organisation commune des régions sahariennes (OCRS; Common Organization of Saharan Regions), went on to head the Délégation interministérielle à l'aménagement du territoire (DATAR; Interministerial Committee for Regional Planning), a national agency for territorial planning in France. Once again, many experts working for this organization had extensive experience in the French empire.[155] These examples provide a compelling case for seeing these metropolitan policies as part of a broader history of colonial development.

While it would be tempting to see the Constantine Plan as a laboratory of modernity where experts developed knowledge that was later applied in France, the circulation of social-scientific tools transcended a strictly colonial frame.[156] As an early crucible for neoliberal thought, the Constantine Plan saw the market as a tool of racial transformation rather than a way to balance supply and demand. Some planners located a specific form of resistance to this project in Islam and drew on postwar social sciences to help overcome this "obstacle" to economic development. Similarly, while the modernization of agriculture in both France and Algeria attempted to change the behavior and practices of the peasantry, French sociologists working in both countries insisted that the Algerian peasant was categorically different from his French counterpart. As the next chapter demonstrates, French planners blamed the day-to-day malfunctioning of the Constantine Plan on the essential characteristics of the Algerian peasantry rather than on the structural features of the colonial system.

4.
FELLAHS INTO PEASANTS

Pierre Bourdieu once remarked that studying the Algerian peasantry was a natural extension of his own upbringing in Béarn, located in the northwest of the Pyrenees mountains.[1] He grew up speaking a dialect of Gascon, and these rural roots caused him to feel alienated from the Parisian cultural codes that dominated the French academy. Conscripted to military service in 1955, he spent one year in Algeria during the War of Independence, staying to undertake ethnographic research on the clash between the traditional values of the Algerian peasantry and the capitalist worldview that colonialism had forced upon them. His time in Algeria was fundamental to his development of concepts such as the *habitus* and field that became hallmarks of social theory.[2] He saw the traditional worldview of the fellah as a bulwark against the encroaching violence of market society, writing that "the foresight of the fellah, a prescient, pre-perceptive vision, differs essentially from the rational foresight of the capitalist entrepreneur."[3] If Bourdieu saw this as a positive attribute, French officials working on the Constantine Plan were more likely to view these antimarket tendencies as an impediment to economic development. Both of these perspectives, however, agreed that Algerian peasants were defined by a set of economic aptitudes or traditions that were incompatible with capitalism.

Attempts to modernize the fellahin under the Constantine Plan were shot through with metropolitan anxieties that the French peasantry, an important symbol of national identity, was vanishing. In France, after World War II, the goal of modernization was to help farmers mechanize and rationalize production in order to maximize yields and bring them into a market economy. The symbol of the French peasant could take on a range of meanings; at times it invoked isolated and traditional rural habits, but it could also represent those who lived in a rural area and engaged in agriculture more broadly. In both cases, the postwar drive to modernize stressed the role of the peasantry in safeguarding the values of "real" France against the onslaught of urbanization.

Planners and sociologists approached the question of agricultural modernization differently in Algeria than in France; in addition to increasing efficiency and food production, they also wanted modernization to introduce new moral and psychological frameworks among Algerian farmers. Many colonial administrators and planners saw the fellah as a particularly stubborn iteration of homo islamicus whose attachment to Islam made social transformation especially difficult. Rather than trying to turn peasants into Frenchmen, in Eugene Weber's phrase, planners sought to transform the Algerian fellah into a French *paysan* (peasant).[4] In the process, they ignored how settler colonialism had restricted access to labor, land, and credit, effectively preventing the majority of rural Algerians from participating in market production. This chapter studies the multiple, and mostly failed, attempts to modernize agriculture in Algeria between 1958 and 1962.

Scholars of colonial agriculture have long noted that the lofty humanist schemes of administrators and planners were rarely successful. The postwar period witnessed a number of attempts to introduce commercial agriculture to Africa and the Middle East, most of which ended in disappointment. These results cannot be attributed solely to the fact that "high modernism" was more convincing when imagined from the planner's office than seen on the ground.[5] Postwar efforts to address land use and soil conservation in the British empire also encountered resistance and provoked farmers' distrust.[6] The Swynnerton Plan in Kenya, for example, aimed to introduce individual land ownership in order to quell the escalating violence of the Mau Mau rebellion.[7] French officials in Algeria followed a similar blueprint, hoping that creating a rural working class, modernizing agriculture, and introducing cooperatives would undercut the FLN insurgency. Given that 87 percent of Muslims depended on farming for their livelihood, and the possibility that farmers would become politically dangerous semiproletariats, it seemed imperative to improve the quality of life of rural Algerians.[8]

The struggles for decolonization in the 1950s strengthened the tendency of colonial officials to view peasants as a security threat to European rule.[9] While agricultural reform had been introduced during the interwar period, the Constantine Plan provided a major boost to postwar efforts at agricultural modernization. It also reflected the technocratic values of the Fifth Republic. Colonial administrators often assumed that the cultural practices of Algerian Muslims were the main obstacle to modernization and believed that market exchange was the key to social evolution; this commitment to a market-based solution allowed planners to blame Muslims' mental capacities for the failure of these reforms. During the War of Independence, the French state pursued the contradictory goals of aiding Algerian peasants and deepening the reach of market society. Their faith in agricultural credit and the modernization of farming equipment overlooked how these incentives tended to promote the interests of settler agriculture. Attempts at land reform also failed to meaningfully alter existing inequalities. Yet many late colonial policies to redistribute land and increase agricultural output were adopted by the Algerian state, which upheld the fellah as a nationalist hero symbolizing resistance to colonial exploitation after independence.

Colonial Theories of the Peasantry

As discussed in the first chapter, the conquest of French Algeria led to the confiscation of the most fertile lands from native Algerians and brought devastating changes to the countryside. In 1954, Muslim Algerians, who composed 89 percent of the total population, possessed just 47.3 percent of the available territory.[10] Moreover, the vast majority of Algerian farmers practiced subsistence agriculture in relative isolation from the market economy.[11] Colonial officials tended to view these farmers as a potential source of political unrest due to their economic precarity. As a result, attempts to define the fellah had long been framed by the specter of political revolt in the Middle East and North Africa.[12] As Timothy Mitchell argues, peasant studies emerged in the interwar period due to the "widespread rebellions that rural populations were able to organize against occupying European powers."[13] In Egypt, colonial observers often described the Arab peasant with a racialized vocabulary that referred to physical traits and psychological structures.[14] Joost Van Vollenhoven, a Dutch-born French soldier and colonial administrator, wrote an essay on the Algerian fellahin in 1903, in which he described them as incapable of general reasoning or progress. It was impossible, he asserted, to teach the fellah modern agricultural methods since his intellectual weakness, laziness, and apathy made him a "deplorable worker."[15]

The criteria for defining Algerian fellahin were often vague. Experts sometimes characterized them as farmers who owned their own—often meager—parcels of land, on which they practiced subsistence agriculture, distinct from those who provided low-cost labor to large European farms. There was no consensus on which category of agriculturalist encompassed the fellahin. This term could be used to describe farmers that had larger parcels of land (51 to 100 hectares of wine or 500 to 1,000 hectares of grain) and were thus on par with European farmers. It could also be used to describe more precarious farmers who had access to smaller parcels (10 to 50 hectares), enough only to satisfy the needs of their families.

In the arrondissement of Aïn Témouchent, in northwestern Algeria, landowners with more than one hundred hectares of wine (or one thousand hectares of grain) were almost all European; of the 174 farms claiming this privileged status, only fourteen belonged to Algerian Muslims in 1960.[16] In the territory as a whole, indigenous Algerians possessed the majority of cultivated farmland (totaling 7,349 thousand hectares, versus 2,727 thousand owned by Europeans). Yet most of these holdings were smaller than 10 hectares. In comparison, 41 percent of European farms exceeded 50 hectares. In addition, the lands owned by Muslims tended to be unfit for modern methods of farming.[17]

Attempts to modernize production and develop rural society gained traction after World War II. The issue of soil erosion had led to the creation of the Service de la défense et restauration des sols (DRS; Service for the Defense and Restoration of Soil), in 1945; a Comission du paysannat (Peasantry Commission) was formed in the same year. In 1946, the Commission supérieure des réformes musulmanes (High Commission for Muslim Reforms) introduced a number of measures to help Algerian farmers, including the creation of Secteurs d'amélioration rurale (SAR; Sectors for Rural Improvement). These cooperative organizations helped fellahin modernize their farming techniques if they agreed to follow the advice of a French technical advisor, respect certain guidelines on which crops to grow, and commit to a minimum number of days of work. Yet the colonial state's financial investment in native agriculture was woefully inadequate: in 1948, there existed a mere 103 agricultural stations, which were supposed to serve seventy-five thousand families.[18]

French administrators were not alone in viewing the peasantry as a political danger. Western governments were alarmed by peasant insurgencies during the Korean War and the French defeat at Dien Bien Phu in 1954. In the 1950s and 1960s, against the backdrop of the Cold War, observers worried that peasants were likely to develop communist sympathies and engage in violence if the material promises of capitalism were not fulfilled.[19] Modernization theory, a self-proclaimed noncommunist manifesto, saw increased agricultural productivity and participation in international markets as key to the takeoff stage that would usher in an age of mass consumption.[20] This attention to the peasant classes was a departure from Marx, who saw them as

Figure 4.1 A drawing from a French tract depicting a fellah surrounded by nationalist "vermin" from 1956. The three scorpions represent Ferhat Abbas, Messali Hadj, and Ahmed Ben Bella. Source: Service historique de la défense, 1H/2504.

a conservative class, famously comparing them to a sack of potatoes. Some analysts—French and Algerian—defined the fellahin in terms of religious fanaticism and claimed they displayed a lack of political maturity.[21] Despite these fatalistic renderings, the uprisings in Sétif and Guelma on May 8, 1945, served as a wake-up call for the colonial state, crystallizing the threat that peasant society posed to colonial rule.[22] With the outbreak of the War of Independence in 1954, the modernization of the peasantry became a key tool in pacifying anticolonial revolt.[23]

In undertaking economic reforms after World War II, colonial experts in Algeria were influenced by debates in the field of rural sociology, whose practitioners studied agricultural modernization in France and the Third World. During the late 1950s and 1960s, Henri Mendras, a leading French rural sociologist, and his colleagues became "obsessed" with defining the peasantry.[24] In 1961, American anthropologist Lloyd A. Fallers raised the question of whether the category *peasant* could be applied outside of Europe, noting that African cultivators failed to meet certain cultural criteria.[25] Fallers alleged that the low literacy rate made the differences between peasant and urban cultures too subtle for the African peasant to exist as a distinct cultural unit. He concluded that "the traditional African villager was, we might say, a peasant economically and politically, but was not a peasant culturally."[26] His commitment to defining peasants collectively as a bastion against the modern high culture of urban centers shows that the category was never defined solely in terms of economic activities but articulated through culturalist analyses of non-Western societies.

Discussions on agricultural development in Algeria raised the question of whether the fellah could be likened to a "real" French paysan. For Bourdieu and Abdelmalek Sayad, the fellah was not an objective category defined by land ownership or a specific form of agricultural production. Instead, they identified the fellah by the cultural values of honor and attachment to land, which implied that this figure existed outside capitalist economic rationality. They wrote, "It is clear that one can externally conform to certain models, as the fellahin do today, without being an authentic fellah."[27] Bourdieu and Sayad also recounted the fellahin's resistance to new forms of calculation, describing how they refused to sell certain products that had a symbolic value, such as olive oil, at the market.[28] The notion that being a fellah was not based in material realities was also expressed in the work of some rural sociologists who upheld the existence of a peasant "soul" or thought about the peasantry as a "race."[29]

Claudine Chaulet, a French sociologist who supported the FLN during the war and stayed in Algeria after independence, took issue with Bourdieu and Sayad's definition. She argued that Algerian patterns of agro-pastoralism and tribal organization fostered a relationship to the land distinct from that of European paysans, who participated in the market economy and engaged in relatively autonomous family-based production.[30] Contra Bourdieu and Sayad, she maintained that Algerian cultivators were able to adapt to colonial structures and develop a "spirit of calculation" based on their situation— including their choice to engage in market production.[31] Algerian-born sociologist Fanny Colonna also criticized Bourdieu and Sayad's analysis for neglecting the role played by Islam. She saw this as symptomatic of the Durkheimian approach that dominated sociology in postwar France, which tended to reduce religious phenomena to "social facts."[32]

Other experts studying rural society found it necessary to account for Islam when designing reforms that targeted the fellahin. Rabah Chellig was a Muslim agricultural expert who worked on the Constantine Plan and the author of *La vie du fellah et du pasteur algériens* (The life of the fellah and the

Algerian shepherd).[33] Chellig argued that the "real fellah" was concerned exclusively with his immediate needs and was incapable of planning for the long term—an understanding that colonial officials shared.[34] He claimed the fellah had "more confidence in his silo than his land" and thus preferred to stock food instead of making improvements to the land that would increase production.[35] Writing for the newspaper *Terre Algérienne* in early 1962, Chellig claimed the fellah felt "an inner sense of love for God and [is defined by] his own equilibrium: he is difficult to manipulate and psychological action has no effect on him. One must help the peasantry to evolve with their consent and with respect, while, at the beginning, offering them the technical prowess that allows them to instigate changes themselves."[36]

Chellig insisted that French planners should officially recognize the role of religion in shaping the worldview of Algerian farmers. During a meeting of the Superior Council of the Plan in 1959, there was a debate over whether the Constantine Plan should mention Islam. The discussion centered on a section of text that discussed the regroupment camps as a tool of "rural renovation," and advocated for the introduction of itinerant teams. This was allegedly to ensure that Algerians living in the camps would enjoy "a sustainable livelihood and thus dignity in their condition as men."[37] Chellig intervened, wanting to change the phrase to express respect not only for their human dignity but also for their religion. While Delouvrier accepted this proposition, it was refused by Laurent Schiaffino, the powerful head of the Algerian chamber of commerce, who claimed that speaking of religion was an "insult" to the French government.[38] Chellig argued that invoking Islam would help the French state accomplish its developmental program, but Delouvrier ultimately sided with Schiaffino. This exchange shows that while experts working for the French state sometimes cited Islam explicitly to explain the fatalism of the fellahin, at other times they denied the relevance of religion in defining France's humanitarian mission in Algeria.[39] As we will see in chapter 6, this dual tendency to either cast Islam as a set of essential cultural attributes or to employ a color-blind stance that refused to engage with the role of religion marked how French actors engaged with Islam after independence.

Assumptions about the social and psychological capacities of Algerians, rooted in Islam, shaped visions of modernization. This was true even among experts who did not explicitly mention religion. Alexis Monjauze, the head of the Forest Service, claimed that living in poverty did not motivate the Algerian fellahin, who displayed "an unfortunate indifference" to development initiatives. He continued:

[The fellah] is slow to adapt to a new situation in which his methods risk being modified. This is natural. It is not enough to improve his land; one must make him hopeful and help him to conceive of managing his lands in new ways. It is necessary to offer him the material means and resources that he does not have. Since his initial poverty is not only tied to the surroundings, the [human dimension] of poverty responds to this [material situation]. The two are in equilibrium. Finally, in this equilibrium, men are indifferent to the concept of growth.[40]

For Monjauze, it was the fellahin's relationship to the soil, rather than the tenets of their religion, that determined their "indifference" to development. Yet as we saw in chapter 1, the notion that Muslims were incapable of engaging in productive modes of economic behavior was a classic Orientalist trope. Monjauze also viewed poverty as an affliction that ran deeper than a mere lack of resources and called for the colonial state to inculcate a psychological appreciation for economic growth. Yet his hope that rural Algerians would learn to live in a state of "equilibrium" with their surroundings was dramatically undermined by the myriad forms of violence they endured during the War of Independence.

Those Who Can Survive Uprooting

Bourdieu and Sayad's well-known work *Le déracinement* (Uprooting) described how French *centres de regroupement* (regroupment centers) eroded traditional Algerian worldviews and caused economic hardship. By calling these settlements *centers*, the French government avoided using the word *camps*, which had become a particularly vexing term after World War II.[41] Planners hoped to isolate Algerian Muslims from the FLN and expose them to a model of rural settlement that would encourage development and pacification.[42] These enclosures first appeared in the Aurès mountains as "hermetic cobwebs of checkpoints, watchtowers, military posts, border fortifications, minefields, and electric fences, all of which enabled constant counterrevolutionary military operations."[43] The *zones interdites* (forbidden zones) were to be emptied of all life—human and animal. In other areas, known as zones of operation, officers had carte blanche to restore order.

Bourdieu and Sayad describe how these camps undermined extended family networks and subjected farmers to the violence of the market.[44] The physical separation of famers from their land and the restrictions placed on their movement forced many Algerians to renounce traditional agricultural practices and turn to salaried employment.[45] French colonization also prompted changes in the kinds of grains Algerians produced and consumed. Durum wheat and barley had traditionally been the basis of rural diets, but European settlers introduced soft wheat (also known as farina), which was almost entirely used for market exchange.[46] Consistent with the unequal access to commercialized crops enjoyed by French settlers and Algerian Muslims, the latter produced the vast majority of Algeria's barley and more than half of its durum wheat but less than a third of its soft wheat. Jean Gernignon, a French agricultural expert who worked in Algeria after independence, reflected on these changes:

> As I see it, France created a catastrophe in making these areas [champs] of regroupment during the Algerian war. Why? Because [they] destroyed the population's relationship to their own dietary habits [alimentation]. They started to eat bread when before they would eat galettes, which was much more suitable to the local crops.... If you are deprived of your traditional structures, you take what is given to you, this is how one breaks cultures [C'est comme ça qu'on casse les cultures].... We extracted these people from their culture and their habits, which is not good because people are like plants, there are those who can survive uprooting (déracinement), and those who cannot.[47]

French colonization and exposure to a market economy destroyed local culture on multiple levels. The transition from barley galettes to wheat bread was just one sign of the general destruction of rural life.

The War of Independence provoked a paradoxical mix of humanitarian concern, military repression, and individual idealism among French actors. Nowhere was this clearer than in the Sections administratives spécialisées (SAS; Specialized Administrative Sections), military units that also had important administrative, economic, and social responsibilities. Created in 1955 by ethnologist and governor general Jacques Soustelle, the SAS were modeled on the nineteenth-century Arab Bureaus as well as on the Indigenous Affairs units in Morocco. Officers in these units were tasked with representing the human face of the French administration on the ground, winning over rural populations, and encouraging economic development.

Jean Vibert, the director of the Constantine Plan, noted that the first contact between Algerians and "modern civilization" generally occurred through the SAS, since it was "often the military who are in the biggest hurry to introduce tractors."[48] Regarding rural underdevelopment, Claude Perret, who worked for the General Planning Commission remarked, "Only technology can allow for the individual to surpass the biological equilibrium [found in the relationship] of 'man-earth' [*homme-terre*]."[49] Rather than positing a romantic link between peasants and soil, officials working on the Constantine Plan sought to transform the fellahin into modern subjects by exposing them to economic markets and agricultural mechanization.

Officers in the SAS served as intermediaries between the army and the SAPs, which were organizations designed to aid Muslim farmers. The SAPs were created in August 1952 as successors to the Sociétés indigènes de prévoyance (SIPs; Native Welfare Societies), which had existed since the end of the nineteenth century. The SIPs had played an important role in interwar development attempts by managing the storage, transport, and marketing of grain. Similar to agricultural societies established by colonial regimes elsewhere in Africa, they aimed to teach Algerians about the values and practices necessary for participation in a market economy. Their overall mission was to effect a "progressive evolution" toward agricultural cooperatives.[50] At the same time, they were tarnished by their proximity to political power in Algeria. The president of each SIP was also the administrator of the mixed commune (*commune mixte*).[51] While the official raison d'être of these administrative units was to help prepare predominantly Muslim territories for municipal rule, in reality they lacked resources and personnel. Their existence was widely seen as inflicting yet another set of draconian measures and exceptional disciplinary practices on indigenous Algerians.[52] Although the SIPs had helped prevent starvation by offering small loans and selling improved seeds, they had nevertheless become the object of peasant opposition by the early 1940s.[53]

The SIPs were renamed, becoming SAPs in 1952.[54] They continued to provide credit, wheat, and equipment to farmers. Their staff also demonstrated modern farming techniques and gave members access to storehouses for grain and equipment. Much of this was in line with the previous activities of the SIPs, but the changed political context of the war prompted colonial officials to reconceptualize these organizations. Notably, direct assistance for Algerian farmers was now deemed paternalistic and outdated. Colonial officials prioritized instilling a taste for progress in farmers, since, as one circular by the Commission of the SAPs noted, "in agriculture, the actions on men are as decisive, if not more so, than a focus on the profession."[55] Similarly, a propaganda brochure for the Constantine Plan described the SAPs as "the best vehicle for [introducing] progress among the fellahin."[56] The SAPs relied on agricultural monitors to create "a real mystique of agricultural development" and introduce "an enterprising spirit" among Algerian farmers.[57] As "propagandists for modern life," they were instructed to teach

Muslim farmers to reflect on the future and be more active in instigating changes in their natural environment.[58]

Despite a significant boost in funding from 1956 to 1961, the SAPs remained seriously understaffed. In 1958, there were just 250 monitors for 105 SAPs. The Constantine Plan aimed to recruit and train 3,000 monitors between 1959 and 1964, a number that would still have been insufficient to serve the 600,000 farmers who fell under the purview of the SAPs. Existing centers for agricultural training, such as the Centre professionnel rural de Rovigo (Professional Rural Center of Rovigo), were subsequently dedicated exclusively to educating monitors. The Institut national de recherche agronomique (INRA; National Institute of Agronomical Research), was built for similar purposes in February 1960. French social sciences featured prominently in these training programs. At Rovigo, the first two weeks of a five-week training program were dedicated to rural sociology. In 1958, Michel Cepède, a professor of economics and rural sociology at the Institut national agronomique (INA; National Agronomy Institute), became president of the Association pour la formation et le perfectionnement des cadres agricoles d'Algérie (AFCAL; Association for the Training and Development of Agricultural Managers in Algeria).[59] Each session trained between twenty-five and thirty students, both European and Muslim, and fourteen sessions were held at Saint Germain en Laye, in the western suburbs of Paris, between 1958 and 1962. They featured classes on the psychological problems associated with agriculture as well as presentations by experts on rural psychosociology.[60] One training session held by AFCAL after independence claimed that there were two kinds of peasants in Algeria: One group that was not evolved acted without reflection, so analogies were a powerful strategy to encourage them to change their behavior.[61] Members of the second group, however, had already received some intellectual training and possessed a higher capacity for reflection.

These programs led to an increase in the number of monitors (from 430 at the end of 1959 to 1,055 at the beginning of 1962). They did not succeed in creating a specifically Muslim corps of monitors, however.[62] In keeping with the general French policy of creating a "third force" of Algerians, French technocrats sought to introduce "a Muslim elite trained for several years in a system of cooperative discipline."[63] Yet Algerians continued to be underrepresented in the agricultural profession.[64] The agricultural school at Sidi Bel Abbès in Oran was intended to train Algerians, but there was still a shortage of indigenous students in the regional agricultural schools.[65] Although technocrats sought to include Algerians in agricultural modernization initiatives and familiarize them with ideas of economic progress, few were attracted by the prospect of working with French organizations.

In order to propagate modern agricultural methods among the Algerian fellahin, most SAPs allowed farmers to borrow tractors and plows. In both France and Algeria, tractors were a powerful symbol of postwar modernization. In 1954, there was one tractor in existence for every 100 hectares of land in France, while in Algeria this number was 160 hectares. Moreover, in France's Algerian departments, most of these tractors were used by European settlers.[66] While over half of the farmers in mainland France owned a tractor in 1963, native farmers in Algeria were dependent on the SAPS to procure these machines.[67] In Algeria, the modernizing zeal of French planners often overstated the need for tractors. An inspection of eleven SAPs in 1955 noted that tractors were used for fewer than 1,200 (and often fewer than 1,000) hours per year in 1954.[68] According to French experts, however, tractors needed to be used for at least 1,350 hours per year to justify the cost of their maintenance; they therefore set the goal of 2,000 hours of use per year.[69] The problem persisted. In 1959, 350 machines were employed for a total of 192,233 hours of work, averaging 549 hours per machine.[70]

These heavy machines were ill-suited for agricultural tasks in areas that were difficult to access, where lighter tractors would have been more appropriate. In addition to being detrimental to the soil, the use of tractors also contradicted a major political goal of the Constantine Plan, which was to maximize work hours in agriculture in order to combat unemployment.[71] It was hard to make an economic argument for purchasing tractors, since they were often sold or traded at a loss to the SAPs. These observations undermined any attempt to justify technical modernization with economic arguments, and many experts focused instead on the social effects of reforms. Yet not all planners were convinced that mechanization would inevitably incite Algerians to become more productive. At one meeting of the Departmental Commission for Agrarian Reform, an official who worked for the DRS worried that mechanized farming would cause the inhabitants of Sobha, in Chlef, to become "parasites [who] watch tractors, which are given by the state, do all the work" rather than the "entrepreneurs" envisioned by agricultural reform.[72] While the French state continued to follow the gospel of agricultural modernization, some experts speculated that increasing output would not suffice. Without the necessary psychological transformations, they argued, Algerians would simply increase their dependence on the colonial state rather than embrace a worldview of productivity and growth.[73]

The Inspection of Finances, a state auditing body, recognized the economic advantages of traditional farming methods, claiming that "the rental of a tractor is more expensive for a fellah than the use of his yoke, even more so since it leaves some work to be done by others. The transition from archaic agriculture to modern agriculture does not lead to an elevation of revenue equal to the increase in production."[74] In Frenda, for example, modern farming methods yielded six to ten quintals of wheat per hectare in normal conditions, while traditional methods produced only three to six. During years with a temperate climate (about one out of every three years) the yields from the traditional and modern sectors were roughly equivalent. During drought years, however, fellahin who had invested less in modern equipment were able to break even, while those who practiced large-scale mechanized agriculture lost money.[75] It was relatively rare for French officials to question the orthodoxy of modernization. Yet Jacques Pélissier, the director of the Ministry of Agriculture and Forests, expressed his regret at this state of affairs: "The fundamental error … is to have replaced sheep farming with caterpillar tractors when we should have concentrated all our efforts on the improvement of forage and animal production."[76] Perhaps due to his training at the National Agronomy Institute, Pélissier championed the need for better agricultural training for officials working with the SAPs and criticized previous policy decisions.

Many colonial experts, however, continued to equate the introduction of machinery such as tractors with the transformation of traditional agriculture.[77] Despite several reports that highlighted the economic illogic of mechanization in Algeria, the 1959 budget allocated 1,740,000 francs (out of a total of 6,250,000 francs) to be spent on machines, including the purchase of ninety-seven additional tractors.[78] The belief that a market economy and technological progress would institute sociological changes proved to be especially seductive. Despite a multitude of reports revealing the fallacy of this approach, the developmental gospel upheld the need to combat "oriental fatalism among the fellahs" and fight against pervasive "mistrust for Western techniques."[79] French administrators, enamored with the purported sociological impact of these machines, predicted that Western technology would vanquish oriental passivity.[80] Debates on the peasant in metropolitan France were marked by a similar tension between a nostalgic celebration of their role in national identity (a source of pride that represented the rural roots of the French nation [*la France profonde*]) and a critical view of farmers as backwards and hostile to modernization.[81] In Algeria, however, discourses on the fellahin reproduced the racial trope of oriental passivity that was fundamental to maintaining the boundary between European settlers and Muslim natives.

There were several indications that issues of production and distribution were rooted in colonial structures rather than in native mentalities. State investment in the SAPs increased under the Constantine Plan, but in 1959 only five hundred thousand people were members of the 105 existing SAPs.[82] Moreover, the SAPs were under the purview of the subprefects, who, according to Pélissier, often failed to prioritize agriculture in plans for economic development.[83] Despite the ambitious hopes of planners, the war made agricultural reform a herculean task; presidents of SAPs wondered how they could prevent the grain distributed by the organization from falling into FLN hands. In the arrondissement of Médéa, just south of Algiers, a military official noted that there were no restrictions on the amount of grain that a single individual could procure. While each individual sale was limited to 50 kilograms, nothing stopped a member from coming back every day to stock grain. Given that 18 kilograms of grain fed one person for an entire month, he calculated that a family of five would need 90 kilograms. If an individual came every day and stocked 1,500 kilograms of wheat over the course of a month, this left 1,410 kilograms that were "likely to pass into rebel hands."[84]

The various solutions envisaged by planners, including asking Algerians to show paperwork such as birth certificates or family record books, were largely impractical.[85] Other administrators argued that military oversight would be the best response, but the prefecture had already refused this solution. Military surveillance of the distribution of grain was clearly at odds with the desired cooperative spirit, yet in certain regions military authorities built stocking depots for family reserves where members of the SAP were obligated to keep their grain.[86] Political circumstances were never far from developmental visions; archival evidence suggests that colonial administrators took loyalty to the French state into account when deciding whether to offer assistance (such as credit or tractors) to rural Algerians.[87]

The war also had devastating effects on mobility. Authorizations were required to move wheat between districts, and prefects were advised to be vigilant about tracking the declared destinations of harvests and surveilling whether Algerian families were stocking grain. The SAPs had previously asked farmers to declare the quantity of their harvests, though this obligation was largely ignored. Annual reports by the General Inspection of Finances repeatedly underlined the fact that the SAPs were badly managed.[88] Some farmers were consistently unable to procure seeds, they noted, also drawing attention to the questionable accounting practices and lax work ethic at the SAPs. Perhaps the most shocking revelation of these reports is the repeated claim that the SAPs helped relatively well-off settlers instead of Algerian fellahin. A study of nine SAPs in 1955 concluded that 75 percent had undertaken more services for Europeans than for Muslim farmers. The many organizations responsible for agricultural reform, and the lack of coordination among them, were also major obstacles to implementing development schemes. The structural impediments to raising agricultural production were thus overwhelmingly political even though planners often identified the mentality of the fellahin as the main target for intervention.

The Banker and the Pioneer

The central mission of the SAPs was based on a contradiction: they were responsible for aiding small farmers even though they sought to make a profit.[89] Remarking on their tendency to lose money, one observer suggested that "Algeria should subsidize the modernization of Muslim agriculture and not the loss-inducing management [*gestion déficitaire*] of the SAPs."[90] The idea that the French state should subsidize Algerian agriculture was controversial. Consistent with the wisdom of postwar modernizing technocracy discussed in the last chapter, some officials argued that the goal of rural renovation was not to help those who were most in need but rather to generate profits by focusing on areas that promised high returns on investment.[91] Planners therefore decided that the goal of the SAPs should be to integrate the so-called Muslim sector into the general economy rather than attempting to uplift Algerians in particular.[92] An external investigation by the Ministry of Finances confirmed that the SAPs were often more attentive to the issue of profitability than social development. Pierre Guichard, who interned with the SAS from July to August of 1958, explained that the risk-averse nature of the SAPs meant that "the banker [would] prevail over the pioneer."[93] These observations shed light on the discursive differences between agricultural development in mainland France and Algeria. While the French state gave generous aid to farmers in the metropole with few qualifications, in Algeria planners worried that charity would weaken the entrepreneurial spirit that the Constantine Plan attempted to instill.

Making the SAPs profitable by extending credit to Algerian farmers was no easy task. Reports by the general inspector of finances in 1955 and 1959 stressed that the most vulnerable farmers required direct aid, noting the "constant confusion between the concept of a loan and the concept of a subsidy" among those who worked for the SAPs.[94] The organizations often lent money, sometimes at high rates of interest that made it impossible for native farmers to repay their debts. Farmers had trouble navigating the SAP bureaucracy and were subjected to long wait times before receiving funds. Moreover, it was difficult to the collect the unpaid debts of individuals who were largely unaccustomed to the idea of credit.[95] Algerians often lacked the down payment required for loans, feared expropriation, or had the faulty impression that their debts would be forgiven. The director of a SAP in northeast Algeria wrote in 1958 that "the notion of credit among local farmers and the substantial debts of the SAP resulting from issued loans that were never reimbursed require that we remain cautious."[96] Regardless of these obvious shortcomings, exposure to credit was seen as a way to acquaint native farmers with economic thinking.

The contradictory goals of the SAPs, which sought to help the fellahin while liberalizing an autarkic economic system, allowed the cultural practices of Muslim Algerians to appear as the main object of reform. The SAPs published the *Almanach du paysan algérien* (Almanac of the Algerian farmer) for the first time in 1959.[97] The brochure was decorated with sketches of Arab families and motifs meant to mimic traditional designs. It detailed the system of social protection for agricultural workers and asked farmers to keep notebooks of accounts (*cahier de comptabilité*) akin to those kept by storekeepers. It also outlined the differences between expenses, revenue, and profit. The almanac offered the same lessons in Arabic and included diagrams that explained the workings of loans that could be repaid in wheat or cash. It described the functioning of a loan, the concepts of yield and profit, and fines that could be imposed by the SAP. The colorful pages included short stories that imitated a traditional genre of storytelling. Whereas one would expect this kind of fable to offer lessons on morality or religion, the almanac provided advice on healthcare and agriculture. For each month, it provided an Arabic proverb or religious saying, albeit sometimes with grammatical mistakes and typos. The cover page of the chapter for March featured the Hadith: "Man radiya bi-l-qalil min al-rizqi radiya Allah ʿanhu bi-l-qalil min al-ʿamal" (He who is satisfied by meager wealth, God will grant him a meager amount of work).[98] Planners thus employed religious vocabulary to induce Algerian farmers to participate in a market economy.

Another obstacle to market production was the organization of credit, which relied on a distinction between small-scale farmers (*petit fellah*) who depended on the SAPs for credit, and medium- or large-scale farmers. The second group was integrated into a separate circuit for obtaining loans,

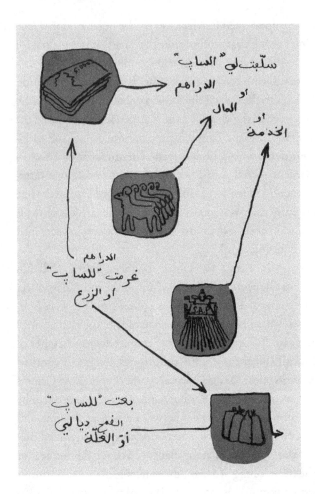

Figure 4.2 An almanac published by the SAP in 1959. Source: Archives nationales d'outre-mer, BIB AOM 46972.

the Caisse algérienne de crédit agricole mutuel (CACAM; Algerian Bank of Cooperative Agricultural Credit).[99] This organization offered long-term loans and was financially autonomous, while the SAPs distributed mostly short- and medium-term loans, the majority of which were used to obtain seeds, replenish livestock, or plant crops.[100] The different forms of credit offered by the SAPs and the CACAM perpetuated a system dating from the interwar period that distinguished "normal credit," which corresponded to the laws of profitability outlined by banks, from "abnormal credit," which posed a higher risk and was dedicated to subsistence farming.[101] In 1957, the CACAM offered forty-five billion francs in credit, yet less than one-third of its thirty-three thousand members were Muslim.[102] Moreover, Algerian natives constituted just 11 percent of those who participated in its governing councils in 1958.[103] Tellingly, despite these inequities, a report outlining the need to reform the CACAM in May 1958 asserted that it was the "degree of evolution of the Algerian Muslim farmers" that explained the differences between agricultural credit in Algeria and in the metropole.[104]

A letter from the General Planning Commission to the governor general acknowledged the need to reform credit structures since "the lack of medium- and long-term credit in the traditional milieu accentuate[d] the differences that exist[ed] between the two economies, whose rapprochement [was] one of the major conditions for any amelioration in the socio-economic equilibrium."[105] Though the lack of long-term credit was repeatedly cited as an obstacle to the development of traditional agriculture, this dual system of credit persisted. The managing council of the SAPs, for example, argued that the organization should prioritize farmers who appreciated the fruit of their labor and who worked to satisfy their thirst for progress. This implied that a certain work ethic, or moral code, should be the criteria for credit. The stated goal was to "get [farmers] used to direct action, to decisions made together and to the collective responsibility of borrowing."[106] Despite the many signs that the SAPs were pervasively mismanaged, it was rare for planners to reconsider their faith in this organization. Instead, they posited that Islamic fatalism and a basic inability to calculate future needs were the real reasons that agricultural modernization had failed to help Algerians.

"He Must Have Callused Hands"

French administrators believed that encouraging Algerians to own land and engage in full-time agricultural employment would help calm political unrest. One agricultural practice was of particular concern: Muslim farmers had historically engaged in a form of sharecropping known as the *khammesat*, whereby the sharecropper (known as a *khammès*) received one-fifth of the harvest. This practice had been outlawed in 1956 but continued to be widespread at the end of the 1950s. In 1957, for example, there were between one hundred thirty thousand and one hundred forty thousand *khammès*, and one million agricultural workers who earned regular salaries.[107] In the eyes of administrators, the *khammesat* resembled a form of serfdom that had existed in the French countryside in the Middle Ages. French officials also worried that the *khammès* could easily become an agent of political agitation since "nothing attaches this farmer to the soil, or encourages him to undertake improvements."[108] As a result, colonial officials sought to transform these sharecroppers into agricultural workers, in part by offering them social services and protection on the condition that their employers declare them to the Caisse mutuelle d'assurances sociales agricoles (Cooperative Bank of Agricultural Social Security).[109]

The creation of CAPER, the body designed to oversee land reform in 1956, aimed to reduce the number of sharecroppers.[110] Pélissier complained that the lack of a clear system of land rights among Muslims prevented the rational use of territory, highlighting the existence of collectively held 'arsh land.[111] The organization also sought to consolidate individual plots of land, safeguard family farms, and increase productivity. In many ways, these efforts resembled those of the Société d'aménagement foncier et d'établissement rural (SAFER; Society for Developing and Settling Rural Land) in mainland France, which sought to enact the policy of *remembrement* to consolidate the heavily fragmented landholdings that had resulted, in part, from the 1803 Civil Code.[112] In 1940, only 4.5 percent of Algerians (as compared to 43 percent of Europeans) had landholdings larger than fifty hectares.[113] In mainland France, planners sought to protect farmers from the encroachments of capitalism, romanticizing the French peasant's link to the soil in the process. In Algeria, however, their main concern was to instill the mental structures needed for market production.

Land reform efforts in Algeria predated the Constantine Plan, however. Under Vichy, the Law of March 18, 1942, had introduced a tax on insufficiently developed large estates. The tax was to be paid in land and would have led to the expropriation of twenty thousand hectares (five thousand from wealthy Algerian landowners and fifteen thousand from Europeans) and the resettlement of fifteen thousand Algerian and one thousand European farmers. In 1943, the Commission for Muslim Reforms envisaged the creation of collective farms (*kolkhozes*) and stations with machinery, but only eighteen hundred families had been resettled by the end of 1954.[114] The Constantine Plan was far more ambitious than either of these measures, committing to the redistribution of two hundred fifty thousand hectares of land in five years.[115] CAPER also had a social role, as it was to discourage undesirable labor practices such as sharecropping. According to the Chamber of Agriculture in Algiers, the "Muslim agricultural worker who has become a landowner should be required to live on his farm. He should be required to work every day like a French peasant. He must have callused hands so that he does not hire a *khammès* or permanent agricultural worker."[116] Planners hoped that agricultural workers would learn to behave as landowners and demonstrate the corresponding respect for private property and long-term economic calculation.

Families who received land from CAPER were given a certificate of possession and a note that outlined the accompanying obligations, which included participation in agricultural modernization schemes and credit initiatives. The administration decided which crops should be grown, expressing a preference for citrus and wine, which were intended for export. The relationship between agricultural profit and land tenure was calculated through the institution of a land quota for each family (*l'unité culturale familiale*), which was the amount of land that permitted a family to earn an annual revenue of 3,500 francs.[117] The spatial organization of these lots was often problematic, however. The village of Mirabeau, like most territories, was divided into lots that were reserved for specific crops. But each parcel of land was cultivated by multiple tenants, since certain crops were more profitable than others, and agricultural specialists had long deplored the tendency toward monoculture. As a result, each farmer had access to several parcels at different distances from the fixed residence of their family.

While many of these attempts at land reform were based on metropolitan models, planners quickly ran into obstacles as European practices were often unsuitable for the climate, soil, and preferences of the Algerian inhabitants. As René Mayer recounted:

> As the director for habitat in Algeria, I commissioned studies on the norms of local low-cost housing and was subsequently reprimanded by the Ministry of Construction [who] thought that they had the right to impose French norms. They would say ... "Algeria is France. You should therefore apply French norms." Can you imagine, in the Algerian south, applying the window requirements that were in accordance with French norms for low-cost housing? You would literally cook everyone, it's completely ridiculous. Also, Algeria is a Muslim country, and you're not supposed to see the women when they are inside. So, when designing bedrooms, you cannot have large windows that offer a view of the interior. This is why I had to come up with my own norms. I organized a call for architects to propose housing models that were adapted to [the Algerian] context.[118]

Archival sources bear out the claim that planners were often ignorant of local realities. One report criticized the error of installing concrete floors for people who were often barefoot at home and complained that the windows of houses built in Chélif faced the sun, making the heat unbearable during the day. The Departmental Commission of Agrarian Reform for Orléansville noted, "Despite some remarkable achievements, the general impression is that shoddy things are constructed anywhere, in any fashion [*n'importe où, n'importe comment, n'importe quoi*]."[119] CAPER also concerned itself with the domestic life of Algerians who lived in these structures, sometimes offering women instructions on how to carry out household tasks. While it was acknowledged that this was largely outside of CAPER's assigned mission, planners encouraged these practices since they acquainted farmers with "modern" life.[120] Indeed, while the economic logic of the expropriation, development, redistribution, and supervision of agricultural holdings was questionable (and often questioned), CAPER's role in social advancement was universally commended by colonial officials. [121]

In introducing land reforms, the French administration attempted to rationalize a number of measures that had been instituted in the mid-nineteenth century, when the state had offered monopolies and properties to private interests in Algeria.[122] By expropriating certain *grands domaines* and forests, the state was no longer to be a direct agent of colonization. Instead, semipublic companies were created to manage these holdings. Despite the negative effects of being the sole buyer on the real estate market, CAPER's activities allowed Europeans to leave Algeria under the best possible conditions. At the same time, the meager amount of land acquired by CAPER reflected the political impossibility of forcibly breaking up large European landholdings.[123] Overall, CAPER's reach was extremely limited; it worked with only five hundred families in 1961.[124] Yet planners put great faith in the possibility of transforming Algerian farming habits, mentalities, and landholdings. The failed attempts to rationalize colonial capitalism in accordance with a market economy subsequently enabled the racial-religious difference of Algerians, encapsulated in Islam, to appear as the main obstacle to agricultural modernization.

"The Eternally Forsaken"

After independence, Algerian president Ahmed Ben Bella celebrated the fellahin as a symbol of the revolutionary character of the Algerian people, calling them "les reprouvés de toujours" (the eternally forsaken).[125] Political discourses also cast this population as an object of social engineering, celebrating the experience of self-management as a way to develop their revolutionary capacities. As Robert Malley has noted, the fellah represented a multitude of conflicting symbols.[126] In opposition to the liberal construction of the Algerian farmer as resistant to market rationality, and the Marxist conception of the peasantry as essentially conservative, Algerian nationalism fabricated the fellah as a heroic figure.

This focus on the peasantry was not unique to the postcolonial Algerian state. Tunisian nationalists did all they could to "reinforce the solidarity of fellah and fellaga."[127] Moroccan nationalist ʿAllal Al-Fassi composed an ode to the Moroccan fellah that included these lines:

> Wayha fallahin asbaha ʿabdan
> Nazaʿu ardahu wa ghallu yadayhi
> Kul yawmin tusibuhu nakbatun
> Sara marma istighlali kulli qawiyyin[128]

> Woe to the peasant who became a slave
> They seized his lands and bound his hands
> Every day a catastrophe befalls him
> He's become the target of exploitation by all forces

These romantic renderings were a response to the economic hardship endured by North African farmers during colonialism. This revolutionary construction of the fellahin as a symbol of Arab nationalism did not necessarily erase the colonial depictions of the peasant. As Omnia El Shakry demonstrates, the Egyptian nation-state transformed colonial discourses on the fellahin, viewing them as paradigmatic actors of modernity, or "peasants made of metal."[129] In Algeria, the revolutionary construction of the fellah built on the tradition of rural sociology but substituted a concern with their revolutionary potential for the colonial state's attempts to instill market behaviors.[130]

"The fellah is satisfied with his situation," Mohammed Dib recounts in his novel, *L'incendie* (The fire), which was published in 1954, the first year of the Algerian War of Independence.[131] The novel portrays the Algerian peasantry's realization that the humiliation, poverty, and injustice of daily life were not "natural [facts] like the rain, wind, or soil" but rather the result of the colonial system.[132] The "awakening" of the peasantry, and their adoption of a revolutionary mentality, were pillars of Algerian nationalism. Indeed, the Martyr's Memorial in Algiers (Maqam al-Shahid), built in 1982 to commemorate the anniversary of Algerian independence, depicts three iconic figures of the war: the soldier, the worker, and the peasant. These figures represent "a social and moral order and organization" that is the foundation of the official narrative of Algerian nationalism.[133]

Initiatives designed to raise the standard of living among Algerian farmers, which had become a priority for colonial officials in the interwar period, intensified after World War II. These reforms were articulated in the framework of a liberal economic structure that sought to integrate native Algerians into a system of market production. In France, too, economic planners sought to increase output and rationalize systems of food production and distribution; these priorities were reflected in the tripling of the agricultural budget in the 1960s.[134] Yet farmers in the metropole often looked unfavorably on state investment in Algeria. One farmer's poster during violent protests in Amiens in 1960 read, "Do I have to become a fellagha in order to get my own Constantine Plan?"[135] Despite the similarities in agricultural reforms on both sides of the Mediterranean, the Algerian fellah and French paysan had different roles in cementing French nationalism after 1945. French peasants, though seen as culturally backward, were nevertheless romanticized. They tended to view state assistance as a right. In Algeria, however, colonial officials were on guard against providing charity to the fellahin, fearing that it would impede their efforts to introduce racial and social transformations through contact with a market economy.

Algerian nationalists viewed the fellah as a symbol of national authenticity. Writing in 1961, Frantz Fanon—the Martinican psychiatrist and FLN militant who wrote on the Algerian War—substituted the fellahin for the proletariat as the motor of revolution. He famously wrote: "The fellah, the unemployed and the starving do not lay claim to truth. They do not say they represent the truth because they are the truth in their very being."[136] This vision was rebuked by Bourdieu, who considered Fanon's writings to be a form of propaganda rather than an accurate description of the Algerian peasantry.[137] After 1962, Ben Bella sought to gain legitimacy through the construction of an authentically Algerian socialism based on Islam. He rejected the colonial notion that the fellah was inherently opposed to capitalist rationality even as he questioned their capacity for agricultural self-management. This policy, which is the subject of the next chapter, was designed to fashion a revolutionary consciousness among Algerians.

5.
COMMUNISM IN A WHITE BURNOUS

After eight years of violent struggle, the GPRA, the political and diplomatic arm of the FLN, signed the Evian Accords.[1] Overwhelmingly approved by Algerians in a referendum held on July 1, 1962, these agreements guaranteed the territorial integrity of the Algerian nation-state and introduced an official cease-fire. Some Algerians expressed reservations about their content, however. The country's first president, Ahmed Ben Bella, wondered if they had opened the door to a neocolonial relationship by securing the rights of French and foreign companies to Algerian oil.[2] In response, his comrade Kaid Ahmed (nom de guerre Commandant Slimane) interrogated the fundamental nature of the FLN: How could an organization founded on armed combat be transformed into a political party?[3] Did most Algerians share the goal of creating a revolutionary society rooted in a "specifically Algerian" socialism?[4] As Algerian nationalists navigated the transition to independence, they reshaped the racial regime of religion and crafted economic policies to encourage the creation of revolutionary citizens.

The construction of a socialist economy regulated the distribution of material resources and established an imagined Algerian community around religion. The 1963 Constitution was especially clear on this point: it asserted that "Islam and the Arab language [had] been the effective forces of resistance against the attempt by the colonial regime to depersonalize the Algerians."[5] This official emphasis on Islam set Algeria apart from countries in the Middle East where a focus on Arabism facilitated the incorporation of Christians. Despite the practical appeal of foregrounding a unitary conception of Algerian identity organized around Arabism and Islam, this definition nevertheless failed to capture the diversity of the country's inhabitants.[6] By 1964, the ideological coalition that had promoted Ben Bella's version of Islamic socialism looked especially fragile, setting the stage for Houari Boumediene's coup the following year.

The establishment of self-proclaimed revolutionary states across the Middle East and North Africa undoubtedly bolstered the monopoly on social and political life held by vanguard parties such as the FLN. This experience can also be viewed as a form of worldmaking, as intellectuals and politicians in the Global South "stretched" Marxism to accommodate their specific cultures and histories.[7] In the 1960s, intellectuals and politicians from formerly colonized countries sought to break free of Eurocentric models for revolution. In this regard, while Ben Bella's articulation of a Muslim socialism undoubtedly instrumentalized religion and established an authoritarian regime, it also attempted to draw on indigenous traditions in organizing economic policies.[8] The first comprehensive outline for the independent nation-state's economic policy, the June 1962 Tripoli Program, adopted at a congress held in Libya, clearly expressed Algeria's commitment to socialism. It claimed that Islam functioned as "more than just a religion" and would be the main source for Algerian culture and national identity.[9] Coupled with a citizenship law that established Islam as a hereditary principle, religion provided a cultural framework and an imaginary of fixed origin that became the cornerstone of Ben Bella's revolutionary governmentality.[10]

As previous chapters have argued, French experts drew on essentialized notions of Islam in their attempts to encourage native Algerians to adopt the behaviors and mentalities necessary for the smooth functioning of liberal capitalism. Decolonization fundamentally changed the politics of development, but it did not erase the essential grammar that posited a natural correspondence between religious principles and economic organization. Government officials, technocrats, and economists had considered Islam as an obstacle to establishing a market economy during the colonial period. After 1962, however, Algerian nationalists turned this vision on its head and presented religion as a source of socialist principles. Questions about the organization of markets, the ownership of the means of production, and the commercialization of agriculture were thus fundamental to the creation of Algerian citizens. Ben Bella reconfigured the colonial tropes of homo islamicus and homo economicus, harnessing religion to a revolutionary project in which Islam was the basis for a socialist economy.

The House Is in Ruins

Violent struggle in Algeria did not end with independence. During the summer of 1962, weary chants of *sab'a snin, barakat!* (seven years of fighting is enough!) replaced the optimistic slogan *vive l'Algérie indépendante!* (long live independent Algeria!). The prospect of a civil war loomed large as divisions among political clans wreaked havoc on Algeria's political life.[11] Some disagreements centered on ideology, while others were rooted in regional attachments. Just months after jubilant crowds took to the streets celebrating independence, Mohammed Boudiaf formed the Parti de la révolution socialiste (Party of the Socialist Revolution), the country's first opposition party, which led to his brief arrest and exile later the same year.[12] Even though the Algerian state banned all political associations in August 1963, the wartime hero Hocine Aït Ahmed founded the Berberist Front des forces socialistes (FFS; Socialist Forces Front) the following month. His brief insurrection led to his imprisonment in 1964; he escaped in 1966 and spent the next two decades in exile.

Ben Bella's rise to power represented a victory over the GPRA for the armed wing of the FLN, the ALN, and the army's general staff (*l'état-major général*). Algeria had suffered staggering human losses during the war. Official estimates claim that over one million Algerians died in the conflict, though the actual number is likely closer to half a million.[13] The end of the war prompted the departure of the majority of Europeans, along with their capital and expertise, leaving vast numbers of farms, factories, and apartments vacant. According to Bachir Boumaza, head of the Ministry of Labor and Social Affairs under Ben Bella, 80 percent of those occupying high-ranking positions in education, engineering, agriculture, and medicine left Algeria after independence.[14]

Filling these positions was a herculean task. Approximately 90 percent of Algerians were illiterate in 1962, and the OAS, a right-wing European paramilitary group, pursued a campaign of civilian violence and vandalism that included bombing and assassinations.[15] The agricultural sector of the economy particularly suffered from the war: overall production dropped by more than one-third, creating a crisis for the historically lucrative wine economy.[16] The only silver lining was the 1956 discovery of oil, a resource that accounted for 63 percent of all export earnings in 1963 and that increasingly financed economic development and social welfare.[17] The Algerian economy was also locked in a pattern of dependency on France that proved difficult to break. In 1963, 75 percent of Algerian exports went to France, and 81 percent of Algerian imports came from the Hexagon. Ben Bella walked a thin line between keeping the economy afloat and asserting Algeria's sovereignty. The Tripoli Program denounced the neocolonial character of the Evian Accords, but some FLN members, such as M'hammed Yazid and Mostefa Lacheraf, took issue with the document's emphasis on religion. Ferhat Abbas also disagreed with Ben Bella's attempt to marry socialist principles to an Islamic identity, later writing that Ben Bella had tried to dress up "communism in the white burnous of religion."[18]

While nationalists in the Middle East sometimes adopted Germanic conceptions of identity that relied on ethnic and cultural heritage, Algeria presented a specific case in that Islam, rather than Arabism or Arabness (arabité, al-'uruba) served as the cement of national belonging.[19] As Abbas wrote, "What matters in Algeria is not race, it's Islam."[20] While this statement reproduces the long-standing dichotomy between race and religion, it nevertheless shows the specificity of Algerian nationalism. The importance of Islam was enshrined in the 1963 Algerian nationality law, which made citizenship contingent on paternal filiation and French personal status law.[21] To obtain Algerian nationality, it was necessary for the father of an individual to have been born in Algeria and been governed by Islamic legal codes during colonial rule.[22] Similarly, the 1964 Algiers Charter stated that the Algerian people had always viewed their religion as a message that promoted the "end of the exploitation of man by man" rather than a "doctrine of resignation."[23] As politicians and intellectuals invoked Islam, they approached religion less as a precise theological corpus than as a broad historical imaginary that denoted a set of origins and bloodlines.

Despite the heady revolutionary ambiance of the first years of independence, there were signs that Algerians were growing weary of the sacrifices made during the war. Ahmed Saber, the Rai singer from Oran, had joined the FLN in Tunisia during the war. His denunciation of the nepotism, corruption, and bureaucracy of the independent nation-state nevertheless landed him in jail under Ben Bella.[24] In addition to delivering a searing critique of the regime, he lamented the impossibility of finding a dignified job. The refrain of "El Khedma" (Work) expressed the feeling that securing employment had become about appearances or personal connections and compared the actions of the administration to those of the French colonizers ("This is the work of colonialism").[25] If only the system would treat Algerians with dignity, the song suggested, they would be able to follow a path to progress (taqaddum). The song also revealed the ways in which anxieties about the future orientation of the nation-state were projected onto gender roles.[26]

Saber implied that writing a woman's name on a CV was a sure way to be hired, lamenting, "look at this tribulation, the system doesn't like men." In another song, "El Khayen" (The imposter), he described how some individuals had unjustly profited from the revolution, asking, "At the time of the revolution, where were you?" and promising retribution ("your day will come, o imposter").[27] This profound sense of disillusionment underscored the fact that Algeria's economic challenges would require a more effective distribution of resources as well as the construction of a new set of national values.

Mohammed Mokrane, who had worked with the FLN in France before returning to Algeria, expressed similar sentiments:

> After 1962, we were discharged from the Federation [of the FLN] and I came back home. What struck and disappointed me [during the summer of 1962] was the conflict between resistors, and between revolutionaries. I was profoundly disappointed to see that some friends supported Ben Bella, while others were for the army, and others were with Aït Ahmed, etc. This disappointed me because during the war, we were a unit [bloc] and that's what allowed for victory. At that time, unity was something really important. We were ready to die for the cause. Weak elements [les défaillants] were considered traitors. To sum up 1962 in Algeria, we were politically divided; it was conflictual.[28]

Mokrane recounted how friends tried to get him to join the FFS, the opposition party to the FLN, but he refused, saying "the house is in ruins; we first have to establish the foundations."[29] The revolution thus engendered intense solidarities and struggles, even as it also introduced deep fissures that threatened to bring the national edifice crumbling down.

"The Land for Those Who Work It"

On November 1, 1962, the anniversary of the outbreak of the War of Independence, Ben Bella gave a speech in Algiers. Speaking to massive crowds in Martyrs' Square, he claimed the government "want[ed] to introduce a revolutionary socialism that [took] into account our Arabo-Islamic traditions."[30] For Ben Bella, the most crucial element of this principle was the policy of self-management (autogestion), which he claimed was the only way to continue the legacy of the revolution. The famous slogan "the land for those who work it" was ubiquitous during his rule.

At the first Fellah Congress in 1963, Ben Bella maintained that farmers shared his enthusiasm for setting the country on a socialist path.[31] This was

Figure 5.1 A cartoon by the Algerian artist Tewfik in the newspaper *Le Peuple* (Ach-Chaab), October 26, 1963, portraying the Congress of Peasants. The inscription on the right reads "The land for those who work it." Source: Bibliothèque nationale de France.

partly true: the occupation of farms and factories by Algerian workers was initially a spontaneous response to the exodus of Europeans. But the reforms were also based on a long-standing European socialist tradition rooted in collective ownership by workers' associations. Arabic propaganda by the FLN defined self-management as a way to give workers "direct power" to run the economy and introduce public ownership of the means of production.[32] Despite this official messaging, it was not always clear what Algerian farmers understood when they heard *al-tasyir al-dhati*, the Arabic term for self-management.[33] Amar Ouzegane claimed that while the French word *socialisme* sounded cold to Algerian ears, the Arabic term *ishtirakiyya* evoked a warmer response.[34]

European comrades and members of the GPRA used Josip Broz Tito's experience with self-management in Yugoslavia as a model for Algeria.[35] Both countries adopted a "third way" of socialism that was not necessarily anti-market, but which introduced a state-led economic sector that existed in parallel with private investments.[36] This has led critics to argue that these countries in fact fostered a system of state capitalism.[37] The bureaucratization of the self-managed sector in Algeria effectively stripped individual workers of any real influence in the day-to-day management of their farms. This process began with the 1963 March Decrees, which formalized land reform and the self-management of farms and factories. The first decree, of March 18, legalized the status quo, officially transferring the ownership of farms left vacant at independence. The decrees nationalized roughly 800,000 hectares of land from about 16,000 farms, as well as approximately 200,000 apartments and houses, 450 industrial enterprises, and hundreds of commercial interests. They also legalized the existence of so-called vacant properties (*biens vacants*), a term that had been in use since the summer of 1962.[38] The second decree, of March 22, specified that vacant enterprises should be run by a general assembly composed of permanent workers who would be responsible for establishing the priorities, goals, and production schedules of each farm or factory.[39] It also outlined the creation of workers' councils, management committees, and communal councils, which in practice had overlapping functions.

The March 18 Decree further incorporated colonial organizations into the system of self-management. For example, the SAPs remained an important source of credit in the early years of independence, and the director of individual autogestion units was often chosen from former SAP workers.[40] The decree established the National Office of Agrarian Reform (ONRA), run by Ahmed Mahsas, which soon came into conflict with the Bureau national d'animation du secteur socialiste (BNASS; National Office of the Socialist Sector). Mahsas also served as the minister of agriculture and agrarian reform from 1963 to 1965, following Amar Ouzegane, who had occupied the position from 1962 to 1963. The BNASS had a reputation for being staffed by leftist Marxists, including the Algerian historian Mohammed Harbi and the leader of the Fourth International, Pablo (a.k.a. Michel Raptis). Mahsas criticized those with secular leanings, claiming they had no real experience in agriculture; he claimed these Marxists considered Algerian farmers to be retrograde "because they constructed mosques and taught their children to read the Qu'ran."[41] Political divisions were built into the very bureaucratic apparatus that was responsible for implementing self-management. According to the Algerian sociologist Ali El Kenz (writing under a pseudonym), even if this period was short-lived, it revealed the "first ideological clashes of independent Algeria."[42]

The self-managed sector included the most fertile lands, which had previously belonged to European settlers.[43] Constituting less than one-sixth of all agricultural territories, these farms produced nine-tenths of the country's wine and five-sixths of its citrus.[44] The socialist sector thus reflected the colonial distinction between "traditional" and "modern" agriculture, which was now evident in the contrast between self-managed and privately owned farms.[45] There was also continuity in the attitudes and working patterns of agricultural laborers, despite the revolutionary intentions of the March Decrees. According to Claudine Chaulet, who conducted extensive fieldwork in the Mitidja region, the attitudes fostered by the colonial regime did not disappear with the transition to independence.[46] Kamel Abdellah Khodja confirmed this account. Trained as an economist, he was the minister of state planning under Boumediene. He attributed the failure of self-management to the state's refusal to offer any real responsibility to members of the management committees; instead, they remained removed from the quotidian tasks of running the farms.[47] Reports by French diplomats asserted that some agricultural workers found life to have been easier during the French period and that the bureaucratization and paternalism of the management committees were sometimes viewed as a continuation of colonial policies.[48]

In adopting a socialist "third way," the regime avoided both the language of class struggle and the Soviet Union's disparaging stance on religion. Self-management was the "most important conquest of the revolution" and would restore the glory of the people "without an army of engineers and technicians," according to Ben Bella.[49] The policy was to provide reparations for 132 years of colonial rule while encouraging a unitary conception of the Algerian people. Discussions of class divisions were practically taboo; Ben Bella warned Algerians against embracing *ouvriérisme* (workerism) or glorifying the manual labor of the proletariat.[50] He spoke of eliminating wage labor, since workers were not salaried employees but rather contributed directly to the revolution. He defended self-management by appealing to the attributes of the Algerian people; when asked by a reporter why he did not follow the Russian example of state-led farms, Ben Bella responded that, while he would have liked to nationalize agriculture immediately, one had to take into account the "psychology and specific characteristics of the Algerian people."[51] Algerian socialism reflected the general climate of the Third World, where various economic programs tried to address the legacies of colonial rule. However, the insistence on an Algerian specificity rooted in Islam set it apart from other pan-Arab and pan-African orientations.

"El Baraka fil Haraka"

The AUMA played a key role in articulating an Algerian identity during the colonial period. [52] Although it was officially dissolved after independence, former members continued to advocate for an Algerian state steeped in their understanding of Islamic principles. These themes found voice among the young, Arabic-speaking members of the group al-Qiyam al-Islamiyya (Islamic Values, hereafter al-Qiyam), which was created in 1963. Their vision was largely inspired by the Arab Renaissance (*al-Nahda*), which sought to formulate a response to the encroachment of European power and capitalist modernity. [53] The Algiers Charter also reflected the role of Islamic modernism; it claimed that the doctrines of Muslim renewal espoused by intellectuals Muhammad 'Abduh and Jamal al-Din al-Afghani had contributed to Algerian nationalism. [54] 'Abduh and al-Afghani had been among the first to articulate a distinctly Arab identity in the Middle East, adapting European ideas of nationalism to confront the Turkification of the Ottoman empire. Yet questions of economic policy and national identity were intimately linked. As Sherene Seikaly has demonstrated, understandings of profit and property were fundamental to the Nahda's project. [55]

Algerian officials working for the Ministry of Habus provided an important source of ideological support for Ben Bella and defended the idea that Islam was a socialist religion. [56] They published an Arabic language journal titled *al-Ma'rifa* (Knowledge) that featured individuals who had been close to the AUMA, including politicians, imams, and intellectuals such as Malek Bennabi. [57] In countering claims that Islam was inherently unproductive—common among French economists in the 1950s—the journal also revisited debates among Orientalists and Islamic modernists that dated from the nineteenth century. [58] Perhaps the best-known example was Ernest Renan's 1883 lecture "Islam and Science" and Jamal al-Din al-Afghani's subsequent response. Their exchange expressed a fundamental disagreement over the nature of Arab identity and the role that Islam had played in the region's material development. [59] Subsequently, some of *al-Ma'rifa*'s articles echoed the argument of Syrian intellectual Abd al-Rahman al-Kawakibi, a student of al-Afghani, that excess wealth would lead to a drop in morality. [60] Inspired by an Islamic worldview that tied together values, religion, and the distribution of material resources, contributors to the journal discussed ideas such as social responsibility (*al-takaful al-ijtima'i*) and social justice (*al-'adala al-ijtima'iyya*). Informed by a late nineteenth-century vocabulary, these concepts had first emerged in response to the rise of global capitalism. They proved to be a useful toolbox for discussing Islamic socialism in the 1950s and 1960s, including among members of the Egyptian brotherhood.[61] The short-lived union between Egypt and Syria from 1958 to 1961 also helped legitimize the once-controversial association of socialism with Islam.[62] Mustafa al-Siba'i, the leader of the Syrian branch of the Muslim Brotherhood, published *Ishtirakiyyat al-Islam* (The socialism of Islam) in 1959. Adopting language that resembled the writings of social Catholics, al-Siba'i foregrounded humanism and the search for dignity (*haqq al-karama*) rather than insisting on class struggle.[63]

One article published in *al-Ma'rifa* claimed that although self-management committees were inspired by the Yugoslav model, they were actually an embodiment of *hisba*, an Islamic concept that harkened back to the Abbasid period, the golden age of Islam. In medieval times, the figure of the *muhtasib* personally controlled the markets (*aswaq*) and performed moral, religious, and economic functions.[64] *Al-Ma'rifa* cast Islam as an antidote to capitalism, featuring Umar al-Khattab, a companion of the Prophet known for his generosity. But rather than propose a return to a glorious past, the journal sought new answers to pressing economic questions. 'Abd al-Qadir Zubadiya, for example, wrote that socialism was not a system (*nidham*) or end in itself (*ghaya*), nor even a precise goal (*hadaf*). Rather, it was a moral orientation that rested on specific principles.[65] In this formulation, socialism had existed prior to the emergence of a capitalist system. Moreover, unlike communism, the journal claimed, Islam was not opposed to prosperity or class differences. Instead, the key to a healthy economic system was to ensure the moral fiber of those who were affluent, which was the basis for distinguishing between permitted and forbidden wealth.[66]

A number of voices close to the regime critiqued capitalism while distancing themselves from scientific socialism. Echoing Ben Bella's defense of self-management, the historian and minister of Habus (religious affairs), Tawfiq al-Madani, inverted the colonial trope that blamed Islamic beliefs for fatalism and economic backwardness. After outlining Islam's role in resisting France's civilizing mission, he continued, "Islam is a religion of work, of diligence, of development and perfection. Islam commands one to work for this world as well as for the next, and it calls us to form an upright (*intègre*) and conscientious society. In addition, Islam will lead people in their struggle for construction and development (*mise en valeur*), and help them form a strong state and virtuous society."[67] Al-Madani's coupling of Islam and mise en valeur is particularly striking given the strong association of the latter term with the secular Third Republic. In appropriating this economic tradition, al-Madani saw strength and virtue—rather than economic growth—as the ordering logic of development. In this sense, the adoption of an Islamic framework was a legacy of the racial regime of religion constructed by the French state. Rather than being an impediment to market-driven development, however, Islam was now depicted as the civilizational foundation for socialism.

For many officials, Islam provided the basis for a new postcolonial model of productivity. Like al-Madani, Amar Ouzegane, minister of agriculture and agrarian reform, also portrayed economic activity in religious terms:

> El baraka fil haraka, there is benediction in movement. The Algerian masses, who were previously prisoners of fatalism and superstition, are not only developing a collective will and a force of energy, but an authority that will replace the destructible colonial power. . . . Islam is thus not a backward "hereditary defect" [tare héréditaire] nor an ideological obstacle that is stuck in the superstructure, but a motor nerve that is as necessary for the revolution as the other determinant elements of the infrastructure.[68]

This critique of capitalism was likely informed by Ouzegane's experience as head of the Algiers branch of the Algerian Communist Party in the 1930s. Yet in arguing that religion could promote a productive workfoce, Ouzegane posited a reconciliation between homo islamicus and homo economicus: rather than being an obstacle to liberal capitalism, Islam could provide the basis for socialism and economic justice once Algeria had freed itself from colonial rule.

Between the Arab Race and Black Africa

While an engagement with Islam was central to Ben Bella's socialist program, his relationships to Arab nationalism and pan-Arabism were more ambiguous.[69] Official discourse insisted that Algerian heritage was rooted in the Arabic language and Arab civilization, but the existence of Berber communities, as well as the extreme deculturation experienced under French colonization, made Islam more appealing as a unifying element. In Algeria, Islam was the marker by which the colonial state structured access to property, citizenship, and livelihood, as seen in chapter 1. In the Arab east, however, where the French mandate governed by introducing divisions between religions and sects, Arabism was a common denominator for unifying various groups after independence.[70] The history of Arab nationalism stretches back to the nineteenth century, when early figures of the Nahda such as Egyptian scholar Rifaʿa al-Tahtawi spoke of an Arab *watan* (fatherland) alongside other geographical and religious attachments.[71] In countries such as Iraq, Lebanon, and Syria, which had been under Ottoman rule until World War I, Arab nationalism appeared in the late nineteenth century as a discourse that supported claims for decentralization and separatism as expressed at the Arab National Congress of 1913. Political claims based on Arab identity accelerated in the interwar period, when the creation of British and French mandates over Ottoman territories culminated in the 1936 Arab Revolt against British control of Palestine.[72]

Though Arab nationalism was conceived as a political weapon to resist imperial powers, some thinkers asserted the existence of an Arab race (*al-ʿunsur al-ʿarabi*). In foregrounding racial purity, these intellectuals may well have been influenced by interwar proto-fascism—one of myriad ideologies available to those who encouraged nationalist revival in the 1920s and 1930s.[73] As Götz Nordbruch writes in his study of responses to Nazism in the Syrian and Lebanese press, "Although race appeared scientifically questionable as a biological concept of a distinct and pure communal entity, essentialized definitions of community based on suprahistorical traits nevertheless furnished alternative concepts that allowed the determination of communal boundaries."[74] Similarly, Omnia El Shakry argues that the concepts of culture (*thaqafa*) and civilization (*hadara*), which underpinned interwar articulations of Egyptian nationalism, contributed to the "ineffable quality of national character" while also connoting "racialist undertones with nebulous biological associations."[75]

Interpretations of Arabness relied on racial understandings of bloodlines and origins, as well as on the cultural and linguistic features of the Arab people. Like most nationalists, Arabs employed various strategies for "rationalizing the bonds that [tied] a community together."[76] Commentators rarely agreed on the role of Islam; some saw Islam and Arabism as inherently linked, while others had a more secular view of Arab nationalism. Yemeni-born intellectual Satiʿ al-Husri, for example, was inspired by German romantic nationalists and saw religious ecstasy—though not Islam per se—as a model for national unity.[77] Similarly, Syrian Christian Michel ʿAflaq, one of the main ideologues of Baʿathism, considered the Prophet Muhammad as the founder of the Arab nation and a source of national genius rather than a divine figure who was destined to guide the Muslim community (*umma*).[78]

The Cold War exposed the fragility of isolated nation-states, encouraging territories to pool their resources into strategic alliances or federations.

Many Arab nationalists were attracted to the idea that individual countries belonged to a broader Arab nation (*qawm*), which assumed a concrete form in the short-lived union between Egypt and Syria from 1958 to 1961. In the eyes of pan-Arabists like al-Husri, regional attachments (*iqlimiyya*) and the imposition of European-drawn borders threatened to undermine Arab unity. Their critique of empire also extended to capitalism as many intellectuals across the region revisited Marxism and centered questions of colonialism and sectarianism rather than class. A wave of official socialism washed over not only Egypt but also Syria, Iraq, South Yemen, Libya, Sudan, and Tunisia in the 1960s.[79]

Many Arab intellectuals on the left—nationalists and communists—were inspired by the Algerian Revolution.[80] Lebanese communist Mahdi 'Amil (a.k.a. Hassan Hamdan) departed for Constantine in 1962, where he influenced a number of Algerian scholars, including sociologist Ali El Kenz.[81] 'Amil believed that the petite bourgeoisie was "not by nature a hegemonic class (*tabaqa muhaymina*)" in colonial society as it had been in Europe.[82] Consistent with the communist critique of Arab nationalist regimes, he saw Arab socialism, including the Algerian variant, as symptomatic of the ruling class's (*tabaqa musaytira*) lack of hegemony.[83] Algeria's struggle against the French galvanized leftists across the Middle East, but tensions arose between pan-Arabist and Algerian interpretations of the revolution.

Geopolitical divisions, as well as the divergent histories of racial formation in the region, made it challenging to assimilate Algeria into the history of Arab nationalism. This did not stop student groups on the politically charged campus of the American University in Beirut from advocating for Algeria's liberation. For them, this was a necessary step toward incorporating the territory into the broader Arab nation. The National Committee for Algerian Victory in Lebanon organized an annual week of support for Algeria on March 6, 1961. One pamphlet for this event presented the 1956 Battle of Algiers as a symbol of the heroism of the Arab person (*ramz li-batalat al-insan al-'arabi*) rather than framing it as a definitive moment on the journey to Algerian independence.[84] Material published in April 1958 by a youth group affiliated with the Ba'th Party argued that support for Algeria was based on the complete harmony (*al-insijam al-tamm*) between the Mashreq and Maghreb, which it described as two shores of the Arab nation.[85]

This vision of Algeria as an integral part of the Arab homeland also appears in texts from Iraq published around the same time. In 1958, the University of Damascus held an "Algeria Week" just a few months after the formation of the United Arab Republic. At these celebrations, Syrian president Shukri al-

Quwatli said that "the Algerian cause is our cause," while Prime Minister 'Abd al-Hamid al-Sarraj proclaimed, "Algeria is not fighting only for herself, but for all of the Arab countries."[86] Speeches by noted Ba'th philosophers Michel 'Aflaq and Muhammad al-Hussein followed. As Ahmed Halawani demonstrates, the Syrian press (across the ideological spectrum) reported on the Algerian Revolution in the context of the greater Arab homeland (*qawm*).[87] Similarly, a 1962 publication from Iraq presented Algeria as part of the Arab *umma*, tied to the region by blood (*dam*), civilization, and religion.[88]

These interpretations often clashed with nationalist views of the Algerian Revolution. In 1956, Egyptian historian Ali al-Shalqani published *Thawrat al-Jaza'ir* (The Algerian revolution), which viewed the French occupation, not an inherent Arab spirit, as the essential catalyst for the emergence of Algerian nationalism.[89] He also highlighted the role of Islam in providing a link between Arab and tribal consciousness, arguing that French colonialism organized racial difference along religious lines.[90] Palestinian critic Naji 'Allush subsequently published a searing critique of al-Shalqani's work in the Lebanese journal *al-Adab*. In it, he offered a different genealogy of Algerian nationalism, claiming that Algeria had been an "organic" part of the Arab body since the seventh-century invasion of North Africa by Muslims from the east. He also drew a parallel between the anticolonial movement of Emir 'Abd al-Qadir and the Algerian Revolution that began in 1954.[91] Rejecting al-Shalqani's portrayal of Algerian nationalism and his class analysis of Algerian society, 'Allush instead emphasized the "great harmony of all factions of the people."[92] In his eyes, the major force for integration among the Algerian population was the Arabic language, not religion. He wrote: "The French did not wage war against the Algerians because they were 'Muslim,' as [al-Shalqani] claims, but because they are part of an Arab civilization with humanistic values and a stronghold of Arabism (*al-'uruba*)."[93] The differences in these two interpretations hinged on whether Algerian identity had been constructed on the basis of racial, civilizational, or linguistic categories.

In many ways al-Shalqani's analysis, which avoided pan-Arab abstractions, more accurately reflected the history of French colonization and the geopolitical obstacles facing the Algerian nation-state. The colonial regime had isolated Algeria from the eastern Mediterranean, and the fact that one-quarter of Algerians were Berber also made the identification of Algeria with Arabism a risky proposition. This was especially true after the 1963 armed rebellion of the FFS.[94] Tellingly, Berber and French speakers sometimes described Arabs from the Mashreq who came to Algeria to support Arabization with the derogatory appellation "Islamo-Ba'thistes."[95] Though the Arab nationalist project envisioned by the Ba'th Party had been organized around modern standard Arabic, mastery of this language was not commonplace among Algerian officials, even after 1962.[96] While Arab identity was undoubtedly a major touchstone for Algerian nationalists, there were nevertheless multiple obstacles to incorporating Algeria into a larger Arab nation.

Ben Bella was certainly not averse to dramatic displays of pan-Arabism, but he deployed them strategically. According to an oft-repeated anecdote, he enthusiastically cried, "We are Arab, we are Arab, we are Arab" at the Tunis airport in April 1962. Yet reflecting on this event in a 1980 interview with *Le Monde*, he reminded readers that he issued this exclamation in a particular context: At the time, Tunisian president Habib Bourguiba seemed dangerously close to rejecting a pan-Maghreb alliance and a radical political orientation. Ben Bella clarified his position, stating, "More than Arabism, Islamism offers the most adequate framework, not only because it is larger and more effective, but also because the cultural concept, the civilizational fact, must determine all the rest."[97] His strategy of using pan-Arabism as a door to Islam differed dramatically from the approach of secular Arab nationalists such as 'Aflaq. For Ben Bella, Islamism, not Arabism, provided a template for nationalism that could alternately signal a political orientation, linguistic investment, or imagined community of shared origins and bloodlines.

Algerian nationalists also insisted on the pan-African orientation of the revolution. Frantz Fanon, the GPRA ambassador to Ghana, famously worked to situate Algeria in an African orbit, rejecting the French imagined geography that had partitioned the continent into "white" and "black" Africa and portrayed lighter-skinned Arabs as more fanatical than their black African neighbors. Fanon's analysis of colonial violence was widely read by leaders of other antiracist struggles, but that does not mean that all groups understood the relationships among pan-Africanism, antiblackness, and decolonization in similar terms. When Algiers became the "mecca of revolution" in the 1960s and 1970s, attracting revolutionaries from Africa and the United States, the Black Panthers at times overlooked the delicate geopolitical positioning of Algeria in the Cold War and overestimated the place of armed struggle.[98] Similarly, discussions of negritude at the 1966 World Festival of Negro Arts in Dakar proved to be controversial: some Algerian radicals objected to the emphasis on blackness and would have preferred a more politically grounded definition of African identity.[99]

In the late 1950s, the FLN pointed to antiblack racism in France to convince the leaders of Mali and Mauritania, who were debating whether or not to remain in the French Community, to break their political and economic ties to the Hexagon.[100] The nationalist paper *El Moudjahid* had particularly harsh words for Chad and Niger, which had decided to participate in the OCRS, an administrative unit established in the oil-rich territories of the Sahel. *El Moudjahid* described the countries as "two unreliable fruits of the balkanization of Western Africa" that had "completely adopted the thesis of their masters in Paris."[101] The same newspaper expressed outrage when racist slogans were shouted during a screening of Claude-Bernard Aubert's 1959 film *Les tripes au soleil* (Checkerboard) in Paris, which featured an interracial American couple (a white paratrooper and an African American woman), claiming that this episode demonstrated "the depravity of French education with regard to the rest of humanity."[102] The article continued, "When racism in France has reached this point, it is time for the negroes to leave the ship. It is for the members of the French Community to decide if their place is still with those who have not rid themselves of either hate or vileness (*bassesse*) vis-à-vis the black race."[103]

Even as French racism toward Africans was cited in FLN propaganda, racism in the Algerian case had been constructed around religion rather than skin color. The GPRA archives suggest that at least some Algerian nationalists were influenced by colonial assumptions regarding so-called black Africa. One memo noted, "Algeria will find itself in a better position than the other African territories to assure its economic evolution due to its geographical situation as well as the *potential capital of its people to adapt to a modern rhythm of production*."[104] While it would be a mistake to generalize the sentiment, especially given the long history of exchange with sub-Saharan Africa, it is clear that some Algerians saw their compatriots as more modern than other Africans. Pan-Africanism, then, was confronted with obstacles that were both historical and political. As one edited volume on pan-Africanism asked in 1962, "Is pan-Africanism basically racial or continental? If the former, how would it embrace Algeria?"[105] The question of racial divisions on the African continent did not disappear from the discourse of African unity, even in its most radical incarnation. While pan-Arabism and pan-Africanism were important orientations for Algerian nationalism, the racial regime of religion constructed by the French occupation presented certain challenges to adopting these ideologies wholesale. These obstacles were not only due to geopolitical calculations, but they were also rooted in the history of colonial racial formations that continued to structure regional politics after decolonization.

From Blood to Sweat

In asserting an indissoluble link between Algerian socialism and Islam, Ben Bella sought to inculcate a revolutionary ethos among the population. The two figures of the *ancien moudjahid* (a veteran of the war of independence) and the fellah show how the revolutionary past determined access to social and economic capital.[106] As part of land reform, the Algerian government created 338 agricultural cooperatives encompassing 333,000 hectares of land that were earmarked for the *anciens moudjahidines*.[107] Often, property owned by those who had fought in the war was spared nationalization. Military service trumped the fact that these individuals often had little experience in agriculture, just as the figure of the fellah papered over considerable class differences among those engaged in agriculture.[108]

Economic policies aimed to create a new Algerian citizen and redistribute material resources. Colonial planners had envisioned a system of liberal capitalism in which individual interest would spur national wealth. Algerian socialism, however, foregrounded solidarity and sacrifice as the motors of collective productivity. It was now the system of self-management, rather than economic markets, that would "stimulate the creative capacities of workers," according to the newspaper of the Union générale des travailleurs algériens (UGTA; al-Ittihad al-'Aam lil-'Ummal al-Jaza'iriyin; General Union of Algerian Workers).[109] Volunteer brigades dedicated their Sundays to constructing a new Algeria, repairing roads and schools.[110] Similarly, the Fonds de solidarité nationale (Fund for National Solidarity) asked women to donate jewelry to augment the national coffers, and Opération labours (Operation Plow) was launched in the fall of 1962 to encourage citizens to sow wheat on abandoned French farms.[111]

The policy of self-management was the centerpiece of Ben Bella's attempts to create revolutionary cadres out of supposedly individualistic workers. The distribution of agricultural salaries in the socialist sector was widely discussed. When farmers complained about the long periods they went without payment, the state reproached them for thinking of themselves as salaried employees and reminded them that they did not work for a boss or company, but for the nation.[112] Ben Bella clarified that the money given to agricultural workers in the socialist sector was not a salary but rather an advance provided by the state.[113] Those still employed by Europeans sometimes appeared better off, since they were more likely to receive regular payment for their labor.[114] Yet the desire for financial security was seen as incompatible with the ideal of the Algerian peasant discussed in chapter 4. As the newspaper *Révolution et Travail* reported, the success of agricultural reforms depended on avoiding the proletarianization of the rural population. It lamented that agriculturalists behaved like salaried workers rather than adopting the values of the fellahin.[115] In short, the Algerian government portrayed labor as a patriotic obligation rather than an activity regulated by market demand.

An important moment in the attempted transformation of agricultural workers into revolutionaries was the Congrès des paysans (Fellah Congress) held from October 25 to 27, 1963, in Algiers. Ben Bella brought together three thousand delegates from the self-managed agricultural sector to discuss their complaints and experiences, hoping the event would silence foreign critiques of self-management.[116] Michel Raptis (Pablo), who had worked with Ben Bella to implement self-management, was in attendance and viewed the meeting as a way "to measure the degree of maturity of the peasants."[117] Similarly, Algerian officials worried about the "individualist and retrograde spirit" of the fellahin and questioned the capacity of Algerian peasants for self-management, citing their lack of revolutionary dynamism.[118] If, as Ben Bella claimed, Algeria could "only do socialism with socialists," the question of instilling a socialist sensibility among the rural masses was fundamental.[119] Despite the generally laudatory tone of the congress, which we can safely assume was due, in part, to coercion by the Algerian regime, farmers still complained about the misfunctioning of self-management.

Grievances were also aired at the December 1964 national meeting of the Workers of the Land. Pre-congresses had been held across the country in preparation for this event. In Algiers, delegates asked for social security as well as for paid vacation and family allocations.[120] The National Office of Commercialization (ONACO) was widely criticized for its inefficiency and incompetence; slow and inadequate marketing structures sometimes allowed crops to perish before they were brought to market.[121] One participant denounced the pricing laws that caused seven hectares of carrots to be left unharvested, demanding more liberal commercialization laws.[122] The continuities between the colonial and postcolonial periods were not lost on the farmers, who complained about the role of the SAPs, which carried on some of their activities after independence.[123] According to the French anarchist Daniel Guérin, the SAPs displayed a "mentality inherited from the colonial era" and displayed condescension toward the management committees.[124] Other observers confirmed that even if the SAPs had been rebranded and were now contributing to the socialist sector, many farmers still viewed these organizations as remnants of the colonial period.[125] Yet when farmers expressed more interest in their own economic situations than the lofty ideology of Algerian socialism, the regime painted them with an ungenerous brush.[126]

Other initiatives focused on replenishing the landscape, which had suffered under colonial rule and during the war. Ben Bella inaugurated a national holiday called the "Day of the Tree," which encouraged citizens to participate in reforestation campaigns. While French colonial discourse had represented the native population as an enemy of cultivation and production, Algerian nationalists celebrated nature as part of the country's natural resources.[127] Amar Ouzegane wrote that these initiatives would recover the North Africa of Ibn Khaldun, the famous fourteenth-century philosopher, and tied the planting of trees to the sacrifices made to secure independence.[128] He noted that in Bainem, twelve kilometers west of Algiers, widows of men who had died in battle cultivated the forest that had been set on fire by the OAS. Banners claimed that *veuves de chouhada* (widows of martyrs) were taking over the work of the revolution.[129] Those engaged in reforestation demonstrated revolutionary commitment by volunteering for the nation, and they also commemorated the land for which Algeria's "most glorious sons" had died, weaving together the logics of wartime sacrifice and environmental recovery.[130] These policies strove to encourage soil preservation and plant trees, both of which had featured prominently in the Constantine Plan.[131] Moreover, some of the same experts who had been involved in colonial development (including Alexis Monjauze, known as the "prophet" of Algerian rural renovation) contributed to reforestation and soil conservation after independence. Christian groups such as the Comité chrétien de service en Algérie (Christian Committee for Service in Algeria) also played an important role in these endeavors.[132]

Increasing agricultural productivity depended on improving distribution networks. Ben Bella thus introduced *magasins pilotes socialistes* (pilot socialist stores), which were supposed to protect customers from the laws of supply and demand by mitigating the high prices that resulted from the scarcity of certain products. Controlled by ONACO, they operated in parallel with the private sector and other low-cost stores including Monoprix and Galeries de France, which had signed contracts with the Algerian government to protect them from nationalization.[133] Just before Ramadan, many basic foodstuffs, such as sugar and black pepper, were exorbitantly expensive.[134] Some stores went without milk for two months; others had no black pepper for six.

There were a number of reasons for these shortages. First, a drop in the production of basic goods such as cereals made Algeria increasingly dependent on imports. Second, ONACO's widely noted dysfunctions were compounded by the fact that it enjoyed a monopoly on the importation of a number of foodstuffs, including meat, coffee, tea, and pepper.[135] Penury seemed to encourage speculation, and there were reports of individuals buying products only to sell them at four to five times the normal price, which prompted officials to begin a propaganda campaign against these activities. In front of the National Assembly, Bachir Boumaza, the minister of the national economy, claimed that speculation was interfering with Algeria's "revolutionary morale," going so far as to suggest that the death penalty would be an appropriate punishment.[136] The March Decrees sought not only to redistribute resources but also to create an economic language that communicated the principles of revolutionary morality.

The vocabulary used to describe the confiscation of land raised fundamental questions about colonization. Confiscated properties were often described as *mal acquis* (wrongly acquired) or depicted as being insufficiently exploited. The wording of the March Decrees outlined the need for the state to take over property that was acquired, managed, or exploited in a way that would trouble the public order or social peace.[137] In one case, the director of the National Office of Vacant Properties, Abdelkader Maachou, accused a proprietor of "economic sabotage," arguing that this was unacceptable in a revolutionary country.[138] In an interview, he enumerated several categories of sabotage, ranging from plowing the land but not sowing it to more drastic acts of negligence.[139] Yet the historical meaning of *mal acquis* remained vague. Was a settler who bought a home on the market at fault? Or did it apply only to lands that had been expropriated by the colonial state? When a European woman wrote to the Algerian authorities in October 1965 to lament the confiscation of her home, she stressed that it had been bought in 1948 after many years of hard work in Algeria.[140] She argued that it could not be considered mal acquis and cited a circular from August 20, 1965, which had never been applied. It stipulated that no furnished property, personal homes, small businesses, or small farms would be confiscated.[141] In other cases it was the political orientation of the individual, rather than the manner in which they had acquired the land, that seemed to pose a problem. Despite suspicions that personal and family feuds sometimes informed these actions, Algerian officials often responded with economistic language, claiming, for example, that "the legislation on vacant properties only seeks to maintain the exploitation of productive capital and end speculation."[142]

As officials working for the ONRA took over estates that had once been intended for redistribution by the colonial state, they sought to replace parasitic landowners with laborers who had been badly treated during the colonial period. One of the largest estates, which had belonged to Henri Borgeaud, an important political figure in French Algeria, was nationalized amid a wave of publicity. Covering 1,800 hectares of land and employing four hundred Algerians, the property was handed over to a management committee (*comité de gestion*) led by twenty-seven-year-old Aissa Lamouri, a member of the FLN who had reportedly been arrested and tortured during the war. Newspaper articles emphasized that even though Lamouri was born on the property, it was only after nationalization that he had been allowed to enter the main residence of the Borgeaud family, which was evidence of the segregated living conditions on the estate. Upon assuming his new role, however, Lamouri claimed to not fully understand the texts that defined his responsibilities.[143]

The link between national identity and Islam also had important ramifications for the place of Christians and Jews in an independent Algeria. A handful of Europeans who had sided with the FLN stayed in Algeria after 1962 and adopted Algerian citizenship. The Catholic church was allowed to remain in the country due to its willingness "to participate in the construction of the Algerian nation."[144] An article in *Alger républicain*, a newspaper close to communist circles, wrote that those who came to Algeria to make an honest living were welcome as long as they had not made fortunes from the "sweat of exploited generations."[145] Some Europeans who opted for Algerian nationality in Djidjelli (Jijel), in northeast Algeria, did not have their lands expropriated, suggesting that legal citizenship informed land reform.[146] Blood is often understood to provide a racial basis for national identity. In Algeria national belonging was also sanctified by political commitments, notably by participation in the War of Independence. Ben Bella often asserted that while Algerians had been joined by a "solidarity of blood" during the war, they would find unity in a "solidarity of sweat" as they built a new nation-state.[147]

As the climate of terror imposed by the OAS led to an increase in generalized violence in the summer of 1962, state confiscation of "vacant" properties was the first step in the expulsion of Europeans. It became clear that the

Algerian state would not—or could not—safeguard French property rights, despite the promises outlined in the Evian Accords. The vast majority of Europeans departed for mainland France. Algerian Jews shared a similar fate; although FLN leaders at the 1956 Soummam Congress had insisted that they were fully part of the nation, Benjamin Stora argues that most Jews openly supported the continuation of a French Algeria in early 1960.[148] This orientation can be explained in part by the French state's legal division between Algerian Jews and Muslims in the 1870 Crémieux Decree. Despite having their nationality stripped under the Vichy regime, ninety-five percent of Algerian Jews opted to immigrate to France rather than to Israel.[149] When they arrived in the metropole, they were lumped in with French settlers as *rapatriés* (or *pieds-noirs* in popular parlance), a classification that erased their connections to the Arabic language and Algerian culture.

Mounting Opposition

As Ben Bella invoked the twinned symbols of blood and sweat, joining wartime military sacrifices to revolutionary consciousness, his authoritarian rule provoked increasing opposition. He was unable to stave off attacks by religious figures who saw him as beholden to the influence of the so-called *pieds-rouges* (red feet), the foreign, secular radicals with communist sympathies featured in chapter 6. On January 5, 1964, al-Qiyam convened a public meeting that drew over three hundred people. Speakers denounced Ben Bella's socialist program, particularly the importation of economic models from Yugoslavia and Cuba, which they blamed for provoking a moral crisis (*azma ruhiyya*) in the country.[150] These comments evoked staunch opposition from leftists, who published a collective letter claiming that members of al-Qiyam "employed a language restricted to the most retrograde form of fanaticism, inspired by the most sectarian and medieval source of the feudal-bourgeois reaction."[151] Signatories of the statement included author Bachir Hadj Ali and doctor Sadek Hadjeres, both of whom were high-ranking members in the Parti communiste algérien (PCA; al-Hizb al-Shiyu'i al-Jaza'iri; Algerian Communist Party) that operated clandestinely after independence. The two dozen figures who signed the article upheld the principle of "*ijtihad*, a creative force, against *taqlid*, which is an argument invoked by authority that leads all societies to decadence, faithful to the traditions of tolerance in Islam."[152] The dispute conjured discussions that had been central to the traditions of Islamic modernism, notably the debate regarding jurists' freedom to use independent reasoning (*ijtihad*) when drafting laws, as opposed to the need to abide by legal precedents and traditional interpretations (*taqlid*).

While it is tempting to see this conflict in purely religious or ideological terms, there were also pragmatic considerations. Arabic speakers felt culturally and professionally sidelined by the continued use of French in official circles after independence. At the January 5 meeting, members of al-Qiyam decried Algeria's linguistic policy and requested that certain jobs be reserved for Muslims, taking a stand against the Franco-Algerian policy of cooperation that offered French experts and scholars high-ranking positions in various domains. The president of al-Qiyam, who was also the head of the Department of Literature at the University of Algiers, exclaimed that it was "inadmissible that we still speak French in this university!"[153] His reaction was similar to that of Tunisian politician Rashid al-Ghannouchi, who described his turn to Islam as a reaction to the alienation he felt after decolonization, when the University of Zitouna remained under Francophone control. In al-Ghannouchi's words, he felt that "this was no longer a foreign occupation, but it was still an occupation. Not by the French this time, but by the Tunisian sons of the French."[154]

These ideological conflicts continued when Djamal Baghdadi, a professor of Arabic, gave a widely publicized talk attended by Mahsas and other government officials in February 1964.[155] The eclectic presentation cited Plato as an influence on socialism and insisted that Arabs should reject Marxism because of its emphasis on class conflict and Islam's refusal of violence. In an Algeria marked by revolutionary fervor, this critique of Marxism and violence provoked widespread indignation. Was the speaker questioning the legitimacy of the Algerian Revolution? A member of the FLN's political bureau pointed to the Egyptian example, arguing that force had been necessary to wipe out feudalism in the 1952 revolution that overthrew King Farouk. Another participant asked, Where did the Qur'an defend private property? Wasn't it true that private ownership of the means of production had always been a source of oppression? The speaker, others noted, did not sufficiently praise Ben Bella or the March Decrees.

Dissatisfaction with the regime mounted in 1964, the same year that the government banned the Algerian Communist Party and put Ferhat Abbas under house arrest. In April, Muhammad Bashir al-Ibrahimi, a founder of the AUMA, gave a speech accusing Algerian leaders of grounding policy decisions in foreign economic doctrines rather than Islamic principles.[156] This came on the heels of a talk by Hadj Ali claiming that Marxism was incompatible with any preestablished or schematic doctrine. While asserting the compatibility of Islam and socialism, he denounced certain "reactionary" elements that sought to use Islam to attack progressive economic doctrines. He also associated Islam with a history of decline in the Arab world that dated to the fifteenth century.[157] Ben Bella seemed partly favorable to this interpretation, as he occasionally repeated the critique of secular Marxists who depicted the ʿulama as bourgeois reactionaries.[158]

In 1964, the holy month of Ramadan raised questions of religion and economics with particular urgency. Arabic posters in the capital, published by the Ministry of Habus, reiterated that wine was forbidden to Muslims.[159] Moreover, Ben Bella asked Algerians to abstain from the sacrificial slaughter of lambs, as the nation needed to reconstitute its animal husbandry.[160] This remark provoked a public disagreement with Mohammed Khider, one of the historic leaders of the FLN, who saw such compromises as a direct affront to Algeria's national identity.[161] The minister of the economy, Boumaza, sided with Ben Bella, claiming that certain traditions were injurious to national development.[162] The issue of whether the economy should be organized to maximize value or as a tool for sociological transformation underpinned the struggle between different interpretations of Islam.

When Houari Boumediene seized power on June 19, 1965, the bloodless coup was labelled a revolutionary adjustment (*redressement révolutionnaire*) and the AUMA was the first group to publicly support the takeover.[163] Ahmed Taleb-Ibrahimi, the son of Mohammed Bashir al-Ibrahimi, became the minister of education. Boumediene also altered Algeria's economic orientation. In the place of Ben Bella's emphasis on agrarian self-management and his reliance on personal charisma, Boumediene adopted a program of industrialization, agricultural revolution, and state-driven investment that mirrored his more austere personality. While "privileged access to goods that were supposed to be collectively owned" became a marker of social distinction in the 1970s, the ideal of common ownership of national resources remained at the core of the postcolonial contract.[164] Boumediene positioned the state, rather than the zeal of the revolution, as the source of economic and religious power. After his mysterious death in December 1978, the feeling of economic injustice crystalized around a populist discourse rooted in Islam that sought to rescue the state from the influence of a corrupt oligarchy.[165]

Boumediene's turn to state-driven industrialization is often said to have been influenced by Gérard Destanne de Bernis. A student of the social Catholic economist François Perroux, de Bernis developed the concept of industrializing industries and believed that Algeria would play a key role in overthrowing global capitalist domination.[166] Boumediene was perhaps less bombastic than Ben Bella, who had flaunted his high-profile foreign advisors, but he nevertheless continued the tradition of soliciting European leftists for economic advice. French Third Worldists watched Algeria with particular interest in the 1960s, seeking to articulate a global theory of anti-capitalist revolution while questioning the role of Islam in Algerian politics. They were accompanied by more liberal colleagues who came to Algeria in the framework of official Franco-Algerian cooperation. The engagements of metropolitan thinkers with the Algerian Revolution shaped economic orthodoxies in France, shedding light on how liberals and radicals under-stood the place of religious and racial categories in development after 1962.

6.
TODAY'S UTOPIA IS
TOMORROW'S REALITY

In March 1964, French anarchist Daniel Guérin arrived in Algiers with a personal invitation from Ben Bella to attend the Conference for Industrial Self-Management. Like many with communist sympathies who arrived after independence, Guérin had been a staunch opponent of French repression during the Algerian War of Independence. During his visit to the capital, he observed street signs that presented cleanliness as a symbol of Islam. They exemplified Ben Bella's attempts to promote civic virtues through religion, but Guérin wondered if it was really necessary to invoke Islam to encourage public hygiene. While certain leftists viewed these appeals to religion as a direct response to the deracination that occurred under colonialism, Guérin disagreed. Instead, he maintained that the Algerian state was using Islam to calm a volatile population at a moment of extreme political tension.[1] On this point he also broke with his Trotskyist comrades, who had organized around Michel Raptis, better known as Pablo, the leader of the Fourth International. While the *pablistes* regarded religion as a superstructure that would be transformed by changes in the economic base, Guérin insisted that revolution was a totality. He thus contested Ben Bella's vision of a specifically Algerian socialism rooted in Islam, claiming that "no revolutionary socialism can be established on a religious basis."[2]

Guérin was one of many anticlerical leftists who came to Algiers to construct a socialist regime in the hope that this experience would be a stepping stone to international revolution. During the first three years of independence, those with more liberal convictions also arrived in the capital. Notably, the policy of Franco-Algerian cooperation brought French officials and experts to Algeria. Sometimes described as a way of defending French interests after Algerian independence, cooperation had been outlined in the Evian Accords.[3] One negotiator of the ceasefire, Robert Buron, had been active in the Resistance and espoused social Catholic values; he had served as the minister of overseas France before becoming the minister of public works under de Gaulle and hoped that the policy of cooperation would serve to build a common future between the two countries.[4] His colleagues who worked toward cooperation also sought to establish a less exploitative relationship between France and Algeria, sharing Buron's belief that "today's utopia is tomorrow's reality."[5]

Other public figures, including the journalist Raymond Cartier, found this attitude naïve. In a televised debate with Buron in 1971, Cartier asked why France should continue cultivating a close relationship with the Algerian state given Ben Bella's radical orientation and bombastic rhetoric.[6] Now that the country had chosen independence, why should France treat Algeria differently from any other foreign country? The conviction that France should focus its resources on developing the Hexagon rather than investing in colonial development had become known as Cartierism in the 1950s. Despite the pragmatic appeal of this argument, however, many French officials echoed Buron's commitment to establishing a new relationship based on humanist values. Moreover, Buron's vision of French cooperation was not entirely altruistic, as it also reflected anxieties about French *grandeur* after the end of empire. Secretary of Algerian Affairs Jean de Broglie saw Algeria as "a 'narrow door' through which [France would] penetrate the 'Third World.'"[7] Despite their political differences, leftist militants and liberal experts viewed economic policies in Algeria as potential blueprints that could be adopted in other countries.

Leftists and liberals disagreed on the role that religion should play in economic development. In line with social Catholic principles, Buron remarked that development could not be effective on the "human level" if planners merely "created abstractions out of spiritual values."[8] He maintained that development should account for Islamic beliefs and culture, harkening back to the colonial policy of association. Radical leftists, on the other hand, were more likely to treat Islam as a set of outdated traditions that would need to be overcome to introduce a truly revolutionary form of socialism. While liberal planners found it necessary to account for the role of Islam in order to ensure that economic development reached its full human potential, radical leftists understood Islam to be an ideology or superstructure that would eventually need to be excised from revolutionary socialism.

An impressive range of intellectuals, politicians, and economists participated in these debates, but this chapter focuses on two groups: first, anticlerical leftists who supported the construction of a socialist Algeria, and second, government officials committed to the liberal policy of Franco-Algerian cooperation (*coopérants*). While both included diverse sets of actors, each group shared certain views. Those who worked on the official policy of Franco-Algerian cooperation wanted to foster a relationship between Algeria and France based on market exchange and trade. While they often carried an intellectual debt to social Catholicism, they also inherited the culturalist approaches to economic development that had been a hallmark of the late colonial period. Those on the anticlerical left, by contrast, positioned themselves in direct opposition to the policy of cooperation, working with Algerian officials to introduce land reform and lessen economic dependence on France. Some played a key role in drafting the policy of self-management even as they remained suspicious of Ben Bella's invocation of a Muslim socialism, which they believed reflected his desire to appease feudal tendencies.

The Algerian War of Independence had conditioned the attitudes of individual coopérants as well as those of anticlerical leftists. The positions taken by those on the far left were influenced by political alliances inherited from the revolution; many radicals backed Messali Hadj over the FLN due to their reservations over the latter's Islamic rhetoric. At the same time, French officials working in the framework of official cooperation rebranded their efforts in the face of geopolitical realities. While Algeria provided a key arena for liberal experts who sought to test strategies for international development, the country also became the site of far-left projections that remained attached to revolution as a necessarily secular horizon. In comparing the approaches of anticlerical leftists and liberal experts, we are faced with two different frameworks for thinking about the relationship between race, religion, and the economy, both of which questioned the older dichotomy between homo islamicus and homo economicus. These genealogies are central to understanding how colonialism in Algeria shaped the traditions of revolutionary anticlericalism and liberal technocracy in France. While liberals cast Islam as an essentialized source of culture, leftists viewed religion as a form of false consciousness that undermined class analysis. In both cases, French observers ignored how racialized understandings of Islam had been fundamental to economic underdevelopment in Algeria.

"We Prefer the 'New' Arrivals"

Franco-Algerian cooperation sent thousands of people to Algeria as a remedy for the the dramatic shortage of expertise that followed the departure of European settlers. The Ministry of Cooperation, created by de Gaulle in

1959, was responsible for providing development and economic assistance following the decolonization of French sub-Saharan and West Africa. In Algeria, the Secrétariat d'État aux affaires algériennes (SEAA; Secretariat of State for Algerian Affairs), which was created in 1959, played a key role in these initiatives.[9] French officials authorized cooperation as a substitute for military service, which facilitated the arrival of twenty-five thousand French functionaries who worked in technical and cultural cooperation in 1963.[10] Coopérants came to Algeria under different conditions; some enjoyed official contracts with the French state, while others arrived with student groups or youth movements. They also arrived at different points in time: some had lived in Algeria before 1954, others came during the war, and a third group arrived after independence. These late arrivals have received more scholarly attention due to their desire to distance themselves from the War of Independence and their more leftist or *progressiste* tendencies.[11] Ben Bella himself differentiated between these categories, proclaiming, "We very much appreciate the French [coopérants] who come to Algeria and their courage. We prefer the 'new' [arrivals] to the old. The new ones come here to forget [the past] or by vocation."[12] Indeed, coopérants sought to establish a fresh relationship between France and Algeria based on mutual interests rather than exploitation, very much in line with Buron's vision of constructing a common future.

Algeria received the lion's share of French overseas aid in the 1960s, securing 1.25 billion French francs in 1963—more than the aid offered to all of sub-Saharan Africa (1.17 billion francs). The 156 million francs given to Morocco and Tunisia seemed paltry in comparison.[13] In Algeria, this financial assistance was delivered in part through channels set up under the Constantine Plan, namely the CEDA, created in 1959 to finance colonial development. After 1962, the CEDA was responsible for the conditional aid (*aide liée*) offered by cooperation, which differed from free aid (*aide libre*), which could be administered by Algerians directly and was managed by the Caisse algérienne de développement (Algerian Development Bank).[14] This is just one example of the continuity between colonial development and cooperation, which was naturally a sensitive issue after the War of Independence. The representatives of the FLN who negotiated the Evian Accords found the word *association* reminiscent of colonialism and thus preferred the term *coopération*.[15]

In many ways, cooperation followed colonial blueprints for development. Some officials had thought the Constantine Plan would safeguard a French Algeria, but more forward-looking planners understood its goal as providing a new basis for Franco-Algerian relations in the case of independence.[16] The Saint-Simonian ideal of achieving a harmony between the Occident and Orient through economic development had informed visions of the Constantine Plan and later became an ideological touchstone for some coopérants.[17] Many aspects of the Constantine Plan, including a faith in the disciplines of sociology and psychology to provide strategies for social engineering, were built into postcolonial development. Far from being considered obsolete, planners often referred to the document after 1962. One former coopérant noted that, paradoxically, the effects of the plan were not felt until after independence.[18]

The overlap between colonial expertise and international development had already taken shape in the last years of the war, as planners viewed cooperation as a technique to soften Algeria's revolutionary fervor and highlight France's prowess in economic planning.[19] Robert Buron, for example, drew on his experiences during the Algerian War to launch a career in international development, becoming president of the Organisation de coopération et de développement économiques (OCDE; Organization for Economic Cooperation and Development) in 1962. Even prior to Algerian independence, it was not unusual for individuals to accentuate their credentials in colonial planning to demonstrate their legitimacy in the realm of international development. In October 1961 the FAO (Food and Agriculture Association of the United Nations) held a conference dedicated to regional development. The French delegates presented their experience in Algeria as a pertinent case in the framework of European regional development. After listing France's many experiences with regional plans, the director of the SEDIA, a consulting firm in Algiers working for the French government, delivered an exposé on the Constantine Plan.[20] Jean de Vaissière, a member of the French delegation, reported with satisfaction that the conference was "a great success for the expansion of French language and thought" since "the value of French methods of planning was entirely recognized and praised."[21] Notes from the meeting asserted that "the methodology of planning in the different countries should bear the characteristics of their political, historical, social, and theoretical environment."[22] This late colonial trend, which emphasized the role of culture in the success of market economies, was later reflected in the policy of cooperation.

After 1962, French development aid continued to prioritize cultural particularity and geopolitics over a strictly economic logic. The Jeanneney Report, for example, was written by a commission established by the French government in 1963 to examine French aid. It highlighted the need to respect the existing social order, signaling the extravagant costs of development in Algeria. De Gaulle nevertheless defended this use of resources, claiming that "the importance of cooperation relates less to figures and immediate results than to the advantages of a general nature which it can ensure in the future for ourselves and our partners."[23] The belief that economic planning could foster affective links was also evident in the 1966 census, which was conducted under the rubric of cooperation. Echoing the principles of the Constantine Plan, the director for cooperation at the INSEE, Albert Ficatier, recommended that the French convey a *mystique du recensement* (mystique of the census), which reiterated the belief that the true goal of development was to shape psychological structures, not to produce concrete results.[24] In the context of the Cold War, the specters of pan-Islamism and communism encouraged European experts to craft development policies in light of geopolitical concerns.

The Emergence of Third Worldism

Just as colonial visions of development influenced cooperation policy, engagements during the War of Independence shaped the positions held by French radical leftists. The increasingly sclerotic nature of the PCF, the discontent of the increasing student population, and the fractures between communist countries led a younger generation to seek novel ideological formulations in the years leading up to 1968. Some far-left groups were formed in response to the traditional left's dismal record on anticolonial organizing in France. For example, the PCF had prioritized international revolution above national independence, and the Section française de l'internationale ouvrière (SFIO; French Section of the Workers' International) was increasingly discredited by its complicity with colonization.[25] This became especially apparent after Guy Mollet and his Socialist-led government passed a law in support of emergency powers in Algeria in 1956.[26] An alternative or radical left thus came into being, whose partisans were often known as *gauchistes* (leftists). This derogatory term was based on Lenin's writings, which were invoked by the PCF in 1968 in order to denounce those who did not toe the party line.[27]

The far left included Trotskyists, Maoists, and Anarchists. The first group emerged around Leon Trotsky, who was expelled from the Soviet Union for his opposition to Stalinism. The movement fractured soon after the founding of the Fourth International in Paris in 1938, when supporters of Pierre Lambert (a.k.a. Pierre Boussel) dissented from the ideology of the organization's secretary, Pablo, who advocated a form of entryism. According to this strategy, Trotskyists would enter into the structures of the working class (namely the PCF and the major union federation, the Confédération générale du travail or General Confederation of Labor) to encourage a break from Stalinism. To Lambertistes, as they came to be called, this was nothing short of treason. A second major current among the far left in France was Maoism. In the wake of the Sino-Soviet split in the early 1960s, Maoism was particularly attractive to those who advocated for Third Worldist revolution and sought to apply Mao's definition of peasant communism to Latin America, Europe, and the Middle East.[28] Yet scholars studying the Gauche prolétarienne (Proletarian Left), a Maoist political party, have argued that their commitments stemmed less from an understanding of China's unique experience with the Cultural Revolution than from a need to revive the concept of revolution in France.[29] Third, alongside Trotskyists and Maoists, there was a wide variety of anarchist groups, such as the situationists and the Fédération anarchiste (FA; Anarchist Federation), which sought to introduce a classless society, opposing state structures and authoritarian hierarchies. Drawing on a long tradition of anarcho-syndicalism, anarchists remained convinced of the need to dissolve capitalism and state structures in order to introduce worker self-management.[30]

The question of the Algerian Revolution was central to the new alliances that emerged in the 1960s as disparate groups united in their opposition to colonialism. In the process, they became known as *Third Worldists* (*tiers-mondistes*).[31] French demographer Alfred Sauvy had coined the term *Third World* in 1952 to designate the bloc of countries that belonged neither to the communist East nor capitalist West. By the 1970s, however, it was used to discredit leftists who opposed the neocolonialist policies of France. According to Maxime Szczepanski-Huillery, it was only in the mid-1980s that this term was adopted by those who, like René Dumont, claimed the mantle of Third Worldism with a sense of pride.[32] The category is still useful in highlighting how the Algerian War brought together individuals with divergent ideological tendencies and fostered the emergence of a far left that decried the PCF's reticence to support anticolonial struggles.

Engagement with the Algerian war helped fashion a new revolutionary constituency in Europe that brought together a number of different networks.[33] For example, in 1960, 121 intellectuals signed a petition in favor of the "right to insubordination in the Algerian War."[34] The Jeanson network, organized around journalist and writer Francis Jeanson, transported money and papers for the FLN. The publishing house Maspero printed a number of subversive books, including Frantz Fanon's *The Wretched of the Earth*.[35]

After independence was achieved, however, it was the more radical fringe of this group—including Pablo and Guérin—that most clearly supported Ben Bella's socialist experiment. Pablo helped pen the 1963 March Decrees, which introduced land reform in Algeria, and Guérin came to Algeria twice under Ben Bella's rule: once to write a report on self-management for the president and a second time in March 1964 to attend the Conference for Industrial Self-Management. Due to their communist sympathies, those like Pablo and Guérin who actively supported self-management came to be known as *pieds-rouges*—a moniker that highlighted their ideological differences from the settler community known as *pieds-noirs*.[36]

During the war, many anarchists and Trotskyists had allied with Messali, who had begun his nationalist mobilization among Algerian factory workers in the metropole and was close to the PCF.[37] In a speech at a meeting of the Committee of Action of Intellectuals against the Continuation of the War in North Africa in 1955, Guérin explained that while Algerian Islamic scholars had invoked religion to raise nationalist consciousness, it was Messali Hadj who had offered the necessary political message.[38] Guérin helped publicize Messali's texts and actively supported his release from prison in the mid-1950s.[39] On a more personal note, Guérin sent Messali Hadj a book that belonged to his father (a study of Ismayl Urbain) and the Emir 'Abd al-Qadir's signature (which was entrusted to Messali's brother but apparently never delivered).[40]

Guérin even wrote to Tunisian president Habib Bourguiba, asking him to intervene against those who slandered Messali.[41] He identified three categories of people who had reasons to betray the nationalist hero: First, he claimed that the PCF opposed Messali because they had not been able to control him. Second, Egyptian president Gamal Abdel Nasser had positioned himself against Messali because he hoped for a "supple" leader in Algeria. And last, landholding Muslims (*possédants musulmans*) in Algeria disliked the "proletarian" character of Messalism.[42] Thus Messali was not just a champion of Algerian nationalism for Guérin, but he was also a valuable opponent of the pan-Arabism associated with Nasser and the allegedly feudal-religious nature of the FLN.

The decision to support Messali was difficult in light of the fratricidal violence between his Mouvement national algérien (MNA; Algerian National Movement) and the FLN, which both claimed to be the sole representative of the Algerian people. By the beginning of 1957, more than half of the MNA members in France had defected to the FLN as violence raged in the metropole.[43] Many radical leftists in France continued to support Messali even after popular support in Algeria had tipped in favor of the FLN. The FA withheld support from the FLN on the grounds that the party merely wanted "to replace the Gospel with the Qu'ran."[44]

The first group to provide aid to the FLN despite its long-standing support for Messali was the Fourth International, led by Pablo. His role in manufacturing weapons and fake currency for the group subsequently led to his arrest and trial in Amsterdam.[45] Despite these acts of solidarity, he nevertheless postulated that the FLN had failed to eradicate the "feudal spirit" that had existed in the Maghreb since the Middle Ages.[46] Like Guérin, he was skeptical of the role of religion in anticolonial revolts, claiming that "it would be an exaggeration to explain the cohesion and resistance at the base of the Algerian Revolution by religion and not by the effects [of colonization] on the entire population."[47] His frustration that the FLN remained a "vague front" rather than a "revolutionary party" only increased after 1962.[48] Commenting on the Tripoli Program, he lamented that the FLN had initially viewed the war as an anticolonial struggle and had not "overcome" the narrow goal of nationalism based on tradition.[49] This was consistent with the tendency of radical leftists to see Algerian customs and beliefs as "dead weight" rather than as a revolutionary vernacular that accounted for the identity and history of the people.[50]

From Colonial Humanism to International Development

The radical changes to the political context after 1962 affected the vocabulary that economists used to discuss economic growth. The terminology of *underdevelopment*, for example, was gradually replaced by the language of *developing countries* in order to avoid creating an "inferiority complex" among inhabitants.[51] The social Catholic ideas discussed in chapter 3 were also forced to adapt to the new language of international development. Louis-Joseph Lebret, who had created the group Economy and Humanism in the 1940s, was deeply influenced by the 1955 Bandung Conference, which convinced him of the need to rethink the prevailing economic order. He subsequently founded the Institut international de recherche de formation éducation et développement (IRFED; International Institute of Research on Education and Development Training) in 1958, which was headed by Buron. The group trained development practitioners working in the Global South and began publishing a journal titled *Tiers Monde* in 1960.[52] Lebret claimed that IRFED continued his initial project of advocating for a humanistic vision of the economy, but he stressed the new context of the late 1950s by stating, "the Third World is now conscious of its unsatisfied needs and its trampled dignity."[53]

Lebret had initially defined Economy and Humanism's approach in terms of Christian values, but the creation of IRFED prompted him to adopt a more secular stance in order to foster collaboration with non-Christians. A decentering of Christian thought and an attempt to consider economic development from a less Eurocentric perspective both contributed to a new vocabulary for development. Even as religion was gradually removed from economic discourses, France's attachment to a liberal economic system based on national values bore the deep imprint of social Catholicism. The early days of postcolonial development elucidate how France's national self-conception, which once hinged on civilizational superiority and colonialism, now relied on economic *rayonnement* (influence) to contain the twin threats of pan-Islamism and communism in the Third World.

Buron was a natural choice to lead IRFED, and his pragmatism tempered Lebret's more idealistic designs. He also had access to key political networks and understood international development in way that that broadened the scope of the organization.[54] By August 1966, the institute had trained 841 individuals of sixty-seven nationalities that were evenly split between industrialized and underdeveloped countries. Most came from Latin America, North Africa, and sub-Saharan Africa. The organization's approach was largely inspired by François Perroux's concept of harmonized development (*développement harmonisé*), which sought to understand individuals as multidimensional beings with a range of social and psychological needs. Though Perroux is best known for his theory of poles of development in Europe, he was also involved in discussions on social and economic development in North Africa. In the late 1950s, he exchanged letters with the Centres sociaux, the social Catholic–inspired organizations designed to help Algerians during the war.[55] In 1961, Perroux edited a special issue of the well-known journal of the Institut de science économique appliquée (Institute for Applied Economic Sciences) dedicated to the relationship among Islam, technology, and the economy."[56]

The special issue on Islam and the economy featured contributions from a wide range of individuals and demonstrated the deep interest in these questions among academics and policy makers in the 1960s. Pierre Rondot, a colonial official who later directed the Centre des hautes études sur l'Afrique et l'Asie modernes (CHEAM; Center for Advanced Studies of Modern Africa and Asia), contributed an article, as did ethnologist Jean Servier, a specialist of Berber culture who had done fieldwork during the War of Independence. The issue also featured a piece by Roger Arnaldez, a French *arabisant* and philosopher of religion who wrote several works on Islam. It also included an article by Perroux's pupil Destanne de Bernis, who played an important role in shaping the economic policy of postcolonial Tunisia and Algeria.[57] Jacques Austruy, a specialist on international development, who wrote a book on Islam and development the following year, also participated.[58] A number of conferences were held to address the topic of Islam and material development in the early 1960s as sociologists of religion increasingly turned their attention to economic questions.[59]

It was likely his fame as an economist and his social Catholic credentials that made Perroux an attractive candidate to head an Algerian École nationale d'administration (National School of Administration) in the eyes of the French Ministry of Cooperation.[60] This institution, established in 1964, reflected France's desire to set up an educational system in Algeria that resembled the elite establishments in the Hexagon. Yet this favorable image of Perroux would not last. When the protests of May 1968 erupted, students occupied the Institut d'études du développement économique et social (IEDES; Institute for the Study of Economic and Social Development) and demanded that someone with more leftist views, and who would express a "militant solidarity with the struggles for emancipation in the Third World," take the reins of the institution.[61] Students complained about Perroux's neocolonial tendencies, "dictatorial" nature, and absenteeism, all of which contributed to the ministerial order that revoked his position. One article in *Le Monde* stated that students "reproached the teacher for diffusing, under the guise of 'technicity,' a neocolonialist ideology and submitting to the official French foreign policy with regards to developing countries."[62] The crisis prompted students to go on strike and form a transitional committee composed of professors and administrators that included Destanne de Bernis.[63] Even though Buron, along with the Catholic intellectuals Jacques Madaule and Gabriel Marcel, came to Perroux's defense, these events were telling. They signaled how Perroux's humanist engagements and economic reflections, which were often showcased in international development and the policy of cooperation, came under fire during May 1968.

Marxist approaches to thinking about Islam and the economy also marked the French intellectual scene in the years leading up to 1968. Maxime Rodinson's watershed 1966 book *Islam et capitalisme* (*Islam and Capitalism*) maintained that there was nothing inherent in Islam that represented an obstacle to capitalist development.[64] Rodinson claimed that Islam could accommodate a number of different economic ideologies, including capitalism. Nor was there an essential link, he argued, between Islam and socialism, despite the claims of Syrian Mustafa al-Siba'i or Algerian Amar Ouzegane. He did not deny that the rural classes in Muslim countries were often attached to Islam, but this reflected the fact that religion was, "above all, a sign of identity and protest, a sign that was more rooted in national and class realities than governed by a spiritual connection to God."[65] Rodinson broke with the Communist Party in 1958. He later asserted that Islamic fundamentalism and communism shared certain characteristics. His fear that the Arabic translation of his work might be used in favor of traditionalist interpretations of Islam was assuaged by his translator, Syrian-born Nazih al-Hakim. Al-Hakim assured Rodinson that his Arabic translation would be a continuation of his own "battle against fanaticism" and described his search for a "non-dogmatic" socialism that was rational and democratic.[66]

Rodinson was one of many French Marxists who followed events in the Third World closely during these years. Fellow travelers included Charles Bettelheim, whose articles appeared in the *Alger républicain*, the journal run by French Communist Henri Alleg, and the sociologist Georges Gurvitch, whose writings on Proudhon were often invoked by theorists of self-management in the 1960s.[67] Gurvitch had trained the Iranian revolutionary Ali Shariati during the latter's studies in Paris, and his public position in favor of Algerian independence made him the target of a bomb attack in 1962. Roger Garaudy, another Marxist who adopted controversial stances on Algeria, had spent part of World War I as a prisoner of war in Djelf. He was expelled from the PCF before converting to Islam. In 1964, Garaudy was invited to speak in Algeria alongside Rodinson and Jacques Berque. All three addressed the link between Islam and socialism in their presentations.[68] As heterogenous thinkers reflected on Algeria's socialist experiment, they generated new constellations of thought in the hope that these utopian visions would provide a model for the Global South.

Colonialism's New Skin

While Marxist intellectuals were critical of colonial policy, the structures that had underpinned French development initiatives did not disappear after 1962. Since World War II, there had been increasing overlap between official and academic circles as policy makers were keen to adopt the new tools provided by the social sciences. This trend intensified in the 1950s, including among the consulting firms that had been created under the aegis of the Caisse des dépôts et consignations (CDC; Deposits and Consignments Fund), the major bank that coordinated investments for the French state. The rise of these consulting firms coincided with the importation of new approaches to planning that sought to make the French economy more flexible. The head of the CDC, François Bloch-Lainé, created the Société centrale d'équipement du territoire (SCET; Central Society for the Equipment of Territories) in 1955 with the explicit aim of "stimulating the development of regions that suffer from unemployment or insufficient economic development."[69] While this organization was primarily concerned with postwar reconstruction in the metropole, SCET-Coopération was created in 1959 to promote the development of territories outside mainland France.[70] Along with other branches of the CDC, such as SEDES, SCET had participated in the Constantine Plan, offering expertise and loans as well as opportunities to invest in real estate. In 1960, SCET-Coopération set up a regional office in Algiers and participated in a number of projects, most of which were never realized due to the war. It had been especially active, however, in developing infrastructure in the oil-rich region of the Sahara and played a central role in attempting to create an agglomeration of "Greater Algiers."[71]

After independence, SCET's expertise contributed to the official policy of cooperation. Moreover, its debt to Gaullism, which had portrayed decolonization as an inevitable transition that would encourage new forms of French influence in the world, remained considerable. On the tenth anniversary of its founding, Yvon Bourges, the last governor general of Equatorial Africa (1958–60) and secretary of state for cooperation, paid homage to the organization. He noted that the success of SCET epitomized the spirit of cooperation and was largely thanks to de Gaulle's vision in courageously leading France down the path of decolonization, thereby transforming the country's relationships with its colonies and demonstrating France's "generous attitude."[72] Some colonial experts—like Jean Fonkenell, who had previously tried to develop the Saharan regions with the OCRS—returned to Algeria in 1963 to work with SCET under the rubric of cooperation.[73]

In the last years of French Algeria, organizations that were under the umbrella of the CDC tried to distance themselves from the history of colonization. SCET-Coopération was rebranded as SCET-International in the hopes that by adopting a "new skin" the organization could hire independent experts and avoid displaying a direct link to France's colonial legacy.[74] Similarly, the SEDES found itself in a delicate position after independence. A 1963 report by its executive committee noted that the organization had adopted a prudent attitude prior to independence in order to avoid "compromising its future chances" of operating in Algeria.[75] The delinking of development from the French state provoked skepticism among traditional civil servants like Delouvrier, but SCET-International witnessed a period of expansion from 1963 to 1971, specifically in Algiers, which had the largest office in France's ex-colonial territories.[76] The Algiers office provided more than one-fifth of the organization's total business (over eight million francs) and employed 102 agents (52 expats and 50 locals) in 1968. This number increased to 700 in 1970 when the geographic scope of SCET-International also expanded.[77]

Even if French officials hoped to establish a monopoly in the realm of cooperation, the changed atmosphere in Algeria after decolonization made this all but impossible. Competition among various developmental actors was fierce, and there were good reasons for French experts to worry that their role was being eclipsed. At a meeting on January 9, 1963, a team of French officials responsible for cooperation that included Stéphane Hessel and Yves Roland-Billecard met to discuss the establishment of a UN office of technical assistance in Algeria. Hessel insisted that the "language of civilization" in Algeria should remain French. Yet despite hopes that the French language would continue to play a dominant role on the continent, the Commission économique des Nations Unis pour l'Afrique (Economic Commission of the United Nations for Africa) had recently adopted a resolution demoting France from a full to an associate member. French officials were resolutely opposed to this change, which they found particularly objectionable given the substantial aid they offered to African countries.[78]

Experts from communist countries in Eastern Europe posed a particular threat to France's dominance, given the ideological proximity of countries such as Yugoslavia to Algeria's quest for a "specific socialism," as we saw in the last chapter. Polish economist Czeslav Bobrowski, known to his Algerian colleagues as *cheikh*, played an important role in Algerian planning until 1978.[79] Hungarian experts were also active in cooperation. During a press conference, one member of INSEE praised Hungary's activities in Algeria, making an implicit comparison with France's "colonial" efforts.[80] Any notion that French *grandeur* was being eclipsed by another country's developmental efforts posed a threat to national pride in the Hexagon. When a team of Hungarian consultants arrived in Algeria to help conduct a census from July 24 to 31, 1962, the head of INSEE, Claude Gruson, wrote to the Algerians to convey his dissatisfaction. Defending the diverse relationships cultivated by the postcolonial state, Algerian authorities emphasized their country's need for international recognition and the reality of national sovereignty. An Algerian official responsible for the census wrote that "the experiences of our young state are not without echo abroad, and it is normal to see foreign delegations and missions come to Algeria to offer us their sympathy and the benefit of their knowledge. Our authorities are the only ones who can judge the appropriateness of [foreign] visits."[81] As Algeria navigated its relationships with its possessive ex-colonial power and new international admirers, the position of French coopérants seemed increasingly precarious.

The tension between international and French expertise was perhaps most marked in the field of agriculture, where Ben Bella's desire for land reform was hampered by a lack of qualified experts. While individuals from all corners of the globe filled positions in agricultural research and development, specialists from Eastern European countries tended to dominate.[82] Despite the ideological preferences of Algerian officials, French experts were not pushed aside so easily. Individuals like Monjauze, who had worked in Algeria prior to independence, were reputed to have good relations with the Algerians. This group comprised a handful of the estimated one hundred French experts who worked in agricultural services in 1964.[83] French experts could—and did—claim one clear advantage over their international socialist competitors: they understood the lay of the land. A report by the French embassy noted that foreign experts had the "heavy handicap of almost total ignorance regarding local conditions."[84] Decades of experience with the specific climatic features of Algeria provided a considerable advantage in envisaging solutions to maximize agricultural production.

Many of the consulting firms that worked on French cooperation had close links to academia and the government. René Mercier, who became the head of SEDES in 1959, had been the director of the Centre de recherches économiques appliquées (CREA; Center of Applied Economic Research), exemplifying the intimate connections between economists, social scientists, and the state.[85] Mercier followed Perroux's work with interest, attending conferences on development with the well-known economist in the 1960s. One such conference, held by UNESCO in Paris, specifically sought to address the dispersion and limitations of the social sciences in France. At another event, dedicated to the "social premises of industrialization," Perroux proposed that economists pay less attention to consumption, savings, and investment, and instead focus on work and innovation.[86] This desire to focus on locally specific variables rather than adopt a universal approach to modernization characterized much of SEDES's approach to development in the 1960s.

The organization's emphasis on the social factors of development is apparent from a number of documents written by those working for SEDES. One 1964 report explained the relevance of the Durkheimian approach to sociology and explored the applications of American social psychology in the field of development. It argued that economic actions were "profoundly influenced by ideological structures (aspirations; protestations; religious, moral, political, or cultural 'fixations,' which is to say judgments of values in the largest sense)."[87] In addition to mentioning sociologists Pierre Bourdieu and Jean Stoezel, the report cited André Ombredane, who had written about the psychology of labor in his article "Principles for a Psychological Study of the Blacks of the Belgian Congo."[88] The report highlighted the role played by social scientists in economic planning after World War II and shed light on how colonial knowledge shaped developmentalist discourse. This was consistent with broader trends in the 1960s when planners increasingly saw cultural traits as important variables for productivity and understood capitalist growth in terms of psychological aptitudes.[89]

Experts who had worked on the Constantine Plan helped create a European aid apparatus, bringing with them culturalist approaches to economic and social development. They often explained poverty by invoking social habits, mental capacities, and religious beliefs. To offer just one example, a report by SCET-Coopération drew on social psychology, behavioral sociology, and "oriental psychology" in an attempt to take into account cultural differences.[90] Religion remained an important explanatory factor for understanding North Africa; Islam, which had once functioned as a racial category that structured access to property and capital, was now part of a culturalist argument that explained the possibilities for economic prosperity. The notion that developmental success depended on cultural aptitudes rather than structural factors, which has become a major critique of post-development approaches, is one of the legacies of the transition from colonial to postcolonial development.[91]

The Tunic of Nessus

Not all French observers were enamored with the policy of cooperation or liberal development models. In 1963, the French government issued an iconic postcard that showed the Algerian and French flags under the text "1963—The Year of Cooperation." This postcard was sent to historian and Third Worldist Pierre Vidal-Naquet with one minor change: two self-proclaimed "retired *fellagas*" (fighters) had drawn the communist hammer and sickle on the French flag. The back of the postcard commented, "the capitalists are at least less serene [in Algeria] than in France. I hope you will attend their definitive burial soon."[92] Defacing the official policy of cooperation was not merely a symbolic act. From June 15 to 19, 1963, 150 delegates met in Algiers for the European Conference for Non-Governmental Assistance to Algeria. Organized by Pablo, the event brought together participants from a dozen countries to discuss how Europeans might provide humanitarian and technical aid outside the rubric of cooperation.[93] Conference organizers, including Alfred Sauvy and the agronomist René Dumont, characterized official French policy as a "Tunic of Nessus" that had been imposed by the Evian Accords. While that lavish garment had been "joyously embellished" by Hercules, it nevertheless "stuck to his body and penetrated it with a venom so vicious that it led to his ultimate destruction."[94] The tone of the conference was in line with Pablo's conviction, broadcast on the government-sponsored radio show *La voix de l'Algérie socialiste* (The voice of socialist Algeria). While enemies of socialism opposed the policy of agricultural self-management, it had to be protected at all costs.[95] Participants agreed that Algeria offered the European left an important source of regeneration and presented a new model for global revolution.[96]

While Algeria provided a testing ground for the principles of international socialism, the country also presented a number of obstacles. For example, when René Dumont visited Algeria as the personal guest of Ben Bella, there was a public clash between socialist theory and revolutionary practice. Dumont, who went on to establish the Green Party in France, had political views that were somewhere between those of the liberal coopérants and radical Third Worldists. While not a Marxist, he was still critical of the official policy of cooperation.[97] Dumont visited Algeria from December 21, 1962, to January 8, 1963, receiving a personal welcome from the president at the airport. On January 7, the Algerian president and French expert spoke in Algiers in front of three thousand people, including high-ranking functionaries such as Rabah Bitat, Amar Ouzegane, and Ahmed Francis. Flaunting his international experience, Dumont remarked, "In Russia one says 'comrade,' in Cuba we say 'compagnero,' but here we say 'brother.'"[98] Despite this friendly remark, his speech was contentious, especially when he mentioned that many of the self-management committees had been put in place by the government and army, implying that authoritarianism threatened to undermine the revolutionary intentions of Ben Bella's policies.

Figure 6.1 René Dumont greeted at the Algiers airport by Ahmed Ben Bella and Amar Ouzegane in December 1962. Photo courtesy of Musée du Vivant-AgroParisTech.

At the end of his talk, as Dumont prepared to take questions, Ben Bella intervened to say that he wished to personally start the exchange. He first responded to Dumont's claim that Algeria suffered from a lack of technicians, saying that while he had taken Dumont's opinions into account, he was more interested in what the peasants and workers in Chélif and Bône had to say.[99] Even if technical skills were important, Ben Bella continued, they were not everything. Ben Bella also responded to Dumont's remark that it was strange to see chauffeur-driven cars for government officials in a revolutionary socialist state. He coyly responded that the reason for his own luxurious transportation was simple: he did not know how to drive. Other critiques went unanswered. Dumont had observed, for example, that students at the school of agriculture at Maison-Carée enjoyed table service, which went against the work ethic that was necessary for the young Algerian state. He also expressed dissatisfaction at a lavish lunch given by one of the prefects.

Ben Bella did not hesitate to show his positional superiority, leaving the hall before Dumont had finished speaking. Those who remained did not appreciate the tone of Dumont's speech either; some Algerians felt that Dumont was talking down to them, with one auditor reportedly complaining that "il nous a pris pour des nègres" (he took us for Negroes).[100] Ben Bella had been reluctant to have Dumont share his findings in a public forum, and subsequently declared that regardless of the advice given by Dumont, Algeria would follow its own trajectory.[101] For Ben Bella to publicly shun a prominent Third Worldist in such a fashion underscored the tension between nationalist convictions and international aspirations. As radical leftists flocked to the "mecca of revolutions," it was also clear that many did not understand local cultural codes or politics. Algeria was certainly a prominent stop on the international trajectory of revolution, but it was not always clear what lessons far-leftists drew from Algeria's anticolonial experience.

While some Third Worldists tended to see Islam through the prism of Stalinism, fearing that it would provide an ideological tool for constructing an authoritarian state, others argued that any and all criticism of Ben Bella was out of place. According to a self-described comrade in Algiers affiliated with the anarchist group Information et correspondance ouvrière (ICO; Worker Information and Correspondence), this was not because the president deserved "blind sympathy," but because the sensitive political environment made it imperative to use the utmost caution when passing judgment.[102] Debates about what constituted a revolutionary movement and questions regarding who had the right to issue such judgments abounded. As Henri Simon, head of the ICO, wrote to Guérin, the French were in no position to decide what was revolutionary or counterrevolutionary in Algeria—that was for Algerians to decide.[103] He nevertheless shared a concern about the authoritarian tendencies of the Algerian state. Echoing Simon's sentiment, another member of the ICO reproached Guérin for displaying a "neocolonial spirit" and for his belief that "only doctrine can save the world."[104]

Some far-left observers could not shake the feeling that they were sacrificing their political principles by defending Ben Bella. Guy Debord wrote to Guérin and harshly denounced his support for the Algerian president. For Debord, Ben Bella could hardly be considered an "enlightened despot"; instead, the situationist characterized the Algerian president as a second-rate, or "poor copy," of Robespierre.[105] Another interlocutor argued that the way in which Ben Bella took power should have been enough to disqualify him as a real revolutionary, especially since his socialism was one of "circumstance" rather than conviction.[106] Humorously, the author compared Ben Bella's socialism to Gruyère cheese because it, too, was "full of holes." Why, the author asked, was the label *specific* applied to the socialism of Nasser and Ben Bella, but not of Franco? Could one not declare that Arab socialisms were, in reality, not socialist at all? He therefore took issue with Guérin's relatively unconvincing attempts to engage with Algeria's Arabo-Muslim specificity.

As Algeria became a *terrain d'expérience* (testing ground) for the far left, questions emerged about the possibility of comparing its Third World-ist experiment to the revolutionary tradition in France. Did the Algerian population have the required maturity to be considered a truly revolution-ary people? Would the spontaneity of the people be sufficiently guided by a political party? Some on the far left also recognized the need to account for Algeria's "specificity," a word that often conveyed the country's Muslim identity. In August 1962, Guérin had written an article for *L'Express* that was initially entitled "A Marxist Explanation of Mohammed," but which he later renamed "A Marxist Portrait of Mohammed."[107] It was hardly a defense of the Prophet. Guérin merely noted that Muhammad was most likely sincere in his revelations, adding that his message was not, "properly speaking," revolutionary. But he also returned to Rodinson's work, adopting the stance that one had to study the relationship between superstructure (Islam) and infrastructure (the economy). Intellectuals on the anticlerical far left were loath to analyze economic development (or underdevelopment) in terms of religion; in their eyes, the latter could only operate as a way of masking the essential contradictions of the economic base.

In September 1964, Pablo also reflected on the role of Arabo-Islamic tra-dition in Algeria's socialist experiment. He conceded that it offered a certain character, but expressed discomfort with the idea that Islam had fashioned a source of resistance against colonization. Instead, he placed the accent on Algerians' material grievances: "Indubitably, one should raise the question of religion in a flexible way before a profound transformation of the country attenuates the current importance of this factor. One would nevertheless be exaggerating to explain the cohesion and resistance of the Algerian Revolu-tion by religion rather than by the effects of secular colonization and the war, and by common revolutionary aspirations, particularly the desire felt by the large majority of Algerians to recover their land."[108] While Pablo thus admitted the influence of religion, he expected it to diminish with time as the country gained experience with genuine revolution. He warned that it would be a mistake to "mask the real national problems under the guise of a religious community."[109] After Boumediene's coup, an author writing in

Pablo's journal, *Sous le drapeau du socialisme* (Under the flag of socialism), under the pen name "Abdel Krim," did a postmortem on Ben Bella's regime. The article proclaimed that colonial society had not been conducive to the emergence of a Marxist-revolutionary movement and Algeria was therefore unable to "fully master its historical and social milieu" and liberate itself from the "defects" (*tares*) of traditional society.[110] The specificity of Algeria's ordeal with settler colonialism, which had constructed a capitalist system around the religious-racial nexus of Islam, went all but unrecognized by many on the radical left. Instead, many far-leftists considered that religion would eventually be excised with the introduction of a genuinely socialist system. This precluded any understanding of Islamic socialism as a set of ideas that expressed a desire for radical material change in an indigenous framework.

Despite the skepticism of those on the far left that Islam could serve as the basis of revolution, it would be unfair to claim that they ignored the function of race in a capitalist economy. Guérin had written about racism in the United States, and Fanon even wrote to Guérin expressing appreciation for this work.[111] In Guérin's analysis, however, racial hierarchies remained a second-order violence that stemmed from capitalism and empire. Far-leftists recognized racism as a phenomenon that divided the working class, as was the case with the North African proletariat in France. In their analysis of Algeria, however, they viewed the line between religion and race as analytically solid; whereas race helped bolster the logic of capitalism, religion shaped culture, providing a superstructure that would have to be rebuilt in the wake of a genuine revolution. Even the most radical critics of the colonial regime failed to account for the role that Islam as a racial category had played in influencing the trajectory and implementation of a capitalist system.

Fanon, whose writings have been foundational for theorizing racial capitalism, was also relatively quiet on the topic of Islam. He viewed the appeals to religion during the War of Independence as mostly strategic, and his writings on peasant spontaneity interpreted a long Islamic tradition of anticolonial resistance in light of Marxist categories.[112] This fact made him an object of critique in postcolonial Algeria, notably by Muhammad al-Mili, who had been a member of the AUMA. In 1971, Milli wrote a number of articles in Arabic on Fanon for the Algerian Ministry of Culture's journal, *al-Thaqafa* (Culture), in which he pointed to Fanon's French intellectual baggage and his estrangement from the Arabo-Islamic personality in order to question the Martiniquais' status as the theorist of the Algerian Revolution.[113]

As radical leftists and liberals engaged with Algerian economic development after 1962, both groups remained tied to specific visions of capitalism
and race that had emerged through colonization: coopérants saw markets
and competition as a way of introducing necessary sociological changes and
viewed Islam in largely cultural terms. Those on the far left, however, were
convinced that true revolution would wash away the archaic structures of
religion. In their diagnoses of underdevelopment, both groups failed to
account for the ways in which understandings of Islam were fundamental
to the process of value creation in (post)colonial Algeria. In other words,
as Algeria became a case study for international experiments, conversations
about the future of capitalism, either in liberal or Marxist terms, continued
to invoke an analytical split between race and religion.[114]

The golden age of foreign advisors in Algeria was short-lived. Boumediene disapproved of Ben Bella's Marxist allies and also turned away from
cooperation with France. His economic policies stridently affirmed Algeria's
economic sovereignty, especially his nationalization of hydrocarbons and
introduction of Arabization. For many observers on the far left, Boumediene's regime represented a Stalinist military dictatorship that deepened
the Arabo-Islamic identity of the country at the expense of international
solidarity. As he cracked down on communists and leftists, he also put Ben
Bella under house arrest. Ben Bella's supporters, including Guérin, formed the
Organisation de la résistance populaire (Organization of Popular Resistance)
to advocate for his freedom.[115] Facing intense repression by the regime, the
group morphed into the Parti de l'avant-garde socialiste (Avant-Garde Socialist Party) in February 1966. This party continued the legacy of the PCA,
operating underground until the introduction of political pluralism in 1989.

The opening of the political field in the late 1980s allowed political movements other than the FLN to see the light of day, leading to the creation of the
Front islamique du salut (FIS; Islamic Salvation Front; al-Jabha al-Islamiyya
li-l-Inqadh). One year later, Ben Bella's own party, the Mouvement pour la
démocratie en Algérie (Movement for Democracy in Algeria) was legalized.
This organization represented an attempt to bring together various ideological traditions including Islamism, nationalism, and the vestiges of Third
Worldism. While some have portrayed Ben Bella as a figure who encouraged
a populist and identitarian Islam, others have criticized him for importing
the doctrines of foreign secular leftists. If these analyses often reflect the
polarized ideological climate that followed the Dark Decade, the intellectual
debates of the 1960s and 1970s were much more fluid and included a good
deal of ideological promiscuity. For example, Algerian philosopher Malek

Bennabi hosted informal study sessions at the University of Algiers that attracted multiple ideological and linguistic currents (modernizers, Islamists, Francophones, and Arabophones). People of diverse political tendencies were attracted to Bennabi's lectures, which discussed how Islam could help Algeria overcome the multiple cultural and economic crises that marked the period after independence. While this chapter has focused on how decolonization shaped the tools available for thinking about race and capitalism in France, the epilogue sheds light on the debates over economic progress, national identity, and Islam that structured Algerian political life in the decades after Ben Bella's presidency.

EPILOGUE

For those familiar with the urban geography of Algiers, the Boulevard Té-
lemly is both a monument and a point of reference. Initially the site of
an Ottoman aqueduct, it connects the surrounding hills to the Bay of Algiers. During the colonial period, it became a major throughway where the
Aérohabitat building, a paragon of French modernist architecture, was constructed in 1955.[1] After 1962, however, the boulevard was named after Salah
Bouakouir. Born in Kabylia in 1908, Bouakouir was the highest-ranking
Algerian member of the French government. Trained as an engineer at the
prestigious École Polytechnique in Paris, he later embarked on a career
dedicated to the economic development of colonial Algeria. He held the
position of adjoint secretary general for economic affairs when he passed
away during a boating accident in September 1961. His role in contributing
to economic development within the framework of the Constantine Plan
made him an ambiguous figure in the Algerian nationalist narrative after
1962. Three decades after independence, President Mohammed Boudiaf declared Bouakouir a traitor and renamed the boulevard after Krim Belkacem,
a revolutionary hero who fought against the French state.

Bouakouir was known for his discretion and generally "avoided talking
about politics like the plague."[2] According to British consular sources, he
seemed "careful not to get too out of step with the nationalists" and turned
down an important position in public works in France to devote himself
to economic development in Algeria.[3] In the 1950s, it was rare to have an
Algerian Muslim occupy such a distinguished position in the French government. The colonial regime had historically prevented Algerians from acquiring advanced scientific knowledge, though the policy of social promotion
aimed to train high-ranking civil servants during the War of Independence.
Jean Morin, the delegate general during the last years of the Constantine

Plan, noted that it was especially important to showcase the talents of the few Muslims working for the French state.

A British consular report written in December 1960 ominously mentioned that many observers believed that Bouakouir's life was in danger due to his delicate position between the French government and the FLN.[4] Although Algerian nationalists invoked Bouakouir's name as evidence that Algeria had the technical expertise necessary to run the country after independence, Bouakouir was generally circumspect when speaking to his French colleagues. According to Jean Guyot, a French official who worked in economic planning, Bouakouir was more preoccupied with securing a prosperous future for Algeria than condemning French sovereignty and did not support an "Algerian Algeria."[5] Given these accounts, it might seem unlikely that Bouakouir would be rehabilitated as a symbol of Algerian nationalism. But in 2010, Minister of the Interior Daho Ould Kablia tried to do exactly that. He claimed that Bouakouir should be viewed as a hero since he had provided the GPRA with sensitive technical information—an act that subsequently prompted the French secret services to carry out his assassination.[6]

Algerian nationalists as well as French politicians pointed to Bouakouir's career as proof that Muslims could play a central role in economic development. This attempt to navigate the relationship between Islamic civilization and the technical skills promoted by colonial modernity was not new. While colonial subjects in the early twentieth century were exposed to European technology on battlefields and in factories, after World War II discussions of modernity were organized around the principle of economic rationality. As a result, the economy came to be understood as a self-contained entity that also implied the "re-imagination of the nation-state."[7] As the idea of a national economy became hegemonic, politicians and planners viewed economic doctrines not only as means of organizing goods and resources but also as essential reflections of national identities that accounted for the aggregated capacities, needs, and desires of the national community.

In Algeria, like in many countries in the Global South, economic orthodoxies were articulated alongside anxieties about deculturation and authenticity provoked by colonization. Bouakouir was committed to the possibility of France bringing economic progress to Algeria, but other figures insisted that material development was impossible if it did not occur within an Islamic framework. This was a major preoccupation for the Algerian intellectual Malek Bennabi, who, like Bouakouir, traveled to Paris in order to receive a technical education. Born in Constantine in 1905 to a religious family (his father worked with the Islamic courts), Bennabi had attended a

Franco-Arab *lycée* (high school) and was equally at home writing in French and Arabic throughout his career.[8] In Constantine, he became interested in Islamic reformism, a movement inspired by Abd al-Hamid Ben Badis, who upheld Arabism and Arabic as core elements of Algerian identity.[9] Bennabi describes his younger self as an *islahiste farouche* (enthusiastic Muslim reformer) in his memoirs.[10] Yet after the 1936 Muslim Congress, where reformers formed alliances with Algerian nationalist parties, his criticism of the ʿulama became especially clear. Bennabi saw this event as a sign that prominent religious figures had renounced their commitment to promoting the spiritual life of Algerians and instead decided to engage in the political antics of winning votes and debating citizenship.[11]

In 1930 Bennabi left for Paris, where he had initially hoped to study at the Institut des langues orientales in Paris (Institute for Oriental Languages, the present-day Institut national des langues et des civilislations orientales, INALCO). When he was denied admission, he claimed the French state had rejected him on political grounds, and was subsequently trained as an electrical engineer. After World War II, he embarked on a career as a writer, spending most of the Algerian War of Independence in Egypt, where he translated a number of his own works into Arabic. On returning to his home country in 1963, he became the director of higher education, though he resigned in 1966. The last years of his life prior to his passing in 1973 were spent writing and giving talks across the Middle East.

Bennabi rejected the "pseudo-technocratic" knowledge produced by the colonial system and would likely have been critical of Bouakouir's contribution to economic planning.[12] Whereas Bouakouir exemplified the Algerian Muslim who had reached the highest echelons of the French administration, Bennabi was skeptical that such a feat was possible. Indeed, despite Bouakouir's prestigious title, it is notable that many of his French colleagues highlighted not only his discretion but also his preference for European company, both of which demonstrated a certain cultural distance from his status as a Muslim native in their eyes. In some ways, this confirms Bennabi's observation that the colonial system refused Algerian natives full acquisition of the scientific skills that represented European modernity.[13] In his memoirs Bennabi presents himself as a Muslim intellectual desperate to advance his future and his technical capacities in the face of a colonial system that wished to destroy both.[14] As we saw in the third chapter, Orientalists such as Jacques Berque diagnosed the Muslim world as suffering from a disjuncture between authenticity and efficiency. Bennabi, however, was committed to reconciling these two principles through a historical and intellectual analysis of Islamic civilization. His two best-known works, *Les conditions de la renaissance* (The conditions of the renaissance) and *Vocation de l'Islam* (Vocation of Islam), investigated the possibility that Muslim civilization could provide the basis for cultural and technical progress. In the former work, he wrote that "it is by accomplishing its own renaissance, and by making its own way toward moral and scientific progress, that Algeria can effectively contribute to the building of the human polity (*cité humaine*)."[15] His assertion that the essential factor for anticolonial resistance was located in Islam, not the region's Arab Berber heritage, was consistent with the central role of religion in defining Algerian nationalism; he claimed that the Moroccan anticolonial hero Abdelkrim found the inspiration for resistance "not in his Arabo-Berber 'skin,' but in his Muslim soul."[16]

Bennabi was critical of Algerian nationalists who believed that the answer to Algeria's crisis lay in the sphere of formal politics, dismissing these initiatives as a caricatural zone of *boulitique* (rather than *politique*). He saw politicians as "indulging in mere words when action is needed, denouncing colonialism instead of colonizability without any effort to really transform the condition of men."[17] This is one of the reasons he had a negative impression of Messali Hadj after meeting his supporters in Paris.[18] For Bennabi, political jockeying lacked the commitment to self-improvement that would enable Islamic civilization to overcome its backwardness. An existential threat to the colonial system would not come from demands for reforms or independence, he argued, but from a deep engagement with Islamic thought and civilization, which would induce a profound spiritual transformation.[19]

Bennabi called on Algerians to "cease to be colonizable" and encouraged them to reflect on the origins of the colonial system rather than getting caught up in political maneuverings such as issuing demands for economic reforms or national autonomy. He argued that it was impossible to condemn colonialism without criticizing the factors that allowed the French to conquer North Africa in the first place: "The Muslim does not even think efficiently using the means that are already available, or produce the extra effort necessary to improve his lifestyle, even in a makeshift way, and on the contrary remains on the level of indigenization and thingification [*chosification*], which thus assures the success of colonizing techniques—this is colonizability."[20] While it would be tempting to read his concept of *colonizability* as a simple statement of collective self-blame or colonial apologia, these remarks reflect the importance that Muslim reformers attached to education, which they understood as a prerequisite for both spiritual and material development. Rather than seeking to recreate the conditions of the first centuries of Islam, Islamic reformists in North Africa were resolutely forward-looking and saved their most virulent criticisms for the marabouts, the rural Islamic networks they viewed as repositories of superstitious and backward traditions. They reconstructed the Islamic past in order to articulate a framework for authenticity, but the validity of these principles could only be judged based on modern criteria. In other words, any adopted doctrine would need to allow Islamic civilization to realize technical efficiency and material prosperity; as Bennabi claimed, "an authentic idea is not always efficient."[21] A true cultural renaissance in the Arab world would therefore require Muslims to adopt the core values of productivity.[22]

Bennabi understood development not only as a series of actions exercised on the material world but also as an internal project.[23] Like many of his contemporaries in the period after World War II—including social Catholic thinkers—he advocated for an economic system that would avoid the extreme individualism of liberalism and the dehumanizing materialism of Marxism. This was the theme of Bennabi's often overlooked work published in Arabic, titled *al-Muslim fi 'Alam al-Iqtisad* (The Muslim in the economic world). In it, he rejected the idea that there was an inherent opposition between the economic and religious spheres. His hope that countries like Algeria, Libya, Egypt, or Syria would find a new economic path imbued with an "Islamic spirit" reflected his conviction that "any economy—no matter its [ideological] orientation—is an embodiment of a civilization."[24] He argued that while all countries required a policy for organizing the production and distribution of material resources, the ideological underpinnings of this program necessarily reflected a county's civilizational characteristics. Similarly, in an essay originally published in 1974, he critiqued the uncritical adoption of economism in the region and lamented that Muslims seemed obsessed with creating a society in the image of homo economicus.[25]

Bennabi's attempts to craft a specifically Islamic form of material progress resonated with a number of political trends in Algeria after independence. In the 1960s, his classes and informal study sessions at the University of Algiers became a meeting place for a diverse group of students. One student later reported that he began to see Islam "not as a way to arrive at an Islamic state, but as a civilizational problem" thanks to these discussions.[26] He pointed to Bennabi's view of religion as an all-encompassing framework for progress rather than a narrow set of theological precepts. Individuals associated with the Ja'zara, a group committed to a specifically Algerian framework for political Islam, were particularly attracted by Bennabi's interest in combining Algerian nationalism, scientific rigor, and Islamic civilization.[27] This intellectual trend later played a key role in the FIS, a heterogenous Islamic political party that won the first free elections in Algeria before a military coup interrupted the electoral process. Abbassi Madani and Abdelkader Hachani, two prominent leaders of the Islamic Salvation Front, attended Bennabi's informal discussions. During these exchanges, Madani claimed that he had found a way to reconcile "universal scientific and technological patrimony" with national "authenticity."[28]

Other politicians who explicitly invoked Islamic ideals, such as Noureddine Boukrouh, a liberal disciple of Bennabi who has translated a number of his works into French, repudiated the Jaz'ara's claim to be the inheritors of Bennabi's intellectual project. Boukrouh's denunciation of the Jaz'ara was founded on an unequivocal rejection of those associated with the FIS after the civil war as well as in his own elitism. Boukrouh argued that Bennabi's reformism was fundamentally at odds with the populism of the Jaz'ara's message.[29] Instead Boukrouh invoked Bennabi as an intellectual touchstone for a liberal and technocratic political project informed by Islam, which he understood as a cultural framework rather than a theological corpus. After the political opening of 1989, Boukrouh created the Parti du renouveau algérien (Party of Algerian Renewal) before occupying various economic posts in the Algerian government from 1999 to 2005. To this day he remains a vocal figure in debates around Bennabi's work and the possibility for reforming Islam in Algeria.

Bennabi's legacy, and the tension between technocratic expertise and Islamic identity, has emerged in more dramatic ways over the last few years. In February 2019, the announcement that President Abdelaziz Bouteflika would run for a fifth term sparked a revolutionary movement known as the Hirak. At the time of writing, protests have been suspended after the dual setbacks of the COVID-19 pandemic and government repression. Since 2013, the plummeting price of hydrocarbons has devastated the Algerian economy and posed serious questions about the sustainability of the current model of development. In this context, economic debates have been an important touchstone for Hirakists and their reflections on the founding mythologies of the Algerian state. On May 3, 2019, a banner in the city of Bouira featured a figure resembling a gladiator cutting Algeria off from an octopus that represented the neocolonial powers of France and Algeria's complicit elite. Text at the bottom stated that the blood of the martyrs of the revolution "fueled" the Hirak, making an explicit comparison between blood and oil—two of Algeria's national resources.[30] The perceived threat of foreign exploitation was hardly far-fetched; five months later, a crowd gathered outside Parliament in Algiers to protest a new energy law that would facilitate foreign investment and was, according to many in the Hirak, a way of selling off the nation's wealth. The law was undoubtedly a response to the imminent economic crisis. Yet rather than invoking the country's Third Worldist legacy, the technocratic elite proposed another model of economic development that encouraged start-ups and the associated values of entrepreneurism.[31]

Algerian journalists have recently analyzed the Hirak in the context of the "contemporary Islamic renaissance" described by Bennabi, even though he remains a marginal figure outside of intellectual circles.[32] Activists have emblazoned his words on signs during protests; in Algiers on October 11, 2019, one sign cited the Arabic translation of his 1959 work *Mushkilat al-Thaqafa* (The problem of culture): "Educators in Islamic and Arab countries should teach the youth how to discover a path in which the march of humanity takes precedence rather than teaching them how to keep up with the Russians or the Americans."[33] This passage, written during the Cold War when the countries in the Middle East and North Africa struggled to maintain a position of nonalignment, took on a different meaning in 2019. It now signaled Algeria's strategic position among global powers that were motivated by security concerns and energy needs. A banner from the protests of April 19, 2019 quoted Bennabi's conviction that "the revolution cannot achieve its goals without changing the human irreversibly with respect to his behavior, his ideas, and his words."[34] Not only does this sentence imply that the revolution is a work in progress; it suggests that individual transformation and political change must be complementary and continue the work of articulating a non-Western humanism. A different banner, shown below, quoted the Arabic translation of *Les conditions de la renaissance*, which referred to the Qur'anic admonishment that "God will only change the condition of a people when they change themselves" (13:11).[35]

Some partisans of a secular Algeria have found Bennabi's place in these protests worrying. They have portrayed his ideas as part of the "badissiyya novembriyya," a conservative Islamic tendency rooted in the principles of Islam and Arabism espoused by Ben Badis.[36] The Ministry of Culture, anxious to claim Bennabi's legacy for the state, co-organized a conference on Bennabi's thought in October 2020.

Born three years apart, Bennabi and Bouakouir represent two different blueprints for reconciling homo islamicus and homo economicus. While Bouakouir sought to accomplish the task within the framework of the colonial system, Bennabi's writings analyzed the unfinished project of Muslim re-

Figure E.1 A sign featuring Bennabi in Bourdj Bou Arreridj, April 26, 2019, that says: "This is divine law: change yourself and you will change history." Source: *Algérie 1*.

form after decolonization. Much like the Constantine Plan, Bennabi's vision for material progress adopted the language of cultural authenticity. Despite their ideological and political differences, both individuals were forced to navigate the alleged tension between technical progress emanating from the West and an Algerian identity rooted in Islam. This dichotomy has structured a broader grammar of colonial modernity that remains committed to the possibility that a universal economism can break from anthropological visions of man. It defines the economy as a universal domain untarnished by the vestiges of society's past, which it relegates to the domain of tradition.[37] In this regard, Algeria is hardly exceptional; the project of consolidating a national character, inherited from the nineteenth century, was taken up across Europe by state experts committed to national planning after World War II. The Algerian case is notable, however, in that this discussion occurred under the sign of religion.

This book has shown how the French state defined Islam as a set of psychological and cultural traits that were decisive for colonial development and introduced an economic system in which the capacities of the Algerian population were central to the creation of civilizational and economic value. Colonial officials could speak of the "Muslim economy" without needing to specify that they were referring to subsistence agriculture. This phrase claimed to be merely descriptive, but it simultaneously created an adjective—Muslim—that was synonymous with noncapitalist forms of calculation. After decolonization, economic categories continued to operate as markers of civilizational difference and revolutionary potential, structuring the founding myths of the Algerian nation-state. The use of Bennabi's work by activists, intellectuals, and politicians during the Hirak reveals how the relationship between homo islamicus and homo economicus continues to be an object of debate in constructing an Algerian national identity.

Capitalist modernity often presents itself as a rational system of production based on wage labor, freedom of contract, and formal equality. This book has told quite a different story by documenting how racial-religious hierarchies were fundamental to the conception and implementation of economic reforms. If homo economicus was the emblem of European culture, colonial planners believed that homo islamicus was inherently resistant to economic reason. This in turn affected how the French state organized markets, modernized agriculture, and standardized labor practices. While capitalist modernity relied on a racial regime of religion to introduce the market as a force that would allegedly promote civilization and prosperity, economic doctrines served as blueprints for the distribution of material resources as well as central nodes for the construction of racial difference. As the figures of Bouakouir and Bennabi make clear, the tropes of homo economicus and homo islamicus did not disappear with decolonization. Instead, they continue to structure competing imaginaries of development in North Africa and the Middle East long after the fall of colonial rule.

Introduction

1 "Address by Professor Rappard at the Opening Meeting" (April 1, 1947), folder 12, box 5, Mont Pèlerin Society Records, Hoover Institution Archives, Stanford University (hereafter HIA). I would like to thank Ola Innset for bringing this source to my attention.

2 Susan Pedersen details Rappard's activities in the mandate section at the League of Nations in *The Guardians*, 52–59.

3 Peter, "William E. Rappard and the League of Nations," 227.

4 "Address by Professor Rappard," 3.

5 "Address by Professor Rappard," 3.

6 "Address by Professor Rappard," 4.

7 Whyte, *The Morals of the Market*, 9–10. For more on the link between civilizational discourse and early neoliberal thought, see Elyachar, "Neoliberalism, Rationality, and the Savage Slot."

8 Grosrichard, *The Sultan's Court*, xvi.

9 Lockman, *Contending Visions of the Middle East*, 74–78.

10 Harris, "Whiteness as Property."

11 There have been rigorous discussions of the definition of economism in colonial contexts as well as of the emergence of a self-evident domain of the economy. See, for example, Jakes, *Egypt's Occupation*, 10–12; Mitchell, *Rule of Experts*; and Goswami, *Producing India*, 335.

12 A number of scholars have studied the role of ethnographic knowledge in colonial governance. See Burke, *The Ethnographic State*. The tendency to use ethnographic knowledge for the purposes of colonial rule in Algeria is documented in Trumbull, *An Empire of Facts*. In *Castes of Mind*, Nicholas Dirks shows how missionaries, anthropologists, and ethnologists fashioned caste as a stable category of rule in India. Ritu Birla demonstrates how colonial administrators and nationalist thinkers turned their attention to "Indian Economic Man" and attempted to reform indigenous merchant capitalists who operated through "ties of kinship, clan, and caste" (*Stages of Capital*, 2).

13 Eckert, Malinowski, and Unger, "Modernizing Missions"; McDougall, "Rule of Experts?," 87–108.

14 Darcie Fontaine argues that the relationship between Christianity and the civilizing mission continued to structure resistance to empire during decolonization in *Decolonizing Christianity*.

15 A number of scholars have highlighted the central role played by the transatlantic slave trade in the development of capitalism. See, for example, Beckert, *Empire of Cotton*.

16 René Jammes, "Études sur l'Islam," July 1960, 151, Inspection générale des affaires algériennes, Ambassade de France à Alger (hereafter 21PO), Centre des Archives diplomatiques de Nantes (hereafter CADN).

17 Whyte, *The Morals of the Market*, 37.

18 Denord, "French Neoliberalism and Its Divisions," 45; Kuisel, *Capitalism and the State in Modern France*, 248–71.

19 Jakes, *Egypt's Occupation*, 5. Andrew Sartori and Brenna Bhandar investigate how Lockean notions of property, specifically the capacity to labor, constituted legitimate claims to ownership and influenced colonial policy in the British Empire. Bhandar, *Colonial Lives of Property*; Satori, *Liberalism in Empire*. My own formulation of a racial regime of religion is derived in part from Bhandar's concept of racial regimes of property. Jennifer Pitts's analysis of James Mill in chapter 5 of *A Turn to Empire* also elucidates how a drive to improve colonial subjects trumped the economic burdens that would result from colonial rule.

20 Lowe, *The Intimacies of Four Continents*; Federici, *Caliban and the Witch*. J. K. Gibson-Graham argue in *The End of Capitalism* that theories of capitalism have reproduced a phallocentric teleology that makes it difficult to imagine alternative languages of opposition.

21 Surkis, *Sex, Law, and Sovereignty in French Algeria, 1830–1930*.

22 Albert O. Hirschman claims that economic interest, a realm that appeals to man's rationality and morality, has historically served as an antidote for the malevolent passions of power and greed in *The Passions and the Interests*, 31–33.

23 Elyachar, *Markets of Dispossession*; Mitchell, *Rule of Experts*, 7.

24 Partha Chatterjee locates a division between an outer domain, where anticolonial nationalism "had to be acknowledged and its accomplishments carefully replicated and studied," and a spiritual "inner domain," which bore the "'essential' marks of cultural identity" (*The Nation and Its Fragments*, 6). For a critique of Chatterjee in light of Algerian nationalism, see McDougall, *History and the Culture of Nationalism in Algeria*, 8–9.

25 Vanaik, "Introduction," 12.

26 Vanaik, "Introduction," 12; Chibber, *Postcolonial Theory and the Specter of Capital*, 213–14; Nilsen, "Passages from Marxism to Postcolonialism."

27 The notion of the "individual" assumes the values of self-possession and sense of self that have historically been constructed as the domain of masculinity. The individual was one who could possess property and participate in civil society. See Scott, *Only Paradoxes to Offer*; and Lowe, *The Intimacies of Four Continents*.

28 Hanebrink, *A Specter Haunting Europe*.

29 Sartre, *Anti-Semite and Jew*, 26.

30 Bell, *Globalizing Race*.

31 One notable exception is the work of Naomi Davidson, who argues that, in twentieth-century France, Muslim immigrants were seen as "unable to free themselves from their faith's domination of their very bodies" (*Only Muslim*, 5).

32 Davis, "'Incommensurate Ontologies'?"

33 Hall, *The Fateful Triangle*, 33–34.

34 Todd Shepard argues that race was not fundamental in determining who could become a French citizen, noting, however, that "racism's most direct effect was economic" (*The Invention of Decolonization*, 35). This departs from Emmanu-elle Saada's claim that questions of filiation, class, and culture were bound to discourses of race in her study of mixed-race children in the French Empire, *Empire's Children*. Emily Marker analyzes the drive to define Europe as white during European integration alongside discussions around the education of Africans in *Black France, White Europe*.

35 Scholars have disagreed as to whether republicanism offered a model for equality or fashioned a set of constitutive discriminations. Conklin, *A Mission to Civilize*; Wilder, *The French Imperial Nation-State*; Fernando, *The Republic Unsettled*. Reflecting on this debate in terms of colonial political economy, Eliz-abeth Heath argues that "the economic development of the colonies and the racialized labor regime it promoted served as the foundation of the Republic's stability" (*Wine, Sugar, and the Making of Modern France*, 3).

36 Gilmore, *Golden Gulag*, 28.

37 Aydin, *The Idea of the Muslim World*; Rana, *Terrifying Muslims*; Puar, *Terrorist Assemblages*.

38 Amin, "The Remainders of Race."

39 Martinez, *Genealogical Fictions*, 39.

40 Guha, *Beyond Caste*, chap. 1.

41 Writing about Irish immigrants in the United States, Bruce Nelson argues that, "like blackness, whiteness was about far more than skin color; it was about laying claim to a set of cultural characteristics that made one respectable and capable of exercising the rights of citizenship" (*Irish Nationalists and the Making of the Irish Race*, 10). Also see Hickman and Walter, "Deconstructing Whiteness: Irish Women in Britain."

42 Robinson, *Black Marxism*.

43 Clancy-Smith, *Rebel and Saint*; Colonna, *Les versets de l'invincibilité*.

44 Clancy-Smith, *Rebel and Saint*, 41.

45 Doumani, *Rediscovering Palestine*; Banaji, "Islam, the Mediterranean and the Rise of Capitalism."

46 This was particularly the case prior to Muhammad Ali's modernizing reforms. Marsot, "The Ulama of Cairo," 153; Mitchell, *Colonizing Egypt*.

47 As Arthur Asseraf notes, colonial rule did not create the marker of Islam ex ni-hilo, but rather built on a "pre-existing peculiarity by flattening Algerians into Muslims" (*Electric News in Colonial Algeria*, 90). The fact that Islam served as a moral framework for actors can be fruitfully analyzed as one manifestation of

the tension between the lived experience of race and state imposition of racial categories (Goldberg, *The Racial State*, 104–9).

48 Goldberg, *The Racial State*, 4.

49 A number of excellent studies document how the Algerian War of Independence informed French politics and intellectual life. Ross, *Fast Cars, Clean Bodies*; Shepard, *The Invention of Decolonization*; Lyons, *The Civilizing Mission in the Metropole*; LeSueur, *Uncivil War*.

50 Historians have debated the relative importance of the *corso* (i.e., privateering) versus agricultural production for the Ottoman economy in North Africa. Sadok Boubaker argues that the rural economy was more important for North African elites in the seventeenth and eighteenth century in *D'une Méditerranée à l'autre*. I would like to thank M'hamed Oualdi for his help on this point.

51 McDougall, *A History of Algeria*, 19.

52 Schreier, *The Merchants of Oran*; Stein, *Plumes*; Jomier, *Islam, réforme et colonisation*.

53 Lydon, *On Trans-Saharan Trails*, 110.

54 Following the work of Patrick Wolfe, settler colonialism has been defined in terms of a "logic of elimination" that seeks to free up land for settlement ("Settler Colonialism and the Elimination of the Native"). Yet in Algeria the removal of the indigenous population was incomplete, and Algerians were an important source of cheap labor. This observation has led theorists of settler colonialism, such as Jürgen Osterhammel, to consider Algeria an "African" style of settler colony similar to Rhodesia, Kenya, and South Africa (*Colonialism*, 7). For a study of Algerian history in light of Wolfe's framework, see Barclay, Chopin, and Evans, "Introduction."

55 Sessions, *By Sword and Plow*, 186. For example, French support for wine produced by European settlers in Algeria should be explained by political rather than economic logics (Henni, *La colonisation agraire*, 127). Laura Maravall shows that colonial policymakers in the early 1900s privileged consolidating settlement over encouraging the ideal of small family farms due to the sparse availability of arable land ("Factor Endowments on the 'Frontier'").

56 The term *colonial capitalism* denotes the ways in which capitalism emerged in the context of violence and coercion, thereby questioning our ability to speak of a universal process of capital accumulation. Dipesh Chakrabarty analyzes a "capitalism of the colonial type" in India, arguing that "the secular languages of law and constitutional frameworks coexisted and interacted with noncommensurable strategies of domination and subordination" ("Subaltern Studies and Postcolonial Historiography," 21). Also see Ince, *Colonial Capitalism and the Dilemmas of Liberalism*. While much of this literature has looked at the particularity of British colonial ideology, the intertwining of capitalism, liberalism, and empire was also fundamental in the French case.

57 Luxemburg, *The Accumulation of Capital*, 357.

58 For a discussion of this model, see Prochaska, *Making Algeria French*, 122.

59 Marseille, *Empire colonial*.

60 Marseille, *Empire colonial*, 136.

61 Lefeuvre, *Chère Algérie*, 68.

62 Elise Huillery's empirical research, contra Marseille, concludes that "French West Africa did not place a significant economic burden on French taxpayers" ("The Black Man's Burden," 34). Also see Clément, "L'analyse économique de la question coloniale"; Fitzgerald, "Did France's Colonial Empire Make Economic Sense?"

63 While the scholarship on this topic is voluminous, Jill Jarvis has engaged with literary texts to think about memory without "center[ing] French experiences and narratives of decolonization" (*Decolonizing Memory*, 13).

64 Lefeuvre, *Pour en finir avec la repentance coloniale*. This work instigated a number of polemics, most notably between Lefeuvre and economic historian Catherine Coquery-Vidrovitch, who deplored the instrumentalization of economic data by Lefeuvre and lamented that he structured an academic study around the theme of repentance, a concept that she argued was eminently political. Lefeuvre, on the other hand, pointed out certain factual errors in her response, accusing her of allowing a Third Worldist orientation to color her analysis. For further discussion of this polemic, see Davis, "Qu'est-ce qu'un échec?"

65 Foucault, *The Birth of Biopolitics*, 225.

66 Thomas, "Albert Sarraut."

67 Woker, "Empire of Inequality," 25.

68 Sewell, "A Strange Career." Owen White and Elizabeth Heath investigate how cultural models influence the writing of economic history in their article, "Introduction: The French Empire and the History of Economic Life."

69 Sewell, "A Strange Career," 157. The term *embedded* is often associated with the work of Karl Polyani, who used it to describe how firms and markets were necessarily informed by social and cultural norms (Polanyi, *The Great Transformation*).

70 Kuisel, *Capitalism and the State in Modern France*, 252.

71 Winant, *The World Is a Ghetto*.

72 Murphy, *The Economization of Life*.

73 Cited in Chenu, *Paul Delouvrier ou la passion d'agir: Entretiens*, 384. Unless otherwise indicated, all translations are my own.

74 This position is known as *cartiérisme*, a reference to the thesis initially proposed by the journalist Raymond Cartier in the pages of the French magazine *Paris Match*. Cartier argued that the skyrocketing cost of developing the colonies was a burden on the metropole (Cooper, *Citizenship between Empire and Nation*, 270).

75 See, for example, Lefeuvre, "L'échec du plan de Constantine"; and Chapman, *France's Long Reconstruction*.

76 Clarno, *Neoliberal Apartheid*, 9.

77 Zimmerman, *Alabama in Africa*, 216.

78 For a study of Weber's writings on Islam in the framework of religious sociology, see Turner, *Weber and Islam*.

79 Weber, *The Protestant Ethic*, xlii.

80 Simmel, *On Individuality and Social Forms*, 192. Similarly, Hayden White notes that the narrative form transforms "events" into "patterns of meaning" ("The Question of Narrative," 22).

81 Guha, *Peasant Insurgency*, 18.

82 Spivak, "The New Subaltern," 325.

83 Two examples of Algerians acquiring notable fortunes are Youssef Hamoud, who started the very successful Hamoud Boualem soda company in the late nineteenth century, and the Tamzali family, which operated an olive oil factory. Gilbert Meynier notes that the visibility and number of Algerian Muslims with significant amounts of capital increased after World War I (*L'Algérie révélée*, 663–64).

84 Weber, *The Protestant Ethic*, xlii.

85 Du Bois used the term *dark proletariat* to describe racialized subjects who undermined the alleged universality of class politics, which was revealed to be based on the white European proletariat (*Black Reconstruction in America*, 30). Roland Barthes makes a similar point regarding the intractable differences between conceptions of the colonial and Western working classes by analyzing the North Africans in the Goutte d'Or area of Paris (*Mythologies*, 164).

86 Goldberg, *The Threat of Race*, 21.

87 "Intervention de M. Layashi Yaker," October 30, 1962, 29QO/33, MAE.

Chapter One: Settling the Colony

1   Karl Marx to Friedrich Engels, February 21, 1882, in Galissot, Engels, and Marx, *Marx, marxisme et Algérie*, 304.

2   Galissot, Engels, and Marx, *Marx, marxisme et Algérie*, 353. For more on Marx's time in Algeria, see Musto, *The Last Years of Karl Marx*, 105–11.

3   Von Sivers, "Rural Uprisings as Political Movements."

4   Galissot, Engels, and Marx, *Marx, marxisme et Algérie*, 296.

5   Daumas and Fabar, *La Grande Kabylie*, 249.

6   Mezzadra, "Marx in Algiers"; Anderson, "Marx's Late Writings."

7   Galissot, Engels, and Marx, *Marx, marxisme et Algérie*, 163.

8   Rosalind Morris argues that Islam functions as a particular kind of difference for Marx, which explains why he can "ask the question of why the history of the East *appears* as a history of religions, and answer it with reference to the absence of private property in land" ("Theses on the Questions of War," 157).

9   Galissot, Engels, and Marx, *Marx, marxisme et Algérie*, 346.

10 Robinson, *Black Marxism*, xxix.

11 Robinson, *Black Marxism*, xxix.

12 Benachenhou, *Formation du sous-développement en Algérie*, 94–106, 225–31.

13 Harvey, *Spaces of Capital*; Harvey, *The Limits to Capital*; Harvey, "Globalization and the 'Spatial Fix.'"

14 Sessions, *By Sword and Plow*, 10.

15 This led many liberal economists to oppose colonization due to its high cost during the July monarchy. The early 1860s saw a "reconciliation between liberals and protectionists in favor of state intervention" along with a "softening of anti-colonial stances" (Clément, "French Economic Liberalism," 51).

16 Aydin claims that Sultan Abdulhamid's emphasis on spiritual sovereignty over the *umma* (Muslim community) helped consolidate this vision and that his

pan-Islamic sensibility "aggravated Islamophobia and paranoia about Muslim revolts" (*The Idea of the Muslim World*, 97).

17 McCluskey, "Commerce before Crusade?"; Touati, *Entre Dieu et les hommes.*

18 Grosrichard, *The Sultan's Court*, chap. 4; Curtis, *Orientalism and Islam.*

19 Montesquieu, *The Spirit of the Laws*, 272.

20 Massad, *Islam in Liberalism*, 15.

21 Thomson, "Arguments for the Conquest of Algiers," 109.

22 Weiss, *Captives and Corsaires*, 9.

23 Though the French republic abolished slavery in 1794, Napoleon Bonaparte restored the slave trade in France and its colonies in 1802 (Brower, "Rethinking Abolition in Algeria").

24 Weiss, *Captives and Corsaires*, 20. The concept of social death was developed by Orlando Patterson to discuss slavery as a global institution that systematically depersonalized and desocialized enslaved persons (*Slavery and Social Death*).

25 Thomson, "La classification raciale de l'Afrique du Nord," 20.

26 Pitts, *A Turn to Empire*, 212.

27 Amichi, Kuper, and Bouarfa, "Tilling the Land," 49.

28 McDougall, *A History of Algeria*, 95; Sessions, *By Sword and Plow*, 254–57; Budin, "La 'reconnaissance' de la propriété rurale."

29 Ageron, *Histoire de l'Algérie contemporaine*, 240.

30 La société algérienne de Paris, *De la colonisation*, 79.

31 This terminology reflects the nineteenth-century debate on the policy options of assimilation, relocation (*refoulement*), and extermination in Algeria (Brower, "Rethinking Abolition in Algeria," 810).

32 Société algérienne de Paris, *De la colonisation*, 86.

33 De Raousset-Boulbon, *De la colonisation et des institutions civiles*, 25.

34 Lucas and Vatin, *L'Algérie des anthropologues*, 104–9.

35 Société algérienne de Paris, *De la colonisation*, 87.

36 Colonial administrators and scholars made a similarly positive assessment regarding Algerian communities in the M'zab region. The doctor Charles Amat, for example, depicted them as being particularly good at commerce and saving in 1888 (*Le M'zab et les M'zabites*). This representation persisted during the Algerian War of Independence, when the Information Services of the Governor General published a report characterizing inhabitants of this region as possessing a "taste for work" (*goût de travail*) and displaying a penchant for individualism and commerce. "Le M'Zab," August 30, 1955, Documents algériens: Service d'information du cabinet du gouverneur général de l'Algérie, No. 16, 4-JO-4238 (6), BNF. I would like to thank Augustin Jomier for discussions on this point.

37 Woker, "Empire of Inequality." Jerome Greenfield crucially underscores the disagreements between metropolitan and colonial authorities on fiscal policy ("The Price of Violence").

38 Todd, "The *Impôts Arabes*," 115.

39 Ageron, *Les algériens musulmans*, 707.

40 Kateb, *Européens, "indigènes" et juifs*, 82–83.

41 Quoted in Todd, "The *Impôts Arabes*," 116.

42 Roughton, "Economic Motives and French Imperialism," 369.

43 Sessions, *By Sword and Plow*, 250.

44 Sessions, *By Sword and Plow*, 272.

45 De Saint-Sauveur, *Encyclopédie des voyages*, 5.

46 Clancy-Smith, "Islam, Gender, and Identities." Ann Laura Stoler writes that the "colonial order coupled sexuality, class and racial essence in defining what it meant to be a productive—and therefore successfully reproductive—member of the nation and its respectable citizenry" (*Race and the Education of Desire*, 178).

47 Taraud, *La prostitution coloniale*, 57.

48 D'Ivry, *L'Algérie*, 15.

49 D'Ivry, *L'Algérie*, 20.

50 D'Ivry, *L'Algérie*, 15–16.

51 Abi-Mershed, "The Mediterranean in Saint-Simonian Imagination."

52 Surkis, *Sex, Law, and Sovereignty*, 7.

53 Sessions, "Colonizing Revolutionary Politics."

54 Drolet, "A Nineteenth-Century Mediterranean Union"; Chevalier, *Système de la Méditerranée.*

55 Régnier, *Les Saints-Simoniens en Egypte*; Emerit, *Les Saint-Simoniens en Algérie*, 56.

56 Abi-Mershed, *Apostles of Modernity*, 32.

57 Emerit, *Les Saint-Simoniens en Algérie*, 25.

58 Abi-Mershed, *Apostles of Modernity*, 156.

59 Guignard, "Conservatoire ou révolutionnaire?," 81.

60 McDougall, *A History of Algeria*, 97.

61 Guignard, "Les inventeurs de la tradition 'melk,'" 66.

62 Mahfoud Bennoune, *The Making of Contemporary Algeria*, 45.

63 Saada, *Empire's Children*, 100; Sessions, *By Sword and Plow*, 3.

64 McDougall, *A History of Algeria*, 122.

65 Surkis, *Sex, Law, and Sovereignty*, chap. 2; Blévis, "La citoyenneté française."

66 Betts, *Assimilation and Association*, 106.

67 In this light, association can be seen as a form of historicist (rather than naturalist) racial thought. Goldberg, *The Racial State*, chap. 3.

68 Shepard, *The Invention of Decolonization*, 26.

69 Weil, "Le statut des musulmans." In a study of requests for naturalization, Blévis demonstrates how ideas of dignity, culture, morality, and patriotism contributed to determining success ("La citoyenneté française," 42).

70 The 1892 Méline tariff set up a double tariff system benefiting countries that had bilateral agreements with France. Smith, "The Méline Tariff."

71 Pomel, *Des races indigènes*, 18.

72 Davis, *Granary of Rome*, 96–99.

73 Surkis, *Sex, Law, and Sovereignty*, 101.

74 Maravall, "Factor Endowments on the 'Frontier.'"

75 The French administration actively encouraged potential settlers to take up wine production in the 1870s, particularly after the 1876 phylloxera crisis (White, *The Blood of the Colony*, 41).

76 Heath, "The Color of French Wine."

77 Davis, *Granary of Rome*, 118.

78 Thénault, *Violence ordinaire dans l'Algérie coloniale*, 163.

79 According to Thénault, administrators meted out at least twenty thousand punishments every year between 1898 and 1920. Thénault, "Le 'code de l'indigénat,'" 205.

80 Isnard, "Vigne et colonisation en Algérie." The phylloxera crisis came to Algeria in 1885.

81 Cross, "The Evolution of Colonial Agriculture," 64–66.

82 Cross, "The Evolution of Colonial Agriculture," 67; For more on the "wine war" between French wine producers in the Midi and European vignerons in Algeria during the 1930s see White, *Blood of the Colony*, chap. 4.

83 Henni, *La colonisation agraire*, 59.

84 This is most famously the case in Pierre Bourdieu's analysis; see Darbel et al., *Travail et travailleurs en Algérie*. The term *agricultural proletariat* refers to those who work for wages on capitalist agricultural farms (Mintz, "The Rural Proletariat," 300).

85 Henni, *La colonisation agraire*, 74.

86 Henni calculates that given the average salary of between 1.25 and 1.5 francs per day, a worker would make 250 francs over 200 days of the year. A small farmer growing barley on five hectares of land would have a gross revenue of 300 francs and a net revenue of 220 francs. This leads Henni to conclude that "the wages paid thus seem barely sufficient to assure, in market terms, a precolonial quality of life in terms of subsistence. Salaried work does not change the situation of the peasants quantitatively but qualitatively: they become integrated in the world of commodities" (*La colonisation agraire*, 66–68).

87 Just before World War I, a European agricultural worker could earn a daily salary of 3 to 4.25 francs, while highly trained Algerian workers such as *cavistes* (cellarmen) would receive between 2 and 2.25 francs. Those without specialized training were paid 1 to 1.5 francs (Meynier, *L'Algérie révélée*, 118).

88 Nancy Fraser highlights the historical distinction between wage labor—a form of exploitation resulting from the sale of labor power—and those who work under the threat of physical coercion, whose labor is expropriated. "Dispensing with the contractual relations through which capital purchases labor power in exchange for wages," she writes, "expropriation works by confiscating capacities and resources and conscripting them onto capital's circuits of self-expansion" ("Roepke Lecture in Economic Geography," 7).

89 Lukács, *History and Class Consciousness*, 149.

90 In Marx's account, a period of "primitive accumulation," which includes brute force, enslavement, and looting, preceded the emergence of a rational economic system (*Capital*, 713–16). The notion that primitive accumulation stands outside capitalism has been critiqued by a number of scholars, who point out

that this violence cannot be placed in historical or conceptual parenthesis (Coulthard, *Red Skin, White Masks*, 9).

91 Chakrabarty notes that his early interest in labor history was rooted in the question of the "world-historical role the proletariat might play in a country such as India that was, still, predominantly rural" (*Provincializing Europe*, x).

92 Sari, *La dépossession des fellahs*, 38–41.

93 Quoted in Ageron, *Les algériens musulmans*, 846.

94 Sari, *La dépossession des fellahs*, 65.

95 Quoted in Benachenhou, *Formation du sous-développement en Algérie*, 239.

96 Ageron claims that the lack of labor rights in Algeria spurred immigration to France (*Les algériens musulmans*, 852–54).

97 Quoted in Sari, *La dépossession des fellahs*, 41.

98 Collot, *Les institutions de l'Algérie*, 218–19. Seventy percent of the delegates to the Financial Delegations, which comprised three bodies, were European. For more on how this institution discriminated against Muslims, see Adda-Djelloul, "Société colonisée et droit colonial."

99 Benachenhou, *Formation du sous-développement en Algérie*, 150–62.

100 Nouschi, *Enquête sur le niveau de vie des populations rurales*, 571.

101 Trumbull, *An Empire of Facts*, 23.

102 Renan, *Qu'est-ce qu'une nation?*

103 Renan, *Études d'histoire réligieuse*, 295.

104 Renan, *Études d'histoire réligieuse*, 235.

105 Leroy-Beaulieu, *De la colonisation chez les peuples modernes*.

106 Leroy-Beaulieu, *L'Algérie et la Tunisie*, 239.

107 Clément, "L'analyse économique de la question coloniale en France," 57–58.

108 Bochard, *Les impôts arabes en Algérie*, 3.

109 For more on how the settler press consolidated a Latin identity while participating in a global conversation, see Chopin, "Pages without Borders."

110 "L'élevage du bétail en Amérique," 2–3.

111 Davis, *Granary of Rome*, 149; Ford, "Anxieties of Empire."

112 Kateb, *Européens, "indigènes" et juifs*, 178.

113 Ageron, *Histoire de l'Algérie contemporaine, Tome II*, 100.

114 Legg, *The New White Race*. Sarah Gualtieri traces how Syrian immigrants to the United States constructed themselves as white in order to make appeals for citizenship in *Between Arab and White*.

115 Ahmed, "A Phenomenology of Whiteness," 150.

116 The native tribunals "designed specifically for the swift trial and easy detention of Algerian Muslims" are another example of a state of exception based on race (Ghabrial, "Reading Agamben from Algiers," 237).

117 Stora, *Algeria, 1830–2000*, 23.

118 Francis, "Catholic Missionaries," 689.

119 Francis, "Catholic Missionaries," 686; Dirèche-Slimani, *Chrétiens de Kabylie*.

120 Saaïdia, *Algérie coloniale*, 144.

121 Jews were emancipated and granted equal citizenship after the French Revolution (in 1790 for Sephardim and 1791 for all Jews); in exchange, they were asked to eliminate particular customs that allegedly made them a "nation in a nation." Napoleon sought to further Jewish assimilation by giving French civil law priority over Jewish law and reinstituting the ancient institution of the Sanhedrin, the Jewish councils in the Roman province of Judea. The integration of Jews into the Republic was thus based on the hope of diluting—or eliminating—Jewish difference. Jewish legal equality was finally achieved under the July Monarchy. While anti-Semitism accelerated in proportion to increased legal gains in France and elsewhere in Europe during the nineteenth century, most French Jews had assimilated to Western European norms and shed traditional religious practices. Indeed, these cosmopolitan Jews, like the namesake of the Crémieux Decree, Adolphe Crémieux, set their sights on the social uplift and acculturation of Jews according to the aims of the French civilizing mission in North Africa, Iran, and the Ottoman Empire.

122 Blévis, "En marge du décret Crémieux."

123 Schreier, *Arabs of the Jewish Faith*.

124 For additional works that examine the place of Algerian Jews in colonial hierarchies see Cole, *Lethal Provocation*; and Stein, *Saharan Jews*.

125 Ageron, *Histoire de l'Algérie contemporaine*, 128.

126 There are several theories about the genealogy of this term, which translates literally to "black feet." Some claim it is an indication of the poverty of many settlers, signaling that they arrived in Algeria without shoes. Others have argued the term derives from the idea of a pioneer (*pionnier*). See Savarese, *L'invention des pieds-noirs*; Shepard, "Pieds-Noirs, Bêtes Noires"; and Plaisant and Assante, "Origine et enjeu du la dénomination 'pied-noir.'"

127 Indigenous Muslims could not be considered foreigners despite their lack of citizenship and were therefore ineligible for naturalization under the 1889 law (Blévis, "La citoyenneté française," 32).

128 Fontaine, *Decolonizing Christianity*, 31; McDougall, "The Secular State's Islamic Empire."

129 Fontaine argues that "'Christianity' had become a mark of European identity" by the end of the nineteenth century (*Decolonizing Christianity*, 24).

130 Fanon, *The Wretched of the Earth*.

131 Laurens, *Orientales II*, 57.

132 Ruscio, *Les communistes et l'Algérie*, 103–4.

133 Quoted in Ageron, "Le Parti communiste algérien," 40.

Chapter Two: A New Algeria Rising

1 Governor General in Algeria, *L'Algérie, pays de la qualité*, film., 21 min., 1948, accessed August 16, 2020, https://www.ina.fr/video/AFE00003973.

2 Institut national de l'audiovisuel, *Voyage au coeur de la Kabylie*, film, 14 min., 1946, accessed August 19, 2020, https://www.youtube.com/watch?v=19iWnNA21xE.

3　Jodi Melamed writes in "Racial Capitalism" that capitalism introduces divisions not only among humans but also between humans and nature. Bruno Latour notes that nature is often seen as a self-evident entity, much as the category of man once was once assumed to be universal (*The Politics of Nature*, 49). For a series of essays that explore nature as a contested terrain, see Cronon, *Uncommon Ground*.

4　Meynier, *L'Algérie révélée*, 405.

5　Marseille, *Empire colonial*, 155; Meynier, *L'Algérie révélée*, 313.

6　Fogarty, "The French Empire," 119.

7　Metcalf, *Imperial Connections*; Moyd, *Violent Intermediaries*; Lunn, "'Les races guerrières'"; Fogarty, *Race and War*.

8　Hassett, *Mobilizing Memory*, 21.

9　Asseraf, *Electric News*, chap. 3.

10　Despite the tendency to isolate separate strands of Algerian nationalist thought, historian Abu al-Qasim Saʿdallah notes the close relationship between Algerian communists and religious scholars in the interwar period (*Hizb al-Shaʿb al-Jazaʾiri*, 3:25).

11　Zack, "Origins of Islamic Activism."

12　Thomas, "Albert Sarraut"; Rosenberg, "Albert Sarraut and Republican Racial Thought."

13　Gary Wilder calls the 1920s and 1930s in France an "ethnological era," claiming that the civilizing mission gave way to a colonial humanism that was expressed through economic development (*The French Imperial Nation-State*, 28).

14　Marseille, *Empire colonial*, 57.

15　Letter to the minister of the interior (signed Marcel Peyrouton), January 19, 1932, Algiers, Office algérien d'action économique et touristique (OFALAC) (90)/1, Gouvernement général de l'Algérie (GGA), Archives nationales d'outre-mer, Aix-en-Provence (hereafter ANOM).

16　On tourism, see Zytnicki, *L'Algérie, terre de tourisme*.

17　Letter from OFALAC to the administrator-director of la société des forêts de Sanhadja et de Collo, March 16, 1934, 90/12, GGA, ANOM; letter from E. Garcin, director of OFALAC, to Mme Sophie de Narbutt, March 29, 1934, 90/1, GGA, ANOM.

18　Algeria exported 1,060,294 metric quintals of fruits and vegetables from 1933 to 1934, versus 2,404,446 from 1936 to 1937 (OFALAC, "Les productions et le commerce," *Nouvelles et informations d'Algérie*, October 28, 1937, no. 12, BNF).

19　Bernard de Raymond, *En toute saison*, 91.

20　The magazine, printed by Baconnier, was suspended from 1959 to 1961 for budgetary reasons. In 1961, there were five hundred copies on sale in Algeria and all but ten were sold. OFALAC meeting notes, July 3, 1961, 23, Cabinet Jean Morin (15CAB)/29, GGA, ANOM.

21　Bernard de Raymond, "Une 'Algérie californienne,'" 26.

22　Bernard de Raymond, "Une 'Algérie californienne,'" 39.

23　Bernard de Raymond, *En toute saison*, 104.

24　Interview with René Mayer, April 4, 2014, St. Cloud.

25 Cohen, "The Colonial Policy of the Popular Front," 386.

26 This discussion comes from Délégation financières algériennes, "Encouragements à l'oléiculture et avances aux industries oléicoles," session of May 27, 1936,
47, GGA, BNF.

27 Délégation financières algériennes, "Encouragements à l'oléiculture," 48.

28 Nord, *France's New Deal*.

29 Bouchard and Ferme, *Italy and the Mediterranean*, 26.

30 Highlighting that European states viewed some Mediterranean populations
more favorably than others, Valerie McGuire describes how Italy tended to
consider Greek communities to be more assimilable than the Turkish inhabitants of the Aegean ("Bringing the Empire Home").

31 Montarsolo, *L'Eurafrique*, 20.

32 Maxime Champ, "Perspectives eurafricaines," *Bulletin économique et juridique*,
November–December 1960, 31, Centre des archives nationales, Algiers (hereafter CANA).

33 Hansen and Jonsson, *Eurafrica*, 65; Steffek and Antonini, "Toward Eurafrica!," 149.

34 Hansen and Jonsson, *Eurafrica*, 67.

35 Dramé and Saul, "Le projet d'Eurafrique en France."

36 Davis, "The Sahara as the 'Cornerstone' of Eurafrica."

37 Hansen and Jonsson, *Eurafrica*, 9.

38 Eirik Labonne, "Politique industrielle et stratégique de l'Union française,"
December 1955, 6, 81F/188, GGA, ANOM.

39 Champ, "Perspectives eurafricaines," 31.

40 The French government sent three African representatives to the Parliamentary
Assembly of the EEC to underline the importance of its colonial territories
for treaties on the Common Market and Euratom (Garavini, *After Empires*).
For more on how empire shaped the Common Agricultural Policy, see Davis,
"North Africa and the Common Agricultural Policy." Megan Brown shows
how central the question of Algeria was to discussions over the Treaty of
Rome in "Drawing Algeria into Europe." Also see Brown, *The Seventh Member
State*.

41 Letter from the governor general of Algeria to the minister of the interior,
Algiers, Feb. 7, 1955, "Normalisation des fruits et des légumes," Ministère d'État
chargé des affaires algériennes (81F)/2301, GGA, ANOM.

42 Muller, "Iconographie de l'Eurafrique." Robert Schuman saw Eurafrica as
"the necessary prolongation of a reconciled Europe" ("Unité europénne et
Eurafrique"). Walter Hallstein, the first president of the commission of the
EEC, was also a proponent of Eurafrica.

43 Wilder, "Eurafrique as the Future Past"; and Cooper, *Citizenship between
Empire and Nation*, 202–10.

44 Lorcin, "Rome and France in Africa," 318. Environmental narratives also intersected with the Kabyle Myth, as explained in Davis, *Granary of Rome*. Benito
Mussolini utilized the idea of a Latin Mediterranean to defend the Italian
empire in Libya in the 1930s (Agbamu, "Mare Nostrum").

45 Moe, *The View from Vesuvius*.

46 Sergi, *The Mediterranean Race*, v–vi.

47 Ripley, *Races of Europe*, 247.

48 Ripley, *Races of Europe*, 247.

49 Audisio, *Sel de la mer*, 103.

50 Audisio, *Sel de la mer*, 121. For critical takes on the Algiers school, see Haddour, *Colonial Myths*; Foxlee, *Albert Camus's "The New Mediterranean Culture"*; Graebner, *History's Place*. Scholars have often studied Audisio's literary activities without reflecting on his role in the colonial administration. See, for example, Clancier et al., *Audisio, Camus et Roblès*.

51 Audisio, *L'Algérie littéraire*, 3.

52 Stenner, *Globalizing Morocco*, 47.

53 Kaufman, *Reviving Phoenicia*, chap. 4; Corm, *La montagne inspirée*.

54 Husain, *Mustaqbal al-Thaqafa fi Misr*.

55 Discussions of Pharaonism had first emerged during the fin de siècle period as Egyptologists articulated "new concepts of place, space, and community that subtly uncouple[d] Egypt from the Islamic and regional traditions of cultural identity" (Colla, *Conflicted Antiquities*, 125). For more on how this discourse was used by Egyptian nationalists during the interwar period, see El Shakry, *The Great Social Laboratory*.

56 Merkel, "Fernand Braudel"; Silverstein, *Algeria in France*. For more on Braudel's view of the Mediterranean, see Liauzu, "La Méditerranée selon Fernand Braudel"; Silverstein, *Algeria in France*, 66; Lorcin, "Rome and France in Africa"; and Carlier, "Braudel avant Braudel?"

57 Dávila, "Gilberto Freyre," 59.

58 Schroeter, "Between Metropole and French North Africa," 27.

59 Daniel Lefeuvre, Jacques Marseilles, and Catherine Coquery-Vidrovitch have all argued for the importance of the Vichy regime to the economic modernization of France's overseas territories. See Lefeuvre, "Vichy et la modernisation de l'Algérie"; Coquery-Vidrovitch, "Vichy et l'industrialisation aux colonies"; Marseille, *Empire colonial*.

60 OFALAC, Comité de gestion, session of March 11, 1943, 4, 90/2, GGA, ANOM.

61 Zarobell, *Empire of Landscape*.

62 Cooper, *Decolonization and African Society*, 173.

63 Vince, *The Algerian War*, 48.

64 'Akkah, "Tafsir al-Sihafa al-Shuyu'iyya wa-Sihafat al-Haraka al-Wataniyya li-Dawr al-Maja'a dimna Asbab Intifadat 8 May 1945."

65 Harbi, "La guerre d'Algérie a commencé à Sétif"; Yacine, "Sétif, Guelma et Dien Bien Phu."

66 Eckert, Malinowski, and Unger, "Modernizing Missions"; and Naylor, *France's Modernising Mission*. Scholars of Africa have considered Europe's increased investment in its colonial territories after World War I a "second colonial occupation" (Berman and Lonsdale, *Unhappy Valley*).

67 Lefeuvre, *Chère Algérie*, 247.

68 Lefeuvre, *Chère Algérie*, 255. According to Jean-Pierre Rioux, between 1948 and 1951, 3.21 percent of the Marshall Plan was allocated for development in Algeria

while 2.56 percent went to Morocco and Tunisia and 1.69 percent to other overseas territories (*The Fourth Republic*, 176).

69 "Istifadat al-Jaza'ir min Barnamij Marshall: Taqaddum Malhuz fi al-Zira'a wa-l-Sina'a," *al-Ahram*, December 18, 1950, 2.

70 Al-Da'im, "Ma'sat al-Jaza'ir."

71 Semley, *To Be Free and French*.

72 Lentin, "Replacing 'Race,' Historicizing 'Culture'"; Brattain, "Race, Racism, and Antiracism"; Shepard, "Algeria, France, Mexico, UNESCO"; Hazard, *Postwar Anti-Racism*. Alice Conklin demonstrates how interwar debates in the social sciences led to the disappearance of "racial science," which was subsequenly replaced by "an alternative sociologically grounded understanding of difference based on such innovative universal concepts as the gift, the person, and historical contact between societies" (*In the Museum of Man*, 4).

73 In 1830, Algeria grew only 420 acres of citrus fruit; by the 1950s, it grew 61,750 acres ("La culture des agrumes en Algérie," July 15, 1948, Documents algériens, Série économique, no. 49, 81F/2302, GGA, ANOM). Only one-fifth of clementines and one-fourth of oranges were produced for internal consumption (Banque de l'Algérie, Bulletin d'information, Agrumes, March 1961, 2, 81F/2302, GGA, ANOM).

74 Association française interprofessionnelle des agrumes, October 25, 1960, compte-rendu, Colloque Paris-Oran-Alger, chamber of commerce (hereafter CC), 186, CANA. Also found in 81F/2255, GGA, ANOM.

75 For a study of how the Californian dream influenced colonial policy in Morocco, see Swearingen, *Moroccan Mirages*.

76 Mendel and Ranta, *From the Arab Other*, 57.

77 Karlinsky, *California Dreaming*, 7.

78 Karlinsky, *California Dreaming*, 26. Arthur Asseraf has shown that French planners saw Israel as a possible model for the partition of Algerian territory during the War of Independence ("'A New Israel'").

79 Voyage d'études en Israël de la promotion 1955–1958, March–April 1958, 133, École Nationale d'Agriculture d'Alger, 8-02F-1654, BNF.

80 OFALAC, "L'exposition: Algérie, Californie française," *Nouvelles et informations d'Algérie*, no. 17, January 10, 1939.

81 Farmer, *Trees in Paradise*, 408.

82 Wine was responsible for 66 percent of the value of Algerian exports in 1933 (Isnard, "Vigne et structures en Algérie," 90).

83 Isnard, "Vigne et structures en Algérie," 77. For additional work on how wine influenced identity in Algeria, see Jansen, "French Bread and Algerian Wine"; Barrows, "Alcohol, France and Algeria"; and Heath, *Wine, Sugar, and the Making of Modern France*.

84 Lequy, "L'agriculture algérienne," 52.

85 For more on how *terroir* intersected with French colonial expansion, see Guy, "Culinary Connections and Colonial Memories."

86 OFALAC, "Nouvelles et informations d'Algérie," *Bulletin*, no. 13, November 10, 1937.

87 Keith Sutton suggests that without this process up to twenty-three million hectoliters of wine were potentially unsalable in 1962 ("Algeria's Vineyards," 52).

88 Joseph Bohling details how the high alcoholic content of wine was invoked during French anti-alcohol campaigns in *The Sober Revolution.*

89 Giulia and Swinnen, "World's Largest Wine Exporter." The struggle between metropolitan and Algerian winegrowers largely predates the interwar period, however; see Strachan, "The Colonial Identity of Wine."

90 Délégation générale du Gouvernement en Algérie, "La vigne et le vin en Algérie," 1959, 15, BIB AOM/2974, ANOM.

91 Délégation générale, "La vigne et le vin en Algérie," 16.

92 Launay, *Paysans algériens: La terre,* 98.

93 Benachenhou, *Formation du sous-développement,* 190–91.

94 Pierre Mayer, Inspecteur des finances, "Note sur l'organisation du marché des huiles d'olive dans le zone Franc," 3, no date but likely 1957, 81F/2297, GGA, ANOM.

95 Gaudry, "Fabrication de l'huile en Aurès," August 8, 1949, Documents algériens, no. 4, BNF.

96 Oulebsir, *L'olivier en Kabylie,* 90.

97 Oulebsir, *L'olivier en Kabylie,* 97.

98 OFALAC experts also postulated that lower-quality oil could be used for purposes other than consumption, including as a motor lubricant ("Rapport sur l'oléiculture algérienne," October 30, 1933, Bougie, 90/12, GGA, ANOM).

99 OFALAC, "Rapport sur l'oléiculture algérienne."

100 Letter from president of the chamber of commerce of Bougie to the director of OFALAC, September 8, 1933, 90/12, GGA, ANOM.

101 Letter from oil producers in Seddouk to the president of OFALAC in Algiers, December 13, 1934, 90/12, GGA, ANOM.

102 Préfecture de Grande-Kabylie, Dra el Mizan, 12, 9150/253, ANOM.

103 Olive oil had been subject to international regulation since the interwar period, and the Fédération internationale d'oléiculture (FIO) had existed in different forms since its creation in Rome in 1934. After suspending its activities during the Spanish Civil War and World War II, the organization was reconstituted in 1949.

104 FIO, "Deuxième conférence internationale des techniciens oléicoles," October 7–11, 1963, Nice, 19879238/48–49, Direction générale de la production et des marchés, Ministère de l'agriculture, Archives nationales de France, Pierrefitte-sur-Seine (hereafter AN).

105 FIO, "Deuxième conférence internationale des techniciens oléicoles."

106 Jacques Pélissier to the head of domestic and international trade, "Réglementation du commerce des huiles d'olive," June 25, 1960, 81F/2297, GGA, ANOM.

107 Note from the chamber of commerce of Bougie to the president of the chamber of commerce of Algiers, March 7, 1960, CC 136, CANA.

108 Letter from Moustafa Tamzali to the president of the chamber of commerce of Algiers, Feb. 15, 1960, CC 136, CANA.

109 Letter from Jacques Pélissier to the secretary general for Algerian affairs, "Participation de l'Algérie à la F.I.O.," December 1, 1958, Cabinet Delouvrier (14CAB)/120, GGA, ANOM.

110 Letter from Oulid Aissa, director of agriculture and forests, "Adhésion de l'Algérie à la Fédération internationale d'oléiculture," December 29, 1961, 81F/2295, GGA, ANOM.

111 Letter from Paul Délouvrier to M. Mohamed Baouya, deputy of Orléansville, February 2, 1960, 81F/2295, GGA, ANOM.

112 M. Chaux, "L'olivier et le figuier en Kabylie," Direction de l'agriculture du paysannat, des forêts et de la restauration des sols, *Bulletin des renseignements agricoles*, no. 49, January 1958, 91, 4-s-5766, BNF.

113 Chaux, "L'olivier et le figuier en Kabylie," 92.

114 Ministère de l'agriculture à messieurs les directeurs départementaux des services agricoles et du paysannat, les inspecteurs départementaux des SAPS, les présidents de SAP, "Encouragement à la culture de l'olivier—Attribution de primes," January 7, 1958, Sous-préfecture de Djidjelli, circulaire no. 69, 9318/41, GGA, ANOM.

115 Ministère de l'agriculture aux directeurs départementaux, "Encouragement à la culture de l'olivier."

116 In 1953, three hundred sixty million new francs of long-term credit was available for olive oil in the metropole, as compared with four hundred million francs in Tunisia and two hundred sixty thousand francs in Morocco. Despite the fact that twenty-two thousand tons of oil were produced in Algeria (as compared with twelve thousand tons in Morocco and seventy thousand in Tunisia), the territory did not receive any long-term credits for this purpose. General Planning Commission, "Commission de modernisation et d'équipement des corps gras, projet de rapport général," 64–65, Agriculture, Direction de la production et des échanges, 19870238/43–45, AN.

117 Dossier on Dra El Mizan, 12, 9150/253, GGA, ANOM.

118 Commission du développement industriel, groupe de travail corps gras, [ca. 1959], F/60/4059, Archives du Plan de Constantine, AN.

119 Commission du développement industriel, groupe de travail corps gras, [ca. 1959].

120 Caisse d'accession à la propriété et l'exploitation rurale, "Domaine d'El Faraoun (Mirabeau), rapport cultural, 1958," March 1959, 81F/2254, GGA, ANOM.

121 Mouloud Sloughi argues that the rare references to agriculture in the Evian Accords served to ensure the financial interests of the settlers ("Agriculture et coopération algéro-française").

122 The nationalist paper *Révolution africaine* claimed that wine exported from the private sector got preferential treatment on French markets ("Qui boira le vin socialiste," no. 79, August 1, 1964, 9). Settlers, on the other hand, complained that France was accepting too much Algerian wine in 1965. Assemblée générale ordinaire, February 25, 1965, Maison des agriculteurs français d'Algérie, Secrétariat d'État aux affaires algériennes (SEAA) 195, Archives du Ministère des affaires étrangères, Nantes (hereafter MAE).

123 Sutton, "Algeria's Vineyards," 57.

124 General Assembly, "Motion sur le sort des vins français," February 25, 1965, Maison des agriculteurs français d'Algérie, SEAA 195, MAE.

125 Ministry of Foreign Affairs, September 12, 1962, 2, SEAA 195, MAE. The memo noted that "stopping the commercialization of wines of a doubtful origin is

one of the rare means we have at our disposal to help the legitimate Algerian authorities stop the acts of pillage that have occurred over the last two months."

126 Telegram sent from the MAE, signed Gorse, August 7, 1963, SEAA 195, MAE.

127 Juliette Minces, "M. Tamzali avait laissé 1.500 fr!," *Révolution africaine*, no. 41, November 1963, 9–10.

128 "Les Mirages de l'EurAfrique," *Révolution africaine*, no. 9, March 30, 1963, 16–17.

129 Decree 63–24 of January 14, 1963 (published in the *Journal official de la République Algérienne Démocratique et Populaire* [*JORA*] on January 25, 1963) stipulated that "the importation of liquid food oil and oilseeds falls under the competence of the Algerian Republic" and that the "ONACO is the only [body] that is authorized to negotiate their purchase or oversee their importation." According to some, this was a punishment against the region of Kabylia, which had been the stronghold of the 1963 insurrection against the state led by Hocine Aït Ahmed (Oulebsir, *L'olivier*, 9).

130 Oulebsir, *L'olivier*, 65.

131 Titouh, Mazari, and Meziane, "Contribution to Improvement."

132 Annuaire économique de l'Algérie, 1964–1965, 256, Ministère de l'économie nationale, Algérie, FOL-03W-181, BNF.

133 Georges Mutin, "Le commerce extérieur de l'Algérie en 1964," *Revue de géographie de Lyon* 40, no. 4 (1965): 345–65; and *JORA* of November 13, 1964, 1213, 21/PO, MAE.

134 "Arrestation de fonctionnaires de l'ONACO," *Alger républicain*, March 31, 1964, 1, archives of Daniel Guérin, F-721–84, LC. The French embassy also reported on these issues: "Application du système de l'autogestion dans les exploitations agricoles de l'Oranie," March 9, 1964, 7, Service de liaison avec l'Algérie (29QO), MAE. Participants in a meeting of the chamber of commerce in the summer 1964 called ONACO a "monster" and went so far as to use expletives describing the organization. Letter from the French consul general in Oran to the ambassador, June 30, 1964, 29QO/80, MAE.

135 "Discours de M. Boumaza à l'occasion de la première foire internationale d'Alger," October 1964, 29QO/67, MAE.

136 OFALAC, Conseil consultatif, 53rd séance, October 29, 1960, 14CAB/24, GGA, ANOM.

137 Letter from Paul Chauvin to the delegate general, January 19, 1960, Algiers, 15CAB/154, GGA, ANOM.

138 "Interview with Paul Delouvrier," published in *Entreprise*, no. 53, September 26, 1959, 30, 81F/965, ANOM.

139 "Questions générales," excerpt of a talk by Jean Vibert, *Travail et méthodes*, April 1961, 33–34, F/12/11810, Commerce et industrie, AN.

140 "Questions générales," 33–34.

Chapter Three: Decolonization and the Constantine Plan

1 Berque, *Les Arabes, d'hier à demain*, 90.

2 Berque and Massignon, "Dialogue sur 'Les Arabes,'" 1506.

3   Berque and Massignon, "Dialogue sur 'Les Arabes,'" 1506.

4   See Meynaud, "Qu'est-ce que la technocratie?" Delphanie Dulong claims that
    this new model of politics "set technical competence in management against
    political representation, economic efficacy against juridical regularity, planning
    against law, and the executive [branch] against the legislative" (*Moderniser
    la politique*, 287). Technocracy was a major source of anxiety and interest in
    the 1950 and 1960s, as evidenced by the plethora of works published on the
    subject, such as Cottier, *La technocratie, nouveau pouvoir*; Duclos, *Gaullisme,
    technocratie, corporatisme*; and Lefebvre, *Position*. For a laudatory analysis of
    industrial civilization, see Nef, *La naissance de la civilisation industrielle*.

5   Harbi, *Une vie debout*, 56.

6   Bourdieu and Sayad, *Le déracinement*, 108.

7   Cohen, "The Algerian War, the French State and Official Memory."

8   Algerian Muslims had been granted French nationality but not citizenship.
    They possessed limited political rights until the constitution of 1958 was
    adopted (Shepard, *The Invention of Decolonization*, 31–33).

9   "Interview with Paul Delouvrier."

10 Ross, *Fast Cars, Clean Bodies*, 170.

11 Kuisel, *Capitalism and the State*, 248.

12 Bourdin, "Des intellectuels à la recherche d'un style de vie."

13 Nord, *France's New Deal*, 8.

14 Clarke, *France in the Age of Organization*, 34.

15 Centre d'études des complexes sociaux, "Manifeste d'Économie et Human-
    isme," 1942, 12, Archives de l' de la revue Économie et Humanisme (EH) 183 II 1,
    Archives municipales de Lyon (hereafter AML).

16 Chamedes, "The Catholic Origins of Development," 62.

17 Centre d'études des complexes sociaux, "Manifest d'économieie et human-
    isme," 16.

18 Lebret, "Avant-projet de manifeste," *Économie et humanisme*, 1955, 59–69, EH
    183 II 1, AML.

19 Lebret, "Avant-projet de manifeste," 66.

20 Lebret, "Avant-projet de manifeste," 66.

21 Lebret, "Avant-projet de manifeste," 44.

22 Chenu, *Paul Delouvrier*, 91; Rouban, "Un inspecteur des finances atypique,"
    17–18.

23 Hellman, *The Knight-Monks of Vichy France*, 234.

24 Massé, "Les principes de la planification française." For more on his approach
    to economic planning, see Massé, *Le plan ou l'anti-hasard*.

25 Massé, "Les principes de la planification française," 113.

26 Ross, *Fast Cars, Clean Bodies*, chap. 4; Foucault, *Les mots et les choses*.

27 Chappel, *Catholic Modern*, 200.

28 Mirowski and Plehwe, *The Road from Mont Pèlerin*, 10.

29 Denord, "French Neoliberalism and Its Divisions," 45.

30 Burgin, *The Great Persuasion*; Denord, "The Origins of Neoliberalism in
    France"; Audier, *Le colloque Walter Lippmann*.

31 Kuisel, *Capitalism and the State*, 249. Michel Foucault defines neoliberalism in terms of the state's drive to ensure the principle of competition and "govern for the market," which he traces to the early example of German ordoliberalism in the 1930s. Foucault, *The Birth of Biopolitics*, 121.

32 CIRL, quoted in Denord, "The Origins of Neoliberalism," 14.

33 Denord, "French Neoliberalism and Its Divisions," 49.

34 Whyte, *The Morals of the Market*, 37.

35 Quoted in Mirowski and Plehwe, "Introduction," in *The Road from Mont Pèlerin*, 25.

36 Boussard, "Roland Maspétiol, une figure marquante de l'économie rurale."

37 This law granted the French state exceptional military powers to "safeguard" the Algerian territory against terrorism. According to Benjamin Stora, the legislation "authoriz[ed] the government to set in place a program of economic expansion, social progress, and administrative reform in Algeria, enabling it to take all exceptional measures in view of reestablishing order, protecting persons and property, and safeguarding the territory" (*Algeria, 1830–2000*, 46).

38 For more on economic modernization under the Fourth Republic, see Rioux, "Pierre Mendès France modernisateur." François Denord mentions the activities of both Robert Lacoste and Robert Maspétiol in "The Origins of Neoliberalism in France."

39 Cotta, "Les perspectives décennales du développement économique de l'Algérie."

40 These individuals included Jean Vibert, Yves LePortz, and Jacques Gabory.

41 Rousso, *De Monnet à Massé*, 11.

42 Massé also headed the steering committee of the Caisse d'équipement du développement de l'Algérie (CEDA; Fund for the Development of Algeria) which was responsible for organizing partnerships between public funds and private investments.

43 Interview with René Mayer.

44 Ordonnance 45–2283 of October 9, 1945, last modified August 4, 2018, https://www.legifrance.gouv.fr/loda/id/JORFTEXT000000521942/2020-10-09/.

45 Suleiman, *Politics, Power, and Bureaucracy*, 46.

46 Nord, "Reform, Conservation, and Adaptation," 117.

47 Lemoine, "Paul Delouvrier et l'Algérie," 46.

48 Massé had been trained at the prestigious École nationale des ponts et chaussés and Bouakouir was also a polytechnicien. Pierre Chaussade, who has been called the spiritual father of the Constantine Plan, was a graduate of the ENA. Michel Piquard, who was in charge of economic affairs, was another prominent *énarque* (ENA graduate). Yves LePortz, the general inspector of finances, was a graduate of Sciences Po. Martin Evans notes the large role played by "specialist civil servants," noting that Piquard and Vibert had been working on welfare policies in mainland France since 1954 (*Algeria*, 242).

49 Suleiman, *Politics, Power, and Bureaucracy*, 127.

50 Jacques Rueff advised de Gaulle in 1958 and was central to the creation of the Pinay-Rueff Plan (1958) and the Armand-Rueff Committee (1959–62). Both initiatives

sought to attenuate the effects of protectionism, leading Denord to view them as a revival of interwar neoliberalism ("French Neoliberalism," 61).

51 Chenu, *Paul Delouvrier*, 35.

52 Yves Mény demonstrates the close cooperation between the ENA, the private sector, and the state in *La corruption de la République*. Also see Bourdieu and Boltanski, "La production de l'idéologie dominante," 53.

53 Nathan and Delouvrier, *Politique économique de la France*.

54 Rouban, "Un inspecteur des finances atypique," 12.

55 Nathan and Delouvrier, *Politique économique de la France*, 254.

56 The hope that private interests would supplement state funding was clear in the organization of the CEDA. The body sought to invest twenty million francs in Algeria over five years, but planners envisioned that only half of this amount would come from public funds. The rest of the money would come from the private sectors.

57 Harbi and Meynier, *Le FLN: Documents et histoire*, 37.

58 Connelly, *A Diplomatic Revolution*, 109–10.

59 Jennifer Johnson shows that health care was a key component of this strategy in *The Battle for Algeria*.

60 Stora, "Le massacre du 20 août 1955."

61 Branche, *La torture et l'armée*.

62 Peterson, "Counterinsurgent Bodies," 12; Leroux, "Promouvoir une armée révolutionnaire."

63 The principles of counterinsurgency played a central role in urban planning, influencing the built environment during the war. See Henni, *Architecture of Counterrevolution*.

64 On December 21, 1958, de Gaulle was elected president by an electoral college.

65 Shepard, *The Invention of Decolonization*, 50.

66 According to Allistair Horne, when Delouvrier said to de Gaulle that he believed Algeria would be independent, the president replied, "in twenty-five years, Delouvrier, in twenty-five years" (*A Savage War of Peace*, 310).

67 "Economic Project for Algeria," December 12, 1958, Foreign Office (FO) Records, 371/131682, National Archives of the United Kingdom, Kew (hereafter NAK).

68 Déclaration Paul Delouvrier sur l'Algérie, December 20, 1958, JT 13h (Radiodiffusion Télévision Française), accessed August 11, 2019, http://www.ina.fr/video /CAF91054810.

69 In an interview conducted in 1988, Delouvrier said that he regularly traveled to Paris and saw Monnet, adding that their discussions focused on the situation in Algeria. P. Delouvrier, Interview by F. Duchêne, May 5, 1988, Jean Monnet Collection, FD/5.5.88/Rév 1, 1, Historical Archives of the European Union, Florence (hereafter HAEU).

70 Commissariat général au plan, "Analyse de la situation générale," [fall 1958?], Archives of CEDA, B-0024875, Centre des archives économiques et financières, Savigny-le-Temple (hereafter CAEF).

71 De Wailly and Gabory, "La protection des industries algériennes," Mission d'études pour l'Algérie, November 10, 1959, Paris, F/60/4012, AN; M. Brillaud, "Établissement du Plan de Constantine," May 5, 1960, 46, B-0024876, CAEF.

72 Delouvrier, interview by Duchêne, 7.

73 Monnet, *Memoirs*, 392.

74 Letter from Pierre Massé to Paul Delouvrier, June 2, 1960, F/60/4011, AN.

75 Conseil supérieur du Plan de l'Algérie, meeting on March 31, 1960, F/60/4014, AN.

76 Interview with René Mayer.

77 Marié, *Les Terres et les mots*, 59.

78 Direction of the Plan and Economic Studies, "Directives pour la préparation des plans régionaux," February 24, 1959, Délégation générale du gouvernement en Algérie, 9150/253, ANOM.

79 Press conference, "Le délégué général du gouvernement à la suite des travaux du Conseil supérieur du plan," February 10, 1959, 9, 81F/345, ANOM.

80 Press conference, "Le délégué général," 9.

81 Jean Vibert quoted in *Travail et méthodes, revue technique de la direction et de l'organisation des entreprises*, no. 155, April 1961, 35, F/12/11810, AN.

82 Lyons, *The Civilizing Mission*.

83 Délégation générale du gouvernement en Algérie, *Plan de Constantine*, 77.

84 Franklin, "A Bridge across the Mediterranean."

85 MacMaster, *Burning the Veil*, 81; Lazreg, *The Eloquence of Silence*.

86 Pulju, *Women and Mass Consumer Society*.

87 Seferdjeli, "French 'Reforms' and Muslim Women's Emancipation."

88 "Note pour M. le Délégué général, Objet: Plan de Constantine," May 18, 1960, 1/Paul Delouvrier Archives (DV)/32, Archives d'histoire contemporaine, Sciences Po, Paris (hereafter AHC).

89 Michel Piquard, "Note pour M. le Délégué général, Objet: Plan de Constantine, Rédaction no. 2," June 3, 1960, 5, 1/DV/32, AHC. See also Giacone, "Paul Delouvrier et le Plan de Constantine," 105.

90 Michel Piquard, "Note pour M. le Délégué général, Objet: Plan de Constantine," May 18, 1960, 3, 1/DV/32/.

91 Foucault, *The Birth of Biopolitics*, 201.

92 Direction of the Plan and Economic Studies, "Directives," February 24, 1959, 1, emphasis in original.

93 Service des études générales, "Slogans sur le Plan de Constantine," July 1959, 15CAB/138, GGA, ANOM. The same document can also be found in Algeria subseries (1H)/2571, Service historique de l'armée de terre (hereafter SHAT).

94 Service des études générales, "Slogans sur le Plan de Constantine."

95 Jean Vibert, "Note," July 13, 1959, Service des études générales, 1H/2571, SHAT, emphasis added.

96 M. Brillaud, "Établissement du Plan de Constantine," May 5, 1960, B-0024876, CAEF.

97 Conseil supéreiur du Plan de l'Algérie, meeting of June 22, 1959, Paris, 56, 14 CAB/239, ANOM.

98 Raymond Peyronnet, "La viticulture nationale à la présente heure: métropole et Algérie," Session of April 16, 1958, Agricultural Office of the Department of Algiers, CC, 185, CANA.

99 Kuisel, "L'*american way of life* et les missions françaises."

100 For more on the role of American social sciences in Algeria, see Davis, "The Transformation of Man."

101 Closon, *Un homme nouveau*, 15.

102 Kateb, "La statistique coloniale en Algérie." For a general history of the INSEE, see Touchelay, "L'INSEE des origines à 1961."

103 Letter from Francis-Louis Closon to the minister of the interior, December 15, 1947, B-0057574/1, CAEF.

104 Commissariat général au plan, "Note sur le Plan de Constantine et l'information," August 12, 1960, F/60/4011, AN.

105 Ministry of Algeria, "Perspectives décennales de développement économique de l'Algérie," March 1958, 23, B-0024875, CAEF.

106 Commissariat général au plan, "Note sur le plan de Constantine et l'information," August 12, 1960, F/60/4011, AN.

107 For example, the Food and Agriculture Organization of the UN (FAO) established a Mediterranean Development Project in the late 1950s. The Economic Conference of Countries in the Franc Zone of the Mediterranean and Africa was held at the chamber of commerce in Marseille in July 1959. Indicative of the new accent on Mediterranean space, the journal of reference for overseas business interests, *Marchés tropicaux* (*Tropical Markets*), was renamed *Marchés tropicaux et Méditerranée* (*Tropical and Mediterranean Markets*) in 1958.

108 Ferguson, *The Anti-politics Machine*.

109 Beirut, AUB (American University of Beirut) Archives, Linda Sadaqa Collection, Algeria Files, Carton 3, Dossier 2, File 209, Hizb al-Sha'b al-Jaza'iri, "Al-Tamyiz al-'Unsuri fi al-Jaza'ir," 1951. The publication seems to have been first written by the Algerian People's Party (PPA) and then reedited by MTLD, its successor organization.

110 René Arrus documents that colonial agriculture relied on a differential rent between lands that benefited from capitalist investment and those inhabited by the native population that served to reproduce labor power (*L'eau en Algérie*, 65).

111 Commissariat général au plan, "Note sur le Plan de Constantine et l'information."

112 Délégation générale du gouvernement en Algérie, "Note sur le projet du Plan de Constantine, 3e partie," June 25, 1960, Algiers, 6, 1/DV/32, AHC.

113 Davis, "The Transformation of Man," 80.

114 Salah Bouakouir, exposé fait devant le Conseil supérieur du plan, February 10, 1959, F/60/4014, AN.

115 Service des études générales, "Notice sur le signe, le label et le slogan du Plan de Constantine," [July 1959], 1H/2571, SHAT.

116 Davidson, *Only Muslim*, 58.

117 10ᵉᵐᵉ Région militaire, Bureau psychologique, "Contrôle et sondage des résultats de la propagande à destination des musulmans," 8, no date but likely March 1957, 1H/2460, SHAT.

118 Service des études générales, "Notice sur le signe, le label et le slogan du Plan de Constantine."

119 10ᵉᵐᵉ Région militaire, Bureau psychologique, "Les Fourberies de Si Djeh'a," no date but likely March 1957, 1H/2560, SHAT.

120 Service des études générales, "Plan de Constantine: Campagne d'information par le 5ᵉᵐᵉ Bureau," July 7, 1959, 1H/2471, SHAT.

121 Service des études générales, "Plan de Constantine: Campagne d'information par le 5ᵉᵐᵉ Bureau," July 7, 1959, 1H/2471, SHAT.

122 "Interview with Paul Delouvrier."

123 Résumée des exposés faits au cours du colloque de la Jonchère, September 1959, 1H/2522, SHAT.

124 Fyot, Dimensions de l'homme.

125 Charrasse, "Considérations sur le Plan de Constantine," 25.

126 M. Lecompte, "Pour une politique de décolonisation en Algérie," December 1959, Mission d'études, general secretary of Algerian affairs, F/12/11805, AN.

127 "Note concernant quelques réflexions sur le Plan," March 9, 1959, Cabinet du préfet d'Alger (91/1K)/1255–1256, ANOM.

128 Commandement en chef des forces en Algérie, "Note de service: Plan de Constantine—Campagne d'information," August 4, 1959, Algiers, Archives of the Sections administratives spécialisées (SAS), 3 SAS 137, ANOM.

129 Morin, De Gaulle et l'Algérie: Mon témoignage: 1960–1962 (Paris: Albin Michel, 1999), 349.

130 "Les 1,000 villages de M. Delouvrier," El Moudjahid, no. 42, May 25, 1959, 277.

131 Thénault, "How about 1958 in Algeria?" 149.

132 Albert O. Hirschman, François Perroux, and Gunnar Myrdal all sought to encourage more even development by encouraging certain poles of development that would then enjoy a trickle-down or spread out effect, discouraging the nation-state as a unit of economic analysis. They also relied on certain culturalist assumptions that explained the psychological or sociological obstacles to development. Hirschman, Strategy of Economic Development; Perroux, "Economic Space"; Myrdal, Rich Lands and Poor.

133 "Plan de Constantine: observations et analyses," June 23, 1961, GPRA 037.03.001, CANA.

134 Mourad Bourboune, "D'abord être nous-mêmes," Révolution africaine, January 4, 1964, 20–21.

135 "Les mirages de l'eurafrique," Révolution africaine, no. 9, March 30, 1963, 16–17.

136 "Plan de Constantine et économie algérienne," El Moudjahid, September 29, 1959, 6–7.

137 This is consistent with Jessica Whyte's argument that early neoliberal thinkers like Wilhelm Röpke tried to divorce colonialism from capitalism: "Against postcolonial demands for economic self-determination, the neoliberals mobilized their dichotomy between the market as a realm of mutuallly beneficial,

free, peaceful exchange, and politics as violent, coercive and militaristic" (*Morals of the Market*, 119).

138 "Politique générale de la révolution," [s.d.], GPRA 5.2, CANA.

139 Abdallah ʿAbd al-Daʾim, "Masir Faransa fi al-Jazaʾir," *Al-Adab*, March 1957, 237.

140 Al-Daʾim, "Masir Faransa fi al-Jazaʾir," 236.

141 "Plan de Constantine: Voici les résultats après un an d'application," *Croix*, Octocber 7, 1959, Fonds du gouvernement general de l'Algérie (2E), 1/320, CANA. Jim House argues that efforts to construct housing for Algerians under the Constantine Plan continued previous initiatives outlined under Mayor Chevallier, which had made use of sociological studies. House, "Intervening on 'Problem' Areas," 144.

142 Direction of the Plan and Economic Studies, "Note sur le plan et l'action économique et social," February 3, 1960, 2, 14CAB/239, ANOM.

143 "Plan de Constantine: Voici les résultats après un an d'application," *Croix*, October 7, 1959, 5, Fonds du gouvernement general de l'Algérie (2 E), 1/320, CANA.

144 Lefeuvre, *Chère Algérie*, 409.

145 This number excludes the appropriation of two major holdings that were concessions under the Second Empire. Elsenhans, *La guerre d'Algérie*, 621.

146 Collot, *Les institutions de l'Algérie*, 252.

147 The factory in Bône was nationalized in the fall of 1964, becoming a source of pride for the Algerian state. Vincent Beylier notes that the Algerian government wanted to create a "psychological shock" and "offer the Algerian people a symbol while drawing on the myth of the steel industry as the French government did previously" ("Le destin d'un grand projet industriel," 106).

148 David Theo Goldberg puts this slightly differently. He connects neoliberalism to antiracialism, which "suggests forgetting, getting over, moving on, wiping away the terms of reference, at best (or worst) a commercial memorializing rather than a recounting and redressing of the terms of humiliation and devaluation" (*The Threat of Race*, 21).

149 Lemoine, "Paul Delouvrier et l'Algérie," 60.

150 Morin, *De Gaulle et l'Algérie*, 7.

151 "Les investissements français en Algérie," [s.d.], GPRA 0032/006/001, CANA. Jeff Byrne makes a similar point in *Mecca of Revolution*, 128.

152 Interview with Mahmoud Ourabah, March 29, 2013, Paris.

153 Chabou, "Retrospective on the Social Housing Policy," 143.

154 Effose, "Paul Delouvrier et les villes nouvelles," 78.

155 Wendeln, "Contested Territory"; Chapman, *France's Long Reconstruction*.

156 Rabinow, *French Modern*.

Chapter Four: *Fellahs* into Peasants

1 Honneth, Kocyba, and Schwibs, "The Struggle for Symbolic Order."

2 Craig Calhoun highlights Algeria's importance for Bourdieu's thought in "Pierre Bourdieu and Social Transformation." Jane E. Goodman and Paul

Silverstein offer a more sustained reflection on how Algeria influenced Bourdieu's theoretical framework in their edited volume *Bourdieu in Algeria*. Also
see Yacine, "Pierre Bourdieu in Algeria"; and Grenfell, "Bourdieu in the Field."

3 Bourdieu, *Esquisses algériennes*, 79. Launay defines the fellahin by their sense of
dignity and relationship to the soil (*Paysans algériens*, 203).

4 I would like to thank Venus Bivar for helping to clarify my thinking on this
point. The canonical work on French attempts to modernize peasants in the
late nineteenth and early twentieth century is Weber, *Peasants into Frenchmen*.
For more on the role of peasants in French history see Wright, *Rural Revolution in France*; and Moulin, *Peasant and Society*.

5 Scott, *Seeing Like a State*.

6 Hodge, *Triumph of the Expert*, 218.

7 Moskowitz, *Seeing Like a Citizen*, 39. A number of historians have analyzed
failed colonial attempts at agricultural development in Africa—see Rizzo,
"Groundnut Scheme"; Anderson, *Histories of the Hanged*; Swearingen, *Moroccan Mirages*; and Ax, *Cultivating the Colonies*.

8 Gendarme, *L'économie de l'Algérie*, 53; Lefeuvre, *Chère Algérie*, 335. Also see
the following report: Commissariat général au plan, "Rapport de la sous-
commission des 'problèmes humains,'" November 1958, 6, 81F/2019, ANOM.

9 Wolf, *Peasant Wars*.

10 Lequy, "L'agriculture algérienne," 48.

11 Elsenhans, *La guerre d'Algérie*, 157.

12 Sivers, "Rural Uprisings as Political Movements," 45.

13 Mitchell, "Invention and Reinvention," 130. El Shakry also traces the work on
the peasantry's collective mentality to the interwar period (*The Great Social
Laboratory*, 100).

14 Mitchell, "Invention and Reinvention." Mitchell also argues in *Rule of Experts*
that the Third World peasant was constructed as backward, timeless, overly
sexualized, and violent.

15 Vollenhoven, *Essai sur le fellah algérien*, 167–70.

16 Launay, *Paysans algériens*, 68.

17 Launay, *Paysans algériens*, 62–64.

18 Lequy, "L'agriculture algérienne," 64.

19 Subaltern studies focused on "peasant consciousness" as a way of undermining
both nationalist and colonialist historiographies in India. A useful overview
of these debates can be found in Chaturvedi, *Mapping Subaltern Studies*. On
attempts to locate a subaltern class in Algeria, see Fanny Colonna's "The Nation's 'Unknowing Other.'" James Scott reflects on "the ordinary weapons of
relatively powerless groups" in *Weapons of the Weak* (xvi).

20 Rostow, *The Stages of Growth*.

21 Harbi, "Massacre in Algeria," *Le Monde diplomatique*, May 2005, http://
mondediplo.com/2005/05/14algeria. Historians of the Algerian War have debated what role rural organizations played in formal politics and the extent to
which their activities were merely responses to material hardships. Stora claims
that the majority of nationalists were urbanites and that French education

played a major role ("Faiblesse paysanne"). As a counterpoint, Neil MacMaster argues for the importance of peasant assemblies in modern forms of politics during the war (*War in the Mountains*).

22 Rey-Goldzeiguer, *Aux origines de la guerre d'Algérie*, 280.

23 LeSueur, *Uncivil War*; Mendras, "L'invention de la paysannerie."

24 Mendras, "L'invention de la paysannerie," 546.

25 Fallers borrowed his definition and rubric from American cultural anthropologist Alfred L. Kroeber ("Are African Cultivators to Be Called 'Peasants'?," 108).

26 Fallers, "Are African Cultivators to Be Called 'Peasants'?" 110.

27 Bourdieu and Sayad, *Le déracinement*, 88; Cote, "Hal Yujad Fallahun Jaza'iriyyun?"

28 Bourdieu, *Esquisses algériennes*, 93.

29 According to David Brion Davis, the dehumanization of the peasantry in medieval Europe was an important precursor to the racism directed against blacks and Jews in the early modern period ("Constructing Race," 12).

30 Chaulet, *La terre, les frères*, chap. 4.

31 Chaulet, *La terre, les frères*, 196. Historians have documented the various strategies employed by rural Algerians in the face of colonial violence. These included maintaining attachments to the extended family group (*'ayla*) that was the foundation of rural society, avoidance of the state, and forms of banditry and sabotage (MacMaster, *War in the Mountains*, 40; Flarier, "Le banditisme rural en Algérie"; Prochaska, "Fire on the Mountain"). Algerian historian Mostefa Lacheraf writes of a "deliberate resistance" that took on different forms in the face of attempts to expropriate land and repress the indigenous population, while Peter Von Sivers argues that rural communities' propensity for revolt in the nineteenth century can be explained in terms of their "partial self-sufficiency coexist[ing] with only a slight market dependency" (Lacheraf, *L'Algérie: Nation et société*, 23; Von Sivers, "Rural Uprisings," 49).

32 The relationship between Islam and tradition in Algeria was taken up by Bourdieu in his letters to the Algerian historian André Nouschi (Bourdieu, *Esquisses algériennes*, 380–82; Colonna, *Eléments d'histoire sociale*, 11).

33 After his career in colonial agriculture, including working for the SAPs, Chellig occupied prominent positions under Algerian presidents Ben Bella and Boumediene.

34 Working Group on Rural Renovation, "Procès-verbal de la réunion du sous-groupe de travail 'finances'," December 22, 1960, 81F/203, ANOM.

35 Rabah Chellig, *La vie du fellah et du pasteur algériens* ([Algiers]: Ministère de l'agriculture et de la réform agraire, [1959]), Délégation générale du gouvernement en Algérie, Bibliothèque du moniteur, École des cadres, Commissariat au paysannat et aux sociétés agricoles de prévoyance, F/60/4016, AN.

36 Rabah Chellig, "L'évolution de la paysannerie algérienne," *Terre algérienne*, January 1, 1962, 7.

37 Conseil supérieur du Plan de l'Algérie, "Compte-rendu," June 22, 1959, F/60/4014, AN.

38 Conseil supérieur du Plan de l'Algérie, "Compte-rendu."

39 As Darcie Fontaine points out, these reforms were only seen as "humanitarian" after the regroupment camps were established, a shift that reflected Delouvrier's conviction that civilian—rather than military—authorities should control these spaces. She also stresses the role of Christian leaders (both Catholic and Protestant) in highlighting the plight of regrouped Algerians (who were labeled "refugees" in official reports). "Refugees, Sovereignty, and Humanitarian Anxiety: Regroupment Camps and the Limits of Universal Rights in the Algerian War of Independence," invited lecture, University of Ottawa, Gordon F. Henderson Series on the History of Refugees, November 11, 2016.

40 Alexis Monjauze, "Rénovation rurale en Afrique du Nord, aspects géographiques et communautaires," Extrait du numéro spécial du développement africain consacré à l'agriculture algérienne, October 1961, Algiers, F/60/4057, AN.

41 Kuby, *Political Survivors*.

42 Feichtinger, "'A Great Reformatory.'"

43 Henni, *Architecture of Counterrevolution*, 26.

44 Bourdieu and Sayad, *Le déracinement*.

45 Sacriste, "Les camps de 'regroupement,'" 404. Bourdieu and Sayad claim that when farmers ceased to see their activity as a real profession associated with the values of the fellah, they began to seek the advantages of salaried work outside of the agricultural sector (*Le déracinement*, 67).

46 Only seventeen percent of soft wheat was used for auto-consumption in 1955, as compared to fifty percent of durum and seventy-five percent of barley ([Ministry of Agriculture?], "Le marché des céréales en Algérie," [c. 1961], 10, SEAA 193, MAE; Henni, *La colonisation agraire*, 153).

47 Interview with Jean Gernignon, May 18, 2013, Algiers.

48 CEDA, "Aménagements à prévoir," April 2, 1962, 27, B-0024876, CAEF.

49 Claude Perret, "Planification et développement rural en secteur sous-développé, application à l'Algérie," May 1960, 1, F/60/4057, AN.

50 "Plan de Constantine, les SAP et les SCAPCO, moyen de développement rural," February 15, 1960, Inspection générale régionale, Cabinet of the Prefect of Algiers (91/1K)/1259, ANOM; National Assembly, "Annexe au procès-verbal de la séance du 4 mars 1954," 81F/2264, ANOM.

51 The mixed communes were administrative units created in 1866 in order to aid the transition from military to civil rule (Mussard, "Réinventer la commune?").

52 McDougall, *A History of Algeria*, 125.

53 MacMaster, *War in the Mountains*, 99–104.

54 See the discussions of this question in the Assemblée algérienne on December 6 and 7, 1951, and again on January 29, 1952.

55 Simoneau, Circulaire no. 125, February 25, 1959, Algiers, Commissariat au paysannat et aux SAP, Délégation générale du gouvernement en Algérie, 91/1K/1259, ANOM.

56 *Bulletin mensuel de la Caisse d'équipement pour le développement de l'Algérie*, no. 10, November 1961, 20327/1962, BIB AOM, ANOM.

57 Jaques Pélissier, "Attributions de l'inspection régionale des SAP," January 15, 1959, Commissariat au paysannat et aux SAP, 91/1K/1259, ANOM.

58 Jacques Herbier, "Les moniteurs du paysannat," *Bulletin mensuel de la Caisse d'équipement pour le développement de l'Algérie*, no. 10, November 1961, 32, 20327/1962, BIB AOM, ANOM.

59 Cepède taught at the INA in France (1947–79) and worked for the Ministry of Agriculture (1957–59) before presiding over the FAO (1969–73).

60 Notable experts included Chellig, Oulid Aissa (head of the Paysannat), André de Cambiare (director of the Laboratory of Rural Economy and Sociology in Algiers), Mouloud Feraoun (novelist and educator), and René Dumont (French ecologist and politician).

61 AFCAL, "Stages 5 juillet–5 aout 1963," F/60/4057, AN.

62 Oulid Aissa, "Perspectives agricoles et développement rural," *Terre algérienne*, January 8, 1962.

63 Letter from General Salan to M. Voilley, President de la Fédération des caisses de crédit agricole mutuel, June 19, 1959, 14CAB/120, ANOM.

64 "Tête-à-tête de Gaulle-Debré, création d'un corps de moniteurs agricoles musulmans," *Le Figaro*, August 11, 1959.

65 Letter from A. Grosrenaud, director of the regional agricultural school at Sidi-Bel-Abbès, to Beni Merzoug, head of the SAS of Fromentin, May 15, 1959, Sidi-Bel-Abbès, 4 SAS 116, ANOM.

66 Lebeau, *L'algriculture algérienne*, 13.

67 Farmer, *Rural Interventions*, 14.

68 CEDA, "Exécution du programme d'équipement public 1959, chapitre 3, agriculture," 23, 81F/2025, ANOM.

69 J. Gonot, "Note d'ensemble concernant les Sociétés agricoles de prévoyance et l'action du paysannat en Algérie," 1955, 8, Inspection générale des finances, F/60/4001, AN.

70 CEDA, "Exécution du programme d'équipement public 1959," 26.

71 Gonot, "Note d'ensemble"; Commission d'études pour la réforme agraire, Département d'Orléansville, "Procès-verbal," February 18, 1959, 6, 4 SAS 119, ANOM.

72 Commission d'études pour la réforme agraire, Département d'Orléansville, "Procès-verbal," February 18, 1959, 9, 4 SAS 119, ANOM.

73 Directive addressed to the head officers of the SAS, "À propos d'une politique de l'arbre," November 19, 1959, Algiers, 2, Inspection général des affaires algériennes, Délégation général du gouvernement en Algérie, 4 SAS 119, ANOM.

74 J. Gonot, inspecteur général des finances, "Note d'ensemble concernant les Sociétés agricoles de prévoyance et l'action de paysannat en Algérie,"1955, 49, F/60/4001, AN.

75 J. Gonot, "Note d'ensemble concernant les sociétés agricoles de prévoyance," 49.

76 Jacques Pélissier, Direction de l'agriculture et des forêts, "L'indispensable révision," Algiers, November 4, 1959, 9314/144, ANOM.

77 "Commission d'études pour la réforme agraire," 8.

78 CEDA, "Exécution du programme d'équipement public 1959," 24.

79 "Note d'ensemble concernant les sociétés agricoles," 8, F/60/4001, AN.

80 Adas, *Machines as the Measure of Man*.

81 Bivar, *Organic Resistance*; Farmer, *Rural Interventions*.

82 The money allotted to the functioning of the SAPs increased from 135 million francs in 1956–57 to 2 billion in 1961 (Collot, *Les institutions de l'Algérie*, 249). Marcel Lanata, "Plan de développement économique et social de l'Algérie. Les Sociétés agricoles de prévoyance," April 1, 1959, Algiers, 2, Inspection régionale des SAP, Région d'Alger, 91/1K/1259, ANOM.

83 Delouvrier repeatedly pointed to the need to democratize the SAPs. See Letter from Paul Delouvrier to Djilali Kaddari, March 17, 1960, 14CAB, ANOM. Economic Committee, "Réunion no. 111," March 14, 1960, Algiers, 6, Délégation générale du gouvernement en Algérie, 14CAB/24, ANOM.

84 Letter from M. Arnaud, president of SAP of Ténès, to the chief of the SAS of Fromentin, July 5, 1958, 4 SAS 116, ANOM.

85 Letter from Captain Juteau, head of the SAS of Oughat Haouara, to the colonel of Médéa, "Contrôle de la vente des céréales par les Docks SAP," November 28, 1959, 3 SAS 137, ANOM.

86 Letter from the prefect of the department of Titteri, "Campagne céréalière—circulation des céréales," November 28, 1959, 3 SAS 137, ANOM.

87 Letter from the colonel of Constantine to the president of the SAP of Constantine, November 16, 1959, 9314/145, ANOM; Launay, *Paysans algériens*, 231.

88 M. Auboyneay, "Report," August 8, 1962, 18, Inspection générale des finances, B-0008706, CAEF.

89 Article 2 of the August 28, 1952 decree that created the SAPs defined the organizations' goals as promoting traditional agriculture and providing credit. As Marius Hautberg and Maurice Parodi write, the president of a SAP was subject to conflicting logics: "His responsibility as a banker [was] measurable and controllable while his responsibility as a promoter of traditional agriculture [was] not quantifiable" (*Étude sur le secteur agricole*, 12).

90 Gonot, "Note d'ensemble."

91 Working Group on Rural Renovation, "Procès-verbal de la réunion du sous-groupe de travail études économiques et techniques du 9 février 1961," February 15, 1961, Algiers, 4, Secrétariat général de l'administration, 81F/203, ANOM.

92 As Sara Berry has shown, opening up colonial economies to globalization was "less a time of transition—from isolation to global incorporation, from social eulogium to turbulence, from collective solidarity to fragmented alienation—than an era of intensified contestation over custom, power, and property" (*No Condition Is Permanent*, 8).

93 Guichard, "Problèmes ruraux en Algérie," 70.

94 "Report on the functioning of the SAPs," 1955, 44, General Inspection of Finances, F/60/4001, AN; M. Auboyneau, "Rapport sur les travaux de l'Inspection générale des finances en Algérie (1959–1962)," August 9, 1962, 15, Inspection générale des finances, B-0008706, CAEF.

95 Letter from André Jacomet, "Commercialisation des céréales—récupération des prêts consentis par les SAP," May 24, 1960, Algiers, 4 SAS 116, SHAT; "Les institutions locales et la mise en valeur du bled algérien," July 5, 1960, Inspection générale des finances, 81F/2250, ANOM.

96 Guichard, "Problèmes ruraux en Algérie," 71.

97 *Almanach du paysan algérien* (Algiers: SAP, 1959), BIB AOM 46972, ANOM.

98 In the Qur'an, the verb *radiya* means to be well-pleased or satisfied, usually in the sense of having the approbation of God. *Rizq* specifically indicates that sustenance has been provided by God. As written above, the Hadith is mistaken, in that it should be "radhiya Allahu minhu" rather than "'anhu." I have corrected the existing typos.

99 Hautberg and Parodi, *Étude sur le secteur agricole*, 3.

100 "Crédit agricole en Algérie," [s.d.], 8, B-0024832, CAEF.

101 Louis Lebeau, director of the CACAM, "Quelques aspects particuliers du crédit agricole en Algérie," [s.d.], 9, B-0024832, CAEF.

102 "Note sur les organismes de crédit agricole en Algérie," [s.d.], B-0024832, CAEF.

103 Letter from General Salan to M. Voilley, June 19, 1958, Algiers, 14CAB/120, ANOM. A third organization for credit, the Caisse de prêts agricoles (CPA; Bank of Agricultural Loans), offered funds to farmers who had experienced natural disasters that prevented them from obtaining funds from the other two organizations.

104 "Projet de décret, portant réforme du crédit agricole mutuel en Algérie," May 31, 1958, 81F/2268, ANOM. In Sidi-Bel-Abbès, a formal complaint was filed by a number of farmers claiming that European members were misusing the credit (to fund agriculture in the metropole, for example) and that they tended to overlook the fellahin and small-scale agriculturalists (Letter from Louis Lebeau, director of CACAM, to Jacques Pélissier, director of agriculture and forests, July 7, 1958, 14CAB/120, ANOM).

105 General Planning Commission to the governor general of Algeria, "Elaboration d'une politique agricole," March 30, 1955, 81F/2268, ANOM.

106 R. Putod, "Les SAP et les SCAPCO, moyen de développement rural," February 15, 1960, 25, Inspection générale de l'agriculture, 5 SAS 241, ANOM.

107 Cabinet of the minister, "Reformes agricoles," 1957, sub-prefect of Greater Kabylia (9150)/180, ANOM.

108 [Commission of Agriculture and Rural Development?], "La réforme de l'agriculture en Algérie et l'aide aux pays sous-développés," June 1960, 4, F/60/4057, AN.

109 Letter from the departmental inspector of social laws in agriculture to the head of the SAS of Frometin, April 24, 1959, Orléansville, 4 SAS 116, ANOM; letter from the secretary of the interior of Algerian affairs to the minister of the state, "Projet de décret: Réforme de certains contrats d'associations agricoles en Algérie," October 8, 1956, 19950236/12, Le Centre des hautes études sur l'Afrique et l'Asie modernes (hereafter CHEAM), AN.

110 For a summary of these previous attempts see Elsenhans, *La guerre d'Algérie*, 620–21.

111 Jacques Pélissier, "La réforme foncière," *Europe-France outremer*, no. 354, May 1959, 54.

112 Bivar, *Organic Revolution*, 29.

113 Kateb, *Européens, "indigènes" et juifs*, 218.

114 Ageron, *Histoire de l'Algérie contemporaine*, 2:498–99.

115 This goal was almost immediately deemed too conservative. Commission de vérification des comptes des entreprises publiques, 1959 et 1960, "Rapport particulier sur les comptes et la gestion de la CAPER," July 1, 1962, 5, 29QO/77, MAE.

116 M. Huet, "État d'avancement des opérations de réforme agraire," April 6, 1958, Chambre d'agriculture d'Alger, 9150/180, ANOM.

117 This area was estimated to represent thirty-five hectares of dry crops on the plateaus, four to ten hectares in irrigated areas, and one hectare in oasis regions ("La réforme agraire est en marche en Algérie," [s.d.], 81F/451, ANOM). In 1956, the Conseil d'administration had fixed this revenue at thirty thousand francs per year for each member of the family, while in 1954, the average net revenue among the Algerian peasantry was twenty-two thousand francs per person per year ("Rapport particulier," 28).

118 Interview with René Mayer.

119 Departmental Commission of Agrarian Reform for Orléansville, "Extrait du procès-verbal: quelques obstacles au développement rurale dans le département d'Orléansville," July 17, 1959, 91/1K/1259, ANOM.

120 Commission de vérification des comptes des entreprises publiques, "Rapport particulier," 51.

121 "Comité économique, réunion no. 2," March 7, 1960, 14CAB/24, ANOM.

122 By two decrees on October 20, 1956, CAPER acquired the domains of Cie Algérienne (66,000 hectares) and the Cie Genevoise (15,000 hectares). The decree of July 13, 1956, also permitted CAPER to acquire forestry domains, most notably those belonging to the Société des Hamendas et de la Petite Kabylie, which totaled fifty-five thousand hectares. In December 1961, CAPER had acquired 165,236 hectares, almost half of which were from these large estates (81F/2333, ANOM).

123 Lefeuvre, *Chère Algérie*, 376. On the eve of independence, the properties belonging to the French were estimated at 2.5 million hectares, while CAPER had acquired 196,000 hectares. Secretary of state, "Note sur l'aide spécifique à la réforme agraire," April 24, 1963, 29QO/78, MAE.

124 Planners acknowledged that high costs prevented CAPER from offering a comprehensive solution. Instead, the stated goal was to pursue these projects as an "example of perfection." Rural Renovation Committee under the Superior Council of Social Promotion for the Constantine Plan, "Principes pour des décisions à prendre sur la rénovation rurale de l'Algérie," January 17, 1961, 2, 81F/203, ANOM.

125 French Embassy in Algeria, "L'autogestion en Algérie, concept et réalité," March 9, 1964, 21, 29QO/80, MAE.

126 Malley, *The Call From Algeria*, 146.

127 Ajl, "Farmers, Fellaga, and Frenchmen," 185. *Fellaga* was a common word for anticolonial fighters in North Africa.

128 Quoted in Hajji, *Mutanaww'at Muhammad Hajji*, 457.

129 El Shakry, *The Great Social Laboratory*, 210.

130 The Bourdieusian tradition heavily influenced the Algerian social sciences after independence, specifically in the creation of the Centre algérien de recherche agronomique, sociologique et économique (Algerian Center for Agronomic, Sociologic, and Economic Research).

131 Dib, *L'incendie*, 40.

132 Dib, *L'incendie*, 40.

133 Driss, "L'irruption de Makkam Ech-Chahid," 66.

134 Bivar, *Organic Resistance*, 92.

135 Bivar, *Organic Resistance*, 91.

136 Fanon, *The Wretched of the Earth*, 13.

137 B. Marie Perinbam argues that Fanon's writings reflected his commitments to the Algerian Revolution and that his image of the peasantry should be read as "a rallying idea, a myth, a symbol of committed action" ("Fanon and the Revolutionary Peasantry," 444).

Chapter Five: Communism in a White Burnous

1 The two main bodies of the FLN were the GPRA, which had had been created in 1958, and the Conseil national de la révolution algérienne (CNRA; National Council of the Algerian Revolution), which had been created in August 1956 at the Soummam Congress.

2 Affaires sociales, Meeting of May 29, 1962, 12.2, CNRA, CANA; Malek, "La place seconde des intérêts économiques," 108. For more on the role of oil during decolonization, see Musso, "Oil Will Set Us Free."

3 He asked, "Until now, unity has been realized due to the fact [of fighting] the enemy; tomorrow, what will we have to replace this factor that has always assured our unity?" (Affaires sociales, meeting of May 29, 1962).

4 "Interview with Ben Bella," 124.

5 "Constitution of Algeria (1963)," Marxist History Archive, 2001, https://www.marxists.org/history/algeria/1963/09/constitution.htm.

6 Ben Bella was elected prime minister in September 1962 and became president in September 1963.

7 Getachew, *Worldmaking after Empire*. The concept of stretching Marxism comes from Fanon, *The Wretched of the Earth*. Sara Salem explores decolonization in Egypt through the lenses of Marxism and the thought of Frantz Fanon in *Anticolonial Afterlives in Egypt*.

8 There are parallels with Julius Nyerere's policy of *ujamaa* in Tanzania, which has also been discounted as a mere example of "state authoritarianism confirming the generalized dysfunction of postcolonial African politics" (Lal, *African Socialism*, 4). Byrne argues that the founders of the FLN were "method men" who were enamored by the "utilitarian abstraction of reality" (*Mecca of Revolution*, 55). Others have claimed that Ben Bella's emphasis on an Arab Islamic identity provided a model for the Islamic Salvation Front (FIS) during the civil war (Bouamama, *Algérie: Les racines de l'intégrisme*).

9   French embassy in Algeria, "Analyse du programme de Tripoli" [early September 1962?], 6, Algiers, 29QO/17, MAE.

10 This is not to deny that social practices embedded in an Islamic worldview also shaped how material life was organized on the ground; Augustin Jomier demonstrates how the ʿulamaʾs interpretation of Islam helped to legitimize the commercial activities of merchants in the M'zab, for example (*Islam, réforme et colonisation*, chap. 6). The use of Islam as a racial marker can be seen in the classifications of Turkish and Greek populations after the dissolution of the Ottoman Empire (Shields, "The Greek-Turkish Population Exchange"). Pakistan and Israel have been described as particular forms of ethno-religious nationalisms; see Devji, *Muslim Zion*; and Shepard, "Algerian Nationalism."

11 Ali Haroun offers a firsthand account of the crisis in *L'été de la discorde*; see also Benkhedda, *L'Algérie à l'indépendance*.

12 Mohammed Boudiaf returned from exile in 1992, when he assumed the role of the chairman of the High Council of State following the annulment of election results. He was assassinated on live television on June 29, 1992.

13 Yacono, "Les pertes algériennes."

14 Boumaza, "Politique économique du gouvernement," speech in front of the National Assembly, December 30, 1963, 11.

15 Thénault, "L'OAS à Alger en 1962."

16 Raffinot and Jacquement, *Le capitalisme de l'État algérien*, 49.

17 Adamson, *Algeria: A Study*, 113.

18 Abbas, *L'indépendance confisquée*, 96. The "white burnous" referred to the traditional hooded cloak worn in Algeria that was associated with religious purity.

19 Dawisha, *Arab Nationalism*, 64–65.

20 Abbas, *L'indépendance confisquée*, 90. For more on the life and career of Ferhat Abbas, see Rahal, *L'UDMA et les Udmistes*.

21 McDougall, *Culture of Nationalism*, 92. For a cautionary tale against reifying legal frameworks, or mistaking them for lived experience, see Oualdi, "Nationality in the Arab World."

22 For a discussion of exceptions in which maternal filiation was accepted as a marker of nationality, see Mahiou, "La nationalité en Algérie," 400.

23 FLN, *La charte d'Alger*, 35.

24 Z. M., "Cela s'est passé un 19 juillet 1971…Décès du chanteur Ahmed Saber," Babzman, July 19, 2016, https://babzman.com/cela-sest-passe-un-19-juillet-1971 -naissance-du-chanteur-ahmed-saber/.

25 The refrain ("al-khidma wallat wujuh") is ambiguous, suggesting that connections and apperances played a role in securing a job. Ahmed Saber, El Khedma, El Feth (album), Productions Fouatih Ibrahim, available on Youtube: https:// www.youtube.com/watch?v=qap5gF1XLGQ.

26 McDougall, *A History of Algeria*, 264; Vince, *Our Fighting Sisters*, chap. 3.

27 Ahmed Saber, El Khayen, El Feth, Productions Fouatih Hrahim, available on Youtube: https://www.youtube.com/watch?v=gi4-GahNoOU.

28 Interview with Mohamed Mokrane, April 11, 2011, Algiers.

29 Interview with Mohamed Mokrane.

30 "Discours du Président Ben Bella du 28 septembre 1962 au 12 décembre 1962," December 4, 1963, 39, République Algérienne Democratique et Populaire, 1H/1799, SHAT.

31 Al-Jumhuriyya al-Jaza'iriyya al-Dimuqratiyya, *Al-Mu'tamar al-Awwal li-l-Fallahin*, October 25–27, 1963, 15, Maison méditerranéenne des sciences de l'homme (MMSH).

32 Jabhat al-Tahrir al-Watani, "Al-Dalil al-'Amali li-l-Tasyir al-Dhati fi al-Jaza'ir," [1963], Dossier 2, Folder 204, Linda Sadaqa Collection, AUB.

33 Chaulet, *La Mitidja autogérée*, 10.

34 Jean-François Kahn, "M. Ouzegane critique vivement les révolutionnaires de la phrase," *Le Monde*, September 2, 1964.

35 Byrne, "Our Own Special Brand of Socialism."

36 Johanna Bockman argues that Yugoslav economists mobilized neoclassical economics in constructing a non-Soviet socialism (*Markets in the Name of Socialism*). For works that analyze Algeria in terms of state capitalism, see Raffinot and Jacquement, *Le capitalisme de l'État algérien*; and Benhouria, *L'économie de l'Algérie*, 28.

37 Raffinot and Jacquement, *Le capitalisme de l'État algérien*; Benhouria, *L'économie de l'Algérie*, 28.

38 Ottaway and Ottaway, *Algeria*, 61.

39 A third and last set of reforms, announced on March 28, outlined measures for revenue distribution and income.

40 Adamson, *Algeria*, 117; Bennoune, *The Making of Contemporary Algeria*, 104.

41 Mahsas, *L'autogestion en Algérie*, 238–39.

42 Benhouria, *L'économie de l'Algérie*, 28.

43 Monique Laks claims that by the spring of 1964, only twelve thousand workers were involved in the other sectors of self-management, representing less than ten percent of the total population working in industry and construction (*Autogestion ouvrière et pouvoir politique*, 17).

44 Teillac, *Autogestion en Algérie*, 18.

45 Isnard, "Les structures de l'autogestion agricole en Algérie," 140.

46 Chaulet, *La Mitidja autogérée*.

47 Interview with Kamel Abdellah Khodja, September 14, 2015, Nice.

48 French embassy in Algeria, "Application du système de l'autogestion," March 9, 1964, 3, 29QO/80, MAE.

49 Letter from the French ambassador to the head of Algerian affairs, "Des difficultés de l'agriculture algérienne," November 30, 1964, Algiers, 16, SEAA 191, MAE.

50 Bouamama, *Algérie*, 11; Mahsas, *L'autogestion en Algérie*, 192.

51 From an interview on November 10, 1962, quoted in a letter from the French ambassador in Algeria to the head of Algerian affairs, January 8, 1963, 12, 21PO/194, CADN.

52 Courreye, *L'Algérie des oulémas*, 41–42. For an account of the organization's participation in the War of Independence, see McDougall, "S'écrire un destin"; and Saoud, *La place de l'Islam dans l'Algérie indépendante*, 127. Scagnetti discusses how the idea of an Algerian "personality" functioned after independence in "Identité ou personnalité algérienne? L'édification d'une algérianité."

53 McDougall discusses the influence that Nahda thinkers had on Tawfiq al-Madani (*Culture of Nationalism*, 235). For more recent works on the Nahda that situate the role of Middle Eastern thinkers in a global age of capital, see Hill, *Utopia and Civilisation*; Sheehi, *Modern Arab Identity*; and Khuri-Makdisi, "Inscribing Socialism into the Nahda."

54 FLN, *La charte d'Alger*, 18.

55 Seikaly, *Men of Capital*.

56 "Socialisme musulman en Algérie," January 1964, 7, 21PO/151, CADN.

57 For additional information on the journal's contributors as well as for more examples of its defense of a Muslim socialism, see Courreye, *L'Algérie des oulémas*, 259–63.

58 Gendarme, *L'économie de l'Algérie*, 132.

59 Renan, for example, claimed that from the late eighth to mid-thirteenth centuries, Arabic speakers in Iran and the south of Spain could not be considered "Arabs by blood" (*L'Islam et la science*, 24). He also claimed that the "inward turn instilled by the Muslim faith is so strong that all differences of race and nationality disappear with a conversion to Islam" (*L'Islam et la science*, 11). Al-Afghani agreed that Islam had hindered material development but did not see this as a logical outcome of religion. He also defended a more capacious understanding of Arabism rooted in the Arabic language ("Réponse du Cheik Gemmal Eddine" in Renan, *L'Islam et la science*, 44).

60 Vallin, "Muslim Socialism in Algeria," 54.

61 Gran, "Islamic Marxism in Comparative History," 119; and Merhavy, "Ecumenical Tendencies in Egypt."

62 Carré, *La légitimition islamique des socialismes arabes*, 247.

63 Al-Siba'i, *Ishtirakiyyat al-Islam*.

64 Reported in a letter from the French ambassador to the head of Algerian affairs, "Des références islamiques dans le socialisme algérien," September 9, 1963, Algiers, 4, 21PO/99, CADN. According to Sami Zubaida, while the *muhtasib* could not fix prices due to a preference in classical Islamic societies for freedom of contract, his main roles were the policing of markets (e.g., making sure that basic goods were not priced unreasonably) and the overseeing of public morals (*Law and Power*, 59).

65 'Abd al-Qadir Zubadiya, "Abhath Tarikhiyya: Ishtirakiyya," *al-Ma'rifa*, no. 1, May 1963, 30, 28–30.

66 Ahmed al-Sharbasi, "Ishtirakiyyat al-Islam," *al-Ma'rifa*, no. 4, August 1963, 3–8.

67 "Interview de M. Ahmed Tewfik al-Madani au quotidien algérois Ach-Cha'b," February 23, 1963, 21PO/99, CADN.

68 Ouzegane, *Le meilleur combat*, 146.

69 Byrne argues that "it was precisely because Algeria's cultural, religious, and human connections with the Maghreb and the Arab world were so profound that its new leaders judged them too dangerous to handle" (*Mecca of Revolution*, 176).

70 Makdisi, *The Culture of Sectarianism*.

71 Dawn, "The Origins of Arab Nationalism," 8.

72 Haim, *Arab Nationalism*.

73 Wien, *Arab Nationalism*, 190.

74 Gershoni, *Arab Responses to Fascism and Nazism*, 45.

75 El Shakry, *The Great Social Laboratory*, 66.

76 Wien, *Arab Nationalism*, 9.

77 Cleveland, *The Making of an Arab Nationalist*.

78 Tibi, *Arab Nationalism*, 206.

79 For the official government view of Algeria, see al-Dib, *'Abd al-Nasir wa-Thawrat al-Jaza'ir*. James Jankowski argues that Nasser identified more strongly with Egypt than with pan-Arabism in the 1950s ("Arab Nationalism in 'Nasserism,'" 151). Stenner describes in chapter 2 of *Globalizing Morocco* the multiple obstacles that Moroccan nationalists encountered in trying to promote their cause from Cairo after the 1952 Free Officers coup.

80 Fadi Bardawil shows that Algeria was an inspiration for a generation of Arab Marxists in *Revolution and Disenchantment*, 37–51.

81 Nasir Jabi, "'Ali al-Kanz, Masira bi-Alwan Balad," *Al-Quds*, November 8, 2020, https://www.alquds.co.uk/علي-الكنز-مسيرة-بألوان-بلد/.

82 'Amil, *Muqaddima Nadhariya*, 70.

83 'Amil, *Muqaddima Nadhariya*, chap. 7; and Guha, *Dominance without Hegemony*.

84 Al-Lajna al-Wataniyya li-Nasr al-Jaza'ir fi Lubnan, untitled document, April 1958, Beirut, file 204, Linda Saddiq Archives, AUB.

85 Shabab al-Ba'th al-'Arabi al-Ishtiraki, *Yawm al-Jaza'ir*, April 1958, Beirut, file 204, Linda Saddiq Archives, AUB.

86 "Al-Quwtali Yaqul Masir al-'Arab Murtabit bi-Masir al-Jaza'ir," *al-Ahram*, March 31, 1958, 4.

87 Halawani, *Al-Thawra al-Jaza'iriyya fi al-Sahafa al-Suriya, 1955–1957*.

88 Al-Adabiyya, *Al-Jaza'ir al-Mujahida*, 7.

89 Al-Shalqani, *Thawrat al-Jaza'ir*, 95.

90 Al-Shalqani, *Thawrat al-Jaza'ir*, 134.

91 'Allush, "Hawl Kitab Thawrat al-Jaza'ir," 78–80.

92 'Allush, "Hawl Kitab Thawrat al-Jaza'ir," 79.

93 'Allush, "Hawl Kitab Thawrat al-Jaza'ir," 78.

94 Although colonial administrators sought to prevent contact between Muslims from different regions, Allan Christelow and Arthur Asseraf show that Algerians participated in larger Mediterranean networks of information and politics (Christelow, *Algerians without Borders*; Asseraf, *Electric News*). It is important to note that what has often been framed as a "Berber crisis" or cultural division within Algerian nationalism was in fact "a political struggle in which culture was weaponized" (Vince, *The Algerian War*, 55). See also Guenoun, *La question Kabyle dans le nationalisme algérien*.

95 Courreye, *L'Algérie des oulémas*, 333.

96 Byrne, *Mecca of Revolution*, 178.

97 Ahmed Ben Bella, "Un Entretien avec Ben Bella," interview by Daniel Junqua, *Le Monde*, December 4, 1980, https://www.lemonde.fr/archives/article/1980/12/04/un-entretien-avec-m-ahmed-ben-bella-bull-je-rejette-un-dialogue-nord-sud-truque-et-moralisateur-bull-l-islamisme-offre-les-meilleures-chances-d-une-liberation-reelle_3072431_1819218.html.

98 Mokhtefi, *Algiers, Third World Capital*.

99 Apter, "Beyond Negritude."

100 "Un film anti-raciste pris à partie," *El Moudjahid*, vol. 2, May 25, 1959, 277.

101 "La question du Sahara: Neutralisme et coopération," *El Moudjahid*, November 1, 1961, 607.

102 "Un film anti-raciste," 277. The screening of the film provoked protests by various fascist groups. On May 11, 1959, commandos attempted to stop its projection in the theaters of Biarritz, Richelieu, and Paris. Censorship was eventually lifted due to popular protest ("Un film maudit?," *Droit et liberté*, June–July 1959, 3).

103 "Un film anti-raciste."

104 Letter from A. Chanderli to the minister of foreign affairs, January 19, 1960, Cairo, GPRA 036.02.002, CANA; emphasis added.

105 American Society of African Culture, *Pan-Africanism Reconsidered*, 13.

106 Mohammed Djeghri, "Premier jour de la tournée du Ministre de l'agriculture et de la réforme agraire," *Alger républicain*, November 13, 1962, 2. Also see *Révolution et travail*, August 12, 1964.

107 Land previously held by CAPER was also transformed into self-managed farms and cooperatives for war veterans under Boumediene. One plot of land owned by the Genevan Company near Sétif had been granted as a concession by the French state in 1853 and was expropriated by CAPER in 1956. It was transformed into a self-managed farm under Ben Bella, and then, finally, unveiled as a cooperative for the *anciens moudjahidines* in 1966 (French embassy in Algeria, "Note d'information: La constitution de coopératives agricoles d'anciens moudjahidines et les résistances du secteur autogéré," April 9, 1966, Algiers, 29QO/80, MAE).

108 On one self-managed property, the majority of the permanent workers were *junud* (ex-soldiers of the ALN) who were paid twelve dinars a day—the standard rate for agricultural workers. As they were "quite uninterested" in the running of the farm, most of the labor was done by seasonal workers (Tidafi, *L'agriculture algérienne et ses perspectives de développement*, 103).

109 "Le Sacrifice de tous est nécessaire à l'édification du socialisme," *Révolution et Travail*, February 6, 1964, 3, and "Volontariat du travail: Le barrage de l'Oued Fodda: 1er chantier national," *Révolution et travail*, February 6, 1964, 2.

110 "La page des brigadiers," *Révolution et travail*, January 9, 1964, 6.

111 "Des humbles par milliers donnent leurs économies au Fonds de solidarité nationale," *Alger républicain*, May 12–13, 1963, 1.

112 "2,500 fellahs au congrès nationale de l'autogestion agricole qui s'ouvre demain à Alger," *Alger républicain*, October 24, 1963, 1. Also see the letter from Bernard Gretter, consul of France in Blida to the ambassador, "Autogestion," February 24, 1964, 21PO/181, CADN, which also notes the dissatisfaction of agricultural workers with their salaries.

113 "Premier congrès des travailleurs agricoles du secteur autogéré: Allocation du Président Ben Bella," October 25, 1963, 8, 21PO/194, CADN.

114 Letter from M. Moreigne, Consul of France in Miliana to the French ambassador, "'Précongrès' du secteur agricole," October 26, 1963, 21PO/194, CADN.

115 "La Réforme agraire dans les comités de gestion," *Révolution et travail*, August 27, 1964, 5.

116 "2,500 fellahs au congrès national," 1.

117 Raptis, "Autogestion et bureaucratie en Algérie," 65.

118 Letter from Jean Thomas, French consul in Batna, to the French ambassador in Algeria, April 7, 1965, and telegram from the French embassy in Algeria, July 15, 1965, both in 21PO/194, CADN. Letter from the French ambassador to the director of Algerian affairs, "De l'autogestion rurale vue par le Ministre de l'agriculture," March 29, 1965, Algiers, French embassy in Algeria, 29QO/80, MAE.

119 For a study of attempts to introduce "socialism without socialists" in Egypt, see Abul-Magd, *Militarizing the Nation*, chap. 1.

120 "Alger: Pré-congrès des travailleurs agricoles," *Révolution et travail*, October 29, 1964, 7.

121 Bennoune, *The Making of Contemporary Algeria*, 106.

122 "Blida: Pré-congrès des travailleurs de la terre," *Révolution et travail*, October 22, 1964, 12.

123 Most notably, as mentioned above, directors of the self-management committees tended to be former SAP officers (Adamson, *Algeria*, 117). According to Mahsas, while the SAPs were gradually transformed into cooperative centers for agrarian reforms, they could not make up for their original sin of having failed to help the fellahin during colonization (*L'Autogestion en Algérie*, 185–86).

124 Daniel Guérin, "Quelques observations faites sur l'autogestion," December 1963, 5, F-721-82, Guérin Archives, LC.

125 Letter from the French ambassador to the director of Algerian affairs, "Les sociétés agricoles de prévoyance dans la révolution agraire," March 4, 1963, Algiers, 21PO/194, CADN. An anonymous report published by Algérie presse service noted the hostility of small farmers toward the SAPs and called for these organizations to disavow the political and psychological actions they had exercised under the Constantine Plan (Letter from the French ambassador in Algeria to the head of Algerian affairs, "Pré-congrès des paysans du secteur socialiste," October 22, 1963, Algiers, 7, 21PO/194, CADN).

126 In 1962 one fellah claimed that they did "not want communism or capitalism" but rather the opportunity to live the lifestyle of the "petit bourgeois" (Launay, *Paysans algériens 1960–2006*, 419).

127 Davis, *Granary of Rome*, chap. 1. For more on the policy of reforestation during the colonial period, see Duffy, *Nomad's Land*.

128 Amar Ouzegane, "Le reboisement: Test socialiste," *Révolution Africaine*, December 5, 1964, 3.

129 "Une grande journée de l'arbre," *Révolution et travail*, December 3, 1964, 5.

130 "Tous ce matin à l'Arbatache avec le frère Ben Bella," *Le Peuple*, April 25, 1965, 1.

131 Inspection générale des affaires algériennes, "À propos d'une politique de l'arbre," November 19, 1959, 3, 2 SAS 140, ANOM.

132 French embassy in Algeria, "L'agriculture algérienne," May 1964, 2, Service de la coopération, 29QO/80, MAE.

133 French embassy in Algeria, "Note sur le grand magasin, 'Les galeries de France' à Bône," February 22, 1964, 21PO/174, CADN.

134 "Les MPS: Une expérience concluante," Révolution et travail, August 13, 1964.

135 Tidafi, L'agriculture algérienne, 55. At one meeting of the chamber of commerce in Oran, a shopkeeper who was an ex-FLN militant proclaimed, "Votre ONACO c'est de la merde! En cent ans les Borgeaud ont fait moins de mal à ce pays que l'ONACO en une seule année." Letter from Jean-Félix Chavret, the French consul general in Oran, to the French ambassador, June 30, 1954, 2, 21PO/174, CADN.

136 République Algérienne Démocratique et Populaire, "Politique économique du gouvernement, exposé de Bachir Boumaza"; Ambassade de France en Algérie, "La nouvelle politique économique algérienne," January 13, 1964, 13, Mission économique et financière, 21PO/174, CADN.

137 Telegram from the French embassy in Algeria, October 17, 1962, 21PO/198, CADN.

138 "Le décret sur les biens vacants a une résonance politique et présente une importance capitale," Alger républicain, March 26, 1963, 2.

139 "Le décret sur les biens vacants."

140 Letter from Mme Fernande Schmitt to H. Boumediene, October 26, 1965, Rovigo, 21PO/198, CADN.

141 Schmitt to Boumediene.

142 French embassy in Algeria to the Ministry of Foreign Affairs in Algiers, April 12, 1963, 3, Algiers, 21PO/198, CADN.

143 "Voici les successeurs de Borgeaud," Révolution Africaine, April 6, 1963, 12.

144 Fontaine, Decolonizing Christianity, 184.

145 Boualem Khalfa, "Maîtres de notre destin," Alger républicain, March 31–April 1, 1963, 2.

146 Letter from J. Merleaud, consul of France in Djidjelli to the French ambassador, "Réforme agraire," October 7, 1963, 3, 21PO/199, CADN.

147 "Congrès des travailleurs du secteur autogéré agricole les 25, 26 et 27 octobre," Alger républicain, October 9, 1963. This is also quoted in Mahsas, L'autogestion en Algérie, 192.

148 Stora, Les trois exils, 149.

149 Stora, Les trois exils, 167.

150 Courreye, L'Algérie des oulémas, 269.

151 "Posons les vrais problèmes," Le Peuple, January 17, 1964, 21PO/151, CADN. The text also appeared in a number of other newspapers under a different title.

152 "Posons les vrais problèmes."

153 Association El Qiyam, "Les valeurs religieuses de l'Islam," Revue de presse, February 1964, 21PO/151, CADN.

154 Quoted in Burgat and Dowell, The Islamic Movement in North Africa, 55.

155 Initial coverage of the event can be found in "Débat sur l'Islam et le socialisme," *Révolution et Travail*, February 20, 1964, 7, as well as in the letter from the French ambassador in Algeria to the head of Algerian affairs, "Islam et Socialisme," February 13, 1964, Algiers, 29QO/17, MAE. For additional criticism of the talk, see "À propos du socialisme et l'Islam," *Révolution et travail*, February 27, 1964, 2.

156 Henri Simon to the French ambassador in Algeria, "Diffusion d'une déclaration du Président des ulémas en Algérie," May 6, 1964, Bône, 21PO/151, CADN.

157 Ambassade de France en Algérie, "Copie d'un article paru dans le journal 'Alger républicain,' 4 Avril 1964, 'L'édification du socialisme en Algérie,'" April 7, 1964, Algiers, Press and Information Services, 29QO/17, MAE.

158 Benzenine, "Les ulémas algériens et leurs positions sous le régime de Ben Bella," 108–10.

159 The posters were reported to say, "Wine is forbidden (*hurrima*) by God and prohibited (*muni'a*) by the government. He who drinks it is not fully Muslim or a pure citizen" (Association El Qiyam, "Les valeurs religieuses de l'Islam").

160 Association El Qiyam, "Les valeurs religieuses de l'Islam."

161 "Une campagne d'intolérance religieuse risque de gêner le gouvernement de M. Ben Bella," *Le Monde*, January 20, 1964.

162 Association El Qiyam, "Les valeurs religieuses de l'Islam."

163 Knauss, *The Persistence of Patriarchy*, 171.

164 Serres, "La réforme du marché du travail"; McAllister, "Algeria's 'Belle Époque,'" 53. This vision of social justice, which saw resources as belonging to the nation rather than a specific economic class, remains a pillar of national identity in contemporary Algeria.

165 Roberts, "Radical Islamism," 575; Phillips and Evans, *Algeria*; Carlier, *Entre nation et jihad*.

166 Destanne de Bernis, "L'Afrique de l'indépendance politique à l'indépendance économique," 26.

Chapter Six: Today's Utopia Is Tomorrow's Reality

1 Guérin, *L'Algérie qui se cherche*, 76–77.

2 Guérin, *L'Algérie qui se cherche*, 77.

3 Naylor, *France and Algeria*, chap. 2.

4 Colin et al., "Des relations entre la France et l'Algérie aux relations entre la France et le Tiers Monde."

5 Colin et al., "Des relations entre la France et l'Algérie aux relations entre la France et le Tiers Monde," 8.

6 Colin et al., "Des relations entre la France et l'Algérie aux relations entre la France et le Tiers Monde," 7.

7 "Une brouille avec l'Algérie risquerait de ruiner les efforts de notre diplomatie dans le monde entier, déclare M. de Broglie," March 2, 1965, F-721–83, Guérin Archives, LC.

8 Launay, *Robert Buron*, 153.

9 This organization was linked to the office of the prime minister. A decree of January 11, 1963, placed de Broglie in control of the organization, which was merged with the Ministry of Foreign Affairs after 1966.

10 "Note: Politique française à l'égard de l'Algérie," May 11, 1963, Direction of General Affairs and Economic and Financial Cooperation, SEAA 177, MAE. In 1965, the French state sent 13,006 coopérants to Algeria, 4,698 of whom were involved in technical cooperation and 8,308 in cultural cooperation (C. Busson de Janssens, chief of the Office of Economic and Financial Cooperation, "Coopération économique entre la C.E.E. et l'Algérie," September 2, 1964, 4, SEAA 177, MAE). This number corresponds to that given in Henry et al., *Le temps de la coopération*, 13.

11 Chaïb, "Les coopérants français en Algérie."

12 Letter from the Délégué pour l'Algérie du Ministère des rapatriés, "Revue de presse des 1 et 2 janvier 1963," January 3, 1963, French embassy, B-0071522/5, CAEF.

13 Bossuat, "French Development Aid," 445.

14 Naylor, *France and Algeria*, 60.

15 M. Rey, "Projet de rapport au Conseil sur les conversations exploratoires entre la Commission et l'Algérie," February 8, 1965, Brussels, Sécrétariat exécutif, Archives of the European Economic Community (BAC) 7/1971/4, Archives of the European Commission, Florence (hereafter ACE).

16 "Les investissements français en Algérie."

17 Michel Levallois, the president of the Society of Saint-Simonian Studies, formerly worked on colonial development initiatives in Algeria. He has noted continuities between Saint-Simonian thought, the Constantine Plan, and the project of cooperation. See Henry, "La recomposition des savoirs au Maghreb à l'époque de la coopération."

18 Interview with Christian Pheline, February 5, 2015, Paris. See also Ammour, Leucate, and Moulin, *La voie algérienne*, 11.

19 "Rapport de mission à Alger de M. Ficatier (26 au 30 juin 1963)," July 12, 1963, 2, B-0057593, CAEF.

20 M. Gueret, "Rapport relatif aux réunions tenues par la FAO à Madrid," October 30, 1961, 25, 19770412/92, AN.

21 Letter from Jean de Vaissière to the minister of foreign affairs, "Réunion sur les zones de développement," February 20, 1962, 19770412/92, AN.

22 De Vaissière to the minister of foreign affairs.

23 Quoted in Naylor, *France and Algeria*, 54.

24 A. Ficatier, "Rapport de la mission de démographes," January 17, 1964, 6, INSEE, B-0057593, CAEF.

25 The PCA had separated from the PCF in 1936. It was first banned by the French state in 1955, though individual members joined the ALN during the war. It was banned for a second time by the Algerian authorities in November 1962 (Ruscio, *Les communistes et l'Algérie*).

26 Joly, *French Communist Party*; and Marynower, *L'Algérie à gauche*.

27 Lenin, *La maladie infantile du communisme*.

28 Sing, "Brothers in Arms"; Bardawil, *Revolution and Disenchantment*, chap. 5. Given that a number of Maoists in the Middle East became adepts of political Islam in the 1960s and 1970s, it would seem that this tendency was more open to questions of religion due to its emphasis on the cultural forms of revolution.

29 Wolin, *French Intellectuals*.

30 Porter, *Eyes to the South*.

31 Szczepanski-Huillery, "'L'idéologie tiers-mondiste,'" 30. Christoph Kalter argues that radical voices on the Third World were central for the left, but he distinguishes the Third World as an academic and political lens of the 1960s from the framing of certain actors as *tiers-mondistes* in the 1970s (*The Discovery of the Third World*, 58).

32 Szczepanski-Huillery, "L'idéologie tiers-mondiste."

33 Shepard, *Sex, France, and Arab Men*, 84.

34 LeSueur, *Uncivil War*, 234.

35 Bush, *Publishing Africa in French*; Brun and Penot-Lacassagne, *Engagements et déchirements*.

36 Simon, *Algérie, les années pieds-rouges*.

37 Moussa, *Algérie, une autre histoire de l'indépendance*.

38 "L'Algérie n'a jamais été la France, déclaration de Daniel Guérin au meeting organisé, le 27 janvier 1956, à Paris par le Comité d'action des intellectuels contre la poursuite de la guerre en Afrique du Nord," F-721–91, Guérin Archives, LC.

39 For more on this committee, see Le Tallec, "L'unité d'action des trotskystes, anarchistes et socialistes de gauche autour de l'anticolonialisme et de l'anti-bonapartisme (1954–1958)."

40 Letter from Daniel Guérin to Messali Hadj, February 16, 1954, F-721–91, Guérin Archives, LC.

41 Letter from Daniel Guérin to Habib Bourguiba, February 10, 1956, F-721–91, Guérin Archives, LC.

42 Guérin to Bourguiba.

43 Aissaoui, *Immigration and National Identity*, 143.

44 Pattieu, *Les camarades des frères*, chap. 4; and for the quotation, Pattieu, "Le 'camarade' Pablo, la IVᵉ internationale, et la guerre d'Algérie," 700. The FA officially refused to take sides in the conflict between the MNA and the FLN, while Trotsky-libertarians and Lambertists supported Messali Hadj unconditionally. The Parti communiste international (International Communist Party), close to Pierre Frank, and the Fédération communiste libertaire (Libertarian Communist Federation) tended to be more open-minded. Ultimately, the Trotskyists organized around Pablo offered the FLN the most significant support.

45 Porter, *Eyes to the South*, 95.

46 Michel Pablo, *Le programme de Tripoli: Impressions et problèmes de la révolution Algérienne: impressions et problèmes de la révolution algérienne* (Paris: Parti communiste internationaliste, IVᵉᵐᵉ internationale, 1962), 11; in F-721–82, Guérin Archives, LC.

47 Pablo, "Impressions et problèmes," 35.

48 Pablo, "Impressions et problèmes," 18.

49 Pablo, "Impressions et problèmes," 9–10.

50 Pattieu, *Les camarades des frères*, 201. Guérin viewed Mahsas and Boumaza, ministers who interpreted Islamic principles to support socialism, as the principal enemies of the policy of self-management. Daniel Guérin, draft of "L'ORP parti d'avant-garde," *Combat* [s.d.], F-721–86, Guérin Archives, LC.

51 Thèse Irani, "Chapter 2: De l'assistance à la coopération," 1976, 16, EH-183 II 143, AML; and Ammour, Leucate, and Moulin, *La voie algérienne*. Buron himself gradually shifted from Christian Democracy to more socialist tendencies, exemplified in his movement *Objectif 72*, which took on the name *Objectif socialiste* in 1971.

52 Raymond Delprat, "La Création de l'IRFED," May 1981, 3, EH-183 172, AML. In 1960 IRFED created the journal *Développement et civilisations*, which printed 4,500 to 5,000 copies three times per year, half of which were sent abroad (Delprat, "La création de l'IRFED," 8–9). The editorial board of the journal mixed liberal and progressive voices, including those of Fernand Braudel, Raymond Aron, Charles Bettelheim, René Dumont, and Georges Balandier.

53 Lebret, "Devant le drame du monde une initiative nécessaire: L'IRFED," *Économie et Humanisme*, 1959, 5, EH 183 II 6, AML.

54 Buron, *Carnets politiques de la guerre d'Algérie par un signataire des accords d'Evian*; Launay, *Robert Buron*, 64.

55 Letter from François Perroux to the head of the Centres sociaux in Algeria, March 4, 1958, Perroux Archives (PRX) 207.4, Institut mémoires de l'édition contemporaine, Saint-Germain-la-Blanche-Herbe (herafter IMEC). He also closely followed events in Tunisia, and corresponded with President Bourguiba in 1957, expressing his admiration for the "historical traditions, refined culture, and sensitive and delicate intelligence of the elites and people of Tunisia." Letter from François Perroux to Habib Bourguiba, December 7, 1957, Paris, PRX 231.11-Tunisia, IMEC.

56 Perroux, "L'Islam, l'économie et la technique." He also edited a volume after independence, *L'Algérie de demain*.

57 For more on Servier's activities during the war see Sacriste, *Germaine Tillion, Jacques Berque, Jean Servier, Pierre Bourdieu*.

58 Austruy, *L'Islam face au développement économique*.

59 Marthelot, "L'Islam et le développement."

60 Letter from the French ambassador in Algeria to the head of technical and cultural cooperation, "Création de l'École nationale algérienne d'administration," September 2, 1963, Algiers, 21PO/84, CADN. The ENA, set up to train Algerian students to work in ministries or engineering as well as in the police and health services, had an enrollment of seven thousand in 1974 (Bossuat, "French Development Aid," 445).

61 "Institut d'étude du développement économique et sociale: Les élèves estiment que l'enseignement doit contribuer à la lutte anti-impérialiste," *Le Monde*, June 13, 1968, PRX 198.6, IMEC.

62 "Institut d'étude du développement."

63 "IEDES: Controverse autour de l'orientation de l'enseignement et de la gestion du directeur," *Le Monde*, June 22, 1968, https://www.lemonde.fr/archives /article/1968/06/22/i-e-d-e-s-controverse-autour-de-1 -orientation-de-1 -enseignement-et-de-la-gestion-du-directeur_2497841_1819218.html.

64 Rodinson, *Islam et capitalisme.*

65 Rodinson, "Le poids de l'Islam sur le développement économique et sociale," 19.

66 Letter from Nazih al-Hakim to Maxime Rodinson, May 4, 1967, Rodinson Archives 334, IMEC. Al-Hakim had translated works by René Dumont, Albert Meister, and Roger Garaudy. The translation was published in 1968 by Dar al-Tali'a in Beirut.

67 Duvingaud, "George Gurvitch."

68 Gadant, "Nationalisme et anticolonialisme dans les sciences sociales," 87–89.

69 "La société centrale pour l'équipement du territoire," [s.d.], 2, SCET 01, CDC, Paris.

70 For more on SCET's role in the metropole, see Newsome, *French Urban Planning*, 108.

71 INTER, "La caisse des dépôts et ses filiales techniques en Algérie," January 1989, Archives of SCET-Coopération (COOP) 202–28, CDC.

72 Service de l'information et de la communication internes, "Trente ans de coopération internationale," 1988, 18, COOP 202–20, CDC. For information on SCET's activities in the Ivory Coast, see Haguenauer-Caceres, "Construire à l'étranger."

73 SCET-Coopération, "Curriculum-vitae de quelques ingénieurs de la SCET-Coopération," 1971, 18, SCET-COOP 202–19, CDC.

74 "2e semestre 70, Bulletin Coop, Avant-Propos," SCET-COOP 202–19, CDC.

75 "Procès-verbal de la réunion du Comité de Direction du 11 février 1963," SEDES 09, 3, CDC.

76 P. Morand, "Note pour R. Mercier," May 16, 1964, SEDES 01, CDC.

77 INTER, "La caisse des dépôts et ses filiales techniques en Algérie," 7.

78 J. M. Soutou, "Mandat de la commission économique pour l'Afrique," telegram sent February 14, 1963, SEAA 147, MAE.

79 Ourabah, *Premiers pas*, 34.

80 Letter from Pierre Elie to Albert Ficatier, November 19, 1964, Algiers, 4, B-0057593, CAEF.

81 Letter from the commissioner of the national census to Claude Gruson, September 9, 1964, Algiers, B-0057593, CAEF.

82 According to a memo, agricultural experts had come to Algeria from Egypt, Yugoslavia, Bulgaria, and Germany, with Sweden expected to send technicians and material. Experts from Yugoslavia tended to be the most respected by the Ministry of Agriculture. "Aide étrangère autre que française à l'Algérie," September 27, 1965, SEAA 177, MAE.

83 French authorities noted that more recent arrivals, "known for their progressivism and loyalty to the FLN" during the war, were "eliminated" by the Algerian authorities themselves. Half of the French experts worked for the

SAPs and were reported to be offered the most difficult positions; it was also reported that ten Egyptian technicians left the country after refusing the jobs that were offered to them. French embassy in Algeria, Service of Cooperation, "L'agriculture algérienne," May 1964, 2, 29QO/80, MAE.

84 "L'agriculture algérienne," 4.

85 According to François Dosse, Perroux "played a fundamental role" in building "bridges" between "economists and the rest of the social sciences" (*History of Structuralism*, 168).

86 "Compte rendu de la réunion sur les prémisses sociales de l'industrialisation," Conseil international des sciences sociales, UNESCO, September 12–15, 1961, Paris, 4, SEDES 60, CDC.

87 Hélène Legotien, "Note de méthode sur une activité sociologique a la SEDES," February 1964, 8, SEDES 44, CDC.

88 Legotien, "Note de méthode."

89 John Carson provides an intellectual history of how understandings of merit and talent were bound up with race in France and the United States in *The Measure of Merit*.

90 "Note by M. Laylay and M. Fonkenell," June 15, 1963, 2, Société d'équipement de la région de Bône, COOP 202–30, CDC.

91 Escobar, *Encountering Development*.

92 Postcard from Si Denis and Hocine to Pierre Vidal-Naquet, April 6, 1963, Algiers, carton 8, Vidal-Naquet Archives, École des hautes études en sciences sociales.

93 A series of preparatory conferences had been held in Europe by branches of the organization in France, Switzerland, Holland, Italy, Germany, and Austria ("Le comité d'Alger dresse un bilan," *Le Peuple*, May 13, 1963, 21PO/ 220, CADN).

94 "Pour la solidarité active des peuples d'Europe avec l'Algérie," [s.d.], 1, F-Res-340(2), Raptis Archives, LC.

95 République Algérienne Démocratique et Populaire, BNASS, Présidence du conseil, "Émission du 14 Mai 1963," [May 1963], 2, F-Res-340(1), Raptis Archives, LC.

96 Présidence du Conseil, "Émission du 14 Mai 1963," 2.

97 When Perroux was expelled from the IEDES in 1968, Dumont was one of the proposed replacements, though he was not ultimately selected due to his reservations regarding the official policy of cooperation. While Dumont had worked for the Ministry of Cooperation, his unorthodox views irritated Michel Debré, who ultimately forced him to resign.

98 A fairly complete account of this speech can be found in "Note concernant la conférence faite par le professeur René Dumont" and the letter from Louis de Guiringaud to the secretary of state of the prime minister of Algerian affairs, "Conférence du M. Dumont et déclarations de M. Ben Bella sur la réforme agraire," January 17, 1963, Algiers, both in 21PO/194, CADN.

99 J. Manachem, "La conférence de M. René Dumont," *La Dépêche d'Algérie*, January 8, 1963, 5.

100 Guiringaud to the secretary of state, 6.

101 Telegram from Mr. Ewart-Biggs of the British embassy, "Agrarian problem and the Govt's attitude to it, advice given by M. Dumont, French left-wing

economist during his visit to Algiers," January 11, 1963, Algiers, Foreign Office Records (FO) 371/173165, Public Records Office, Kew (hereafter PRO). British observers noted that Dumont was even more outspoken in his criticism behind closed doors.

102 Letter from J. Kokiq to Daniel Guérin, July 2, 1964, F-721–94, Guérin Archives, LC.

103 Letter from Henri Simon to Daniel Guérin, February 19, 1964, F-721–84, Guérin Archives, LC.

104 Letter from J. Kokiq to Henri Simon, June 23, 1964, F-721–94(1), Raptis Archives, LC.

105 Letter from Guy Debord to Daniel Guérin, May 3, 1966, F-721–86, Guérin Archives, LC.

106 Letter from Al. Decaune to Daniel Guérin, April 7, 1964, F-721–94/2, Guérin Archives, LC.

107 Daniel Guérin, draft of "Une explication portrait Marxiste de Mahomet," *L'Express*, August 3, 1962, F-721–90, Guérin Archives, LC.

108 Michel Pablo, "Le programme de Tripoli," October 1962, 35, F-721–82, Guérin Archives, LC.

109 Pablo, "Le programme de Tripoli," 34.

110 Krim, "La chute de Ben Bella," 3.

111 Guérin, *Où va le peuple américain?*; Letter from Frantz Fanon to Daniel Guérin, November 26, 1955, F-721–91, Guérin Archives, LC. The archives also reveal other links between Guérin and Fanon: Guérin offered to help Fanon get his work published and even offered to send Fanon's work to Sartre.

112 Slisli, "Islam."

113 Al-Mili, "Fanon wa-l-Fikr al-Gharbi"; Al-Mili, "Al-Thawra al-Jaza'iriyya wa Fanon."

114 See, for example, issues of the *Cahiers d'études anarchistes-communistes* from 1966, or the 1967 issue of the journal *Autogestion*, which was edited by Pablo and dedicated to Algeria.

115 Other notable members included Mohammed Harbi and Bachir Hadj Ali. According to Guérin, 120 supporters of the group were imprisoned at El-Harach. The group was ideologically vague, with Guérin claiming that it was "neither Communist nor non-Communist" and that, in Algeria, the real enemies were the forces of imperialism and reaction ("L'ORP parti d'avant-garde").

Epilogue

1 Stambouli, "L'aéro-habitat, avatar d'un monument classé?" 117–27.

2 E. B. Boothby, "Conversation between M. Zevans and M. Bouakouir," December 22, 1960, British Consulate General in Algiers, FO 371/147341, PRO.

3 Boothby, "Conversation."

4 Boothby, "Conversation."

5 Giacone, *Jean Guyot.*

6 L. M., "Salah Bouakouir, traître ou héros?" *Le matin d'Algérie*, December 12, 2010, www.lematindz.net/news/3534-salah-bouakouir-traitre-ou-heros-rappels.html.

7 Mitchell, "Fixing the Economy," 89.

8 The French administration had created Franco-Arab schools to train native interlocutors to work with the colonial state (Colonna, "Educating Conformity," 346–72). For more on Bennabi's educational trajectory, see Naylor, "Life and Thought of Malek Bennabi"; and Jebari, "Colonial Education."

9 Bennabi, *Pourritures*, 50.

10 Bennabi, *Pourritures*, 50.

11 Bennabi, *Pourritures*, 34.

12 Bennabi, *Vocation de l'Islam*, 10.

13 Bennabi, *Pourritures*, 112.

14 Bennabi, *Pourritures*, 103–4.

15 Bennabi, *Conditions de la renaissance*, 165.

16 Bennabi, *Conditions de la renaissance*, 23.

17 Bennabi, *Vocation de l'Islam*, 89.

18 Bennabi, *Pourritures*, 50.

19 Bennabi, *Vocation de l'Islam*, 26.

20 Bennabi, *Vocation de l'Islam*, 85.

21 Bennabi, *Les problèmes des idées dans le monde musulman*, 113. For a study of the link between efficiency and revolution in Bennabi's thought, see Badreddine, "Dawr al-Faʿaliyya fi Binaʾ al-Dhat al-Thawriyya fi Mandhur Malik Bennabi."

22 Bennabi, *Al-Muslim fi ʿAlam al-Iqtisad*, 82.

23 Sarah Pursley frames development as carrying both transitive and intransitive meanings in *Familiar Futures*, 18.

24 Bennabi, *al-Muslim fi ʿAlam al-Iqtisad*, 61.

25 Bennabi, "Le mal nouveau: L'économisme," 107.

26 Labat, *Les islamistes algériens*, 169.

27 Serres, *L'Algérie face à la catastrophe suspendue*, 50; and Walsh, "Killing Post-Almohad Man."

28 Abbassi Madani's interview in *La tribune d'octobre*, March 15–31, 1989, 31. Quoted in Carlier, *Entre nation et jihad*, 363. The FIS had been poised to emerge victorious after the legislative elections of January 1992, prompting the Algerian army to cancel the electoral process. The ensuing conflict led to the death of between 150,000 and 200,000 people and is known as the Dark Decade.

29 El-Hamri, *La vocation civilisationnelle de l'Islam dans l'œuvre de Malek Bennabi*.

30 Yasmina (@yassmiin95), Twitter, May 3, 2019, 4:39 p.m., https://twitter.com/yassmiin95/status/1124322642683662336/photo/1.

31 Serres, "Algerian Counter-Revolution."

32 "Sawfa Aʿud Baʿda 30 Sana . . . Kayfa Yuʾathir Malik Bennabi fi al-Hirak al-Jazaʾiri al-ʾAn?," Sasapost, September 24, 2019, https://www.sasapost.com/malek-bennabi-and-algerian-demonstrations; Ahmed Ouabel, "Kayfa Yufassir Malik Bennabi al-Hirak al-Shaʿbi bi-l-Jazaʾir?" Aljazeera.net, March 10, 2019, https://www.aljazeera.net/blogs/2019/3/10/كيف-يفسر-مالك-بن-نبي-الحراك-الشعبي.

33 Photos provided by Awel Haouati from Algiers, Hirak protests of October 11, 2019. The sign cited Bennabi, *Mushkilat al-Thaqafa*, 118.

34 "Mouvement populaire: Vendredi acte 10 (Vidéo)," *Algérie 1*, April 26, 2019, available at https://www.algerie1.com/societe/mouvement-populaire-vendredi -acte-10-video.

35 The image, published by the website *Algérie 1* on April 26, 2019, is available online at https://algerie1.com/societe/mouvement-populaire-vendredi-acte-10 -video. The quote from Bennabi can be found in *Shurut al-Nahda*, 35.

36 Fabbiano, "Le temps long du hirak."

37 Foucault, *Les mots et les choses*; Zakariya, *Malek Bennabi*. As Talal Asad notes, rather than being the sole domain of history, tradition is also a commentary on desired futures: "An Islamic discursive tradition is simply a tradition of Muslim discourse that addresses itself to conceptions of the Islamic past and future, with reference to a particular Islamic practice in the present" (*Anthropology of Islam*, 14).

BIBLIOGRAPHY

Archives

Algeria

Centre des archives nationales (CANA), Algiers
  Archives de la Chambre de commerce (CC)
  Archives du Conseil national de la révolution algérienne (CNRA)
  Archives du Gouvernement provisoire de la République algérienne (GPRA)
  Fonds du Gouvernement general de l'Algérie (2E)

France

Archives d'AgroParisTech, Musée du vivant, Grignon
  Fonds de René Dumont (FRD)
Archives d'histoire contemporaine, Sciences Po, Paris
  Archives de Paul Delouvrier (DV)
Archives du Ministère des affaires étrangères (MAE)
  Afrique du Nord, Service de liaison avec l'Algérie (29QO)
  Secrétariat d'Etat aux affaires algériennes (SEAA)
Archives municipales de Lyon (AML), Lyon
  Fonds de l'association Economie et Humanisme (EH)
Archives nationales de France (AN), Paris
  Archives du Plan de Constantine (F/60)
  Bureau du droit civil général et section du sceau
  Commerce et industrie (F/12)
  Inspection générale de l'agriculture
  Ministère de l'agriculture
Archives nationales d'outre-mer (ANOM), Aix-en-Provence
  Bibliothèque (BIB AOM)
  Cabinet du préfet d'Alger (91/1K)
  Gouvernement général de l'Algérie (GGA)
    Cabinet Delouvrier (14CAB)
    Cabinet Jean Morin (15CAB)
  Ministère d'État chargé des affaires algériennes (81F)

Office algérien d'action économique et touristique (90)
Préfecture de Grande Kabylie (9150)
Sous-préfecture de Djidjelli (9318)
Sous-préfecture de Constantine (9314)
Bibliothèque nationale de France (BNF), Paris
Caisse des dépôts et consignations (CDC), Paris
    Société centrale d'équipement du territoire (SCET)
    Société d'études pour le développement économique et sociale (SEDES)
Centre des archives diplomatiques de Nantes (CADN), Nantes
    Archives rapatriées de l'ambassade de France à Alger (21PO)
Centre des archives économiques et financières (CAEF), Savigny-le-Temple
    Archives de la Caisse d'équipement pour le développemenmt de l'Algérie
    (CEDA)
École des hautes études en sciences sociales (EHESS), Paris
    Archives de Vidal-Naquet
Institut mémoires de l'édition contemporaine (IMEC),
La Contemporaine (LC), Nanterre
    Archives de Daniel Guérin
    Archives de Michel Raptis
Saint-Germain-la-Blanche-Herbe
    Archives de François Perroux (PRX)
    Archives de Maxime Rodinson (RDS)
Service historique de l'armée de terre (SHAT), Paris
    Sous-série Algérie (1H)
    Archives des sections administratives spécialisées en Algérie (SAS)

Italy
Historical Archives of the European Union (HAU), Florence
    Archives of the European Commission
    Archives of the European Economic Community
    Jean Monnet Collection

Lebanon
American University of Beirut Archives (AUB), Beirut
    Linda Sadaqa Collection

United Kingdom
National Archives of the United Kingdom (NAK), Kew
    Foreign Office Records (FO)
    Public Records Office (PRO)

United States
Hoover Institution Archives (HIA), Stanford University, Stanford, CA
    Mont Pèlerin Society Records (MPS)

Published Sources

Abbas, Ferhat. *L'indépendance confisquée, 1962–1978*. Paris: Flammarion, 1984.

Abi-Mershed, Osama W. *Apostles of Modernity: The Saint-Simonians and the Civilizing Mission in Algeria*. Stanford, CA: Stanford University Press, 2010.

Abi-Mershed, Osama W. "The Mediterranean in Saint-Simonian Imagination: The 'Nuptial Bed.'" In *The Making of the Modern Mediterranean: Views from the South*, edited by Judith E. Tucker, 149–73. Berkeley: University of California Press, 2019.

Abul-Magd, Zeinab. *Militarizing the Nation: The Army, Business, and Revolution in Egypt*. New York: Columbia University Press, 2017.

Adamson, Kay. *Algeria: A Study in Competing Ideologies*. London: Cassell, 1998.

Adas, Michael. *Machines as the Measure of Men: Science, Technology, and Ideologies of Western Dominance*. Ithaca, NY: Cornell University Press, 1989.

Adda-Djelloul, Mohammed. "Société colonisée et droit colonial: Les élus des délégations arabe et kabyle face au projet Albin Rozet." *Insaniyat* 5, no. 187 (1998): 171–86.

Agbamu, Samuel. "Mare Nostrum: Italy and the Mediterranean of Ancient Rome in the Twentieth and Twenty-First Centuries." *Fascism* 8 (2019): 250–74.

Ageron, Charles-Robert. *Les algériens musulmans et la France, 1871–1919, Tome 2*. 1968. Reprint, Saint-Denis, France: Editions Bouchène, 2005.

Ageron, Charles-Robert. *Histoire de l'Algérie contemporaine*. Paris: Presses universitaires de France, 1964.

Ageron, Charles-Robert. *Histoire de l'Algérie contemporaine, Tome II: De l'insurrection de 1871 au déclenchement de la guerre de libération*. Paris: Presses Universitaires de France, 1979.

Ageron, Charles-Robert. "Le Parti communiste algérien de 1939 à 1943." *Vingtième siècle: Revue d'histoire* 12 (1986): 39–50.

Ahmed, Sara. "A Phenomenology of Whiteness." *Feminist Theory* 82, no. 2 (2007): 149–68.

Aissaoui, Rabah. *Immigration and National Identity: North African Political Movements in Colonial and Postcolonial France*. London: Tauris Academic Studies, 2009.

Ajl, Max Smith. "Farmers, Fellaga, and Frenchmen: National Liberation and Post-Colonial Development in Tunisia." PhD diss., Cornell University, 2019.

'Akkash, 'Abd al-Salam. "Tafsir al-Sihafa al-Shuyu'iyya wa-Sihafat al-Haraka al-Wataniyya li-Dawr al-Maja'a dimna Asbab Intifadat 8 May 1945." *Majallat al-Adab wa al-'Ulum al-Ijtima'iyya* 12, no. 2 (2015): 89–104.

Al-Da'im, 'Abdallah 'Abd. "Ma'sat al-Jaza'ir." *al-Adab* 5, no. 9 (1957): 828–32.

Al-Dib, Muhammad Fathi. *'Abd al-Nasir wa-Thawrat al-Jaza'ir*. Cairo: Dar al-Mustaqbal al-'Arabi, 1984.

Al-Mili, Muhammad. "Al-Thawra al-Jaza'iriyya wa Fanon." *al-Thaqafa* 2 (May 1971): 40–54.

Al-Mili, Muhammad. "Fanon wa-l-Fikr al-Gharbi." *al-Thaqafa* 1 (March 1971): 10–25.

Al-Rabita al-Adabiyya. *Al-Jaza'ir al-Munahida*. Najaf: Matba'at al-Nu'man al-Najaf 1960.

Al-Shalqani, ʿAli. *Thawrat al-Jazaʾir*. Cairo: Dar al-Nadim, 1956.

Al-Sibaʿi, Mustafa. *Ishtirakiyyat al-Islam*. Cairo: al-Dar al-Qawmiyya li-l-Tibaʿa wa-l-Nashr, 1961.

ʿAllush, Naji. "Hawla Kitab Thawrat al-Jazaʾir." *al-Adab* 5, no. 3 (1957): 78–80.

Amat, Charles. *Le Mʾzab et les mʾzabites*. Paris: Challamel, 1888.

American Society of African Culture, ed. *Pan-Africanism Reconsidered*. Berkeley: University of California Press, 1962.

Amichi, Hichem, Marcel Kuper, and Sami Bouarfa. "The Legitimacy of Tilling the Land versus Land Use Rights: Algerian Farmers' Land Appropriation Processes on Public Land." In *Law and Property in Algeria: Anthropological Perspectives*, edited by Yazid Ben Bounet, 43–59. Leiden: Brill, 2018.

ʿAmil, Mahdi. *Muqaddima Nazariyya li-Dirasat Athar al Fikr al-Ishtiraki fi-Harakat al-Taharrur al-Watani*. 1972. Reprint, Beirut: Dar al-Farabi, 2013.

Amin, Ash. "The Remainders of Race." *Theory, Culture, and Society* 27, no. 1 (2010): 1–23.

Ammour, Kader, Christian Leucate, and Jean-Jacques Moulin. *La voie algérienne: Les contradictions d'un développement national*. Paris: François Maspero, 1974.

Anderson, David. *Histories of the Hanged: The Dirty War in Kenya and the End of Empire*. London: Weidenfeld and Nicolson, 2005.

Anderson, Kevin B. "Marx's Late Writings on Non-Western and Pre-capitalist Societies and Gender." *Rethinking Marxism* 14, no. 4 (2002): 84–96.

Apter, Andrew. "Beyond Negritude: Black Cultural Citizenship and the Arab Quesiton in FESTAC '77." In *The First World Festival of Negro Arts, Dakar 1966: Contexts and Legacies*, edited by David Murphy, 151–65. Oxford: Oxford University Press, 2016.

Arrus, René. *L'eau en Algérie: De l'impérialisme au développement (1830–1962)*. Grenoble: Presses universitaires de Grenoble, 1985.

Asad, Talal. *The Idea of an Anthropology of Islam*. Washington, DC: Center for Contemporary Arab Studies, 1986.

Asseraf, Arthur. *Electric News in Colonial Algeria*. Oxford: Oxford University Press, 2019.

Asseraf, Arthur. "'A New Israel': Colonial Comparisons and the Algerian Partition That Never Happened." *French Historical Studies* 41, no. 1 (2018): 95–120.

Audier, Serge. *Le colloque Walter Lippmann: Aux origines du néo-libéralisme*. Lormont, France: Le Bord de l'eau, 2012.

Audisio, Gabriel. *Sel de la mer*. Paris: Gallimard, 1936.

Audisio, Gabriel. *L'Algérie littéraire*. Paris: Éditions de l'Encyclopédie coloniale et maritime, 1943.

Austruy, Jacques. *L'Islam face au développement économique*. Paris: Les Éditions ouvrières, 1961.

Ax, Christina Folke. *Cultivating the Colonies: Colonial States and Their Environmental Legacies*. Athens: Ohio University Press, 2011.

Aydin, Cemil. *The Idea of the Muslim World: A Global Intellectual History*. Cambridge: Cambridge University Press, 2017.

Badraddine, Marzuqi. "Dawr al-Faʿaliyya fi Binaʾ al-Dhat al-Thawriyya fi Mandhur Malik Bennabi." *Dirasa Insaniyya wa Ijtimaʿiyya* 9, no. 3 (2020): 255–66.

Banaji, Jairus. "Islam, the Mediterranean and the Rise of Capitalism." *Historical Materialism* 15 (2007): 47–74.

Barclay, Fiona, Charlotte Ann Chopin, and Margin Evans. "Introduction: Settler Colonial Studies and French Algeria." *Settler Colonial Studies* 8, no. 2 (2017): 115–30.

Bardawil, Fadi A. *Revolution and Disenchantment: Arab Marxism and the Binds of Emancipation*. Durham, NC: Duke University Press, 2020.

Barrows, Susanna. "Alcohol, France and Algeria: A Case Study in the International Liquor Trade." *Contemporary Drug Problems* 11 (1982): 525–43.

Barthes, Roland. *Mythologies*. Paris: Éditions du Seuil, 1957.

Beckert, Sven. *Empire of Cotton: A Global History of Capitalism*. New York: Knopf, 2014.

Bell, Dorian. *Globalizing Race: Antisemitism and Empire in French and European Culture*. Evanston, IL: Northwestern University Press, 2018.

Benachenhou, Abdellatif. *Formation du sous-développement en Algérie*. Algiers: Office des publications universitaires, 1976.

Benhouria, Tahar. *L'Économie de l'Algérie*. Paris: François Maspero, 1980.

Benkhedda, Benyoucef. *L'Algérie à l'indépendance: La crise de 1962*. Algiers: Dahleb, 1997.

Bennabi, Malek. *Al-Muslim fi 'Alam al-Iqtisad*. 1979. Reprint, Damascus: Dar al-Fikr, 1987.

Bennabi, Malek. *Les conditions de la renaissance: Problème d'une civilisation*. 1949. Reprint, Algiers: Éditions ANEP, 2005.

Bennabi, Malek. "Le mal nouveau: l'économisme." In *Pour changer l'Algérie*, 103–7. Algiers: Edition Benmerabet, 2011.

Bennabi, Malek. *Le Problème des idées dans le monde musulman*. Beirut: Albouraq, 2006.

Bennabi, Malek. *Pourritures: Mémoires*. Algiers: Dar el Oumma, 2007.

Bennabi, Malek. *Shurut al-Nahda*. 1961. Reprint, Damascus: Dar al-Fikr, 2013.

Bennabi, Malek. *Vocation de l'Islam*. 1954. Reprint, Algiers: Éditions ANEP, 2006.

Bennoune, Mahfoud. *The Making of Contemporary Algeria, 1830–1987*. Cambridge: Cambridge University Press, 1988.

Benzenine, Belkacem. "Les ulémas algériens et leurs positions sous le régime de Ben Bella." In *Le Maghreb et l'indépendance de l'Algérie*, edited by Amar Mohand-Amer and Belkacem Benzenine, 103–14. Oran: CRASC, 2012.

Berman, Bruce, and John Lonsdale. *Unhappy Valley: Conflict in Kenya and Africa*. Athens: Ohio University Press, 1992.

Bernard de Raymond, Antoine. "Une 'Algérie californienne'? L'économie politique de la standardisation de l'agriculture coloniale (1930–1962)." *Politix* 24, no. 95 (2011): 23–46.

Bernard de Raymond, Antoine. *En toute saison: Le marché des fruits et légumes en France*. Tours: Presses universitaires François-Rabelais de Tours, 2013.

Berque, Jacques. *Les Arabes d'hier à demain*. Paris: Éditions du Seuil, 1960.

Berque, Jacques, and Louis Massignon. "Dialogue sur 'Les Arabes.'" *Esprit* 288, no. 10 (1960): 1505–19.

Berry, Sara. *No Condition Is Permanent: The Social Dynamics of Agrarian Change in Sub-Saharan Africa*. Madison: University of Wisconsin Press, 1993.

Betts, Raymond F. *Assimilation and Association in French Colonial Theory, 1890–1914*. New York: Columbia University Press, 1961.

Beylier, Vincent. "Le destin d'un grand projet industriel: La société bônoise de sidérurgie." In *Les accords d'Évian: En conjoncture et en longue durée*, edited by René Galissot, 165–70. Algiers: Casbah Éditions, 1997.

Bhandar, Brenna. *Colonial Lives of Property: Law, Land, and Racial Regimes of Ownership*. Durham, NC: Duke University Press, 2018.

Birla, Ritu. *Stages of Capital: Law, Culture, and Market Governance in Late Colonial India*. Durham, NC: Duke University Press, 2009.

Bivar, Venus. *Organic Resistance: The Struggle over Industrial Farming in Postwar France*. Chapel Hill: University of North Carolina Press, 2018.

Blévis, Laure. "La Citoyenneté française au miroir de la colonisation." *Genèses* 4, no. 54 (2003): 25–47.

Blévis, Laure. "En marge du décret Crémieux: Les Juifs naturalisés français en Algérie (1865–1919)." *Archives Juives* 45, no. 2 (2012): 47–67.

Bochard, Arthur. *Les impôts arabes en Algérie*. Paris: Guillaumin et Cie, 1893.

Bockman, Johanna. *Markets in the Name of Socialism: The Left-Wing Origins of Neoliberalism*. Stanford, CA: Stanford University Press, 2011.

Bohling, Joseph. *The Sober Revolution: Appellation Wine and the Transformation of France*. Ithaca, NY: Cornell University Press, 2018.

Bossuat, Gérard. "French Development Aid and Co-operation under de Gaulle." *Contemporary European History* 12, no. 4 (2003): 431–56.

Bouamama, Saïd. *Algérie: Les racines de l'intégrisme*. Brussels: Éditions Aden, 2000.

Boubaker, Sadok. *D'une Méditerranée à l'autre: Espaces maritimes et échanges commerciaux*. Vol. 1. Tunis: Latrach éditions, 2019.

Bouchard, Norma, and Valerio Ferme. *Italy and the Mediterranean: Words, Sounds, and Images of the Post–Cold War Era*. New York: Palgrave Macmillan, 2013.

Bourdieu, Pierre. *Esquisses algériennes*. Edited by Tassadit Yacine. Paris: Éditions du Seuil, 2008.

Bourdieu, Pierre, and Abdelmalek Sayad. *Le déracinement: La crise de l'agriculture traditionnelle en Algérie*. Paris: Les Éditions de Minuit, 1964.

Bourdieu, Pierre, and Luc Boltanski. "La production de l'idéologie dominante." *Actes de la recherche en sciences sociales* 2, no. 2–3 (1976): 3–73.

Bourdieu, Pierre, et al. *Travail et travailleurs en Algérie*. Paris: Mouton, 1963.

Bourdin, Janine. "Des intellectuels à la recherche d'un style de vie: L'école nationale des cadres d'Uriage." *Revue française de science politique* 9, no. 4 (1959): 1029–45.

Boussard, Isabel. "Roland Maspétiol, une figure marquante de l'economie rurale." *Économie rurale* 223 (1994): 3–5.

Branche, Raphaëlle. *La torture et l'armée pendant la guerre d'Algérie (1954–1962)*. Paris: Gallimard, 2016.

Brattain, Michelle. "Race, Racism, and Antiracism: UNESCO and the Politics of Presenting Science to the Postwar Public." *American Historical Review* 112, no. 5 (2007): 1386–1413.

Brower, Benjamin Claude. "Rethinking Abolition in Algeria: Slavery and the 'Indigenous Question.'" *Cahier d'études africaines* 195, no. 3 (2009): 805–28.

Brown, Megan. "Drawing Algeria into Europe: Shifting French Policy and the Treaty of Rome (1951–1964)." *Modern and Contemporary France* 25, no. 2 (2017): 191–208.

Brown, Megan. *The Seventh Member State: Algeria, France, and the European Community*. Cambridge, MA: Harvard University Press, 2021.

Brun, Catherine, and Olivier Penot-Lacassagne. *Engagements et déchirements: Les intellectuels et la guerre d'Algérie*. Paris: Gallimard, 2012.

Budin, Jacques. "La 'reconnaissance' de la proprété rurale dans l'arrondissement de Bône (Annaba) en application des ordonnances des 1er octobre et 21 juillet 1846." In *Propriété et sociéte en Algérie contemporaine: Quelles approaches?*, edited by Didier Guignard and Isabelle Grangaud, 95–114. Aix-en-Provence: IREMAM, 2019.

Burgat, François, and William Dowell. *The Islamic Movement in North Africa*. Austin: University of Texas Press, 1997.

Burgin, Angus. *The Great Persuasion: Reinventing Free Markets since the Depression*. Cambridge, MA: Harvard University Press, 2015.

Burke, Edmund, III. *The Ethnographic State: France and the Invention of Moroccan Islam*. Berkeley: University of California Press, 2015.

Buron, Robert. *Carnets politiques de la guerre d'Algérie par un signataire des accords d'Evian*. Paris: Librarie Plon, 1965.

Bush, Ruth. *Publishing Africa in French: Literary Institutions and Decolonization 1945–1967*. Liverpool: Liverpool University Press, 2016.

Byrne, Jeffrey James. *Mecca of Revolution: Algeria, Decolonization, and the Third World*. Oxford: Oxford University Press, 2016.

Byrne, Jeffrey James. "Our Own Special Brand of Socialism: Algeira and the Contest of Modernities in the 1960s." *Diplomatic History* 33, no. 3 (2009): 427–47.

Calhoun, Craig. "Pierre Bourdieu and Social Transformation: Lessons from Algeria." *Development and Change* 37, no. 6 (2006): 1403–15.

Carlier, Omar. "Braudel avant Braudel? Les années algériennes (1923–1932)." *Insaniyat* 19–20 (2003): 143–76.

Carlier, Omar. *Entre nation et jihad: Histoire sociale des radicalismes algériens*. Paris: Presses de Sciences Po, 1995.

Carré, Olivier. *La légitimition islamique des socialismes arabes: Analyse conceptuelle combinatoire de manuels scholaries égyptiens, syriens, et irakiens*. Paris: Presses de la Fondation Nationales des Sciences Politiques, 1979.

Carson, John. *The Measure of Merit: Talents, Intelligence, and Inequality in the French and American Republics, 1750–1940*. Princeton, NJ: Princeton University Press, 2007.

Chabou, Meriem. "Retrospective on the Social Housing Policy in Algeria—Glances on the Cultural Referents of Algerian Architects." In *Architecture and Identity*, edited by Peter Herrle and Erik Wegerhoff, 137–48. Berlin: Lit Verlag, 2008.

Chaïb, Sabah. "Les coopérants français en Algérie (1962–1966): Récits croisés pour une ébauche de portrait." *Mobilités et migrations européennes en (post) colonies* 56, no. 221–22 (2016): 243–65.

Chakrabarty, Dipesh. *Provincializing Europe: Postcolonial Thought and Historical Difference*. Princeton, NJ: Princeton University Press, 2000.

Chakrabarty, Dipesh. "Subaltern Studies and Postcolonial Historiography." *Nepantla: Views from South* 1, no. 1 (2000): 9–32.

Chamedes, Giuliana. "The Catholic Origins of Development after World War II." *French Politics, Culture, and Society* 33, no. 2 (2015): 55–75.

Chapman, Herrick. *France's Long Reconstruction: In Search of the Modern Republic.* Cambridge, MA: Harvard University Press, 2018.

Chappel, James. *Catholic Modern: The Challenge of Totalitarianism and the Remaking of the Church.* Cambridge, MA: Harvard University Press, 2018.

Chatterjee, Partha. *The Nation and Its Fragments: Colonial and Postcolonial Histories.* Princeton, NJ: Princeton University Press, 1993.

Chaturvedi, Vinayak, ed. *Mapping Subaltern Studies and the Postcolonial.* London: Verso Books, 2012.

Chaulet, Claudine. *La Mitidja autogérée: Enquête sur les exploitations autogérées agricoles d'une région d'Algérie, 1968–1970.* Algiers: SNED, 1971.

Chaulet, Claudine. *La Terre, les frères, et l'argent: Stratégie familiale et production agricole, tome I.* Algiers: Office des publications universitaires, 1987.

Chenu, Reselyn. *Paul Delouvrier ou la passion d'agir: Entretiens.* Paris: Éditions du Seuil, 1994.

Chevalier, Michel. *Système de la Méditerranée.* Paris: Aux bureaux du Globe, 1832.

Chibber, Vivek. *Postcolonial Theory and the Specter of Capital.* London: Verso Books, 2013.

Chopin, Charlotte Ann. "Pages without Borders: Global Networks and the Settler Press in Algeria, 1881–1914." In "Settler Colonialism and French Algeria," edited by Fiona Barclay, Charlotte Ann Chopin, and Margin Evans. Special issue, *Settler Colonial Studies* 8, no. 2 (2018): 152–74.

Christelow, Allan. *Algerians without Borders: The Making of a Global Frontier Society.* Gainesville: University Press of Florida, 2012.

Clancier, Georges-Emmanuel. *Audisio, Camus et Roblès, Frères de soleil: leurs combats.* Aix-en-Provence: Édisud, 2005.

Clancy-Smith, Julia. "Islam, Gender, and Identities in the Making of French Algeria, 1830–1962." In *Domesticating the Empire: Race, Gender, and Family Life in French and Dutch Colonialism*, edited by Julia Clancy-Smith and Frances Gouda, 155–74. Charlottesville: University of Virginia Press, 1998.

Clancy-Smith, Julia. *Rebel and Saint: Muslim Notables, Populist Protest, Colonial Encouters (Algeria and Tunisia, 1800–1904).* Berkeley: University of California Press, 1997.

Clarke, Jackie. *France in the Age of Organization: Factory, Home, and Nation from the 1920s to Vichy.* New York: Berghahn Books, 2011.

Clarno, Andy. *Neoliberal Apartheid: Palestine/Israel and South Africa after 1994.* Chicago: University of Chicago Press, 2017.

Clément, Alain. "L'Analyse économique de la question coloniale en France (1870–1914)." *Revue d'économie politique* 123, no. 1 (2013): 51–82.

Clément, Alain. "French Economic Liberalism and the Colonial Issue at the Beginning of the Second Colonial Empire (1830–1870)." *History of Economic Ideas* 21, no. 1 (2013): 47–75.

Cleveland, William L. *The Making of an Arab Nationalist: Ottomanism and Arabism in the Thought of Sati' al-Husri.* Princeton, NJ: Princeton University Press, 1971.

Closon, Francis-Louis. *Un homme nouveau: L'ingénieur économiste.* Vendome: Presses universitaires de France, 1961.

Cohen, William B. "The Algerian War, the French State and Official Memory." *Historical Reflections/Réflexions Historiques* 28, no. 2 (2002): 219–39.

Cohen, William B. "The Colonial Policy of the Popular Front." *French Historical Studies* 7, no. 3 (1972): 368–93.

Cole, Joshua. *Lethal Provocation: The Constantine Murders and the Politics of French Algeria.* Ithaca, NY: Cornell University Press, 2020.

Colin, Roland, Robert Bruton, Raymond Cartier, L. V. Thomas, Guy Belloncle, Alain Reder, Momique Piettre, and Hamid Temmar. "Des relations entre la France et l'Algérie aux relations entre la France et le Tiers Monde, débat entre Robert Buron et Raymond Cartier." *Développement et Civilisations* 43 (March 1971): 7–14.

Colla, Elliot. *Conflicted Antiquities: Egyptology, Egyptomania, Egyptian Modernity.* Durham, NC: Duke University Press, 2007.

Collot, Claude. *Les institutions de l'Algérie durant la période coloniale: 1830–1962.* Paris: Éditions du CNRS, 1987.

Colonna, Fanny. "Educating Conformity in French Algeria." In *Tensions of Empire: Colonial Cultures in a Bourgeois World,* edited by Frederick Cooper and Ann Laura Stoler, 346–72. Berkeley: University of California Press, 1997.

Colonna, Fanny. *Eléments d'histoire sociale sur l'Algérie rurale.* Algiers: Office des publications universitaires, 1987.

Colonna, Fanny. "The Nation's 'Unknowing Other': Three Intellectuals and the Culture(s) of Being Algerian, or the Impossibility of Subaltern Studies in Algeria." *Journal of North African Studies* 8, no. 1 (2003): 155–70.

Colonna, Fanny. *Les Versets de l'invincibilité: Permanence et changements religieux dans l'Algérie contemporaine.* Paris: Presses de la Fondation nationale des sciences politiques, 1995.

Conklin, Alice. *A Mission to Civilize: The Republican Idea of Empire in France and West Africa, 1895–1930.* Stanford, CA: Stanford University Press, 1997.

Conklin, Alice. *In the Museum of Man: Race, Anthropology, and Empire in France, 1850–1950.* Ithaca, NY: Cornell University Press, 2013.

Connelly, Matthew. *A Diplomatic Revolution: Algeria's Fight for Independence and the Origins of the Post–Cold War Era.* Oxford: Oxford University Press, 2002.

Cooper, Frederick. *Citizenship between Empire and Nation: Remaking France and French Africa, 1945–1960.* Princeton, NJ: Princeton University Press, 2014.

Cooper, Frederick. *Decolonization and African Society: The Labor Question in French and British Africa.* Cambridge: Cambridge University Press, 1996.

Coquery-Vidrovitch, Catherine. "Vichy et l'industrialisation aux colonies." *Revue d'histoire de la deuxième guerre mondiale* 29, no. 114 (1979): 69–94.

Corm, Charles. *La montagne inspirée.* Beirut: Édition de la Revue Phénicienne, 1934.

Cote, Marc. "Hal Yujad Fallahun Jaza'iriyyun?" *Insaniyat* 7 (1999): 5–9.

Cotta, Alain. "Les Perspectives décennales du développement économique de l'Algérie et le plan de Constantine." *Revue économique* 10, no. 6 (1959): 913–46.

Cottier, Jean Louis. *La technocratie, nouveau pouvoir*. Paris: Éditions du Cerf, 1959.

Coulthard, Glen. *Red Skin, White Masks: Rejecting the Colonial Politics of Recognition.* Minneapolis: University of Minnesota Press, 2014.

Courreye, Charlotte. *L'Algérie des oulémas: Une histoire de l'Algérie contemporaine (1931–1991)*. Paris: Éditions de la Sorbonne, 2020.

Cronon, William, ed. *Uncommon Ground: Rethinking the Human Place in Nature.* New York: W. W. Norton and Company, 1996.

Cross, Kolleen M. "The Evolution of Colonial Agriculture: The Creation of Algerian 'Vignoble,' 1870–1892." *Proceedings of the Meeting of the French Colonial Historical Society* 16 (1992): 57–72.

Curtis, Michael. *Orientalism and Islam: Thinkers on Muslim Government in the Middle East and India*. Cambridge: Cambridge University Press, 2009.

Daumas, M., and M. Fabar. *La Grande Kabylie: Études historiques*. Paris: L. Hachette, 1847.

Davidson, Naomi. *Only Muslim: Embodying Islam in Twentieth-Century France.* Ithaca, NY: Cornell University Press, 2012.

Dávila, Jerry. "Gilberto Freyre: Racial Populism and Ethnic Nationalism." In *Luso-Tropicalism and Its Discontents: The Making and Unmaking of Racial Exceptionalism*, edited by Warwick Anderson, Ricardo Roque, and Ricardo Ventura Santos, 45–67. New York: Berghahn Books, 2019.

Davis, David Brion. "Constructing Race: A Reflection." *William and Mary Quarterly* 54, no. 1 (1997): 7–18.

Davis, Diana K. *Resurrecting the Granary of Rome: Environmental History and French Colonial Expansion in North Africa*. Athens: Ohio University Press, 2007.

Davis, Muriam Haleh. "'Incommensurate Ontologies'? Anti-Black Racism and the Question of Islam in French Algeria." *Lateral* 10, no. 1 (2021). https://doi.org/10.25158/L10.1.XX.

Davis, Muriam Haleh. "North Africa and the Common Agricultural Policy: From Colonial Pact to European Integration." In *North Africa and the Making of Europe: Governance, Institutions and Culture*, edited by Muriam Haleh Davis and Thomas Serres, 43–66. London: Bloomsbury Academic, 2018.

Davis, Muriam Haleh. "Qu'est-ce qu'un échec? Histoire économique et mémoire colonial." In *Mémoires algériennes en transmission*, edited by Giulia Fabbiano, 51–67. Algiers: Barzakh Press, 2022.

Davis, Muriam Haleh. "The Sahara as the 'Cornerstone' of Eurafrica: European Integration and Technical Sovereignty Seen from the Desert." *Journal of European Integration History* 23, no. 1 (2017): 97–112.

Davis, Muriam Haleh. "'The Transformation of Man' in French Algeria: Economic Planning and the Social Sciences, 1958–1962." *Journal of Contemporary History* 52, no. 1 (2017): 73–94.

Dawisha, Adeed. *Arab Nationalism in the Twentieth Century: From Triumph to Despair*. Princeton, NJ: Princeton University Press, 2003.

Dawn, C. Ernest. "The Origins of Arab Nationalism." In *The Origins of Arab Nationalism*, edited by Rashid Khalidi, Lisa Anderson, Muhammad Muslih, and Reeva S. Simon, 3–30. New York: Columbia University Press, 1991.

d'Ivry, Théodore Fortin. *L'Algérie: Son importance, sa colonisation, son avenir*. Paris: Rignoux, 1845.

Délégation générale du gouvernement en Algérie. *Plan de Constantine, 1959–1963: Rapport général*. Algiers: Direction du plan et des études économiques, 1960.

Denord, François. "French Neoliberalism and Its Divisions: From the Colloque Walter Lippmann to the Fifth Republic." In *The Road from Mont Pèlerin: The Making of the Neoliberal Thought Collective*, edited by Philip Mirowski and Dieter Plehwe, 45–67. Cambridge, MA: Harvard University Press, 2009.

Denord, François. "The Origins of Neoliberalism in France: Louis Rougier and the 1938 Walter Lippmann Conference." *Le Mouvement social* 2, no. 195 (2001): 9–34.

de Raousset-Boulbon, Gaston. *De la colonisation et des institutions civiles en Algérie*. Paris: Dauvin et Fontaine, 1847.

de Saint-Sauveur, Jacques Grasset. *Encyclopédie des voyages contenant l'abrégé historique des mœurs, usages, habitudes domestiques, religions [...]*. [Paris?]: Deroy, 1796.

Destanne de Bernis, Gérard. "L'Afrique de l'indépendance politique à l'indépendance économique." In *L'Afrique de l'indépendance politique à l'indépendance économique*, edited by Gérard Destanne de Bernis and John D. Esseks, 19–61. Paris: François Maspero, 1975.

Devji, Faisal. *Muslim Zion*. Cambridge, MA: Harvard University Press, 2013.

Dib, Mohammed. *L'incendie*. Paris: Éditions du Seuil, 1954.

Dirèche-Slimani, Karima. *Chrétiens de Kabylie 1873–1954: Une action missionaire dans l'Algérie coloniale*. Paris: Bouchène, 2004.

Dirks, Nicholas. *Castes of Mind: Colonialism and the Making of Modern India*. Princeton, NJ: Princeton University Press, 2011.

Dosse, François. *History of Structuralism: The Rising Sign, 1945–1966*. Translated by Deborah Glassman. Minneapolis: University of Minnesota Press, 1998.

Doumani, Beshara. *Rediscovering Palestine: Merchants and Peasants in Jabal Nablus, 1700–1900*. Berkeley: University of California Press, 1995.

Dramé, Papa, and Samir Saul. "Le Projet d'Eurafrique en France (1946–1960): Quête de puissance ou atavisme colonial?" *Guerres mondiales et conflits contemporains* 216 (2004): 95–114.

Driss, Nassima. "L'irruption de Makkam Ech-Chahid dans le paysage algérois: Monument et vulnérabilité des représentations." *L'Homme et la société* 4, no. 146 (2002): 61–76.

Drolet, Michael. "A Nineteenth-Century Mediteranean Union: Michel Chevalier's *Système de la Méditerranée*." *Mediterranean Historical Review* 30, no. 2 (2015): 147–68.

Du Bois, W. E. B. *Black Reconstruction in America, 1860–1880*. New York: Free Press, 1935.

Duclos, Jacques. *Gaullisme, technocratie, corporatisme*. Paris: Éditions sociales, 1963.

Duffy, Andrea. *Nomad's Land: Pastoralism and French Environmental Policy in the Nineteenth-Century Mediterranean*. Lincoln: University of Nebraska Press, 2019.

Dulong, Delphine. *Moderniser la politique: Aux origines de la Ve République*. Paris: L'Harmattan, 1997.

Duvingaud, Jean. "George Gurvitch: Une théorie sociologique de l'autogestion." *Autogestion: Études, débats, documents* 1 (1966): 5–12.

Eckert, Andreas, Stephen Malinowski, and Corinna R. Unger. "Modernizing Missions: Approaches to 'Developing' the Non-Western World after 1945." *Journal of Modern European History* 8, no. 1 (2010): 5–135.

Effose, Sabine. "Paul Delouvrier et les Villes Nouvelles (1961–1969)." In *Paul Delouvrier, un grand commis de l'État*, edited by Sébastien Laurent, 75–86. Paris: Presses Sciences Po, 2005.

El Hamri, Jamel. *La vocation civilisationnelle de l'Islam dans l'œuvre de Malek Bennabi*. Paris: Les Éditions du Cerf, 2020.

Elsenhans, Hartmut. *La guerre d'Algérie 1954–1962: La transition d'une France à une autre*. Paris: Publisud, 2000.

El Shakry, Omnia. *The Great Social Laboratory: Subjects of Knowledge in Colonial and Postcolonial Egypt*. Stanford, CA: Stanford University Press, 2007.

Elyachar, Julia. *Markets of Disposession: NGOs, Economic Development, and the State in Cairo*. Durham, NC: Duke University Press, 2005.

Elyachar, Julia. "Neoliberalism, Rationality, and the Savage Slot." In *Mutant Neoliberalism: Market Rule and Political Rupture*, edited by William Callison and Zachary Manfredi, 178–95. New York: Fordham University Press, 2020.

Emerit, Marcel. *Les Saint-Simoniens en Algérie*. Paris: Les Belles Lettres, 1941.

Escobar, Arturo. *Encountering Development: The Making and Unmaking of the Third World*. Princeton, NJ: Princeton University Press, 1995.

Evans, Martin. *Algeria: France's Undeclared War*. Oxford: Oxford University Press, 2012.

Fabbiano, Giulia. "Le temps long du *hirak*: Le passé et ses présences." *L'Année du Maghreb* 21 (2019): 117–30.

Fallers, L. A. "Are African Cultivators to Be Called 'Peasants'?" *Current Anthropology* 2, no. 2 (1961): 108–10.

Fanon, Frantz. *The Wretched of the Earth*. Translated by Richard Philcox. New York: Grove Press, 2004.

Farmer, Jared. *Trees in Paradise: A California History*. New York: W. W. Norton and Company, 2013.

Farmer, Sarah. *Rural Interventions: The French Countryside after 1945*. Oxford: Oxford University Press, 2020.

Federici, Sylvia. *Caliban and the Witch: Women, the Body and Primitive Accumulation*. Brooklyn, NY: Autonomedia, 2014.

Feichtinger, Moritz. "'A Great Reformatory': Social Planning and Strategic Resettlement in Late Colonial Kenya and Algeria." *Journal of Contemporary History* 51 (2017): 45–72.

Ferguson, James. *The Anti-politics Machine: Development, Depoliticization, and Bureaucratic Power in Lesotho*. Minneapolis: University of Minnesota Press, 1994.

Fernando, Mayanthi L. *The Republic Unsettled: Muslim French and the Contradictions of Secularism*. Durham, NC: Duke University Press, 2014.

Fitzgerald, Edward Peter. "Did France's Colonial Empire Make Economic Sense? A Perspective from the Postwar Decade, 1946–1956." *Journal of Economic History* 48, no. 2 (1988): 373–85.

Flarier, Antonin. "Le banditisme rural en Algérie à la période coloniale (1871–années 1920)." PhD diss., Université Panthéon-Sorbonne–Paris I, 2020.

FLN–Commission Centrale d'Orientation. *La Charte d'Alger—Ensemble des textes.* Algiers: Imprimerie Nationale Algérienne, 1964.

Fogarty, Richard. "The French Empire." In *Empires at War, 1911–1923*, edited by Robert Gerwarth and Erez Manela, 109–29. Oxford: Oxford University Press, 2014.

Fogarty, Richard. *Race and War in France: Colonial Subjects in the French Army.* Baltimore, MD: Johns Hopkins University Press, 2013.

Fontaine, Darcie. *Decolonizing Christianity: Religion and the End of Empire in France and Algeria.* New York: Cambridge University Press, 2016.

Fontaine, Darcie. "Refugees, Sovereignty, and Humanitarian Anxiety: Regroupment Camps and the Limits of Universal Rights in the Algerian War of Independence." Lecture, University of Ottawa, Gordon F. Henderson Series on the History of Refugees, November 11, 2016.

Ford, Caroline. "Reforestation, Landscape Conservation, and the Anxieties of Empire in French Colonial Algeria." *American Historical Review* 113, no. 2 (2008): 341–62.

Foucault, Michel. *The Birth of Biopolitics: Lectures at the Collège de France, 1978–1979.* Edited by Michel Senellart. Translated by Graham Burchell. New York: Palgrave Macmillan, 2008.

Foucault, Michel. *Les mots et les choses: Une archéologie des sciences humaines.* Paris: Éditions Gallimard, 1966.

Foxlee, Neil. *Albert Camus's "The New Mediterranean Culture": A Text and Its Contexts.* Bern: Peter Lang AG, 2010.

Francis, Kyle. "Catholic Missionaries in Colonial Algeria." *French Historical Studies* 39, no. 4 (2016): 685–715.

Franklin, Elise. "A Bridge across the Mediterranean: Nafissa Sid Cara and the Politics of Emancipation during the Algerian War." *French Politics, Culture, and Society* 36, no. 2 (2018): 28–52.

Fraser, Nancy. "Roepke Lecture in Economic Geography—From Exploitation to Expropriation: Historic Geographies of Racial Capitalism." *Economic Geography* 94, no. 1 (2018): 1–17.

Fyot, Jean-Louis. *Dimensions de l'homme et science économique.* Paris: Presses universitaires de France, 1952.

Gadant, Monique. "Nationalisme et anticolonialisme dans les sciences sociales." *Lignes* 30 (1997): 77–91.

Galissot, René, Friedrich Engels, and Karl Marx. *Marx, marxisme, et Algérie: Textes de Marx-Engels.* Paris: Union générale d'éditions, 1976.

Garavini, Giuliano. *After Empires: European Integration, Decolonization, and the Challenge from the Global South, 1957–1986.* Oxford: Oxford University Press, 2012.

Gendarme, René. *L'Économie de l'Algérie: Sous-développement et politique de crois-sance.* Paris: Librarie Armand Colin, 1959.

Gershoni, Israel, ed. *Arab Responses to Fascism and Nazism: Attraction and Repulsion.* Austin: University of Texas Press, 2014.

Getachew, Adom. *Worldmaking after Empire: The Rise and Fall of Self-Determination.* Princeton, NJ: Princeton University Press, 2019.

Ghabrial, Sarah. "Reading Agamben from Algiers: The Racial Meonymy of Perma-nent Exception." *Comparative Studies of South Asia, Africa and the Middle East* 40, no. 2 (2020): 237–42.

Giacone, Alessandro. *Jean Guyot: Le financier humaniste.* Paris: Éditions du CNRS, 2015.

Giacone, Alessandro. "Paul Delouvrier et le Plan de Constantine." In *Michel Debré et l'Algérie, acts du colloque, Assemblée Nationale, 27 et 28 avril 2006,* edited by Association des amis de Michel Debré, 93–108. Paris: Éditions Champs Elysees, 2007.

Gibson-Graham, J. K. *The End of Capitalism (As We Knew It).* Minneapolis: Univer-sity of Minnesota Press, 2006.

Gilmore, Ruth Wilson. *Golden Gulag: Prisons, Surplus, Crisis, and Opposition in Globalizing California.* Berkeley: University of California Press, 2006.

Goldberg, David Theo. *The Racial State.* Malden, MA: Blackwell, 2002.

Goldberg, David Theo. *The Threat of Race: Reflections on Racial Neoliberalism.* Mal-den, MA: Wiley-Blackwell, 2009.

Goodman, Jane E., and Paul Silverstein, eds. *Bourdieu in Algeria: Colonial Politics, Ethnographic Practices, Theoretical Developments.* Lincoln: University of Ne-braska Press, 2009.

Goswami, Manu. *Producing India: From Colonial Economy to National Space.* Chi-cago: University of Chicago Press, 2004.

Graebner, Seth. *History's Place: Nostalgia and the City in French Algerian Literature.* Lanham, MD: Lexington, 2007.

Gran, Peter. "Islamic Marxism in Comparative History: The Case of Lebanon, Re-flections on the Recent Book of Husayn Muruway." In *The Islamic Impulse,* edited by Barbara Freyer Stowasser, 106–20. London: Croon Helm in associaiton with the Center for Contemporary Arab Studies, Georgetown University, 1987.

Greenfield, Jerome. "The Price of Violence: Money, the French State, and 'Civiliza-tion' during the Conquest of Algeria, 1830–1850s." *French Historical Studies* 43, no. 4 (2020): 537–69.

Grenfell, Michael. "Bourdieu in the Field: From the Bearn and to Algeria—A Timely Response." *French Cultural Studies* 17, no. 2 (2006): 223–39.

Grosrichard, Alain. *The Sultan's Court: European Fantasies of the East.* Translated by Liz Heron. London: Verso Books, 1998.

Groupes anarchistes d'action révolutionnaire. *Noir et rouge: Cahier d'études anarchistes-communites* 36 (December 1966).

Gualtieri, Sarah. *Between Arab and White: Race and Ethnicity in the Early Syrian American Diaspora.* Berkeley: University of California Press, 2009.

Guenoun, Ali. *La question kabyle dans le nationalisme algérien, 1949–1962*. Vulaines-sur-Seine: Éditions du Croquant, 2021.

Guérin, Daniel. *L'Algérie qui se cherche*. Paris: Présence Africaine, 1964.

Guérin, Daniel. *Où va le peuple américain?* Paris: Éditions Julliard, Collection les Temps Modernes, 1952.

Guha, Ranajit. *Dominance without Hegemony: History and Power in Colonial India*. Cambridge, MA: Harvard University Press, 1997.

Guha, Ranajit. *Elementary Aspects of Peasant Insurgency in Colonial India*. Durham, NC: Duke University Press, 1999.

Guha, Sumit. *Beyond Caste: Identity and Power in South Asia, Past and Present*. Leiden: Brill Academic Publishers, 2014.

Guichard, Pierre. "Problèmes ruraux en Algérie." PhD diss., L'institut d'études politiques de Lyon, 1962.

Guignard, Didier. "Conservatoire ou révolutionnaire? Le sénatus-consulte de 1863 appliqué au regime foncier d'Algérie." *Revue d'histoire du XIXe siècle* 41, no. 2 (2010): 81–95.

Guignard, Didier. "Les inventeurs de la tradition 'melk' et 'arch' en Algérie." In *Les acteurs des tranformations foncières autour de la Méditerranée au XIXe siècle*, edited by Didier Guignard and Vanessa Guéno, 49–94. Paris: Karthala, 2013.

Guy, Kolleen M. "Culinary Connections and Colonial Memories in France and Algeria." *Food and History* 8, no. 1 (2010): 219–36.

Haddour, Azzedine. *Colonial Myths: History and Narrative*. Manchester: Manchester University Press, 2000.

Haguenauer-Caceres, Lucie. "Construire à l'étranger: Le rôle de la SCET Coopération en Côte d'Ivoire de 1959 à 1976." *Histoire urbaine* 3, no. 23 (2008): 145–59.

Haim, Sylvia G., ed. *Arab Nationalism: An Anthology*. Berkeley: University of California Press, 1962.

Hajji, Muhammad. *Mutanaw'at Muhammad Hajji*. Beirut: Dar al-Maghrib al-Islami, 1998.

Halawani, Ahmad. *Al-Thawra al-Jaza'iriyya fi al-Sihafa al-Suriyya, 1955–1957: Dirasa li-Mawaqif al-Tayyarat al-Siyasiyya*. Damascus: Manshurat al-Hay'a al-ʿAmma al-Suriyya li-l-Kitab , 2017.

Hall, Stuart. *The Fateful Triangle: Race, Ethnicity, Nation*. Cambridge, MA: Harvard University Press, 2017.

Hanebrink, Paul. *A Specter Haunting Europe: The Myth of Judeo-Bolshevism*. Cambridge, MA: Harvard University Press, 2018.

Hansen, Peo, and Stefan Jonsson. *Eurafrica: The Untold History of European Integration and Colonialism*. London: Bloomsbury, 2014.

Harbi, Mohammed. *Une vie debout: Mémoires politiques, Tome 1: 1945–1962*. Paris: Éditions La Découverte, 2001.

Harbi, Mohammed. "La guerre d'Algérie a commencé à Sétif le 8 mai 1945. " *Le Monde diplomatique*, May 2001. https://www.mondediplomatique.fr/2005/05/HARBI/12191.

Harbi, Mohammed, and Gilbert Meynier. *Le FLN: Documents et histoire, 1954–1962*. Paris: Librarie Arthème Fayard, 2004.

Haroun, Ali. *L'été de la discorde: Algérie 1962*. Algiers: Casbah, 1999.

Harris, Cheryl I. "Whiteness as Property." *Harvard Law Review* 106, no. 8 (1993): 1707–91.

Hautberg, Maurius, and Maurice Parodi. *Étude sur le secteur agricole sous-développé en Algérie*. Aix-en-Provence: Librairie de l'Université, 1960.

Harvey, David. "Globalization and the 'Spatial Fix.'" *Geographische Revue* 2 (2001): 23–30.

Harvey, David. *The Limits to Capital*. 1982. Reprint, London: Verso Books, 2006.

Harvey, David. *Spaces of Capital: Towards a Critical Geography*. Edinburgh: Edinburgh University Press, 2001.

Hassett, Dónal. *Mobilizing Memory: The Great War and the Language of Politics in Colonial Algeria, 1918–39*. Oxford: Oxford University Press, 2019.

Hazard, Anthony Q., Jr. *Postwar Anti-Racism: The United States, UNESCO, and "Race," 1945–1968*. New York: Palgrave Macmillan, 2012.

Heath, Elizabeth. "The Color of French Wine: Southern Wine Producers Respond to Competition from the Algerian Wine Industry in the Early Third Republic." *French Politics, Culture, and Society* 35, no. 2 (2017): 89–110.

Heath, Elizabeth. *Wine, Sugar, and the Making of Modern France: Global Economic Crisis and the Racialization of French Citizenship*. Cambridge: Cambridge University Press, 2014.

Hellman, John. *The Knight-Monks of Vichy France: Uriage, 1940–1945*. Liverpool: Liverpool University Press, 1997.

Henni, Ahmed. *La colonisation agraire et le sous-développement en Algérie*. Algiers: Ahmed Zabana, 1982.

Henni, Samia. *Architecture of Counterrevolution: The French Army in Northern Algeria*. Zürich: Zürich gta Verlag, 2017.

Henry, Jean-Robert. "La recomposition des savoirs au Maghreb à l'époque de la coopération." *L'Année du Maghreb* 5 (2009): 573–87.

Henry, Jean-Robert, et al., eds. *Le temps de la coopération: Sciences sociales et décolonisation au Maghreb*. Aix-en-Provence: IREMAM, 2012.

Hickman, Mary J., and Bronwen Walter. "Deconstructing Whiteness: Irish Women in Britain." *Feminist Review* 50 (1995): 5–19.

Hill, Peter. *Utopia and Civilisation in the Arab Nahda*. Cambridge: Cambridge University Press, 2019.

Hirschman, Albert O. *The Passions and the Interests: Political Arguments for Capitalism before Its Triumph*. Princeton, NJ: Princeton University Press, 1977.

Hirschman, Albert O. *The Strategy of Economic Development*. New Haven, CT: Yale University Press, 1958.

Hodge, Joseph Morgan. *Triumph of the Expert: Agrarian Doctrines of Development and the Legacies of British Colonialism*. Athens: Ohio University Press, 2007.

Honneth, Axel, Hermann Kocyba, and Bernd Schwibs. "The Struggle for Symbolic Order: An Interview with Pierre Bourdieu." *Theory, Culture, and Society* 3 (1986): 35–51.

Horne, Allistair. *A Savage War of Peace: Algeira, 1954–1962*. London: Macmillan, 1987.

House, Jim. "Intervening on 'Problem' Areas and their Inhabitants: The Socio-Political and Security Logics behind Censuses in the Algiers Shantytowns, 1941–1962." *Histoire et Mesure* 35, no. 1 (2019): 121–50.

Huillerly, Elise. "The Black Man's Burden—The Cost of Colonization of French West Africa." *Journal of Economic History* 74, no. 1 (2013): 1–38.

Husain, Taha. *Mustaqbal al-Thaqafa fi Misr*. 1938. Reprint, Cairo: Dar al-Ma'arif, 1996.

Ince, Onur Ulas. *Colonial Capitalism and the Dilemmas of Liberalism*. Oxford: Oxford University Press, 2018.

"Interview with Ben Bella." In *Man, State, and Society in the Contemporary Maghrib*, edited by I. William Zartman, 124–26. New York: Praeger, 1973.

Isnard, Hildebert. "Les Structures de l'autogestion agricole en Algérie." *Méditerrannée* 9, no. 2 (1968): 139–63.

Isnard, Hildebert. "Vigne et colonisation en algérie: 1880–1947." *Annales: Histoire, sciences sociales* 2, no. 3 (1947): 288–300.

Isnard, Hildebert. "Vigne et structures en Algérie." *Diogène* 27 (1959): 76–96.

Jakes, Aaron. *Egypt's Occupation: Colonial Economism and the Crises of Capitalism*. Stanford, CA: Stanford University Press, 2020.

Jankowski, James. "Arab Nationalism in 'Nasserism' and Egyptian State Policy, 1952–1958." In *Rethinking Nationalism in the Arab Middle East*, edited by Israel Gershoni and James Jankowski, 150–67. New York: Columbia University Press, 1997.

Jansen, Willy. "French Bread and Algerian Wine: Conflicting Identities in French Algeria." In *Food, Drink, Identity: Cooking, Eating, and Drinking in Europe since the Middle Ages*, edited by Peter Scholliers, 195–218. New York: Berg, 2001.

Jarvis, Jill. *Decolonizing Memory: Algeria and the Politics of Testimony*. Durham, NC: Duke University Press, 2021.

Jebari, Idriss. "When Malek Bennabi Recollected His Colonial Education: Cultural Authenticity, Nostalgia, and Renaissance in Algeria." In *Cultural Entanglements in the Pre-independence Arab World: Arts, Thought, and Literature*, edited by Anthony Gorman and Sarah Irving, 239–60. London: I. B. Tauris, 2020.

Johnson, Jennifer. *The Battle for Algeria: Sovereignty, Health Care, and Humanism*. Philadelphia: University of Pennsylvania Press, 2016.

Joly, Danièle. *The French Communist Party and the Algerian War*. Basingstoke: Macmillan, 1990.

Jomier, Augustin. *Islam, réforme et colonisation: Une histoire de l'Ibadisme en Algérie (1882–1962)*. Paris: Éditions de la Sorbonne, 2020.

Julien, Charles-André. *Histoire de l'Algérie contemporaine: La conquête et les débuts de la colonisation (1827–1871)*. Paris: Presses universitaires de France, 1964.

Kalter, Christoph. *The Discovery of the Third World: Decolonization and the Rise of the New Left in France, 1950–1976*. Cambridge: Cambridge University Press, 2016.

Karlinsky, Nahum. *California Dreaming: Ideology, Society, and Technology in the Citrus Industry of Palestine, 1890–1939*. Albany: State University of New York Press, 2005.

Kateb, Kamel. *Européens, "Indigènes" et Juifs en Algérie (1830–1962)*. Paris: Institut national d'études démographiques, 2001.

Kateb, Kamel. "La Statistique coloniale en Algérie (1830–1962), entre la reproduction du système métropolitain et les impératifs d'adaptation à la réalité algérienne." *Courrier des statistiques* 112 (2004): 3–17.

Kaufman, Asher. *Reviving Phoenicia: The Search for Identity in Lebanon*. London: I.B. Tauris, 2004.

Khuri-Makdisi, Ilham. "Inscribing Socialism into the Nahda: Al-Muqtataf, al-Hilal, and the Construction of a Leftist Reformist Worldview, 1880–1914." In *The Making of the Arab Intellectual: Empire, Public Sphere and the Colonial Coordinates of Selfhood*, edited by Dyala Hamzah, 63–89. London: Routledge, 2012.

Knauss, Peter R. *The Persistence of Patriarchy: Class, Gender, and Ideology in Twentieth-Century Algeria*. New York: Praeger, 1987.

Krim, Abdel. "La chute de Ben Bella." *Sous le drapeau du socialisme*, nos. 19–20 (1965): 1–5.

Kuby, Emma. *Political Survivors: The Resistance, the Cold War, and the Fight against Concentration Camps after 1945*. Ithaca, NY: Cornell University Press, 2019.

Kuisel, Richard. "L'*American way of life* et les mission françaises de productivité." *Vingtième Siècle: Revue d'histoire* 17 (1988): 21–38.

Kuisel, Richard. *Capitalism and the State in Modern France*. New York: Cambridge University Press, 1981.

Labat, Séverine. *Les islamistes algériens—entre les urnes et le maquies*. Paris: Seuil, 1995.

Lacheraf, Mostefa. *L'Algérie: Nation et société*. Paris: François Maspero, 1965.

Laks, Monique. *Autogestion ouvrière et pouvoir politique en Algérie (1962–1965)*. Paris: Études et documentation internationales, 1970.

Lal, Priya. *African Socialism in Postcolonial Tanzania: Between the Village and the World*. New York: Cambridge University Press, 2015.

Latour, Bruno. *The Politics of Nature: How to Bring the Sciences into Democracy*. Cambridge, MA: Harvard University Press, 2004.

Launay, Marcel. *Robert Buron: Témoignages de Pierre Pfimlin and Jean Offredo*. Paris: Beauchesne, 1993.

Launay, Michel. *Paysans algériens 1960–2006*. 1963. Reprint, Paris: Éditions Karthala, 2007.

Laurens, Henry. *Orientales II: La 3e république et l'Islam*. Paris: Éditions du CNRS, 2004.

Lazreg, Marnia. *The Eloquence of Silence: Algerian Women in Question*. New York: Routledge, 2014.

Lebeau, Louis. *L'Algriculture algérienne*. Algiers: Baconnier, 1954.

Lefebvre, Henri. *Position: Contre les technocrats*. Paris: Éditions Gonthier, 1967.

Lefeuvre, Daniel. *Chère Algérie: Comptes et mécomptes de la tutelle coloniale, 1930–1962*. Saint-Denis: Société française d'histoire d'outre-mer, 1997.

Lefeuvre, Daniel. "L'Échec du plan de Constantine." In *La Guerre d'Algérie et les Français*, edited by Jean-Pierre Rioux, 320–27. Paris: Fayard, 1990.

Lefeuvre, Daniel. *Pour en finir avec la repentance coloniale*. Paris: Flammarion, 2006.

Lefeuvre, Daniel. "Vichy et la modernisation de l'Algérie: Intention ou réalité?" *Vingtième Siècle: Revue d'histoire* no. 42 (1994): 7–16.

Legg, Charlotte Ann. *The New White Race: Settler Colonialism and the Press in French Algeria, 1860–1914.* Lincoln: University of Nebraska Press, 2021.

Lemoine, Hervé. "Paul Delouvrier et l'Algérie, comment servir et représenter l'État dans une guerre d'information?" In *Paul Delouvrier, un grand commis de l'État,* edited by Sébastien Laurent, 41–71. Paris: Presses Sciences Po, 2005.

Lenin, Vladimir. *La maladie infantile du communisme, le "gauchisme."* 1920. Reprint, Moscow: Éditions du Progrès, 1982.

Lentin, Alana. "Replacing 'Race,' Historicizing 'Culture' in Multiculturalism." *Patterns of Prejudice* 39, no. 4 (2005): 379–96.

Lequy, Roger. "L'agriculture algérienne de 1954–1962." *Revue de mondes muselmans et de la Méditerranée,* no. 8 (1970): 41–99.

Leroux, Denis. "Promouvoir une armée révolutionnaire pendant la guerre d'Algérie: Le centre d'instruction pacification et contre-guérilla d'Arzew (1957–1959)." *Vingtième Siècle: Revue d'histoire* 120, no. 4 (2013): 101–12.

Leroy-Beaulieu, Pierre Paul. *L'Algérie et la Tunisie.* Paris: Librarie Guillaumin, 1887.

Leroy-Beaulieu, Pierre Paul. *De la colonisation chez les peuples modernes.* Paris: Guillaumin, 1874.

LeSueur, James D. *Uncivil War: Intellectuals and Identity Politics during the Decolonization of Algeria.* Lincoln: University of Nebraska Press, 2001.

Le Tallec, Mathieu. "L'unité d'action des trotskystes, anarchistes et socialistes de gauche autour de l'anticolonialism et de l'anti-bonapartisme (1954–1958)." *Diacronie* 9, no. 1 (2012). https://doi.org/10.4000/diacronie.3077.

Liauzu, Claude. "La Méditerranée selon Fernand Braudel." *Confluences Méditerranée* 31 (1999): 179–87.

Lockman, Zachary. *Contending Visions of the Middle East: The History and Politics of Orientalism.* Cambridge: Cambridge University Press, 2013.

Lorcin, Patricia M. E. "Rome and France in Africa: Recovering Colonial Algeria's Latin Past." *French Historical Studies* 25, no. 2 (2002): 295–329.

Lowe, Lisa. *The Intimacies of Four Continents.* Durham, NC: Duke University Press, 2015.

Lucas, Philippe, and Jean-Claude Vatin. *L'Algérie des anthropologues.* Paris: François Maspero, 1975.

Lukács, George. *History and Class Consciousness: Studies in Marxist Dialectics.* Translated by Rodney Livingstone. Cambridge, MA: MIT Press, 1971.

Lunn, Joe. "'Les races guerrières': Racial Preconceptions in the French Military about West African Soldiers during the First World War." *Journal of Contemporary History* 34, no. 4 (1999): 517–36.

Luxemburg, Rosa. *The Accumulation of Capital.* 1913. Reprint, London: Routledge, 2003.

Lydon, Ghislaine. *On Trans-Saharan Trails: Islamic Law, Trade Networks, and Cross-Cultural Exchange in Nineteenth-Century Western Africa.* Cambridge: Cambridge University Press, 2012.

Lyons, Amelia H. *The Civilizing Mission in the Metropole: Algerian Families and the French Welfare State during Decolonization.* Stanford, CA: Stanford University Press, 2013.

MacMaster, Neil. *Burning the Veil: The Algerian War and the "Emancipation" of Muslim Women*. Manchester: Manchester University Press, 2012.

MacMaster, Neil. *War in the Mountains: Peasant Society and Counterinsurgency in Algeria*. Oxford: Oxford University Press, 2020.

Mahiou, Ahmed. "La nationalité en Algérie." In *Regards critiques et perspectives sur le droit et la fiscalité*, edited by Cyrille David, 395–407. Paris: LGDJ, 2005.

Mahsas, Ahmed. *L'autogestion en Algérie: Données politiques de ses premières étapes de son application*. Paris: Éditions Anthropos, 1975.

Makdisi, Ussama. *The Culture of Sectarianism: Community, History, and Violence in Nineteenth-Century Ottoman Lebanon*. Berkeley: University of California Press, 2000.

Malek, Redha. "La place seconde des intérêts économiques." In *Les accords d'Évian en conjoncture et en longue durée*, edited by René Gallissot, 11–20. Algiers: Casbah Editions, 1997.

Malley, Robert. *The Call from Algeria: Third Worldism, Revolution, and the Turn to Islam*. Berkeley: University of California Press, 1996.

Maravall, Laura. "Factor Endowments on the 'Frontier': Algerian Settler Agriculture at the Beginning of the 1900s." *Economic History Review* 73 (2020): 758–84.

Marié, Michel. *Les terres et les mots: Une traversée des sciences sociales*. Paris: Méridiens Klincksieck, 1989.

Marker, Emily. *Black France, White Europe: Youth, Race, and Belonging in the Postwar Era*. Ithaca, NY: Cornell University Press, 2022.

Marseille, Jacques. *Empire colonial et capitalisme français: Histoire d'un divorce*. Paris: Albin Michel, 1984.

Marsot, Afaf Lufti al-Sayyid. "The Ulama of Cairo in the Eighteenth and Nineteenth Centuries." In *Scholars, Saints, and Sufis: Muslim Religious Institutions in the Middle East since 1500*, edited by Nikki R. Kedie, 149–66. Berkeley: University of California Press, 1972.

Marthelot, Pierre. "L'Islam et le développement: Essai sur quelques publications récentes." *Archives de sociologie des religions* 14 (1962): 131–38.

Martinez, Maria Elena. *Genealogical Fictions: Limpieza de Sangre, Religion, and Gender in Colonial Mexico*. Stanford, CA: Stanford University Press, 2008.

Marx, Karl. *Capital: A Critique of Political Economy, Volume 1: The Process of Capitalist Production*. Edited by Frederick Engels. Translated by Samuel Moore and Edward Aveling. New York: International Publishers, 1967.

Marynower, Claire. *L'Algérie à gauche (1900–1962)*. Paris: Presses universitaires de France, 2018.

Massad, Joseph Andoni. *Islam in Liberalism*. Chicago: University of Chicago Press, 2016.

Massé, Pierre. *Le plan ou l'anti-hasard*. Paris: Gallimard, 1965.

Massé, Pierre. "Les principes de la planification française." *Weltwirtschaftliches Archiv* 92 (1964): 113–40.

McAllister, Ed. "Algeria's 'Belle Époque': Memories of the 1970s as a Window on the Present." In *Algeria: Nation, Culture, and Transnationalism: 1988–2015*, edited by Patrick Cowley, 46–62. Liverpool: Liverpool University Press, 2017.

McCluskey, Philip. "Commerce before Crusade? France, the Ottoman Empire, and the Barbary Pirates (1661–1669)." *French History* 32, no. 1 (2008): 1–21.

McDougall, James. *History and the Culture of Nationalism in Algeria*. Cambridge: Cambridge University Press, 2006.

McDougall, James. *A History of Algeria*. Cambridge: Cambridge University Press, 2017.

McDougall, James. "Rule of Experts? Governing Modernisation in Late Colonial French Africa." In *France's Modernising Mission: Citizenship, Welfare, and the Ends of Empire*, edited by Ed Naylor, 87–108. London: Palgrave Macmillan, 2018.

McDougall, James. "S'écrire un destin: L'association des 'ulama dans la révolution algérienne." *Bulletin de l'Institut d'histoire du temps présent* 83 (2004): 38–52.

McDougall, James. "The Secular State's Islamic Empire: Muslim Spaces and Subjects of Jurisdiction in Paris and Algeria, 1905–1957." *Comparative Studies in Society and History* 52, no. 3 (2010): 553–80.

McGuire, Valerie. "Bringing the Empire Home: Italian Fascism's Mediterranean Tour of Rhodes." *California Italian Studies* 8, no. 2 (2018): 1–27.

Melamed, Jodi. "Racial Capitalism." *Critical Ethnic Studies* 1, no. 1 (2015): 76–85.

Meloni, Giulia, and John Swinnen. "The Rise and Fall of the World's Largest Wine Exporter—and Its Institutional Legacy." *Journal of Wine Economics* 9, no. 1 (2014): 3–33.

Mendel, Yonathan, and Ronand Ranta. *From the Arab Other to the Israeli Self: Palestinian Culture in the Making of Israeli National Identity*. New York Routledge, 2016.

Mendras, Henri. "L'invention de la paysannerie: Un moment de l'histoire de la sociologie française d'après-guerre." *Revue française de sociologie* 41, no. 3 (2000): 539–52.

Mény, Yves. *La corruption de la République*. Paris: Fayard, 1991.

Merhavy, Menahem. "Arab Socialism and Ecumenical Tendencies in Egypt." *British Journal of Middle Eastern Studies* 43, no. 4 (2016): 472–85.

Merkel, Ian. "Fernand Braudel, Brazil, and the Empire of French Social Science: Newly Translated Sources from the 1930s." *French Historical Studies* 40, no. 1 (2017): 129–60.

Metcalf, Thomas R. *Imperial Connections: India in the Indian Ocean Arena, 1860–1920*. Berkeley: University of California Press, 2007.

Meynaud, Jean. "Qu'est-ce que la technocratie?" *Revue économique* 11, no. 4 (1960): 497–526.

Meynier, Gilbert. *L'Algérie révélée: La guerre de 1914–1918 et le premier quart du XXᵉ siècle*. Algiers: Éditions Bouchène, 2015.

Mezzadra, Sandro. "Marx in Algiers." *Radical Philosophy* 2, no. 1 (2018): 79–86. https://www.radicalphilosophy.com/article/marx-in-algiers.

Mintz, Sidney W. "The Rural Proletariat and the Problem of Rural Proletarian Consciousness." *Journal of Peasant Studies* 1, no. 3 (1974): 291–325.

Mirowski, Philip, and Dieter Plehwe, eds. *The Road from Mont Pèlerin: The Making of the Neoliberal Thought Collective*. Cambridge, MA: Harvard University Press, 2009.

Mises, Ludwig von. *Human Action: A Treatise on Economics*. 1963. Reprint, San Fransisco: Fox and Wilkes, 1996.

Mitchell, Timothy. *Colonizing Egypt*. Berkeley: University of California Press, 1988.

Mitchell, Timothy. "Fixing the Economy." *Cultural Studies* 21, no. 1 (1998): 82–101.

Mitchell, Timothy. "The Invention and Reinvention of the Egyptian Peasant." *International Journal of Middle East Studies* 22, no. 2 (1990): 129–50.

Mitchell, Timothy. *Rule of Experts: Egypt, Techno-politics, Modernity*. Berkeley: University of California Press, 2002.

Moe, Nelson J. *The View from Vesuvius: Italian Culture and the Southern Question*. Berkeley: University of California Press, 2006.

Mokhtefi, Elaine. *Algiers, Third World Capital*. New York: Verso Books, 2018.

Monnet, Jean. *Memoirs*. Translated by Richard Mayne. Garden City, NY: Doubleday, 1978.

Montarsolo, Yves. *L'Eurafrique: Contrepoint de l'idée d'Europe; Le cas français de la fin de la deuxième guerre mondiale aux négociations des traités de Rome*. Aix-en-Provence: Publications de l'Université de Provence, 2010.

Montesquieu, Charles de Secondat. *The Spirit of the Laws*. 1748. Reprint translated by Thomas Nugent. Kitchener, ON: Batoche Books, 2001.

Morin, Jean. *De Gaulle et l'Algérie: Mon témoignage: 1960–1962*. Paris: Albin Michel, 1999.

Morris, Rosalind C. "Theses on the Questions of War: History, Media, Terror." *Social Text* 20, no. 3 (2002): 149–75.

Moskowitz, Kara. *Seeing Like a Citizen: Decolonization, Development, and the Making of Kenya, 1945–1980*. Athens: Ohio University Press, 2019.

Moulin, Annie. *Peasant and Society in France since 1789*. Cambridge: Cambridge University Press, 1991.

Moussa, Nedjib Sidi. *Algérie, une autre histoire de l'indépendance*. Paris: Presses Universitaires de France, 2019.

Moyd, Michelle R. *Violent Intermediaries: African Soldiers, Conquest, and Everyday Colonialism in German East Africa*. Athens: Ohio University Press, 2014.

Muller, Karis. "Iconographie de l'Eurafrique." In *L'Europe unie et l'Afrique: De l'idée d'Eurafrique à la Convention de Lomé I*, edited by Marie-Thérèse and Gérard Boussat Bitsch, 9–33. Brussels: Bruylant, 2005.

Murphy, Michelle. *The Economization of Life: Calculative Infrastructures of Population and Economy*. Durham, NC: Duke University Press, 2017.

Mussard, Christine. "Réinventer la commune? Genèse de la commune mixte, une structure administrative inédite dans l'Algérie coloniale." *Histoire@Politique* 3, no. 27 (2015): 93–108.

Musso, Marta. "'Oil Will Set Us Free': The Hydrocarbon Industry and the Algerian Decolonization Process." In *Britain, France, and the Decolonization of Africa: Future Imperfect?*, edited by Andrew W. M. Smith and Chris Jeppesen, 62–84. London: UCL Press.

Musto, Marcello. *The Last Years of Karl Marx: An Intellectual Biography*. Stanford, CA: Stanford University Press, 2020.

Mutin, Georges. "Le commerce extérieur de l'Algérie en 1964." *Revue de géographie de Lyon* 40, no. 4 (1965): 345–65.

Myrdal, Gunnar. *Rich Lands and Poor: The Road to World Prosperity.* New York: Harper, 1958.

Nasiali, Minayo. *Native to the Republic: Empire, Social Citizenship, and Everyday Life in Marseille since 1945.* Ithaca, NY: Cornell University Press, 2016.

Nathan, Roger, and Paul Delouvrier. *Politique économique de la France.* Paris: Les Cours de Droit, 1949.

Naylor, Ed, ed. *France's Modernising Mission: Citizenship, Welfare, and the Ends of Empire.* London: Palgrave Macmillan, 2018.

Naylor, Philip Chiviges. "The Formative Influence of French Colonialism on the Life and Thought of Malek Bennabi (Malik bn Nabi)." *French Colonial History* 7 (2006): 129–42.

Naylor, Philip Chiviges. *France and Algeria: A History of Decolonization and Transformation.* Gainesville: University Press of Florida, 2000.

Nef, John Ulric. *La naissance de la civilisation industrielle et le monde contemporain.* Paris: Librairie Armand Colin, 1954.

Nelson, Bruce. *Irish Nationalists and the Making of the Irish Race.* Princeton, NJ: Princeton University Press, 2012.

Newsome, W. Brian. *French Urban Planning, 1940–1968: The Construction and Deconstruction of an Authoritarian System.* New York: Peter Lang, 2009.

Nilsen, Alf Gunvald. "Passages from Marxism to Postcolonialism: A Comment on Vivek Chibber's *Postcolonial Theory and the Specter of Capital.*" *Critical Sociology* 43, no. 4–5 (2015): 559–71.

Nord, Philip. *France's New Deal: From the Thirties to the Postwar Era.* Princeton, NJ: Princeton University Press, 2012.

Nord, Philip. "Reform, Conservation, and Adaptation: Sciences-Po, from the Popular Front to the Liberation." In *The Jacobin Legacy in Modern France: Essays in Honour of Vincent Wright,* edited by Sudhir Hazareesingh, 115–46. Oxford: Oxford University Press, 2002.

Nouschi, André. *Enquête sur le niveau de vie des populations rurales constantinoises de la conquête à 1919, essai d'histoire économique et sociale.* Paris: Presses Universitaires de France, 1961.

Osterhammel, Jürgen. *Colonialism: A Theoretical Overview.* Translated by Shelly L. Frisch. Princeton, NJ: Markus Wiener, 1999.

Ottaway, David, and Marina Ottaway. *Algeria: The Politics of a Socialist Revolution.* Berkeley: University of California Press, 1970.

Oualdi, M'hamed. "Nationality in the Arab World, 1830–1960: Negotiationg Belonging and the Law." *Revue des mondes musulmans et de la Méditerranée* 137 (2015). https://doi.org/10.4000/remmm.9108.

Oulebsir, Rachid. *L'olivier en Kabylie: Entre mythes et réalités.* Paris: L'Harmattan, 2008.

Ourabah, Mahmoud. *Premiers pas: Souvenirs autour d'un projet de développement de l'Algérie, 1963–1980.* Paris: L'Harmattan, 2012.

Ouzegane, Amar. *Le meilleur combat.* Algiers: Éditions ANEP, 2006.

Patterson, Orlando. *Slavery and Social Death: A Comparative Study.* Cambridge, MA: Harvard University Press, 1982.

Pattieu, Sylvain. "Le 'camarade' Pablo, la IVe Internationale, et la guerre d'Algérie." *Revue Historique* 3, no. 619 (2003): 695–729.

Pattieu, Sylvain. *Les camarades des frères: Trotskistes et libertaires dans la guerre d'Algérie*. Paris: Syllepse, 2002.

Pedersen, Susan. *The Guardians: The League of Nations and the Crisis of Empire*. Oxford: Oxford University Press, 2015.

Perinbam, B. Marie. "Fanon and the Revolutionary Peasantry: The Algerian Case." *Journal of Modern African Studies* 11, no. 3 (1973): 427–45.

Perroux, François. "Economic Space: Theory and Applications." *Quarterly Journal of Economics* 64, no. 1 (1950): 89–104.

Perroux, François. "L'Islam, l'économie et la technique." *Cahiers de l'Institut de Science Economique Appliquée,* no. 106 (1961): 65–86.

Perroux, François, ed. *L'Algérie de demain*. Paris: Presses Universitaires de France, 1962.

Peter, Ania. "William E. Rappard and the League of Nations: A Swiss Contribution to International Organization." In *The League of Nations in Retrospect*, edited by United Nations Library and the Graduate Institute of International Studies, 221–41. Berlin: United Nations, 1983.

Peterson, Terrence G. "Counterinsurgent Bodies: Social Welfare and Psychological Warfare in French Algeria, 1956–1961." PhD diss., University of Wisconsin-Madison, 2015.

Phillips, John, and Martin Evans. *Algeria: Anger of the Dispossessed*. New Haven, CT: Yale University Press, 2008.

Pitts, Jennifer. *A Turn to Empire: The Rise of Imperial Liberalism in Britain and France*. Princeton, NJ: Princeton University Press, 2005.

Plaisant, Odile, and Michèle Assante. "Origine et enjeu du la dénomination 'pied-noir.'" *Language et Société* 60 (1990): 49–65.

Polanyi, Karl. *The Great Transformation: The Political and Economic Origins of Our Time*. 1944. Reprint, Boston: Beacon Press, 2001.

Pomel, Auguste. *Des races indigènes de l'Algérie et du rôle que leur réservent leurs aptitudes*. Oran: Typographie et Lithographie Veuve Dagorn, 1871.

Porter, David. *Eyes to the South: French Anarchists and Algeria*. Edinburgh: AK Press, 2011.

Prochaska, David. "Fire on the Mountain: Resisting Colonialism in Algeria." In *Banditry, Rebellion, and Social Protest in Africa*, edited by Donald Crummey, 229–52. London: James Currey, 1968.

Prochaska, David. *Making Algeria French: Colonialism in Bône, 1970–1920*. Cambridge: Cambridge University Press, 1990.

Puar, Jasbir K. *Terrorist Assemblages: Homonationalism in Queer Times*. Durham, NC: Duke University Press, 2007.

Pulju, Rebecca. *Women and Mass Consumer Society in Postwar France*. Cambridge: Cambridge University Press, 2013.

Pursley, Sara. *Familiar Futures: Time, Selfhood, and Sovereignty in Iraq*. Stanford, CA: Stanford University Press, 2019.

Rabinow, Paul. *French Modern: Norms and Forms of the Social Environment*. Chicago: University of Chicago Press, 1995.

Rahal, Malika. *L'UDMA et les udmistes: Contribution à l'histoire du nationalisme algérien*. Algiers: Barzakh, 2017.

Raffinot, Marc, and Pierre Jacquement. *Le capitalisme d'État algérien*. Paris: François Maspero, 1977.

Rana, Junaid. *Terrifying Muslims: Race and Labor in the South Asian Diaspora*. Durham, NC: Duke University Press, 2011.

Raptis, Michel. "Autogestion et bureaucratie en Algérie—le congrès des fellahs." *Autogestion: Études, débats, documents* 3 (1967): 59–69.

Régnier, Phillippe. *Les Saints-Simoniens en Egypte*. Cairo: Bank of the European Union, 1989.

Renan, Ernest. *Études d'histoire réligieuse*. Paris: Michel Lévy Frères, 1857.

Renan, Ernest. *L'Islam et la science, avec la réponse d'Afghâni*. Montpellier: L'Archange Minotaure, 2003.

Renan, Ernest. *Qu'est-ce qu'une nation? Conférence faite en Sorbonne le 11 mars 1882*. Paris: Galmann Levy, 1882.

Rey-Goldzeiguer, Annie. *Aux origines de la guerre d'Algérie, 1940–1945: De Mers-El-Kébir aux massacres du Nord-Constantinois*. Paris: La Decouverte, 2002.

Rioux, Jean-Pierre. *The Fourth Republic, 1944–1958*. Translated by Godfrey Rogers. Cambridge: Cambridge University Press, 1987.

Rioux, Jean-Pierre. "Pierre Mendès France modernisateur." *Vingtième Siècle: Revue d'histoire* 15 (1987): 81–92.

Ripley, William Z. *Races of Europe: A Sociological Study*. New York: Appleton and Company, 1899.

Rizzo, Matteo. "What Was Left of the Groundnut Scheme? Development Disaster and Labour Market in Southern Tanganyika, 1946–1962." *Journal of Agrarian Change* 6, no. 2 (2006): 205–38.

Roberts, Hugh. "Radical Islamism and the Dilemma of Algerian Nationalism: The Embattled Arians of Algiers." *Third World Quarterly* 10, no. 2 (1999): 556–89.

Robinson, Cedric. *Black Marxism: The Making of a Black Radical Tradition*. 1983. Reprint, Chapel Hill: University of North Carolina Press, 2000.

Rodinson, Maxime. *Islam et capitalisme*. Paris: Éditions du Seuil, 1966.

Rodinson, Maxime. "Le poids de l'Islam sur le développement économique et sociale." *Frères du Monde* 33 (1965): 9–20.

Rosenberg, Clifford. "Albert Sarraut and Republican Racial Thought." *French Politics, Culture, and Society* 20, no. 3 (2002): 97–114.

Ross, Kristin. *Fast Cars, Clean Bodies: Decolonization and the Reordering of French Culture*. Cambridge, MA: MIT Press, 1996.

Rostow, W. W. *The Stages of Growth: A Non-communist Manifesto*. Cambridge: Cambridge University Press, 1960.

Rouban, Luc. "Un inspecteur des finances atypique." In *Paul Delouvrier, un grand commis de l'État*, edited by Sébastien Laurent, 11–32. Paris: Presses Sciences Po, 2005.

Roughton, Richard A. "Economic Motives and French Imperialism: The 1837 Tafna Treaty as a Case Study." *Historian* 47, no. 3 (1985): 360–61.

Rousso, Henri, ed. *De Monnet à Massé: Enjeux politiques et objectifs économiques dans le cadre des quatre premiers plans (1964–1965)*. Paris: Éditions du CNRS, 1986.

Ruscio, Alain. *Les Communistes et l'Algérie: Des origines à la guerre d'indépendance, 1920–1962*. Paris: La Découverte, 2019.

Saada, Emmanuelle. *Empire's Children: Race, Filliation, and Citizenship in the French Colonies*. Translated by Arthur Goldhammer. Chicago: University of Chicago Press, 2012.

Sa'dallah, Abu al-Qasim. *Hizb al-Sha'b al-Jaza'iri*. Vol. 3. Cairo: Ma'had al-Buhuth wa-l-Dirasat al-'Arabiyya, 1977.

Saaidia, Oissila. *Algérie coloniale: Musulmans et chrétiens; Le contrôle de l'État (1830–1914)*. Paris: Éditions du CNRS, 2015.

Sacriste, Fabien. "Les camps de 'regroupement': Une histoire de l'État colonial et de la société rurale pendant la guerre d'indépendance algérienne (1954–1962)." PhD diss., University of Toulouse II, 2014.

Sacriste, Fabien. *Germaine Tillion, Jacques Berque, Jean Servier, Pierre Bourdieu: Des ethnologues dans la guerre d'indépendance algérienne*. Paris: L'Harmattan, 2011.

Salem, Sara. *Anticolonial Afterlives in Egypt: The Politics of Hegemony*. Cambridge: Cambridge University Press, 2020.

Saoud, Tahar. "La place de l'Islam dans l'Algérie indépendante: La période des présidences Ben Bella et Boumediene comme modèle de référence." In *Les indépendences au Maghreb*, edited by Amar Mohand-Amar and Belkacem Benzenine, 121–39. Paris: Karthala, 2012.

Sari, Djilali. *La dépossession des fellahs (1830–1962)*. Algiers: Société nationale d'édition et de diffusion, 1975.

Sartori, Andrew. *Liberalism in Empire: An Alternative History*. Berkeley: University of California Press, 2014.

Sartre, Jean-Paul. *Anti-Semite and Jew*. Translated by George J. Becker. 1944. Reprint, New York: Schocken Books, 1976.

Savarese, Eric. *L'invention des pieds-noirs*. Paris: Séguier Editions, 2002.

Scagnetti, Jean-Charles. "Identité ou personnalité algérienne? L'édification d'une algérianité (1962–1988)." *Cahiers de la Méditerranée* 66 (2003): 367–84.

Schreier, Joshua. *Arabs of the Jewish Faith: The Civilizing Mission in Colonial Algeria*. New Brunswick, NJ: Rutgers University Press, 2010.

Schreier, Joshua. *The Merchants of Oran: A Jewish Port at the Dawn of Empire*. Stanford, CA: Stanford University Press, 2018.

Schroeter, Daniel J. "Between Metropole and French North Africa: Vichy's Anti-Semitic Legislation and Colonialism's Racial Hierarchies." In *The Holocaust and North Africa*, edited by Aomar Boum and Sarah Abrevaya Stein, 19–49. Stanford, CA: Stanford University Press, 2018.

Schuman, Robert. "Unité européenne et eurafrique: Politique révolutionnaire." *Union française et parlement* 79 (1957): 1–3.

Scott, James C. *Seeing Like a State: How Certain Schemes to Improve the Human Condition Have Failed*. New Haven, CT: Yale University Press, 1999.

Scott, James C. *Weapons of the Weak: Everyday Forms of Peasant Resistance*. New Haven, CT: Yale University Press, 1985.

Scott, Joan W. *Only Paradoxes to Offer: French Feminists and the Rights of Man*. Cambridge, MA: Harvard University Press, 1996.

Seferdjeli, Ryme. "French 'Reforms' and Muslim Women's Emancipation during the Algerian War." *Journal of North African Studies* 9, no. 4 (2004): 19–61.

Seikaly, Sherene. *Men of Capital: Scarcity and Economy in Mandate Palestine.* Stanford, CA: Stanford University Press, 2015.

Semley, Lorelle. *To Be Free and French: Citizenship in France's Atlantic Empire.* Cambridge: Cambridge University Press, 2017.

Sergi, Giuseppe. *The Mediterranean Race: A Study of the Origins of European Peoples.* London: Walter Scott, 1901.

Serres, Thomas. "The Algerian Counter-Revolution or the Obsolescence of Authoritarian Upgrading." *Georgetown Journal of International Affairs* (February 2021), https://gjia.georgetown.edu/2021/02/02/the-algerian-counter-revolution-or-the-obsolescence-of-authoritarian-upgrading/.

Serres, Thomas. *L'Algérie face à la catastrophe suspendue.* Paris: Karthala, 2019.

Serres, Thomas. "La réforme du marché du travail, entre néolibéralisation et héritage tiers-mondiste." In *L'Algérie au présent*, edited by Karima Dirèche, 233–49. Tunis: IRMC, 2019.

Sessions, Jennifer E. *By Sword and Plow: France and the Conquest of Algeria.* Ithaca, NY: Cornell University Press, 2011.

Sessions, Jennifer E. "Colonizing Revolutionary Politics: Algeria and the French Revolution of 1848." *French Politics, Culture, and Society* 33, no. 1 (2015): 75–100.

Sewell, William H., Jr. "A Strange Career: The Historical Study of Economic Life." *History and Theory* 49, no. 4 (2010): 146–66.

Sheehi, Stephen. *Foundations of Modern Arab Identity.* Gainesville: University Press of Florida, 2004.

Shepard, Todd. "Algeria, France, Mexico, UNESCO: A Transnational History of Antiracism and Decolonization, 1932–1962." *Journal of Global History* 6, no. 2 (2011): 273–97.

Shepard, Todd. "Algerian Nationalism, Zionism, and French Laïcité: A History of Ethnoreligious Nationalisms and Decolonization." *IJMES* 45 (2013): 445–67.

Shepard, Todd. *The Invention of Decolonization: The Algerian War and the Remaking of France.* Ithaca, NY: Cornell University Press, 2006.

Shepard, Todd. "Pieds-Noirs, Bêtes Noires: Anti-'European of Algeria' Racism and the Close of French Empire." In *Algeria and France, 1800–2000: Identity, Memory, Nostalgia*, edited by Patricia Lorcin, 150–63. Syracuse, NY: Syracuse University Press, 2006.

Shepard, Todd. *Sex, France, and Arab Men, 1962–1979.* Chicago: University of Chicago Press, 2017.

Shields, Sarah. "The Greek-Turkish Population Exchange: Internationally Administered Ethnic Cleansing." *Middle East Report*, no. 267 (2013): 2–6.

Silverstein, Paul A. *Algeria in France: Transpolitics, Race, and Nation.* Bloomington: Indiana University Press, 2004.

Simmel, Georg. *On Individuality and Social Forms: Selected Writings.* Chicago: University of Chicago Press, 1971.

Simon, Catherine. *Algérie, les années pieds-rouges: Des rêves de l'indépendance au désenchantement (1962–1969).* Paris: La Découverte, 2009.

Sing, Manfred. "Brothers in Arms: How Palestinian Maoists Turned Jihadists." *Die Welt des Islams* 51, no. 1 (2011): 1–44.

Slisli, Fouzi. "Islam: The Elephant in Fanon's *Wretched of the Earth*." *Middle East Critique* 17, no. 1 (2008): 97–108.

Sloughi, Mouloud. "Agriculture et coopération algéro-française." In *Les accords d'Évian en conjoncture et en longue durée*, edited by René Gallissot, 171–85. Algiers: Casbah Éditions, 1997.

Smith, Michael S. "The Méline Tariff as Social Protection: Rhetoric or Reality?" *International Review of Social History* 37, no. 2 (1992): 230–43.

La Société algérienne de Paris. *De la colonisation: Question des travailleurs; Solution pour l'Algérie.* Paris: Bureau de la Société Algérienne, 1848. https://gallica.bnf.fr/ark:/12148/bpt6k5697363n.texteImage.

Spivak, Gayatri Chakravorty. "The New Subaltern: A Silent Interview." In *Mapping Subaltern Studies and the Postcolonial*, edited by Vinayak Chaturvedi, 324–40. London: Verso, 2000.

Stambouli, Nabila. "L'Aéro-habitat, avatar d'un monument classé?" *Livraisons de l'histoire de l'architecture* 27 (2014): 117–27.

Steffek, Jens, and Francesca Antonini. "Toward Eurafrica! Fascism, Corporatism, and Italy's Colonial Expansion." In *Radicals and Reactionaries in Twentieth-Century International Thought*, edited by Ian Hall, 145–70. New York: Palgrave Macmillan, 2015.

Stein, Sarah Abrevaya. *Plumes: Ostrich Feathers, Jews, and a Lost World of Global Commerce.* New Haven, CT: Yale University Press, 2010.

Stein, Sarah Abrevaya. *Saharan Jews and the Fate of French Algeria.* Chicago: University of Chicago Press, 2014.

Stenner, David. *Globalizing Morocco: Transnational Activism and the Postcolonial State.* Stanford, CA: Stanford University Press, 2019.

Stoler, Ann Laura. *Race and the Education of Desire: Foucault's "History of Sexuality" and the Colonial Order of Things.* Durham, NC: Duke University Press, 1995.

Stora, Benjamin. *Algeria, 1830–2000: A Short History.* Translated by Jane Marie Todd. Ithaca, NY: Cornell University Press, 2004.

Stora, Benjamin. "Faiblesse paysanne du mouvement nationaliste algérien avant 1954." *Vingtième Siècle: Revue d'histoire* 12 (1986): 59–72.

Stora, Benjamin. "Le massacre du 20 août 1955: Récit historique, bilan historiographique." *Historical Reflections/Réflexions Historiques* 36, no. 2 (2010): 97–107.

Stora, Benjamin. *Les trois exils: Juifs d'Algérie.* Paris: Pluriel, 2011.

Strachan, John. "The Colonial Identity of Wine: The *Leakey Affair* and the Franco-Algerian Order of Things." *Social History of Alcohol and Drugs* 21, no. 2 (2007): 118–37.

Suleiman, Ezra N. *Politics, Power, and Bureaucracy in France.* Princeton, NJ: Princeton University Press, 2016.

Surkis, Judith. *Sex, Law, and Sovereignty in French Algeria, 1830–1930.* Ithaca, NY: Cornell University Press, 2019.

Sutton, Keith. "Algeria's Vineyards: A Problem of Decolonisation." *Méditerranée* 65, no. 3 (1988): 55–66.

Swearingen, Will D. *Moroccan Mirages: Agrarian Dreams and Deceptions, 1912–1986.* Princeton, NJ: Princeton University Press, 1987.

Szczepanski-Huillery, Maxime. "'L'idéologie tiers-mondiste': Constructions et usages d'une catégorie intellectuelle en 'crise.'" *Raisons politiques* 2, no. 18 (2005): 27–48.

Taraud, Christelle. *La Prostitution coloniale: Algérie, Maroc, Tunisie (1830–1962).* 2003. Reprint, Paris: Éditions Payot and Rivages, 2009.

Teillac, Jean. *Autogestion en Algérie.* Edited by CHEAM. Paris: J. Peyronnet and Cie, 1965.

Thénault, Sylvie. "Le 'code de l'indigénat.'" In *Histoire de l'Algérie à la période coloniale,* edited by Abderrahmane Bouchène et al., 200–206. Paris: Éditions La Découverte, 2012.

Thénault, Sylvie. "How about 1958 in Algeria?" In *The Middle East in 1958: Reimagining a Revolutionary Year,* edited by Jeffrey G. Karam, 141–52. London: I. B. Tauris, 2021.

Thénault, Sylvie. "L'OAS à Alger en 1962." *Annales: Histoire, Science Sociales* 4 (2008): 977–1001.

Thénault, Sylvie. *Violence ordinaire dans l'Algérie coloniale: Camps, internements, assignations à résidence.* Paris: Odile Jacob, 2011.

Thomas, Martin. "Albert Sarraut, French Colonial Development, and the Communist Threat, 1919–1930." *Journal of Modern History* 77 (2005): 917–55.

Thomson, Ann. "Arguments for the Conquest of Algiers in the Late Eighteenth and Early Nineteenth Centuries." *Maghreb Review* 14, no. 1–2 (1989): 108–18.

Thomson, Ann. "La classification raciale de l'Afrique du Nord au début du XIXe siècle." *Cahier d'études africaines* 33, no. 129 (1993): 19–36.

Tibi, Bassam. *Arab Nationalism: Between Islam and the Nation-State.* Basingstoke: Palgrave Macmillan, 1997.

Tidafi, Tami. *L'agriculture algérienne et ses perspectives de développement.* Paris: François François Maspero, 1969.

Titouh, Khayreddine, Azzedine Mazari, and Mohand Zine Aït Meziane. "Contribution to Improvement of the Traditional Extraction of Olive Oil." *Oilseeds and Fats, Crops and Lipids* 27, no. 23 (2020): 1–7.

Todd, David. "The *Impôts Arabes*: French Imperialism and Land Taxation in Colonial Algeria, 1930–1919." In *Studies in the History of Tax Law,* vol. 3, edited by John Tiley, 113–38. Oxford: Hart Publishing, 2009.

Touati, Houari. *Entre Dieu et les hommes: Lettrés, saints et sorciers au Maghreb (17e siècle).* Paris: Éditions de l'EHESS, 1994.

Touchelay, Béatrice. "L'INSEE des origines à 1961, évaluation et relation avec la réalité économique, politique et sociale." PhD diss., Paris XII, 1993.

Trumbull, George R., IV. *An Empire of Facts: Colonial Power, Cultural Knowledge, and Islam in Algeria, 1870–1914.* Cambridge: Cambridge University Press, 2009.

Turner, Bryan S. *Weber and Islam: A Critical Study.* New York: Routledge, 1978.

Vallin, Raymond. "Muslim Socialism in Algeria." In *Man, State, and Society in the Contemporary Maghreb*, edited by I. William Zartman, 50–64. New York: Praeger, 1973.

Vanaik, Achin. "Introduction." In *The Debate on Postcolonial Theory and the Specter of Capital*, edited by Rosie Warren. London: Verso Books, 2017.

Van Vollenhoven, Joost. *Essai sur le fellah algérien*. Paris: Rousseau, 1903.

Vince, Natalya. *The Algerian War, the Algerian Revolution*. London: Palgrave Macmillan, 2020.

Vince, Natalya. *Our Fighting Sisters: Nation, Memory and Gender in Algeria, 1954–2012*. Manchester: Manchester University Press, 2016.

Von Sivers, Peter. "Rural Uprisings as Political Movements in Colonial Algeria, 1851–1914." In *Islam, Politics, and Social Movements*, edited by Edmund Burke III and Ira M. Lapidus, 39–59. Berkeley: University of California Press, 1988.

Walsh, Sebastian J. "Killing Post-Almohad Man: Malek Bennabi, Algerian Islamism, and the Search for a Liberal Governance." *Journal of North African Studies* 12 (2007): 235–54.

Weber, Eugene. *Peasants into Frenchmen: The Modernization of Rural France, 1870–1914*. Stanford, CA: Stanford University Press, 1976.

Weber, Max. *The Protestant Ethic and the Spirit of Capitalism*. Translated by Peter Baehr and Gordon C. Wells. New York: Penguin, 2002.

Weil, Patrick. "Le statut des Musulmans en Algérie coloniale: Une nationalité française dénaturée." *Histoire de la Justice*, no. 16 (2005): 93–109.

Weiss, Gillian. *Captives and Corsaires: France and Slavery in the Early Modern Mediterranean*. Stanford, CA: Stanford University Press, 2011.

Wendeln, Matthew. "Contested Territory: Regional Development in France, 1934–1968." PhD diss., New York University and EHESS, 2011.

White, Hayden. "The Question of Narrative in Contemporary Historical Theory." *History and Theory* 23, no. 1 (1984): 1–33.

White, Owen. *The Blood of the Colony: Wine and the Rise and Fall of French Algeria*. Cambridge, MA: Harvard University Press, 2020.

White, Owen, and Elizabeth Heath. "The French Empire and the History of Economic Life." *French Politics, Culture and Society* 35, no. 2 (2017): 76–88.

Whyte, Jessica Stephanie. *The Morals of the Market: Human Rights and the Rise of Neoliberalism*. London: Verso Books, 2019.

Wien, Peter. *Arab Nationalism: The Politics of History and Culture in the Modern Middle East*. London: Routledge, 2017.

Wilder, Gary. "Eurafrique as the Future Past of 'Black France': Sarkozy's Temporal Confusion and Senghor's Postwar Vision." In *Black France/France Noire: The History and Politics of Blackness*, edited by Tricia Danielle Keaton, T. Dennan Sharpley-Whiting, and Tyler Stovall, 57–87. Durham, NC: Duke University Press, 2012.

Wilder, Gary. *The French Imperial Nation-State: Negritude and Colonial Humanism between the Two World Wars*. Chicago: University of Chicago Press, 2005.

Winant, Howard. *The World Is a Ghetto: Race and Democracy after World War II*. New York: Basic Books, 2009.

Woker, Madeline. "Empire of Inequality: The Politics of Taxation in the French Colonial Empire, 1900–1950s." PhD diss., Columbia University, 2020.

Wolf, Eric R. *Peasant Wars of the Twentieth Century*. Norman: University of Oklahoma Press, 1969.

Wolfe, Patrick. "Settler Colonialism and the Elimination of the Native." *Journal of Genocide Research* 8 (2006): 387–409.

Wolin, Richard. *The Wind from the East: French Intellectuals, the Cultural Revolution, and the Legacy of the 1960s*. Princeton, NJ: Princeton University Press, 2010.

Wright, Gordon. *Rural Revolution in France: The Peasantry in the 20th Century*. Stanford, CA: Stanford University Press, 1964.

Yacine, Kateb. "Sétif, Guelma et Dien Bien Phu." *L'algérien en Europe* 59 (May 1968): 12–18.

Yacine, Tassadit. "Pierre Bourdieu in Algeria at War: Notes on the Birth of an Engaged Sociology." *Ethnography* 5, no. 4 (2004): 487–509.

Yacono, Xavier. "Les pertes algériennes de 1954 à 1962." *Revue de l'Occident musulman et de la Méditerranée* 34, no. 1 (1982): 119–34.

Zack, Lizabeth. "Early Origins of Islamic Activism in Algeria: The Case of Khaled in Post–World War I Algiers." *Journal of North African Studies* 11, no. 2 (2006): 205–17.

Zakariyya, Yahya Abu. *Malek Bennabi: Faylasuf Mushkilat al-Hadara*. Beirut: Dar al-Rawafid, 2017

Zarobell, John. *Empire of Landscape: Space and Ideology in French Colonial Algeria*. University Park: Pennsylvania State University Press, 2010.

Zimmerman, Andrew. *Alabama in Africa: Booker T. Washington, the German Empire, and the Globalization of the New South*. Princeton, NJ: Princeton University Press, 2010.

Zubaida, Sami. *Law and Power in the Islamic World*. London: I. B. Tauris, 2005.

Zytnicki, Colette. *L'Algérie, terre de tourisme*. Paris: Éditions Vendémiaire, 2016.

Boumediene, Houari, 95, 120, 126, 142–43, 163, 214n107

Bourdieu, Pierre, 16, 70, 96, 101, 103, 118, 159, 185n84, 201n2–2n2, 209n130; critiques of, 101

Bourguiba, Habib, 133, 151, 220n55

Bouteflika, Abdelaziz, 172

Braudel, Fernand, 54, 220n52

Bugeaud, Thomas Robert, 19

Buron, Robert, 144–45, 147–48, 152–54, 220n51; debate with Cartier, 145

Byé Commission, 75

Camus, Albert, 41, 92

CAPER, 94, 114–16, 208nn122–23, 214n107

Cara, Nafissa Sid, 83

Cartier, Raymond, 145, 181n74; Cartierism, 145, 181n74

caste, 7, 177n12

Cepède, Michel, 106, 205n59

Challe, Maurice, 79–80; Challe Plan, 79

Chaulet, Claudine, 101, 126

Chaussade, Pierre, 196n48

CHEAM, 153

Chellig, Rabah, 101–2, 203n33, 205n60

Christianity, 5, 20, 22, 24–25, 54, 72, 119, 137, 152–53, 178n14, 187n129; Catholic, Catholicism, 39–40, 76, 139, 204n39; Protestant, Protestantism, 13–14, 204n39. *See also* social Catholicism

citrus, 43–44, 47, 57–59, 64, 115, 126, 191

civilizing mission, 27, 29, 39, 53–54, 56, 83, 127, 178n14, 187n121, 188n13

Closon, Francis-Louis 87–88

Colonna, Fanny 101

communism, 4, 41, 46, 56, 71–73, 75, 99, 122, 128, 153, 160, 215n126, 223n115; Communist International (Comintern), 41; PCA, 140–41, 165, 218n25; PCF, 41, 149–51, 155, 218n25

Constantine Plan, 3, 13, 16, 18, 70–71, 75–76, 78–79, 81–87, 89–97, 101–2, 104–7, 109–10, 114, 118, 137, 147–49, 156, 159, 167, 174, 196n48, 201n141, 215n125, 218n17; propaganda for, 82–83, 85, 89–90, 105; precursors to,

75; FLN reaction to, 78–79; disagreements over, 84–86

cooperation (policy), 17, 141, 143–49, 154, 156–60, 165, 218n10, 218n17, 222n97; *coopérants*, 17, 145–48, 158, 160, 165, 218n10

De Broglie, Jean, 145, 218n9

De Gaulle, Charles, 13, 55–56, 68, 70, 76, 79–80, 92, 94, 145–46, 149, 156, 196n50, 197n64, 197n66; Gaullism, 156

De Saint Simon, Henri, 29; Saint-Simonian principles, 28–30, 37, 148, 218n17

De Tocqueville, Alexis, 24

Debord, Guy, 162

Debré, Michel, 222n97

Decennial Perspectives, 75, 85, 88

Delavignette, Robert, 52

Delouvrier, Paul, 13, 16, 59, 71, 73, 75–77, 79–82, 84–87, 89–91, 93–95, 102, 157, 197n66, 204n39, 206n83; training, 71, 73, 76–77; vision of development, 77, 80–81, 85–86; activities after 1962, 95

Despois, Jean, 59

Destanne de Bernis, Gérard, 142, 154

Dib, Mohammed, 117

Dumont, René, 150, 160–62, 205n60, 220n52, 221n66, 222n97, 223n101

École polytechnique, 71, 76, 167

economic planning, 3, 10–12, 14–17, 41–42, 44, 46, 50, 56–57, 60, 64, 68, 71–75, 77–78, 80–88, 90–92, 94–95, 97–98, 102, 104–11, 113–16, 118–20, 125, 135, 138, 141–43, 145–49, 152, 154, 156–59, 165, 167–69, 172–75, 191n78, 195n24, 196nn37–38, 197n56, 200n132, 211n36

Economy and Humanism, 72, 152–53

Egypt, 5, 8, 29, 54, 78, 98, 117, 128, 131, 141, 169, 171, 190n55, 209n7, 213n79, 215n118, 221n82, 222n83

El Kenz, Ali, 125, 131

ENA, 71, 73, 76–77, 154, 196n48, 220n60

Engels, Friedrich, 19–20

European integration, 3, 12, 44, 51–52, 62; EEC, 3, 12, 52, 77, 189n40; European Union, 51; Eurafrica, 15, 42, 44, 51–52, 60, 64, 66, 92, 189n42; Paneuropa movement, 51; Treaty of Rome, 12, 59, 77, 189n40

Evian Accords, 65, 119, 122, 140, 144, 147, 160, 193n121

Fanon, Frantz, 16, 93, 118, 133, 150, 164, 209n137, 223n111

FIS, 165, 172, 209n8, 224n28

Fourastié, Jean, 70

Fourth International, 125, 144, 149, 152

Fourth Republic, 13, 16, 45, 55–56, 75–76, 78, 196n38

Francis, Ahmed, 160

Fyot, Jean-Louis, 90

Gabory, Jacques, 196n40

Garaudy, Roger, 155, 221n66

gauchistes, 145, 149–52, 162–65, 219n31

GPRA, 91–92, 119, 121, 124, 133–34, 168, 209n1

Gruson, Claude, 157

Guérin, Daniel, 136, 144, 151–52, 162–65, 220n50, 223n111

Guichard, Olivier, 95

Hadj Ali, Bachir, 140–41, 223n115

Hadj, Messali, 46, 55, 78, 100, 146, 151–52, 170, 219n44; Messalism, 151

Hadjeres, Sadek, 140

Hall, Stuart, 6, 8

Harbi, Mohammed, 56, 70, 125, 223n115

Hayek, Fredrick, 1, 74

Hessel, Stéphane, 157

Hirak, 18, 172–73, 175

human capital, 15, 68, 81

humanism, 73, 128, 173,

Husain, Taha, 54

al-Husri, Satiʿ, 130–31

hydrocarbons, 165, 172

Ibn Khaldun, 137

al-Ibrahimi, Muhammad Bashir, 141–42

INSEE, 87–88, 149, 157, 199n102

Islam, 3–9, 14–17, 19, 21–26, 28, 30–31, 37, 40–41, 46, 54–55, 60, 65, 69, 72, 78, 83–84, 90–91, 95, 97–98, 100–103, 113, 116, 118–20, 122–23, 125–30, 132–35, 138, 140–46, 151–55, 159, 162–66, 168–74, 179n31, 179n47, 182n8, 182n16–83n16, 190n55, 203n32, 207n98, 210n10, 212n59, 212n64, 217n159, 219n28, 220n50, 225n37; Islamophobia, *Islamophobie savante*, 6–7, 37–38, 183n16; Islamic modernism, 16, 93, 118–20, 122–23, 126–29, 133, 135, 140–42, 144, 162–64, 166, 169–72, 174, 220n50; Marxist approaches to studying, 154–55, 182n8; *Nahda*/Arab Renaissance, 127, 130, 212n53; pan-Islamism, 4, 182n16–83n16; Qur'anic law, 8, 23, 27, 30, 83, 141, 217n159; *umma*, 130, 132, 182n16

Israel, 57–58, 140, 191n78, 210n10

Italian reunification, 52–53

Jeanneney Report, 148

Jeanson, Francis, 150; Jeanson network, 150–51

Jews (in Algeria), 9, 15, 31, 37, 39, 54, 138, 140, 187n121; anti-Semitism, 5–6, 39, 54–55, 187n121, 203n29; French nationality, 9, 37, 39, 54, 140, 187n121; Algerian nationality, 31, 39, 140

Jonnart, Charles, 45

July Monarchy, 24, 28, 41, 182n15, 187n121

Kabylia, 26, 43, 50, 60, 64, 167, 194n129

al-Kawakibi, Abd al-Rahman, 127

Khaled, Emir, 46

al-Khattab, Umar, 128

Khider, Mohammed, 142

Labonne, Eirik, 51

Lacheraf, Mostefa, 122, 203n31

Lacoste, Robert, 75, 196n38

land reform: after Algerian independence, 125, 135, 138–40, 146, 158, 214n107; under the Constantine Plan, 93–94, 98, 114–15, 208n122

Latin America, 7, 150, 153

Popular Front, 49, 77

Property, 4, 8–10, 13, 20–22, 24–26, 30–33, 36, 79, 111, 113–16, 124–25, 135, 138–41, 178n19, 180nn54–55, 182n8, 203n31, 214n107; *'arsh*, 9, 30, 33, 114; *beylic*, 9, 24–25; collective land tenure, 20, 33, 114; dispossession, 10, 15, 21, 24, 30, 31, 33, 36; expropriation, 21, 35, 111, 114, 116, 138–39, 203n31, 214n107; family farms, 33, 114, 180n55; *hubus*, 8, 25; Lockean notions, 26, 178n19; *milk*, 9, 30; ownership, 9, 30, 113, 124–25, 141, 178n19; private property, 16, 21, 25, 32–33, 115, 141, 182n8

primitive accumulation, 21, 35, 185n90–86n90

proletariat, 14–15, 28, 30, 34–36, 46, 58, 97, 118, 126, 136, 164, 182n85, 185n84, 186n91; industrial proletariat, 35; sub-proletariat, 34–35, 46, 58; foreclosed in Algeria, 34, 36

al-Qadir, 'Abd, 29, 46, 132, 151
qawmiyya. *See* pan-Arabism
al-Qiyam al-Islamiyya/Islamic values, 127, 140–41

race, racism, 3–9, 11–13, 15–17, 20–27, 30–32, 34–42, 44–46, 50–56, 58–59, 64–65, 70–71, 75, 78, 82–83, 88–89, 91–92, 94–95, 98, 102, 108–9, 116, 118–20, 122, 127, 129–35, 139, 143, 146, 159, 164–66, 169, 173–75, 178n19, 178n24, 179n31, 179nn34–35, 179n41, 179n47–80n47, 182n85, 184n46, 184n67, 186n114, 186n116, 201n148, 203n29, 209n8, 210n10, 212n59, 222n89; anti-black racism, 17, 23, 133–34, 179n41, 203n29; Arabism, Arabness, 15, 17, 25–26, 32, 34, 53, 70–72, 93, 98, 119, 122, 127, 129–33, 165, 169, 173, 209n8, 212n59; black-ness, 8, 23, 133, 179n41; color-blind framework, 6, 16, 71, 88, 91, 102; essential markers, 37, 71, 78, 82–83, 91, 102, 108–9, 120, 130, 159, 174–75, 178n24, 179n31, 210n10, 212n59; "racial

fix," 15, 21, 41; racial hybridity, 41–42, 54; racial integration, 41–42, 50, 53; racialized differentiation, 30, 34, 44–45, 52, 134, 182n85; racial-religious discrimination, 20–22, 25–26, 30–32, 35, 37, 39–41, 51, 55–56, 64, 71, 83, 88–89, 92, 94, 116, 132, 159, 164, 175, 178n19, 179n31, 186n116; UNESCO, 56, 158; whiteness, 38–40, 58–59, 179n34, 179n41, 186n114. *See also* Islam

Rappard, William, 1–2
Raptis, Michel. *See* Pablo
reforestation, 137, 215n127; Day of the Tree, 137
regroupment camps, 13, 102–4, 204n39
Renan, Ernest, 37, 127
repatriation, 140
rapatriés, 140
republicanism, 6, 32, 45, 72, 179n35
Resistance (World War II), 76, 144,
Robinson, Cedric, 7, 20
Roland-Billecard, Yves, 157
Rondot, Pierre, 153
Rougier, Louis, 73
Rueff, Jacques, 76, 196n50

Saber, Ahmed, 122–23
Salan, Raoul, 79
Sarraut, Albert, 46–47
Sartre, Jean-Paul, 223n111
SAS, 104–5, 110
Sauvy, Alfred, 150, 160
Say, Jean-Baptiste, 10
Sayad, Abdelmalek, 101, 103
Schiaffino, Laurent, 102
Schuman, Robert, 52
self-management, 16, 65, 94, 116, 118, 123–26, 128, 135–37, 139, 142, 144, 146, 150–51, 155, 160, 211n43, 214nn107–8, 215n123, 220n50
Sénatus-Consulte, 30–31, 33, 46, 70
Senghor, Léopold Sédar, 52
Sergi, Giuseppe, 52
Servier, Jean, 153
sexuality, 4, 22, 27–28 31, 184n46, 202n14; deviance, 22–23, 28, 31; polygamy, 4, 28, 31; promiscuity, 27–28